NEWS, GENDER AND POWER

Edited by Cynthia Carter,
Gill Branston and Stuart Allan

London and New York

First published 1998
by Routledge
11 New Fetter Lane, London EC4P 4EE

Simultaneously published in the USA and Canada
by Routledge
29 West 35th Street, New York, NY 10001

Typeset in Bembo by Routledge
Printed and bound in Great Britain by TJ International Ltd, Padstow, Cornwall

British Library Cataloguing in Publication Data
A catalogue record for this book is available from the British Library

Library of Congress Cataloguing in Publication Data
News, gender and power/[edited by] Cynthia Carter, Gill Branston
and Stuart Allan
Rev papers of a symposium
Includes bibliographical references and index
1. Women and journalism. 2. Women in the press. 3. Television broadcasting of
news. 4. Mass media and women. 5. Feminism. I. Carter, Cynthia. II. Branston,
Gill. III Allan, Stuart.
PN4784.W7N48   1998
070.4082–dc21   98-12179

ISBN 0–415–17015–X (hbk)
ISBN 0–415–17016–8 (pbk)

CONTENTS

CONTENTS

CONTRIBUTORS

Stuart Allan lectures in media and cultural studies at the University of Glamorgan. He has published primarily in the areas of news media studies, cultural theory, and nuclear issues, including (co-edited with Barbara Adam) *Theorizing Culture: An Interdisciplinary Critique After Postmodernism* (UCL Press/NYU Press 1995). Currently, he is writing a book on news culture for Open University Press.

Patricia Bradley is Associate Professor in the School of Communication and Theater at Temple University, Philadelphia, where she also directs the American Studies program in the College of Arts and Sciences. She is author of *Slavery, Propaganda and the American Revolution* (University Press of Mississippi 1998).

Gill Branston lectures in film and television studies in the School of Journalism, Media and Cultural Studies, Cardiff University. She is co-author of *The Media Student's Book*. She is currently writing a book on film and culture, and researching the voice in the technologies and ideologies of cinema and television.

Rod Brookes is a lecturer in the School of Journalism, Media and Cultural Studies, Cardiff University. His research interests are the media and national identity, press coverage of BSE, and the media and the environment.

Cynthia Carter lectures in the School of Journalism, Media and Cultural Studies, Cardiff University. She is currently completing her doctoral research on British press reporting of sexual violence and has published historical research on news and gender, as well as analyses of familial ideology and the media.

John Hartley is Professor and Head of the School of Journalism, Media and Cultural Studies at Cardiff University, and Director of the Tom Hopkinson Centre for Media Research. His books include *Popular Reality: Journalism, Modernity, Popular Culture* (Arnold 1996), *The Politics of Pictures: The Creation* *of the Public in the Age of Popular Media* (Routledge 1992) and *Tele-ology: Studies in Television* (Routledge 1992).

Beverley Holbrook lectures in information technology and social research in the School of Social and Administrative Studies at Cardiff University. Her research interests are gender and consumption, green consumption issues and the use of consumer applications within social research.

Patricia Holland is a freelance writer and lecturer. Her 1983 essay 'The Page Three girl speaks to women, too' has been reprinted in several collections. She is also the author of *What is a Child?: Popular Images of Childhood* (Virago 1992) and *The Television Handbook* (Routledge 1997).

Jenny Kitzinger is senior research fellow at the Glasgow University Media Research Unit where she has conducted research into a wide range of feminist issues including AIDS, sexual violence, risk and breast cancer. She is co-author of *The Mass Media and Power in Modern Britain* (Oxford University Press 1997) and *The Circuit of Mass Communication: Media Strategies and Audience Understandings in the AIDS Crisis* (Sage 1998). She is co-editor of *Developing Focus Group Research* (Sage 1998).

Myra Macdonald lectures in communication and media at Glasgow Caledonian University. She is the author of *Representing Women: Myths of Femininity in the Popular Media* (Edward Arnold 1995).

Lisa McLaughlin is on the faculty at Miami University, Ohio, where she teaches courses in media history, mass media research, and gender and race studies. She has published several scholarly articles on women, media and the public sphere, and a book titled *Public Excess: Feminism, Media and the Public Sphere* (University of Minnesota Press 1998).

Paula Skidmore is a senior lecturer in the Department of Social Sciences at the Nottingham Trent University. Her postgraduate research has been in the field of criminology and media studies, and she was previously a researcher with the Glasgow University Media Group. She has published in the areas of crime and media, the sociology of punishment, media ethics, local media and adult education.

Linda Steiner is Assistant Professor of Journalism and Mass Media at Rutgers University, in New Brunswick, New Jersey. She has published widely on the history and structure of alternative and feminist media, media ethics, and the history of journalism education; one of her current projects addresses reforms in reporting about sex crimes. She serves on the editorial boards of six journals.

Janet Thumim is a senior lecturer in Film and Television Studies at the University of Bristol Department of Drama. Her publications include *Celluloid Sisters: Women and Popular Cinema* (Macmillan 1992) and the co-edited anthologies *You Tarzan* and *Me Jane* (Lawrence & Wishart 1993 and 1995). She is currently writing a book about early television in Britain for *Oxford Television Studies*, and editing an anthology of essays on television in the 1950s for Duke University Press.

Liesbet van Zoonen is a senior lecturer in media studies at the University of Amsterdam. She has been president of the gender section of the International Association of Mass Communication Research since 1994. She is the author of *Feminist Media Studies* (Sage 1994) and co-editor of *The Media in Question* (Sage 1998) and *Women, Politics and Communication* (Hampton 1998). She has published widely on gender and journalism in various international academic journals.

C. Kay Weaver lectures in the Department of Film and Television Studies at the University of Waikato, New Zealand. She is co-author of *Cameras in the Commons* (Hansard Society 1990) and *Women Viewing Violence* (BFI 1992). Kay has published articles on media representations of crime, violence and gender and on the debates surrounding these fields of inquiry.

Maggie Wykes is a lecturer in the Department of Journalism, University of Sheffield, where she teaches and researches media discourse. She is currently working on a book on news, crime and culture for Pluto Press, and developing analytical approaches to internet news texts.

ACKNOWLEDGEMENTS

The editors would like to take this opportunity to thank a number of people who have made working on this book such a pleasure. Our first word of appreciation goes to our contributors, who met all of our editorial requests with considered patience and understanding. Next, we wish to express our gratitude to the people who helped us to co-organise the symposium upon which this book found its initial basis. Warmest thanks to Louise Godley, Ewa Chomka-Campbell, Fran Godwin and Carole Bulman, whose enthusiastic professionalism ensured that everything ran smoothly. We are similarly pleased to acknowledge the rôle of John Hartley (Cardiff University), as well as Frances Mannsåker and Alan Salisbury (University of Glamorgan), in providing institutional support for this event. Brian Winston (now at the University of Westminster) also played a key rôle in the early stages of our planning. An appreciative thank you, as well, to everyone who participated in the symposium's debates – we wish that we could have included all of your voices on these pages. At Routledge, we are grateful to Rebecca Barden and Christopher Cudmore for their commitment to this project. And, finally, as clichéd as it may sound to some ears, our sincere thanks to our students who have taught us many important things about the media politics of gender over the years. May this book help to advance those discussions a little bit further.

SETTING NEW(S) AGENDAS

An introduction

Cynthia Carter, Gill Branston and Stuart Allan

'The story of modern journalism', declared British journalist Emilie Hawkes Peacocke in her book *Writing for Women* published in 1936, 'is that of the rise of the Woman's Story' (Peacocke 1936: 129). By a 'woman's story', she was referring both to the late nineteenth-century development of the newspaper 'Woman's Department', responsible for covering such topics as 'beauty', 'fashion', 'shopping', 'social affairs', 'gossip', 'home decoration' and 'child care', as well as to a corresponding rise in the number of women working in journalism as a vocation.[1] These sweeping changes were largely derivative of the 'New Journalism' which was also developing at that time. In general terms, this emergent form of presenting the news sought to emphasise 'human interest' stories, particularly those which were likely to appeal to the 'uneducated mass of all classes'. In the words of Matthew Arnold, who was arguably the first to coin the phrase, writing in the May 1887 issue of *The Nineteenth Century* magazine:

> It has much to recommend it . . . it is full of ability, novelty, variety, sensation, sympathy, generous instincts, its one great fault is that it is feather-brained. It throws out assertions at a venture because it wishes them true; does not correct either them or itself, if they are false; and to get at the seat of things as they truly are seems to feel no concern whatever.
>
> (Arnold 1887: 638–9; see also Griffiths 1992)

The emergent news values which informed the New Journalism were explicitly gendered at a number of different levels, in part so as to direct journalistic attention beyond the preoccupations of propertied, educated and leisured male readers. A range of factors were responsible for this shift, not least of which was the fact that newspaper proprietors and advertisers (especially in the domestic goods markets) alike were becoming increasingly inclined to regard women consumers as an important audience on their own terms. This movement also

1

created spaces for the re-articulation of bourgeois definitions of 'femininity' at a time when longstanding power-differentials based on sexual difference were undergoing extensive transformations across British society. 'The new press,' as Margaret Beetham writes, 'came to be associated with a range of characteristics which were traditionally "feminine", especially its tendency towards sensation and the personalising of information' (Beetham 1996: 118; see also Bateson 1895; Carter and Thompson 1997; Fry 1929; Grieve 1964; Head 1939; Hunter 1992; Knight 1937; Leslie 1943; Mills 1990; Sebba 1994).

Tellingly, though the contemporary 'story of modern journalism' now includes both press and broadcast histories, it continues to refer to similar types of developments, albeit often employing (in our view inappropriately) a language of 'post-feminism'. In Britain at the beginning of the 1990s, for example, many media commentators were insisting that this would be 'The Decade of Women'. Demographic statistics appeared to indicate that there would not be enough graduates to fill job demand, thus 'the female factor' suddenly became an important issue for employers, including those in the media industries (see Dougary 1994: xi). The Conservative government launched its 'Opportunity 2000' programme in 1990 to facilitate the movement of women into 'top jobs' so as to shatter the 'glass ceiling'. That same year would see three women appointed to editorial positions on national newspapers. As the recession started to take grip, however, the optimism of the beginning of the decade began to fade. Those women who had been successful in negotiating senior media posts were increasingly being portrayed in news accounts in either ambivalent or hostile terms.[2] More to the point, they were often the first to be 'let go' as 'efficiency gains' began to dictate moves toward 'downsizing' news organisations (at the time of writing, there is only one female national-newspaper editor, at the *Daily Express* and *Express on Sunday*).

Today, as we approach the start of a new century, the day-to-day culture of most newsrooms is still being defined in predominantly male terms. Whilst there has been a dramatic increase in the number of women securing jobs in journalism, white middle-class men continue to occupy the vast majority of positions of power throughout the sector. Women are still not being promoted to senior decision-making posts in proportion to the overall rôle they play in the profession. At a time when both broadcast and print news organisations are facing ever more intensive (and increasingly globalised) forms of competition, and when female readers, listeners and viewers remain as elusive as ever, the costs of this failure to treat women fairly in the journalistic workplace continue to mount. A study of British journalism by Anne Sebba documents the varied types of discrimination female newsworkers often encounter with their male counterparts, 'some of whom may feel themselves threatened by the star status accorded to several women reporters, others of whom resent what they see as special privileges granted them; a few merely patronise their female colleagues' (Sebba 1994: 9; see also Christmas 1997; Tunstall 1996). Still, this is not to deny that women have made crucial gains in the field of news reporting which have fundamentally altered the types of sexist dynamics which once characterised the profession, as described by Peacocke (1936) above. Nevertheless, Sebba (1994: 10) is not alone when she looks forward to the day when 'women reporters are working in sufficient numbers that they are no longer judged by their looks, their personalities or their private lives and when we, the audience, are able to absorb merely the news they are reporting'.

Critical modes of enquiry

To point out that journalism is central to the study of the modern mass media across a range of academic disciplines is to state the obvious. Even a cursory glance at the research literature, however, confirms that insufficient consideration is being given to an array of pressing questions regarding how gender relations shape its forms, practices, institutions and audiences. It was a commitment to addressing this exigency which led, in turn, to the project that would eventually culminate in this volume.

The contributors to *News, Gender and Power* were invited to demonstrate from their respective analytical perspectives precisely why the media politics of gender deserve much more critical attention than they have typically received to date. Shared by each of the following chapters is a specific politics of intervention, that is, a desire to disrupt the familiar assumptions characteristic of conventional thinking about these issues. In highly varied ways, each of them draws upon the rich resources of feminist and gender-sensitive critique with the aim of providing fresh insights into a vigorous set of debates. A common thread running throughout the collection is a recognition of the need to rethink the organising tenets of earlier research with an eye to facilitating new work in this rapidly developing area of enquiry.

In this introductory essay, we would like to briefly highlight a series of important research problematics which underpin many of the themes later taken-up in a substantive way across a range of the chapters. Although we can offer only a sketch of several of the attendant conceptual and methodological issues here, it is hoped that the general contours of distinct modes of enquiry will begin to emerge as they inform the multiple interconnections between 'news', 'gender' and 'power'. Accordingly, we can identify, in schematic terms, eight interrelated problematics as follows.

1 Ownership and control

Feminist and gender-sensitive studies of journalism are becoming increasingly concerned with the changing patterns of news media ownership, especially with regard to the growing levels of concentration, conglomeration and integration, within local, national and global contexts. The dynamics of ownership are directly linked to a range of issues associated with control over journalistic content: media power is being restricted to an ever smaller number of (white male) hands; the corporate priority of profit maximisation is leading to a commercialisation of news formats whereby content becomes ever more uniform and the spaces available to articulate dissent are being reduced; and, fears over 'the bottom line' are reshaping news values in ways which frequently define feminist concerns as 'controversial', and thus potentially threatening to 'market sensitive' news organisations and their advertisers. The implications of reducing news to a commodity form like any other are profound, particularly when women's voices are struggling just to be heard within the confines of ideological parameters conditioned by these competing logics of capital. Proposed strategies for change call for a fundamental re-organisation of the current dynamics of media ownership and control, a process to be achieved through the radical re-structuring of state regulatory frameworks (see Domhoff 1978; Gallagher 1981; Jallov 1996; Mattelart 1986; Riaño 1994; Simonton 1995; Soothill and Walby 1991; Valdivia 1992; Wasko 1996).

2 Employment

At this level, and in light of the developments described above, new investigations are focusing on the changing nature of women's occupational status within news organisations. In general, the growing commodification of news has led these organisations to 'trim back' the number of journalists they employ, just as women are beginning to make serious inroads into the profession (a language of 'efficiency' is similarly used to justify a shift away from investigative reporting so as to focus on 'pre-packaged' news events which are easier, and cheaper, to cover). An organising assumption of much of this research is that the increased presence of women in the newsroom will necessarily encourage substantive changes in newswork practices: women, it is often argued, are more inclined than men to endorse informal, non-hierarchical management structures and to support collectively-based decision-making processes. In terms of news content, more female reporters means that the lines between 'hard' and 'soft' news will continue to blur, leading to a news agenda defined more closely with 'human interest' news (see Beasley 1993; Buresh 1984; Christmas 1997; Cramer 1993; Deakin 1984; Dougary 1994; Fritz 1979; Gallagher 1995; Grist 1984; Higgins 1997; Lafky 1993; Mills 1990, 1997; Norris 1997; Schulman 1995). At the same time, however, other researchers have questioned the extent to which arguments such as these can be supported as a general rule (see B. Smith 1989; van den Wijngaard 1992; van Zoonen 1991, 1994). Many are sceptical of the claim that there is a 'woman's perspective' which female journalists inevitably bring to their reporting. In any case, as Jane Arthurs contends in her discussion of the televisual industry in Britain: 'More women in the industry is not enough: there need to be more women with a politicised understanding of the ways in which women's subordination is currently reproduced, and with the will to change it' (Arthurs 1994: 100).

4

3 Professional identity

Feminist studies of the processes of socialisation, which reporters undergo when learning the skills necessary for their job, continue to raise awareness of how gender relations underwrite journalism as a profession (see Baehr 1996; Epstein 1978; Foote 1995; Gill 1993; Lafky 1995; Makins 1975; Mata 1994; Molotch 1978; Rhodes 1992, 1995; Schultz-Brooks 1984; Smith 1980; Stott 1973; van Zoonen 1994; Weaver 1997). In the 1930s, Emilie Peacocke (1936) told aspiring female journalists that reporters learnt their craft through a system of reward and punishment. Rewards included being given the 'good assignments' ('serious' news stories), peer acknowledgement, praise, promotion and acclaim; punishments included increased demands for story re-writes as well as the outright rejection of their work, being given less prestigious assignments ('Society news', the women's department, obituaries), and being relegated to 'trite' beats such as 'Lifestyles'. Today, feminist researchers have sought to elucidate how certain 'common sensical' attitudes, values and beliefs about gender inform the criteria underpinning what counts as 'professionalism' and how they, in turn, shape the forms of sexism regularly encountered by female journalists both in the newsroom and in the field (see Bradley 1995; Christmas 1997; Coles 1997; Dougary 1994; Elwood-Akers 1988; Graham 1997; Higgins 1997; Hoffman 1970–1; Kaufman 1995; Mills 1990; Sanders and Rock 1988; Sebba 1994; Skard 1989; Skidmore 1995; Smith et al. 1993; Steiner 1997b; Walkowitz 1993). As much of this work suggests, it is the very taken-for-grantedness of the professionalised norms that govern journalistic routines and conventions which makes them difficult to identify, let alone challenge.

4 News sources

News sources, routinely organised by the journalist into a 'hierarchy of credibility' (Hall et al. 1978), are encouraged to speak the social world in certain preferred ways. Studies of media–source relations show that journalists tend to rely primarily upon white, middle-class, middle-aged, professional males as sources, particularly when 'expert' opinions are being accessed (see Beasley 1993; Bridge 1995; Croteau and Hoynes 1992; Holland 1987; Rakow and Kranich 1991). 'News is not simply mostly . . . about and by men', John Hartley writes, 'it is overwhelmingly seen through men' (1982: 146). When women are included as news sources, as several feminist researchers have argued, they tend to be defined in terms of their status vis-à-vis the principal (typically male) news actor in a particular story. As Patricia Holland points out, women are routinely presented:

> either as an anonymous example of uninformed public opinion, as housewife, consumer, neighbour, or as mother, sister, wife of the man in the news, or as victim – of crime, disaster, political policy. Thus not only do they speak less frequently, but they tend to speak as passive

reactors and witnesses to public events rather than as participants in those events.

(Holland 1987: 138–9)

This gendered division is linked, in turn, to an alignment of 'serious' news values with public-sphere events deemed to be of interest to men, whilst so-called 'women's issues' are more likely to be framed in relation to the 'private' or domestic sphere (see C.F. Epstein 1978; Finn 1989–90; Hanmer and Saunders 1993; Lees 1995; McCormick 1995; Meyers 1994; Nava 1988; Norris 1997; Pingree and Hawkins 1978; Robinson 1978; Rupp 1980; Simpson 1979; Skidmore 1995; Tuchman 1978a, 1978c; van Zoonen 1991, 1992; Voumvakis and Ericson 1984).

5 Representation

Feminist research has long been concerned with how women are portrayed in news media texts, and much of this work has employed the notion of 'stereo-types' to advantage (see Allen *et al.* 1996; Baehr 1980; Baehr and Spindler-Brown 1987; Barr 1977; Benedict 1992; Caputi 1987; Davies *et al.* 1987; C.F. Epstein 1978; Gist 1993; King and Stott 1977; Koerber 1977; Lang 1978; Luebke 1989; McNeill 1996; Robinson 1978; Root 1986; Soothill 1995; Steenland 1995; Stratford 1987; Tuchman 1978b; Tunks and Hutchinson 1991). It is often argued that the journalist's deployment of these stereotypes, far from being harmless, is instead likely to result in 'negative and undesirable social consequences' for women (Lazier and Kendrick 1993). Stereotypes are usually defined as standardised mental pictures which provide sexist judgements about women such that their subordinate status within patriarchal society is symboli-cally reinforced. Demands to reform these types of stereotypical practices in journalism have tended to centre on the need to make news texts more 'accu-rate' or 'true to real life' in their depiction of women's experiences. At the same time, however, some feminists query the value of this notion of 'stereotyping', arguing that it succeeds in obscuring the fluidly contradictory, and often contested, dynamics that it should otherwise be at pains to render visible (see Beetham 1996; Brake 1994; Cirkensa and Cuklanz 1992; Creedon 1993; Douglas 1994; Ganguly 1992; Holland 1983, 1987; Houston 1992; Macdonald 1995; Rakow 1992; Shevelow 1989; Steeves 1987; van Zoonen 1994; Wykes 1995; see also Adam and Allan 1995; Weedon 1997; Women's Studies Group 1978). Much of this work has initiated a conceptual shift to rethink the attendant issues of representation in terms of the ideological gendering of news as an androcentric form of discourse.

6 Narrative forms and practices

Another line of feminist research, as suggested by the problematic above, has sought to argue that news discourse constitutes a 'masculine narrative form'. Lana F. Rakow and Kimberlie Kranich maintain, for example, that in these masculinised narratives, women function not as speaking subjects but as 'signs'. In examining these narrative structures, they argue that 'since women are found so infrequently in news stories, and since they always sign as "woman" (unlike men, who do not ordinarily carry meaning as "man" because the culture assumes maleness as given), their function as sign is unique' (Rakow and Kranich 1991: 13). Moreover, they point out that the meaning of the sign 'woman' is similarly bound up with the assumption of whiteness: 'Both race and gender depend on linguistically categorising people, ostensibly to reflect biological (e.g., skin colour) differences but actually to create a political and hierarchical system of difference' (1991: 19–20). Also relevant here is John Fiske's critique of televisual news as 'masculine soap opera', where he observes that news and soap opera share several characteristics, including 'lack of final closure, multiplicity of plots and characters, repetition and familiarity' (Fiske 1987: 308). It follows from these modes of analysis that the narrative forms and practices routinely held to constitute 'news' will have to undergo critical reconsideration if the imperatives of male hegemony are to be challenged (see Carter and Thompson 1997; Clark 1992; Cuklanz 1996; Holland 1987; Kitzinger and Skidmore 1995; Meyers 1997; Rakow and Kranich 1991; Sanders 1993; Steiner 1992; Valdivia 1992; van Zoonen 1988; 1991; see also Tolson 1977). The same is true for the research process itself, as certain alternative forms of news discourse which often claim to speak more directly to women's experiences, such as talk shows, documentaries, magazines, and breakfast television, have tended to be overlooked – frequently being dismissed by male researchers as being 'infotainment' rather than 'proper news', and hence unworthy of scholarly attention.

7 Feminisation and sexualisation

'There is a move right across the media towards making the news more fun, more sexy, more entertaining', writes British journalist Suzanne Moore, 'as though there is an implicit understanding that news on its own is just too straight, too dull and too boring to attract those peculiar minorities, women and young people' (1997: 21). It would appear that for many different news organisations the division between 'hard' ('serious'; 'fact-based') news and 'soft' ('light' or 'human interest'; 'interpretation-based') news is slowly being dissolved or 'feminised', in part as a response to demands from advertisers that female readers be more actively pursued as a distinct audience-demographic group (see Branston 1993; Christmas 1997; Dougary 1994; Grindstaff 1997; Hartley 1996; Mills 1990; Rapping 1995; Shuttac 1997; Squires 1997; van Zoonen 1991). Several researchers maintain that this process of feminisation is dramatically recasting 'mainstream' (or 'malestream') news narratives. One recent example of such a shift has been the coverage of the death and global mourning of Princess Diana. Specifically, some argue that it illustrates the ways in which the

7

representation of certain highly privileged news celebrities allows a range of feminist debates to be articulated, and in a way which retains an emphasis on expressive feelings and emotions that would otherwise be disallowed under the constraints of 'objective' reporting or 'dispassionate' and 'detached' commentary. Feminised forms of reporting this tragic event elicited worldwide tributes from women for whom certain personal concerns (bulimia, the experience of divorce, very gender-specific feelings of worthlessness) had been given a greater public voice.

8 News audiences

Researchers interested in investigating the actual ways in which people relate to news discourse have drawn upon a range of methodological strategies, including interviews, participant observation and ethnography (see Bird 1997; Brunsdon and Morley 1978; Gillespie 1995; Grindstaff 1997; Hobson 1980, 1990; Morley 1980, 1986; Philo 1990; Reid 1989; Schlesinger *et al.* 1992; see also Allan 1998, 1997b). Evidence drawn from these ethnographic accounts often indicates that how people watch televisual news, for example, is much less determined by the actual programming than it is conditioned by the social relations of its consumption. In tracing the contours of the social contexts of viewing within everyday domestic life in the household, a range of studies have highlighted the need to explicate the gendered nature of both televisual technology and the practices by which it is negotiated. In an early study, entitled 'Housewives and the mass media', Dorothy Hobson (1980) examines how a range of factors inform a sexual division of household labour which, in turn, conditions a gender-specificity with regard to programming preferences. Her female interviewees (young working-class mothers of small children) revealed a tendency to demarcate televisual news into a 'masculine' domain. In Hobson's words:

> There is an *active* choice of programmes which are understood to constitute the 'woman's world', coupled with a complete *rejection* of programmes which are presenting the 'man's world' [predominantly news, current affairs, 'scientific' and documentary programmes]. However, there is also an acceptance that the 'real' or 'man's world' is important, and the 'right' of their husbands to watch these programmes is respected: but it is not a world with which the women in this study wanted to concern themselves. In fact, the 'world', in terms of what is constructed as of 'news' value, is seen as both alien and hostile to the values of women.
>
> (Hobson 1980: 109)

The social world, as represented in news discourse, is generally seen by the women in this study to be 'depressing' and 'boring'. Still, Hobson points out that 'the importance of accepted 'news values' is recognised, and although their own world is seen as more interesting and relevant to them, it is also seen as secondary in rank to the 'real' or 'masculine' world' (1980: 111). As more recent research studies have similarly argued, the varied social uses to which televisual news is put need to be examined in association with the (usually unspoken) rules by which the very 'normality' of everyday life, especially its patriarchal structures, is defined and reproduced (see also Brunsdon and Morley 1978; Dines and Humez 1995; Gillespie 1995; Gray 1992, 1996; Grindstaff 1997; Hobson 1978, 1980; Lull 1990; Mattelart 1986; Morley 1980, 1986; Nightingale 1990; Press 1991; Silverstone 1996).

Overall, then, this brief sketch of several particularly salient problematics (located, as they are, amongst a host of others) illuminates some of the rudimentary features of the ongoing debates we regard as being central to this volume's analytical and strategic agendas. In electing to outline them in this fashion, it has been our intention to help establish a conceptual point of departure for the critical discussions to follow in the various contributions. As will quickly become apparent, each of the respective chapters provides a unique vantage point from which its author(s) engages with the challenge of extending these types of problematics into new areas of concern.

Notes

1 Similarly, Kay Mills (1990: 24), in her account of US journalism at about this time, argues that female reporters tended to be restricted to these same types of stories to cover. There were exceptions to this general rule, however, and she describes how a limited number of female reporters became their newspaper's 'stunt girl'. Such women wrote about controversial subjects, such as divorce and prostitution, and often placed themselves in physically dangerous situations to get 'sensational' stories on topics like the failure of social welfare programmes for women and children. Still others assumed the rôle of 'sob sister', whose function it was to report on court trials where they would "watch for the tear-filled eye, the widow's veil, the quivering lip, the lump in the throat, the trembling hand" (Ross cited in Mills 1990: 26; see also Banks 1902; Beasley and Gibbons 1993; Carpenter 1946; Furman 1949; Henry 1993; Marzolf 1977, Ross 1936; Schlipp and Murphy 1983; Steiner 1992, 1997a; Steiner and Gray 1985).

2 At that time, a BBC report on the first three women newspaper editors was broadcast under the title: 'Killer Bimbos on Fleet Street'. Ginny Dougary (1994: xiii) claims that 'the shorthand has stuck, and set the trivialising tone for subsequent articles on Eve Pollard. When she moved from the *Sunday Mirror* to become the first female editor of a mid-market newspaper, the *Sunday Express*, the *Observer's* interviewer described her as "A 'Killer Bimbo' who knows how to use her bosom as cosh" '.

Part I

THE GENDER POLITICS
OF JOURNALISM

INTRODUCTION

In July 1889, a British trade newspaper published a report on the growing prominence of women reporters. It announced the 'invasion of Fleet Street's sanctity [by] journalistic damsels everywhere taking their place at the reporters' table, or hurrying up to the offices about midnight with their "copy" – chiefly Society news'.[1] If, from the vantage point of today, the use of this type of language to describe the work of female newsworkers is so anachronistic as to be almost amusing, this is not to deny that many of the gendered inequalities it inadvertently identifies are still with us in the 1990s.

Neatly pinpointed in this quotation are a number of themes which inform the chapters presented in this section of the book. In the first instance, for example, there is the notion of female journalists *invading the sanctity* of the newsroom – today it is still a predominantly male domain of work, the dynamics of which are largely shaped by patriarchal norms, values and traditions. Recurrently it is the case, as several of the following contributions document, that women are being denied an equal place at the *reporters' table*. Similarly, the pejorative connotations of the phrase *journalistic damsels*, echoes of which are arguably discernible in the use of quotation marks around the word *copy* above, highlight sexist assumptions about women's professional capacities as journalists. These assumptions, moreover, appear to be contingent upon a hierarchical division between the 'hard' news (serious and important) to be covered by male journalists and, in marked contrast, the *Society* or 'soft' news (trivial and insignificant) reported by female journalists. There is little doubt, of course, which type of news is to be understood as being consistent with the ethos of Fleet Street, and which type threatens its proclaimed journalistic integrity.

It is precisely this issue of the gendering of news across a 'hard'/'soft' division which is addressed by Patricia Holland in her chapter, 'The politics of the smile: "Soft news" and the sexualisation of the popular press'. She begins by pointing out that in Britain during the 1880s and 1890s, when popular newspapers first sought out a mass readership, they needed to be acceptable to women readers. Hence the newspapers became *feminised* with 'soft' as well as 'hard' news. This process of 'feminisation', she argues, was a move which aimed to boost the sales of the papers, but it also opened a more democratic, public space for the discussion of issues of concern to women. Following Rupert Murdoch's transformation of the *Sun* in the 1970s, the popular tabloids became *sexualised* with the use of explicit sexual material. The image of the 'Page Three' girl became the symbol of a readership divided on sex and gender grounds. Holland contends that sexualisation came to structure news stories as well as entertainment items. The discursive use of a woman's body, underpinning the view of the world presented by the 'downmarket' tabloids, makes radical, democratic content less possible. Although women continue to contest the masculine definition of the Page Three image, their public participation is called into question when a sexualised difference remains as a constant potential discipline on their actions. In this way, then, Holland seeks to problematise the democratic status of sexualised news in publications like the *Sun*.

Several related questions regarding the gendering of 'hard' and 'soft' news typfications are taken-up by Liesbet van Zoonen in her chapter, 'One of the girls?: The changing gender of journalism'. More specifically, she argues that journalism as a profession is undergoing important changes as the relative power of female journalists improves. At issue is the extent to which market-driven journalism both depends on and exploits topics and angles usually associated with 'femininity', such as 'human interest', emotions, audience needs and desires, and sensationalism. This type of journalism, van Zoonen suggests, seems to be more open to women and their supposedly particular journalistic rôle conceptions than 'traditional' news journalism. Theoretically, this means that the usual link between media professionals and media texts is turned around. That is to say, it is not the number of women or men in journalism that determines what the news looks like – as is suggested in many feminist studies on journalism – but it is the nature of the genre which allows for a masculine or feminine style of journalism. She argues that this style, in turn, is not necessarily tied to men and women, nor does it necessarily signal a feminist improvement of current newswork practices.

John Hartley's chapter, 'Juvenation: News, girls and power', seeks to problematise several of the key presuppositions which tend to inform discussions about the media politics of gender. On the basis of evidence of 'juvenation' in the news media, he argues that *power* in this context is not a helpful concept, and that *gender* is not the site of most intense semiotic activity in the 1990s. It follows, in his view, that 'power' needs to be rethought in terms of *readership*, 'gender' in terms of *age* (juvenation), and the relations between journalism and the public as *teaching*. From this position, he proceeds to suggest that journalism, both broadsheet and tabloid, gathers populations into readerships, and it teaches social identities and civic proprieties, using young girls as a newly significant semiotic and political figure. It is Hartley's contention that the news media rely on positive juvenation to appeal communicatively to their readership, but at the same time they use the figure of the young girl negatively, as a marker of the boundary between 'Wedom' and 'Theydom'. While 'the young girl' has entered history, he argues, stories display features that treat children as a 'virtual internal colony'.

'Gender, privacy and publicity in "media event space"' by Lisa McLaughlin examines several pertinent issues in relation to news coverage of the O.J. Simpson case as both a 'mass' phenomenon and a spectacle of particularity. Following an evaluative appraisal of Habermas's (1989) *The Structural Transformation of the Public Sphere*, she turns to consider the recent critiques of feminist scholars attempting to document the exclusions constitutive of the normative and historical dimensions of the 'public sphere'. In her view, coming to an understanding of the Simpson case and other contemporary mediated events requires integrating the concerns of Habermas and his feminist critics in such a way as to foreground concerns about how differences are produced, circulated and managed through the judging, selecting, ordering and framing practices of the mass media. Reconciling these two lines of critique, she contends, offers an opening for new insights into the deleterious effects of media spectacle on both privacy and publicity. McLaughlin's analysis of the spectacular representation of domestic violence in the Simpson murder case reveals that the problem was narrowly constructed as a couple of events in the life of a woman, rather than as a profoundly gendered, ongoing form of violence against women.

A historical perspective is provided by Janet Thumim's chapter, ' "Mrs Knight *must* be balanced": Methodological problems in researching early British television'. In focusing on the formation of the television institution in Britain, she takes us back to the period of 1955–65, the beginning of which is marked by the launch of the independent television network (ITV) as a commercial rival to the BBC. Attention first turns to three memos from the BBC archives which, she argues, resonate with questions about the early forma-tion of the television institution and about the thorny and complex question of women and 'the feminine' in this period. There follows a discussion of the BBC Talks Department and the growth of news and current affairs coverage, with particular reference to the gender hierarchy apparent in this prestigious area of broadcasting. A detailed discussion of the BBC current affairs programme *Panorama* follows, in which she speculates on the problematics of gender politics both during this period and for today's feminist scholar operating with the benefit of hindsight. Throughout the chapter, Thumim draws attention to the particular problems of access and of method confronting the researcher.

Myra Macdonald's chapter, 'Politicizing the personal: Women's voices in British television documentaries', examines how women's voices are incorpo-rated in television documentary. Of particular importance, in her view, is the need to assess the relevance to television aesthetics of feminist reworkings of the concept of 'experience', and the conditions these propose for successfully politicising the personal. Three modes of presenting women's voices in docu-mentary are identified and evaluated: the 'confessional', the 'case study' and 'testimony'. Macdonald then proceeds to show that only the mode of 'testi-mony' actually succeeds in unsettling the conventional boundaries between the personal and the political, namely by drawing attention to the movement between the ontological and the epistemological. Testimony also undermines the traditional gendering of these terms, she argues, as well as providing a basis for challenges to the rigidity of documentary's wariness about the legitimacy of subjectivity as evidence.

Part I of the book concludes with Stuart Allan's chapter, '(En)gendering the truth politics of news discourse'. In attempting to contribute to current discussions about the gender politics of news 'objectivity', he highlights for exploration what may be termed, after Mikhail Bakhtin, 'the dialogics of truth'. Allan argues that a gender-sensitive engagement with Bakhtin's conceptual project encourages a sustained reconsideration of many of the ostensibly 'common sensical' precepts underpinning conventional journalistic procedures for dealing with conflicting truth-claims. To this end, a number of the rationales informing different feminist assessments of the heuristic value of Bakhtin's writings are addressed so as to accentuate the basis for a critique of 'monologic' notions of truth as they inform journalistic appeals to 'objectivity'. Allan then proceeds to elaborate a Bakhtinian approach to the news account as a gendered site of dialogic interaction, one which is inextricably caught-up in matrices of definitional power. In this way he aims to help facilitate further efforts to investigate the ideological inflection of truth in news discourse precisely as it appropriates 'the world out there' into an androcentric constellation of 'impartial facts'.

Note

1 This quotation is cited in Hunter (1992: 688); additional discussions of the working practices of female journalists in the early days of the British and US news media include: Bateson 1895; Banks 1902; Beasley and Gibbons 1993; Carpenter 1946; Fry 1929; Furman 1949; Grieve 1964; Hardt and Brennen (eds) 1995; Head 1939; Henry 1993; Knight 1937; Leslie 1943; Marzolf 1977; Mills 1990; Ross 1936; Schlipp and Murphy 1983; Sebba 1994; Steiner 1992, 1997a; Steiner and Gray 1985.

1

THE POLITICS OF THE SMILE

'Soft news' and the sexualisation of the popular press

Patricia Holland

'What makes a woman smile?'

The *Sun* newspaper aims to make women smile. Where it has total control, in the photographs which give its pages such graphic impact, its success is, literally, spectacular. Smiling women appear on the news pages and the celebrity pages. They appear in the glamour pictures; the pictures of royalty and of television personalities; in the pictures of ordinary people whose everyday lives have brought them good fortune, and, above all, they appear on Page Three. The woman who proudly displays her breasts is almost always smiling.

The *Sun* gave a decisive twist to the very meaning of a popular paper when, following its purchase and re-launch by Rupert Murdoch in 1969, editor Larry Lamb set about exploiting entertainment values with unprecedented panache. He based the paper's appeal on irreverence, scandal, 'saucy' humour and sex. Above all he introduced the daily image of a half clad woman. The Page Three 'girls', 'those luscious lovelies you drool over at breakfast time' (*Sun* 20 September 1982) became a shorthand reference for all the paper stood for.

Popular newspapers seek to amuse as much as to inform, to appeal to the emotion as much as to the intellect. The smile has been established as part of a package which continues to reach out to real women and men in an invitation to buy the paper and engage with its informal address. Increasingly over the twentieth century the aim of the popular press has been to 'tickle the public' with entertainment values. Matthew Engel took the title of his book on the history of the British popular press from an anonymous verse that went round Fleet Street in the nineteenth century:

> Tickle the public, make 'em grin,
> The more you tickle the more you'll win.
> Teach the public, you'll never get rich,
> You'll live like a beggar and die in a ditch.

> (Engel 1996: 17)

From the 1880s and 1890s, the introduction of lightweight features and all types of trivia, including the domestic, as well as a move to a 'softer' more ticklish type of news, has been seen as a *feminisation* of the new mass-circulation press, brought about by its desire for a broad appeal. In seeking out a mass audience, there was a need to recognise women as an influential segment of the potential readership, and the feminine had long been identified with the popular and accessible. But the changes initiated by the *Sun* in the 1970s pushed the meaning of 'popular' in a new direction. The *Sun* was no longer feminised, but *sexualised*.[1] Central to its appeal was the provocative image of a woman's body. Breasts were added to the smile. Instantly this implied a readership sharply divided along gender lines. Men and women readers were separately addressed, through a language and imagery which carried the full power of sexual, as well as gender, difference. The smile on the face of the Page Three girl conveyed a double message, 'After a lifetime of learning to establish eye to eye contact during conversation, the glamour girl has to learn to accept eye to breast contact' explained ex-Page Three girl, Jackie Sewell (Wigmore 1986: 13).

A changing relationship between the public and the private spheres of activity has been acted out in the pages of the twentieth-century press. Areas of life, constructed as private in the nineteenth century were now drawn back into public view. At first, the new mass-circulation papers sought to make visible the domestic and the personal. They circulated gossip, scandal, human-interest stories and a wealth of material on household management, cooking, childcare and other domestic issues. 'Softer' news brought a more personal, more human face. Then, in the last decades of the twentieth century, the even more private world of sexual activity became uninhibitedly publicised. Sexual material had long been part of popular imagery, but the nineteenth century and early twentieth century had taken for granted that this was something for men only, and it was concealed from general public view. Now sex brazenly invaded the news columns and dominated the entertainment pages. The concept of 'privacy' can no longer imply 'invisibility', although the terms of its visibility remain hotly contested.[2]

Women's democratic participation, and the role of a newspaper in furthering democratic involvement, is also at issue. A democratic press must also appeal to women and, by the end of the nineteenth century, women were already demanding the space to express their public concerns. Democratisation *entails* feminisation. By the 1970s, the *Sun* was claiming that the sexualisation of the press also brought greater democratic freedoms – for women as well as for men. But the pivotal image of a woman's body brought those claims up against the boundaries of sexual difference. In 1986 MP Clare Short introduced a Parliamentary Bill to ban the use of the Page Three pin-up on the grounds that it was embarrassing and degrading for women. In the heated debates which followed – in Parliament, in the media and around the country – the relationship of women's sexualised image to women's public presence became an issue which divided feminists as well as the public at large. Many suggested that the circulation of the image made women less secure in all sorts of public arenas, from the daily experience of walking in public places to the wider sense of playing a role in public life (Tunks and Hutchinson 1991). Since women were ever more assertively establishing their presence in all spheres of public life, including journalism, it was clear that the movement from feminisation to sexualisation in the pages of the downmarket tabloids had a political dimension.

The shift in emphasis poses questions about the nature of women's presence in the public sphere of discourse and decision making in a new way. It also poses questions about the nature of news itself. Tabloid editors continue to ask, 'what makes women smile?', but *we* should be asking how do women participate. What would it mean for the presentation of news to be properly 'engendered' – to use the term Anne Phillips (1991) used of democracy – in order to achieve a popular media that would be equally potent and meaningful for both sexes?

Some years ago I wrote an article which looked at Page Three from the point of view of women readers, and suggested that its claims to address ordinary women in a new way had some foundation (Holland 1983). I now want to explore more fully the politics of those claims.

The feminisation of the press

The evolution of the popular press has brought with it a changing relationship between readers and text. It has also, from its earliest days, helped to create an expanding sphere of public discourse which, of necessity, involved increasing numbers of women. As part of the mass audience, women were to make a public appearance on terms which had hitherto been denied (Benhabib 1994; Ryan 1996).

The new technologies of the late nineteenth century for the first time enabled daily newspapers to address a huge and varied readership spread across the nation. Editors and interventionist proprietors aimed to please a wider range of people, many of whom had little time and less inclination to plough through the convoluted metaphors and classical allusions which characterised nineteenth-century newspaper prose. Readers were now to be pampered and 'tickled' rather than challenged or patronised. This 'new journalism' moved away from writing which indulged in ponderous self-importance towards a clearer, more accessible use of language, seeking to eliminate the sense of strain between readers and text created by more demanding reading.

> 'We shall do away with the hackneyed style of obsolete journalism: and the men and women that figure in the forum or the pulpit or the law court shall be presented as they are – living, breathing and in blushes or in tears – and not merely by the dead words that they utter' wrote the editor of the *Star*, T.P O'Connor in January 1888.
>
> (Engel 1996: 45)

For Evelyn March Phillips writing in the *New Review* (1895), the new journalism meant 'that easy personal style, that trick of bright, colloquial language, that determination to arrest, amuse and startle' (Hunter 1991).

Verbal attractiveness was accompanied by a move towards a more visual mode of presentation, led by the needs of advertisers. The new dailies depended on advertising revenue to keep their prices to a level their readers could afford (Curran and Seaton 1991). Advertising in itself was becoming an important new medium as the modern consumer-based, leisure economy began to get under way. The mosaic layout of a popular newspaper developed partly to accommodate illustrated and boxed advertisements, while the use of exclamatory and hortatory advertising slogans prefigured the use of striking headlines. There was a recognition that the newspaper purchaser 'doesn't read, he [sic] glimpses' (Engel 1996: 132; see also Allen and Frost 1981; Postman 1985).

It was thought that the less educated readers in the wider market would respond to a 'direct appeal to the eye'. The editor of the *Daily Illustrated Mirror,* the first British newspaper to use photographs, wrote, in January 1904:

> Our pictures do not merely accompany the printed news, they are a valuable help to the understanding of it. . . . the direct appeal to the eye, wherever it is possible, will supplement the written word, which is designed in a more cumbrous fashion to penetrate the mind.
> (quoted in Wombell 1986: 76: see also Holland 1997a, 1997b)

Importantly, a more visual style was also thought to appeal to that other group of new readers, women. A contemporary commentator is on record as saying 'Men naturally think in abstract concepts, women think in pictures' (Ryan 1996).

Women found themselves at the heart of the new society. Their economic influence was growing, as the aspirant working and lower-middle classes gained more purchasing power. The 'new woman' of the turn of the century was more independent, more likely to have a job which would bring her enough money to follow fashion, to make trips to the seaside and to buy magazines and other reading matter. At the same time, women were at the centre of a consumer economy which was increasingly based in the home. A more comfortable domestic life was becoming possible for those lower down the social scale, and homes began to be furnished with labour-saving and leisure goods. Even if they did not control the purse strings, women were the home-makers, and advertisers were anxious to reach an ever larger number of them.

A permissive address to women as consumers helped to open up the space for their public participation as readers. At the same time, women journalists were campaigning for recognition. Barred from the raucous male world of the newsrooms, women who aspired to a journalistic career lacked the means to acquire a basic training. In response, *Atlanta* magazine ran a 'school of practical journalism' for women in 1896 and organised writing competitions. A Society for Women Journalists was set up in 1884 to challenge women's exclusion from the clubs and societies through which members of the journalistic fraternity built up their networks and secured their status. The Society had its own offices and a club in Pall Mall for the benefit of the 2,000 women estimated to be practising (Hunter 1991; Sebba 1994; see also Calhoun 1992: 115, 284).

The changes in editorial policy opened the way for women writers, who could now be valued for bringing a personal touch to the pages of a paper. The powerful editor W.T. Stead, proponent of the 'new journalism', was amongst the first to employ women writers, appointing a woman, Hulda Friederichs, as chief interviewer on the *Pall Mall Gazette* in 1882. It was a short step from the personal to the disreputable. In the 1890s, the American Elizabeth L. Banks became notorious for her scandalous reporting of her life as a maid 'in cap and apron' for the *Weekly Sun*. ' "Oh, but we do not want the ordinary sort of writing from you" the editors would say' she wrote in her *Autobiography of a Newspaper Girl* (1902). ' "You've started this newer and more entertaining kind of journalism over here and you must keep it up!" '

The mass circulation press began to explore ways of appealing to different strata of women. The pioneer *Daily Mail,* launched in 1896, sought out the middle-class wife in the expanding suburbs through its personality and gossip pages. Discreet and respectable in appearance, it was designed to attract the upwardly mobile – or at least upwardly aspirant – with features on homemaking and household management for 'intelligent women'. In 1908 the paper set up the *Ideal Home* exhibition as a celebration of the domestic values to which the paper still adheres. 'All the world and her husband' flocked to its displays of domestic goods and consumer fantasies (Ryan 1996).

Following the success of the *Daily Mail*, its proprietor Alfred Harmsworth, soon to become Lord Northcliffe, was ready to move into new territory. In 1903, he launched the *Daily Mirror* specifically as a women's paper. It had a woman editor, Mary Howarth, and an all-woman staff. The experiment did not last long, killed by what sounds very much like misogyny as well as by the failure of its narrow formula of tittle-tattle and gossip for wealthy women. 'Women can't write and don't want to read' was Northcliffe's sour comment. The paper was denied the opportunity to live through its teething problems, and the replacement editor described sacking the female staff as 'a horrid experience – like drowning kittens' (Engel 1996: 150; Allen and Frost 1981).

Northcliffe's impatience was symptomatic. The aim appears to be to include 'feminine' values without handing over any power to women. In a memo to the editor of the *Daily Mail* he once wrote, 'the magazine page is getting less feminine. It should be a woman's page without saying so' (Ryan 1996). But while the appeal of the popular press was opening up the democratic scope of news information and widening the base of public debate to women as well as men, a link between femininity and a low public status was already engrained.

Andreas Huyssen has described the 'notion which gained ground in the 19th century that mass culture is somehow associated with women, while real, authentic culture remains the prerogative of men'. Women were seen as readers of 'inferior literature, subjective, emotional and passive, while man . . . emerges as a writer of genuine authentic literature – objective, ironic and in control of his aesthetic means' (Huyssen 1986: 47, 46). The 'feminine' remained linked to the visual, which seemed more easily accessible and less susceptible to rational thought than the verbal. Feminine discourse was not only outside the discourse of the educated classes, but was marginal to the universal claims of modernity and the political and public world.

The 'vulgar' tastes of a working class which was gradually acquiring facilities for leisure and cultural activities seemed equally separate from the masculine seriousness of the middle classes. For Huyssen, 'the problem is . . . the persistent gendering as feminine of that which is devalued' (1986: 53). This judgement falls into the very trap that Huyssen is describing, since 'gendering as feminine' is seen to be a 'problem'. For us the reverse problem is of concern, not the 'gendering as feminine of that which is devalued', but the devaluation of that which is gendered as feminine and, indeed, the devaluation of any move towards the incorporation of women's concerns, especially if this is done under the control of women themselves.

At issue is not just the seriousness and authenticity of popular news media, but the nature of their address to the reader. The move towards accessibility in the new journalism developed along two parallel paths, as the split between fact and opinion, reporting and feature writing, accuracy and 'colour' began to gape more widely, dividing the 'serious' papers from the tabloids as well as marking divisions within each individual newspaper. An informational address which claimed to be gender-neutral was set against an entertainment address which developed as feminised, lighter, less demanding and more entertaining. For 'factual' reporting, 'hard news', a language that was clear and to the point came to replace rolling Victorian clauses and circumlocutions. This was a language which made plain its claims to truth, accuracy and universality. The 'soft news' of the entertainment sections and the feature pages was to be judged by different criteria. Yet, despite the claim that 'hard news' made for universality, the distinction remained gender-marked, with women providing the colour and the human touch and men seeking out the reliable facts (Sebba 1994).

More complex difficulties arose as the century progressed and increasing numbers of women insisted on their right to be part of the world of 'hard news'. In a quite different way, 'softer' entertainment values continued to invade the news pages.

The sexualisation of the *Sun*

'What I like to do first thing in the morning is to sit up in bed and have a really good look at Vanya' wrote Colin Dunne in the *Sun* in September 1977.

> Sometimes she has a rose in her hair. Sometimes she wears a dainty necklace. Occasionally, the odd ribbon. Those apart she is always naked

22

and I wonder how it is that she and Ena Sharples can possibly share the same sex.

A sea change in the very definition of a newspaper came about when Rupert Murdoch bought the *Sun* in 1969 and decreed that its selling points should now be 'sex, sport and contests' (Engel 1996: 253). A year later, editor Larry Lamb introduced the topless models which became the paper's best known feature. Its predecessor, the trade-union backed *Daily Herald,* had endeavoured to create a sense of tough working-class community amongst its readers in the interwar years (Curran and Seaton 1991). From the 1970s, the *Sun* set out to create a different sort of communality by addressing the new working class prosperity, in which pleasure was legitimised and the culture of deference put aside. The promise of uninhibited personal gratification was compatible with a rapidly expanding consumer-based economy, and went together with an open contempt for established authority and those who would keep you in your place (Holland 1983).

Larry Lamb decreed that sex in the pages of the *Sun* was to be linked not to pornographic images, nor to highly groomed models, not even, primarily, to celebrities, but to tastefully posed, ordinary young women, smiling at the reader and revealing their breasts. They must be 'nice girls', he is on record as saying (Chippendale and Horrie 1992). In those days of innocence, the *Sun's* brash hedonism seemed to be sharing something of the freedoms argued for by feminism. Despite its unashamed commercialism, the change in style and content was in tune with the liberatory mood of the times. This was the era of *Cosmopolitan* magazine which opened up a public discussion of sex for women. Sex was explicitly dealt with in feminist magazines, notably *Spare Rib,* and even *Parents* magazine, which dealt with childcare issues, indulged in daring presentations featuring natural childbirth and a considerable amount of nudity. Rupert Murdoch was said to admire the 'serious' broadsheet, the *Guardian,* because of that newspaper's readiness to deal with issues of sexual behaviour on its women's pages. (The *Guardian* was later referred to by *Sun* writers as 'the World's Worst'.)

The *Sun's* class and gender realignments echoed a wider set of social changes, resisting the 'discourses of sobriety', trade unions, BBC news and old fashioned politics. It valued itself as a rebel, in reaction to the remnants of post-war stringency and narrow morality. Page Three was launched as an image of defiant liberation. Its message to men was age-old, but its message to women was that women are now free to be sexual. Generations of Page Three 'girls' encouraged women readers to join them, to be proud of their bodies and to have fun. The address to women, often in major features such as the amply illustrated adaptation of Joan Garrity's *Total Loving* (July 1977), was along the lines of, 'loosen up, discover sexual pleasure'. Images of naked men joined those of naked women.

The brashness, visual excitement and downmarket appeal of the *Sun* meant that no newspaper that aimed for a mass readership could ignore it. It was imitated by the long-established *Daily Mirror* – which introduced Page Three-type topless models for a brief period – and the newly established *Daily Star* which determinedly scattered bulging breasts throughout its pages. Finally it opened the way for the *Sport*, a tabloid which claimed to be a newspaper but which dispensed with all pretence to offer anything but fantasy and soft porn. The 'softening' of the news had taken a new turn with the reassertion of the female body as spectacle. The sexualisation of the popular press had brought a different set of alignments between public and private domains, and between masculine and feminine concerns in its pages.

On the one hand, sexualisation could be seen as a logical development of feminisation, continuing to draw into the wider debate issues of sexuality and sexual relations that had been hidden but which women themselves, not least in the feminist movement, now insisted were of public importance. On the other hand, there was a deep contradiction in the presentation. Although women were invited to enjoy themselves, to follow their desires and to drop their inhibitions, the divided address, accompanied by many a nudge and a wink, made it clear that *this* women's pleasure is above all a pleasure for men. In this context, the visual is no longer associated with women and with a less linear style of under-standing, but with a masculine insistence on the inalienable right to a lustful gaze.

The *Sun*'s visible culture of sex invaded every part of the paper, including the pages it has from time to time run for women. In the paper's own version of its history:

> The *Sun* called its women's pages 'Pacesetters' and filled them with sex. They were produced by women *for* women. But they were subtitled 'The pages for women that men can't resist' acknowledging that there are plenty of topics that fascinate both men and women. Like sex.
> (Grose 1989: 94)

But the sex remained male oriented. Chippendale and Horrie write of the 'laddish' culture amongst young women journalists on the paper, outdoing the 1990/1992).

As the years progressed, the *Sun*'s assertive vulgarity became differently aligned to the cultural and political map of the day. When Kelvin MacKenzie took over the editorship in 1981 the paper became strident in its radical Conservative sympathies, expressed as two fingers to the establishment and an insolent individualism. The Page Three image was part of a rightward move in a political and cultural consciousness confirmed by the years of Conservative Government. The central image of the semi-naked 'nice girl' and her welcoming smile was developed as a politics of disengagement. 'Page Three is good for you' was the caption which headed a Page Three picture in 1984.

24

P3's titillating tit-bits are just what the doctor ordered – as a tonic against all the world's gloomy news. Research has shown that the *Sun's* famous glamour pictures are a vital bit of cheer for readers depressed by strikes, deaths and disasters.

'A London psychologist' is quoted as saying:

> When you think how gloomy and threatening most of the news has been lately – strikes, assassinations, hijacks, starving millions and the falling pound – you need Page Three as a shot in the arm. I am sure the *Sun's* famous beauties are a vital safely valve for the country's men when things in general seem to be getting out of hand.

The embrace of the 'loadsamoney' culture, of jingo and bingo, was in tune with a mood which crossed the social classes. Other popular papers and the burgeoning magazine market had followed suit. The culture of sex-for-fun was echoed in advertisements and on television. By the mid-1990s, the *Sun* had lost its rebellious spice. Now its sexual obsessiveness had been overtaken by a host of 'laddish' magazines on the news stands, and by raunchy imagery on the advertising hoardings. On television *The Good Sex Guide* (1993–4) had kicked off the schedules of the new ITV company, Carlton, and inaugurated a genre of 'trash television' which was partly youth-oriented, partly masculine sex fantasy. Kelvin MacKenzie himself left the *Sun* and launched *Topless Darts* (1996–) on the cable channel, Live TV. In the pages of the *Sun* the humour could all too easily harden into malice and the sexual fun into a leery, sneery soft misogyny.

A relaxation of restraint also came to mean less restraint on intolerance. It made possible the intemperate abuse of those whose sexuality and lifestyle does not conform. In the daily mosaic of the newspaper, the image of the sexy woman continues to be laid against female demons like single mothers, lesbian teachers and ugly women, such as Ena Sharples, the *Coronation Street* character whom Colin Dunne had thought could not possibly share the same sex as Page Three girl Vanya. Although the excesses of the Kelvin MacKenzie years are now rare, the obverse of the culture of hedonism remains a theatre of cruelty, which takes pleasure in the distress of the targeted individual.

Women's visibility in the public realm has involved repeated reminders that (hetero)sexuality is always an issue between men and women, from the demand to see newsreader Angela Rippon's legs (Holland 1987), to a preoccupation with Prime Minister Margaret Thatcher's wardrobe. Which brings us back to the image of the smile and to the relationship between the body and the face in the iconic Page Three image.

Body and face

Much has been written about the use of the female body as spectacle and as commodity (Mulvey 1989; Coward 1984). Carole Pateman has drawn the issue even more firmly into the political realm in the unlikely context of the theory of contract which, for liberal thinkers, secures the legitimation of civil society. The theory proposes that free social relations take the form of a series of contracts freely entered into between autonomous individuals. Contracts, such as those involving employment, are governed by law, and structure daily life. Pateman points out that women have been largely overlooked by classical contract theorists, and that, although a contract is seen as the paradigm for an equal agreement, in those contracts which are of necessity between women and men – as in marriage – the parties begin from an unequal position. Such contracts always imply a politicised *sexual* difference and reinforce what she describes as men's 'sex-right' over women's bodies (Pateman 1988: 3).

It is important for her argument that we should not lose sight of this potent *sexual* inequality, as its specificity can too easily be lost in a discussion of other categories of inequality less subject to taboo, such as those of power or gender. Men's sex-right is central to contracts, from marriage to prostitution and surrogacy, 'in which the body of the woman is precisely what is at issue' (Pateman 1988: 224). Despite the liberal doctrine that 'everyone owns the property in their capacities and attributes' men still 'demand that women's bodies in the flesh and in representation should be publicly available to them' (1988: 13–14). A fanciful analogy might pose the Page Three smile as a form of contract which reaches out to the male reader. It appears to secure an unproblematic agreement between men and women which promises access to a sexualised body.

There are many possible types of smile. The *Sun* specialises in the 'lovely to see you!' smile, one which comes straight off of the page, the gaze of the smiler entangling with that of the viewer. It is cheerful, commonplace and relaxed, and it aims to elicit smiles from the readers, men and women.

> Try to avoid a toothy grin or a Bardot pout. This sort of expression can make you look self-conscious. It's best not to copy anyone. Just be yourself.

was the advice given to aspiring Page Threes (*Sun* October 27 1981).

This smile is familiar from the snapshots of friends and family treasured by almost everyone in the Western world. Ever since the introduction of the Box Brownie in 1900, the domestic snapshot, taken 'as quick as a wink', has sought to capture a smile which builds a bond of companionship between photographer and subject, quite different from the confrontational tension created in formal portraits taken by a professional photographer (Holland 1997a; Parr 1997).

This pictured smile is part of the familial ritual, a family masquerade. It is a welcome convention which expresses a longing for happiness and togetherness even when, tragically, it may conceal the opposite (Williams 1994; Spence and Holland 1991). It is an affirmation of belonging and fitting into place, an acquiescence underpinned by pleasure. The work of the newspaper smile is to create an engagement with its own special public, built on the analogy of family warmth.

Much of the text of the *Sun* is organised around the presence and absence of such a smile. In the tradition of the popular press it seeks out good news in contrast to the 'gloomy and threatening' news of the 'serious' broadsheets. As an object lesson to its readers it offers contrasting images of women who will not smile ('Mrs Misery', a betting-shop cashier, 'was sacked because she was so grumpy she drove punters away' (*Sun* 3 September 1996). Such surly refusal on the part of spoilsports, moralists and the bad tempered deprives every one else of their pleasure and undermines the security of the metaphorical family structure.

With this relaxed and familiar smile firmly in place, the *Sun* has gone on to forge an indissoluble link between the welcoming face and the revelation of women's breasts. 'Lovely to see you!' was the headline over a Portsmouth crowd greeting the fleet on its return from the Falklands in June 1982. A smiling young woman, an ordinary girl, just one of the crowd, pulls up her shirt to reveal her breasts. 'A pretty girl reveals how happy she is to see Britain's heroes home – by baring her charms for the delighted sailors', the text confirms (*Sun* 12 June 1982). Sexuality is both affirmed and its danger defused in the ordinariness of the presentation.

For those who refuse the link between smile and female sexuality, the threat of humiliation is always present. When, in 1986, Labour MP Clare Short brought in a Parliamentary Bill to ban Page Three, the response was personalised abuse against 'killjoy Clare'. The *News of the World*, at the time edited by ex-Page Three caption writer, Patsy Chapman, set out to find a picture of the MP in her night-dress (Tunks and Hutchinson 1991; Snoddy 1992: 110). This metaphorical attempt to undress Clare Short was symptomatic. Women who refuse to smile tend to be fully clothed, but once the clothes come off the message of the body cannot be denied. A face, even a smiling face, carries the potential of speech. The revealed body calms and defuses the challenge of that potential.

The Page Three image is an active, working image, layered with mythological resonance (Warner 1987). It displays a 'body that matters', to echo the title of Judith Butler's exploration of the discursive construction of real, material bodies. It works to reiterate the 'regulatory norms with which sex is materialised'. But as Butler goes on to point out 'sex is both produced and destabilised in the course of this reiteration' (Butler 1993: 10). The exposure of a woman's breasts needs strong legitimation, and that legitimation is achieved by the acquiescent smile. Page Three models repeatedly emphasise the point by speaking of the pleasure they take in the role.

Page Three has changed over the years. The models have become more knowing and the presentation has lost something of the exuberant celebration of the early days. Perhaps more importantly, the context in which it is to be understood is different. The women in the pictures are no longer timeless. The well-known models have grown older, and their public personae have developed. Some have had children; some, like Linda Lusardi and Sam Fox, have tried to build up show business careers; others have become unemployed and disillusioned. Their personal accounts of their experiences, published from time to time in newspapers as diverse as the *News of the World* and the *Guardian Weekend*, range from the maudlin to the insightful. Many give a very different picture from that portrayed in the jokey features which fill the pages of the *Sun*.

The highly visible image of a sexualised woman has brought into question the role of the popular press as a potential space for the expression of women's democratic aspirations and public participation. And yet an army of invisible women, journalists, photographers, researchers and editors has been steadily encroaching into hitherto-protected masculine preserves. Could it be that the reassertion of the irreducible differences on which *sexual* relations are based is partly a response to an increasing equality in *gender* relations?

Democracy, women and the public sphere

Rozsika Parker and Griselda Pollock have documented the historic relationship through which the status of male painters has depended on a distinct role for women in the world of art. While women were excluded as artists – the eighteenth-century Royal Academy banned them from its prestigious life-classes – their visible presence was necessary to the very concept of 'art'. The idealised image of 'woman' for centuries represented the archetypal subject for easel painting (Parker and Pollock 1981).

Just like the painted odalisque, the baroque visibility of women in the *Sun* is part of a fantastic excess with which the paper engages its readers. Repeating many similar ironies, the transformation of the popular press into a more accessible, more democratic medium – potentially more feminine – has been carried out through an image which works to temper women's equal participation in those public spaces. A vocal feminist opposition to Page Three has argued that the circulation of the image, as a fantasy for men, would put real women at risk in the physical spaces of the streets. My argument is that by reinforcing sexual difference, the nature of the democratic discursive space is brought into question. Democratic discourse, which needs to be feminised, reaches a different sort of limit when it becomes sexualised. This limit will always need to be negotiated, but negotiation is closed off if sexual difference is always presented in a way that reinforces sexual inequality.

It has been demonstrated in relation to a variety of historical contexts that the exclusion of women from public activities has been structural rather than a mere contingency. This means that the imbalance cannot easily be rectified by equal-opportunities legislation or positive-discrimination programmes, however important such initiatives may be. Carole Pateman has mapped out the ways in which the very concept of a liberal 'individual' implies a notion of sexual subordination, and 'civil freedom depends on patriarchal right' (Pateman 1988: 38, 219). In Hannah Arendt's account of the Greek polis, the private

domestic base was needed to create a public space in which *men* could participate as citizens (Arendt 1989). For Nancy Frazer, the concept of a 'public
sphere' which could make possible a free and equal exchange of views, was a
'masculinist ideological notion' (Calhoun 1992: 116). Joan Landes argued that
'the exclusion of women was constitutive of the very notion of the public
sphere' in the age of the French Revolution (Thompson 1995: 254).

It is consistent with these analyses that the 'serious' broadsheets, with their
claims to objectivity and universal values, have excluded women even more
firmly from positions of power. The first women to become editors of national
newspapers (apart from the first, abortive, *Daily Mirror*) have run the most scandalous of scandal sheets, rather than upmarket papers with liberal credentials.
Wendy Henry and Patsy Chapman, both editors of *News of the World*, learned
their trade on the *Sun*. Hence the paradoxical position that women who lay
claim to the exercise of power in the public arena of tabloid news must themselves oversee the fantasy image of a sexy woman.

The entertainment values which, in the popular press, now invade all parts of
the paper, need to be reconciled with 'public sphere' objectives, where participation depends on the restrained statement of competing opinions, and where
there is an assumption that all can contribute without regard to status or other
identity factors (Calhoun 1992). A viable 'public sphere' would be a democratic
space where, in the words of Anne Phillips, we can 'leave ourselves behind', and:

> We do want to 'leave ourselves behind' when we engage in democratic
> politics: not in the sense of denying everything that makes us the
> people we are, but in the sense of seeing ourselves as constituted by an
> often contradictory complex of experiences and qualities, and then of
> seeing the gap between ourselves and others as in many ways a product
> of chance.
>
> (Phillips 1991: 59)

The sexualised image of a woman is a constant reminder of the utopian nature
of this goal.

Excess and the politics of fun

A consideration of the position of women in the popular press points to the
need for an evaluation of the *political* implications of this interplay between fact
and fantasy, 'information' and entertainment. This means that the visual presentation of a newspaper, the size of the headlines, the style of language used are
never side issues. Hard news is always dependent on soft.

For that reason, rather than exploring the accuracy, bias or otherwise of the
popular press, I have, in this chapter, been concerned with other aspects of its
democratic role. Its role in circulating vocabularies, images and concepts with
which to make sense of the contemporary world and the place of men and

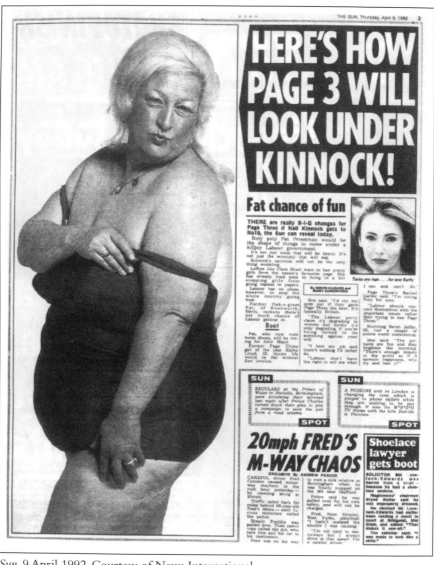

Sun, 9 April 1992. Courtesy of News International.

women within it, is of prime importance, but it also plays a role in offering a space in which people may see themselves, their views and their interests reflected, both as individuals and as groups. Bearing in mind these two aspects, rather than trying to isolate the informational content of the popular press from its entertaining presentation, a political critique would note the ways in which the news content is structured and shaped by entertainment values, while the information is itself filtered through the entertainment material (Curran and Sparks 1991). 'News' and 'entertainment' become ever more entwined as the entertainment matter colours the reader's understanding and itself carries important forms of information. James Curran has made this point in relation to the media in general, arguing that 'Media entertainment is one means by which people engage at an intuitive and expressive level in a public dialogue about the direction of society. Media entertainment is in this sense an integral part of the media's "informational" role' (Curran 1991a; 1991b: 102). Far from neglecting the political role of newspapers, this refocusing of attention is essential to an understanding of the downmarket tabloids as the most influential media of political communication .

The relentless push towards entertainment values has meant that the definition of what makes 'news' is itself constantly changing. The carefully established distinction between fact and opinion is now less easy to maintain. The need for accuracy has become dissolved into the excess of the headline, through a joke, an ironic exaggeration or an expression of outrage. It is part of my argument that, in the downmarket tabloids, the 'Page Three principle' has been a crucial element in this transformation. Images of women – seductive, spectacular yet naturalistic – have been central to a cultural and economic change which is also a political one. 'Samantha waving from the top of an armoured car as it was driven through the picket lines at Wapping was one of the defining moments of the 1980s', wrote journalist Peter Martin of Page Three icon Samatha Fox (Martin 1997: 16).

The long association made by the *Sun* between spoilsports, sexual puritans and a Labour Party now rejected as 'old Labour', has been a highly political campaign, filtered through the association of sexuality and a hedonistic lifestyle. As part of its violently anti-Labour stance during the 1992 election, the *Sun* replaced its usual Page Three with a bulgingly fat 'flabbogram lady', captioned 'Here's how Page Three will look under Kinnock! Fat chance of fun' (Seymour-Ure 1995). Political discourse of this kind appears to transcend party politics. The *Sun* dramatically changed allegiance for the 1997 election, supporting the Labour Party in its 'modernised' form under Tony Blair. On that occasion, its latest Page Three 'superstar', Melinda Messenger, 'Blairs all' and tells readers why she backs Tony Blair. Clearly the party-political switch had had no impact on the 'Page Three principle'. A politics of sexual fantasy which opens up a gap between women and men by reinforcing men's 'sex-right' over women's bodies continues to imply a political allegiance which ultimately undermines democratic participatory rights, and which continues to link the feminine with the trivial.

31

The *Sun* continues to reiterate that women's bodies matter, and it repeatedly demonstrates that the materiality of those bodies will always subvert women's claims to seriousness in a world where they need not smile. And yet, in the spirit of a sexuality which aims to be less under male control, many ordinary women have made it clear that they value the right to smile, even if, for the moment, they cannot smile entirely on their own terms. In a 1987 television debate, ex-Page Three model Linda Lusardi asserted that she had turned the Page Three image to her own advantage. She used it as a sign of the proud independence it had brought to her, rather than a sign of subordination to men's fantasies (BBC Community Programmes Unit 1987). That smile continues to be directed at women, too, even if it is instantly recuperated into the service of a masculine framework of understanding (Norris 1997).

But while real, embodied – if invisible – women continue to have only minimal roles in the shaping of our popular media, the men who produce the pages will continue to build their power on the decorative excess of the women who are pictured on them – just like the eighteenth-century academicians and their voluptuous models. Interestingly, a debate in the pages of the serious broadsheets during June and July of 1997 on whether a lightening of the news content of those papers constituted a 'dumbing down' or a feminisation, was largely conducted by women journalists and quickly took up the issue of women's writing. Smiling or not, the need is for participation on women's own terms. This, of course, will have consequences for the concept of 'news' and for that of 'entertainment'.

Notes

1 It is possible that 1998 will prove to be another turning point in the history of the *Sun* and the popular press in general. Following an underlying decline in the number of readers, which accelerated alarmingly from 1996, the *Sun* decided to change direction once again. It appointed a young woman, 29-year-old Rebekah Wade, as Deputy Editor, abandoned the Page Three pin-up and moved to a generally less laddish approach. The *Sun* felt the need to seek a new niche as, on the one side, magazines such as *Loaded* developed the raunchy style with spectacular success and, on the other, the mid-market *Daily Mail*, with its more serious journalism, increased its readership.

2 The Press Complaints Commission, the self-regulatory body which monitors the ethics of the British press, covers issues of privacy in its Code of Practice. The Commission responds to complaints from members of the public. Disputes regularly arise over the ethics of such issues as intrusive photography and intrusion on grief or shock. These issues are important, but the point that I am making here is a broader one about the general tenor of news values.

2

ONE OF THE GIRLS?

The changing gender of journalism

Liesbet van Zoonen

Introduction

More than a decade ago, in the early 1980s, Norwegian female journalists working in the daily press and television news were asked in an in-depth examination of their working conditions how they appreciated their jobs and what they thought of working in a male dominated environment. The majority of them said they did not have special problems in their daily contacts with their male colleagues. The expression they most frequently used was: 'I think I have been accepted as one of the boys' which implied that they felt they were treated as equals. But obviously, it also meant that they had adjusted to the unwritten rules and expectations of a male environment, 'the boys' being the invisible yardstick to which they had to live up (Skard 1989). In the same period, the early 1980s, Dutch female journalists working for daily newspapers were asked in a similar large-scale research project about their experiences and they too reported the need to adjust to the culture of the newsroom which most of them defined as *masculine*. One of them remembered the initiation she had to go through when she just started her job: 'My male colleagues were continuously making dirty jokes and covert sexual allusions and waiting to see me react to it. I ignored it basically but that did not satisfy them, so after a while they asked me what I thought of it. And I said, if you have to talk about it that much you are probably not very good at it. This was obviously witty enough because after that I was accepted as "one of the boys" ' (Diekerhof *et al.* 1985). To mention one other example still from that same period of the early 1980s, German female newspaper journalists also were subjected to an extensive examination of their experience in journalism and they too observed many masculine features in journalism to which they felt they had to adjust in order to be accepted as 'real' journalists. The high alcohol intake of German male journalists was mentioned as a particular problem (Neverla and Kanzleiter 1984).

Looking back, it seems as if the early and mid-1980s produced a wave of research about female newspaper and television journalists throughout the world. And whether the research came from Norway, the Netherlands and Germany, or from the USA, India or Senegal, basically a similar story was told

33

over and over again: daily journalism, whether it is print or broadcasting, is dominated by men; the higher up the hierarchy or the more prestigious a particular medium or section is, the less likely it is to find women; women tend to work in areas of journalism that can be considered an extension of their domestic responsibilities and their socially assigned qualities of care, nurturing and humanity; regardless of difference in years of experience, education level and other socio-economic factors, women are paid less for the same work. These inequalities were shown to stem from discriminatory recruitment procedures and from discriminatory attitudes among decision makers. Moreover, most women in these professions have experienced sexist behavior from their male colleagues. Finally, daily journalism and motherhood were apparently impossible to combine because very few women with children worked in journalism as compared to a considerable number of men with children (for an extensive summary, see van Zoonen 1994).

Such data are not unique to newspaper and television journalism but hold for a variety of other male-dominated professions, whether it is the police and the army, or surgeons and pilots. The debate about women in journalism has taken on an additional relevance, however, because of the particular tasks and requirements of journalism in democratic societies, one of which is believed to be the production and distribution of balanced and fair information. It was and is often said that the minority position of women in journalism affects the quality of the news product, be it the press or television. Because the news is made by men, it is thought to reflect the interests and values of men too, and therefore news cannot serve very well the needs of this famous other fifty percent of the population, namely women.

Men, women, male, female, masculinity and femininity are terms that have been and still are quite easily used in this debate. But what exactly is meant by the male and masculine character of news and journalism? How do female journalists and femininity fit into this picture and what would more 'female' or 'feminine' news look like? These questions were high on the agenda in the 1980s and the early 1990s, and whereas the debate now seems to have died somewhat, there is still a widespread assumption among many female journalists and feminist scholars that the news would change into new directions more relevant to women if only there were more female journalists. Two questionable issues are at the heart of this assumption: one is that journalists have sufficient autonomy in their day-to-day work to perform in a uniquely individual (and in this case gendered) manner. However, there is ample research that suggests the profession is organized in such a manner that different individuals will operate in much the same way, whether they are women or men. The second questionable issue is that female journalists are distinguished more by their femininity than by any other dimension of identity, like professionalism or ethnicity. However, the contested and contradictory nature of gender has become common sense in most feminist theory, thus undermining any possibility of a definitively 'feminine' input to the news by female journalists (van Zoonen 1988).

Recently, substantial changes in print, but in particular in television journalism, show that the gender of journalists is relatively unimportant for the way the news looks. What I will argue in this chapter is that news and journalism at present, with its increase of 'human interest' topics and angles, is becoming more and more 'feminine' despite the ongoing minority position of women in journalism. I will also argue that it is exactly those changes that may open up journalism as a profession for women. Thus I will turn around the debate some 180 degrees: I will not discuss the question of whether an increase in the number of female journalists will change the news, but will instead show how changes in the news genre allow for more female journalists to enter the profession.

'Feminine' values in journalism

Of course we cannot objectively define what is meant by male and 'the masculine.' Nevertheless, we can have a look at how journalists themselves perceive the gender of their profession, taking into account that some elements of journalism are not specifically gendered, like deadlines, space or broadcast hours. Survey and interview data from various Western countries suggest that it is in the definition of newsworthiness, particular angles and styles, professional norms and values that the masculine nature of journalism expresses itself (Creedon 1989; Diekerhof et al. 1985; Gallagher 1995; Neverla and Kanzleiter 1984; Skard 1989; UNESCO 1987; van den Wijngaard 1992; van Zoonen 1989, 1994; van Zoonen and Donsbach 1988). Female journalists often criticize the selection of newsworthy topics, claiming that topics that are relevant to women are often neglected in the press or relegated to marginal sections. The examples often mentioned are 'human interest' news, consumer news, culture, education and upbringing, and social policy. A Dutch female journalist, for instance, said: 'My colleagues and I used to fantasize about an alternative little paper that would appear besides the real one and which would only contain news we would really want to read: Funny events, unusual people that have interesting stories to tell, the ones you find in every little village; readers love that. Nobody is interested in this excess of political facts' (Diekerhof et al. 1985: 156, translation by this author). The fetishization of facts and factuality is indeed another common concern of female journalists who would appreciate more emphasis on causes and impacts, instead of another accumulation of new facts. In addition, many of them despise the search for scoops and sensationalism which may take on very blatant forms, as in crime reporting, but which can also express itself in the horse-race character of political reporting.

The masculine character of the news is also recognized in the choice of sources and spokespersons who are overwhelmingly male, despite the growing numbers of female politicians, public officials and other professionals. The choice of sources and spokespersons is seen as reflecting the personal networks of male journalists rather than being a representation of actual gender divisions among sources. Again, the expressions of journalists as 'boys' comes up when female journalists observe the existence of what they call 'old boys' networks.' Another element of masculinity in the news lies in male worldviews which underlie the actual reporting. Many female journalists mentioned the issue of unemployment as an example in which they would also focus on the impact of unemployment on family life, whereas their male colleagues supposedly would look at general employment patterns and the immediate victims only. Another interesting case to consider here is the reporting on senior citizens. In most countries they are primarily women; nevertheless reporting usually focuses on the older man, questioning whether he can still be an active citizen, for instance. Finally, many female journalists claim that they hold a set of ethical values different to that of their male colleagues. Female journalists feel they show more respect to their readers and their readers' needs than do their male colleagues. They also scorn the detachment and insensitivity in many of their male colleagues, believing they are hiding behind the idea of objectivity to exclude all compassion and humanity that one should bring to journalism.

The gendered nature of journalism then – as many female journalists throughout the world perceive it – can be summarized as follows:

Table 2.1 The gendered nature of journalism

	Masculine	**Feminine**
Topics	politics	'human interest'
	crime	consumer news
	finance	culture
	education and upbringing	social policy
Angle	facts	backgrounds and effects
	sensation	compassion
	male	general
Sources	men	women
Ethics	detached	audience needs

Sources: Creedon 1989; Diekerhof *et al.* 1985; Neverla and Kanzleiter 1984; Skard 1989; UNESCO 1987; Gallagher 1995; van den Wijngaard 1992; van Zoonen 1989, 1994; van Zoonen and Donsbach 1988.

Although male journalists interviewed in the research projects mentioned are less outspoken about the gendered nature of journalism, and certainly not critical of it, many of them also feel that female journalists do have another approach to news. This is demonstrated, of course, because part of these feelings are expressed in stereotypical views on what female journalists should do: cover fashion, babies and cooking, and in stereotypical views on what they cannot do: write tough stories on rising crime. Male journalists also assume that women are better at and more interested in 'human interest' stories, or in caring about audience needs.

Research results reveal what female and male journalists think and feel about their own professional values and conduct, what they think they do or would like to be doing. Whereas it may also seem that the data tell something about differences between women and men in journalism, they actually tell something about self-perceptions and self-images, which interestingly enough border on the stereotypical. Information on self-images, however, does not tell much about actual professional conduct. In fact, research on professional practices has found very little evidence of women performing differently from men in journalism, with the exception of women looking for female spokespersons (van Zoonen 1994). In addition, large-scale surveys found only one – albeit quite a revealing one – significant difference in role conceptions: women are indeed more oriented to audience needs than men (Weaver 1997).

Yet, when the perception of female and male journalists regarding their profession is so profoundly gendered, what does that mean for working conditions and professional performance? Obviously, it may and does result in discriminatory attitudes toward women. While 'femininity' and what is considered professional journalism are not inherently at odds with each other, the current definitions of femininity and the historically specific requirements of journalism produce tensions which – while expressed in different forms – are felt by many female journalists. Women, for instance, often get very stereotypical assignments which relegate them to marginal areas of journalism. They also have to live up to a double requirement: they have to show in their daily performance that they are good journalists as well as 'real' women. In the Netherlands, many female journalists feel that they are primarily judged as women; they are subject to ongoing comments on their looks and they have to regularly confront friendly heterosexual invitations or unfriendly sexual harassment. Playing the game of heterosexual romance means that women will lose their prestige as professional journalists. But women who ignore it – or worse, criticize it – will not be accepted by their male colleagues as real women; instead they are seen as bitches, viragos or – the worst – 'feminists'. From a country as vastly different as Senegal similar tensions between what is considered appropriate for women and professional journalism have been reported: Senegalese female journalists are accused by their colleagues and their environment of having lost their femininity because their jobs require them to be away from home and 'neglect' their husband and children (van den Wijngaard 1992).

Given such very strong social prescriptions and restrictions on femininity, and by omission on masculinity, the almost stereotypical self-perceptions of female and male journalists make more sense. Apart from reflecting their ideas about journalism, female views may also be seen as efforts to show that despite their professionalism they are still very much 'true' women. This does produce a very awkward situation, of course, because the other way around, they also have to prove that despite their femininity they are good professional journalists. Since masculinity as it is currently defined in Western societies accords so much better with journalism's values, men's professional identities are much less fragmented and problematic than those of women in journalism. This, then, is the predicament in which female journalists have found themselves. It is the result of the minority position of women and the particular professional values of journalism. There are, however, a number of structural developments in journalism that suggest that the situation may change in the decades to come.

Market-driven journalism

To begin with, the number of women in journalism is steadily rising: according to a recent UNESCO report on employment patterns in the media, women now make up the majority of journalism students, especially in Europe and the Americas (Gallagher 1995). In my own department of Communication Studies in Amsterdam some sixty-five percent of the students are female; in the Netherlands as a whole this figure is fifty percent. In Norway, fifty-five percent of journalism and communication students are women, in the UK this figure is about fifty-two percent and in the USA it is forty-nine percent, to mention some arbitrary examples. This does not mean of course that these female students all end up in news journalism. Almost to the contrary, it seems there are still many barriers between having graduated from journalism school and becoming a news journalist. Recent European figures on the employment of women in television and print news confirm this point (see Table 2.2).

Table 2.2 Female employees in news media

	Press reporter/editor	TV journalist
Netherlands	26%	20%
Sweden	★	44%
Finland	★	44%
Denmark	24%	29%
UK	23%	25%
USA	34%	25%

Source: Gallagher 1995.

Note: ★ indicates figures not available

Whereas these figures are definitely higher than some fifteen years ago, improvements are still not very impressive, especially if we consider that most female journalists are young, leaving the profession in their early thirties when they decide to have children. As mentioned earlier, research shows that, by and large, it is nearly impossible for women in journalism to combine their career with children, whereas for men this is much easier.

Given that women are a majority in the schools for journalism and communication, but that they do not work very often in the daily press or television news, where then do they end up? Partly, they tend to find employment in communication sectors which are not considered to be journalism, such as public relations and information management. In addition, women tend to (find) work in what are perceived as the low-status fields of journalism (at least when looked at from the traditional press angle) like magazine publishing and infotainment television.

British media scholar Colin Sparks (1991) has related the position of men and women in journalism to changes in the media industry as a whole. In Britain, the number of newspapers has been falling over the century. On the other hand, the number of magazines in the UK is rapidly rising, thus the balance in journalism is clearly away from newspaper employment towards the magazine sector. This change does not only involve a shift towards another kind of medium, there is a related shift in content also. Because whereas newspapers are aimed at a general public and concerned with general social and political issues, magazines are mostly directed at special-interest groups, the two main growth areas in magazine publishing being publications aimed at particular occupational groups and those aimed at special leisure activities such as travel and sports. Sparks concludes, therefore, that fewer and fewer journalists are what we traditionally think of as journalists (the reporter of political and social information necessary for democracy to function), but more and more journalists are working in the entertainment or specialized information provision of the magazine sector. And, for a variety of reasons, the magazine sector has always been more open to women than the press and television news sector.

This development, then, does suggest an incipient feminization of journalism as a result of the shift from newspaper to magazine publishing. A possible counter-argument – that magazine publishing is not part of journalism – does not hold. To begin with, most magazine journalists consider themselves journalists but, more importantly, the present distinction between, for instance, press and television journalism or the news and magazine sector signifies mainly an acceptance of a hierarchy of journalisms rather than a useful division between truly different kinds of journalism, especially with the increasingly blurred genre divisions and the way audiences use an intertextual mix of genres to make sense of the world (van Zoonen 1998).

Next to the industry as a whole being in transformation, news journalism itself is also undergoing tremendous changes, many of which have a gendered subtext. In the USA, for instance, the struggle for readers and audiences has had a tremendous effect on the substance and style of the news. Whereas commercial logic has always been strong in US journalism, it has not completely dominated the profession until very recently. But it seems that nowadays journalism in the US has become completely market-driven. In the newspaper industry this is expressed by shorter stories, an increase in the use of color pictures and graphics, more attention to lifestyle features and news that is useful to audiences, and a shift away from traditional public affairs reporting, i.e. international and national politics. In other words, more and more papers are becoming like *USA Today*, the classic consumer-oriented newspaper (Hallin 1996: 247).

In television journalism, commercial pressure has had even more dramatic results. US local-television news, in particular, is based on input from market research telling what audiences would like to see in the news rather than on democratic or professional journalistic imperatives of what would be in the public service. This has resulted in a set of new concepts in journalism that all testify to the entertainment product that journalism in the USA has become: there is for instance a new kind of reporter, the helicopter journalist who covers sensational action live from the helicopter (car chases are very popular). The marketing-based imperative that there should be action in the first eighteen seconds of a news bulletin is therewith fulfilled. Another new phenomenon is what has been derisively called 'Ken and Barbie journalism' which refers to the local anchor teams of a woman and a man whose physical attractiveness seems to be more important than their professional qualities as journalists; Ken and Barbie engage in another new journalistic trend, namely 'happy talk.' As the name suggests, these are merry little dialogues between the anchors showing how much they like each other and how much they love their audiences. All this is done in order to 'people-ize' the news, as one news editor has put it, and to suggest that journalists and audiences are one big happy family.

The immense success of local television news in terms of its ratings has forced the traditional and prestigious national news bulletins of CBS, NBC and ABC to adjust their style too, much to the annoyance of their journalists. Not so long ago, the anchor of *CBS Evening News,* Dan Rather, complained: 'They've got us putting on more and more fuzz and wuzz on the air, cop-shop programs, so as to compete not with other news programs but with entertainment programs, including those posing as news programs, for dead bodies, mayhem and lurid tales' (quoted in Hallin 1996: 242). Dan Rather obviously complains about the management of CBS, but he also criticizes the reality-based programs such as *Rescue 911, America's Most Wanted* and *Cops.*

In Western Europe there has been an upsurge of similar programs: *Rescue 911,* for instance, has its local varieties like *06-11 Weekend* in the Netherlands, *999* in Britain and *SOS- 'pao liv eller deud'* in Sweden. Interestingly enough though, according to a Danish researcher, the European varieties seem to adopt a somewhat more informational and didactic approach than the US originals (Bjondeberg 1996). Reality-based programming has gained ground in Europe especially with the arrival of the commercial satellite stations which have crushed public broadcasting monopolies and their public-service ideals of journalism. In fact, last year in the Netherlands the most conspicuous development in the programming schedules of the seven national channels, both public and commercial, was the dominance of reality TV. Whereas these programs are widely different in their thematic content and style – they range from cop shows to coverage of intimate dialogues between people taking a taxi – they all suggest a direct and unmediated relation to people's daily lives and concerns.

In this, they are similar to that other journalistic format so often fiercely criticized but also immensely popular: the talkshow.

Apart from the emergence of new informative genres which are usually labeled 'infotainment', the traditional news bulletins in Western Europe themselves have changed too. Anchorpersons have become all important for the establishment of a lasting and meaningful relationship with audiences, 'human interest' has become an integral part of the news and the audience interest in a topic has become a much more influential criterion for selection than it used to be.

'Feminization' of journalism?

All these developments – reality-based programming, infotainment, the 'people-izing' of the news, Ken and Barbie journalism, the consumer-oriented newspaper – are fiercely criticized by scholars and traditional news journalists who feel that their professional ideals have been sold to market forces. MBAs (Masters of Business Administration) are said to rule the newsroom. Whereas the actual implementation of these new journalistic formats may vary from country to country – in the UK, for instance, television news in its BBC and ITN variety has not (yet) succumbed to market forces – its force as a horrific vision of the future is unmistakable and 'Americanization' influences many a contemporary debate on journalism (and politics) in Western Europe. I shall come back to that discussion later; first, however, I want to draw attention to the usually unnoticed gendered subtexts and implications of market-driven journalism. If we try to summarize the commercial logic of journalism in a couple of key terms we may construct the following list:

- 'human interest'
- audience needs and desires
- emotional investment
- sensationalism

It is interesting to see that three of these four keywords relate exactly to the norms and values that many traditional news journalists, men and women alike, think are typical of female journalists. As discussed earlier, more attention to 'human interest' news, a greater care for audience needs and desires, and a less detached and rational mode of reporting are three elements that female news journalists have expressed in many research projects as typical for their role-conception. It does seem somewhat far fetched, however, and very undeserved to say that infotainment and other forms of consumer-oriented journalism as we witness them today in newspapers and television, match the criticism that female journalists began to express a decade ago. It is even more unlikely that consumer-oriented journalism is the result of this criticism or that it is a specific 'feminine' kind of journalism. Nevertheless, there are clear, gendered elements

41

in these developments and I want to illustrate these by examining a specific Dutch case in a little more detail (van Zoonen 1991).

Dutch television news was first broadcast in 1956 as a part of the public service broadcasting system. Because of technical limitations, the focus was on timeless 'human interest' stories; newsreaders were almost absent because they were thought to stand in the way of objectivity. Although newsreaders appeared ever more frequently in the following years, they read the news in a very uninvolved and detached manner. Their personalities had to be denied. As one TV critic put it in the mid-1970s, 'In the first place a newsreader, be it a woman or a man, must not be too attractive and – although this is less relevant – not too bad looking either. Of course it is strictly forbidden to read bad news in any other way than good news. Objectivity would be endangered by it' (NRC Handelsblad, 8 August 1975).

At the same time in the 1970s, the executive producer decided that the news would focus on politically and socially important issues and that – as he put it – he would not do news that is fun to watch anymore. Dutch TV news acquired a reputation for being serious and objective, but a little dull and uninteresting to watch. This situation lasted until 1985 with the appointment of a new executive producer who had been a correspondent for the Dutch news in the UK. His name was Peter Brusse and he had ideas that were revolutionary in the Dutch context. He wanted to change the news into a popular television program with natural transitions between one item and the other. Brusse felt that the news should become more than a dull listing of events offering audiences the opportunity to identify with events and people. 'Human interest' stories, therefore, had to become a major ingredient of Dutch TV news and newsreaders were urged to transform their serious mode of address into a more personal and intimate style. Brusse said: 'Anchors should be more than people who merely read the news. They must inspire confidence. You must be able to trust them like the neighbor next door, who is familiar to you and who keeps an eye on things while you are away.' This new approach became immediately subject to heavy criticism from Brusse's own staff and from newspaper journalists. His effort 'to make news entertaining by a light and populist approach' as it was called, was looked upon with contempt. Brusse did not remain very long, and later his two-year regime was characterized as a 'reckless period of experiments and failures.' But Brusse's attempts did pave the way for his successor, who managed to develop many of his ideas.

There are now several news bulletins during the day, of which the 8 o'clock news is the most important. It is aimed at a family audience and is supposed to have a smooth and informal mode of address. It is presented by either a woman or a man, and they alternate each week. Both are experienced newsreaders who were assigned to this bulletin because of their popularity. As one newspaper put it: they are reliable, cozy and familiar (Parool 3 March 1988). As an internal policy statement of the TV news said: 'attempts to produce a more inviting and personal news have to motivate audiences to watch the news and to enlarge their pleasure in watching it' (NOS 1987). As Brusse already had argued, newsreaders were now seen as crucial in constructing a particular image for each news bulletin and in establishing an intimate and stable relationship with the audience. His successor said in a newspaper interview: 'We looked for journalists that can present a program. As far as their appearance is concerned . . . they must look like ordinary people. They are not supposed just to read the news, but to tell it from their own personal involvement' (*Parool* 3 March 1988). Thus, the Dutch TV news is now characterized by the personal involvement of its anchors, an intimate mode of address, by attempts to provide pleasure to the audience, and by considerable attention to 'human interest' stories. Again these are the themes and styles that female journalists have been said to appreciate.

It must come as no surprise, then, that the transformation of Dutch TV news coincided with a remarkably high number of female anchors; in fact they form a majority. Although all of the female anchors have an impressive background in traditional news journalism, the fact that they are women must have been an important factor in their recruitment. Officially this always has been (and still is) denied in the television newsroom, and it is quite likely that it is not a conscious factor. However, the cultural expectations implicit in this phenomenon have been made clear by Brusse who had no problems with looking for what he called the 'women's touch' in the news. In another interview he said : 'men's news is to write on the front page that a fire happened, women's news is to write inside why the guy lit a fire for the third time.' During his brief period as an executive editor, Brusse incessantly questioned the rationalistic underpinnings of news and he emphasized its entertainment and emotional qualities instead. 'One tear on TV tells you so much more than an ever so well described tear in a newspaper. Television made us communicate and participate in world affairs with tears. A news bulletin without a tear is not a really good one and that is what they have to learn here' (*Elsevier* May 1988).

The Dutch case is indicative of the way in which the transformations in TV news journalism has opened up the profession for women. Within the new contexts of 'human interest', emotional involvement and entertainment, anchoring the news has actually become a suitable profession for women which accords well with traditional cultural expectations of women. There are, however, different aspects of femininity that are being exploited in TV news, depending for instance on cultural context. The British media observer Patricia Holland notes that newsreading in Britain might become a women's job because the newsreader's task has become that of a decorative performer. She concludes that female newsreaders have been constructed as pleasurable objects for men to look at (Holland 1987).

Whereas this may sound obvious, for instance, when looking at the glamorous presence of US and British anchorwomen, it is not that simple in the case of Dutch female newsreaders. Whereas they are all good looking women, there is more to their presence than just good looks; some of them are in their mid-forties and even fifties. The older women newsreaders are obviously not constructed as the all-knowing male authority who guides you through a complex and confusing world, but theirs may be a model of traditional female authority: in their case a comparison with the caring and never-failing mother who tucks you in after a day of emotional arousal seems more appropriate. Other female newsreaders are too young for the motherly impact. What other element of femininity may mark their presence? Although they are all good looking, they are not spectacularly beautiful. As you may remember, the internal policy statement of Dutch TV news said that its presenters have to look like ordinary people. In addition, Brusse suggested that newsreaders should be like the neighbor you can trust. In fact the Dutch popular press often complains about the main female newsreader, Pia Dijkstra, who is said to look dull in her attempts to look like a common woman. With a little irony then, we may want to consider that the Dutch female newsreader is the embodiment of yet another feminine stereotype: the neighbor's wife: very plain and very ordinary, yet very desirable.

Whereas one may not and does not have to 'buy' the particular versions of femininity (the caring mother and the neighbor's wife) that I have constructed for Dutch TV news, the example does substantiate my claim that the market forces in journalism which bring 'human interest', audience needs and desires, and emotional investment to the fore may open up the profession for women journalists. Obviously the new market-driven values of journalism accord better with mainstream conceptions of femininity than the objective and rational standards of traditional news journalism. There is one element however, that may seem to negate my claim: the sensationalism present in commercial journalism seems to be at odds with female journalists' values and with mainstream conceptions of femininity. But here too, it seems that femininity can be exploited. The British journalist Anne Sebba, who has described the ascent of the woman reporter over the past century, was struck by the high presence of female journalists during the Gulf War (Gallagher 1995). She argues that the danger of war on television is given added drama when it is reported by a woman and that the presence of a woman on screen is a pleasant distraction from the horror of the events themselves. The phenomenon of female war reporters was noticed by the London *Times* too, which sneered: 'The world's war zones are chock-a-block with would-be Kate Adies risking their lives for minor stations in the hope of landing the big story because they know that what the major networks want is a front-line account from a (preferably pretty) woman in a flakjacket' (quoted in Gallagher 1995: 2). So while 'femininity' seems to have just recently become an unmistakable ingredient of market-driven war journalism, crime reporting has a historical tradition of sensationalism carried by female reporters. In the nineteenth-century US press, female reporters were often so-called 'stunt girls' who went undercover in hospitals and jails to report on the conditions there. Another typical women's role in journalism of that time was that of the sob-sister who covered lurid trials

(Mills 1997), and this is the role we may recognize from contemporary commercial TV journalism.

Conclusion

Research results from different Western countries have demonstrated the minority position of women in traditional news journalism. In addition, many female journalists feel a tension between the requirements of objective and detached professional values and the cultural demands one faces as a woman. As journalists, women would favor a more human and involved approach to the news that is seemingly at odds with professional values of objectivity and detachment. Many female journalists thus experience a very awkward position: on the one hand they have to show that despite being women they are good journalists, but on the other hand they have to show that despite being journalists they are still real women too. Female journalists working in traditional news journalism therefore have a much more fragmented and contradictory professional identity than men.

It is often hoped and argued that an increase in the number of female journalists would change the news text as well. However, as I have argued in this chapter, the relation is in fact the other way around, as we can see in present-day journalism: the news genre is changing and therefore more women can enter journalism as a profession. These changes in journalism as a whole may transform the field from a male-dominated domain into an area that has the potential of becoming dominated by women, just as public relations or government communications have become. The transformation of journalism is characterized by changes from newspaper employment to magazine employment, by new reality-based types of programs and by traditional news journalism becoming more and more consumer-oriented and market driven.

In general terms, most of the key elements in these shifts – 'human interest', audience needs and desires, emotional investment and sensationalism – accord quite well with the criticism that female journalists have expressed of traditional news journalism. Paradoxically, although market-driven journalism is not what they had in mind in envisaging a new journalism, it has opened up possibilities for women, as was illustrated by the Dutch television news case. It suggested that the content and style of the news as a genre is determining whether men or women will work in journalism – to put it in somewhat black and white terms – and that it is not men or women journalists who determine what the content and style of news will be.

How does one evaluate these developments? To begin with, it is tempting to suggest that the professional identities of women working in the new kind of journalism will be less schizophrenic than their colleagues in traditional news journalism. This is because it is exactly the traditional cultural prescriptions of femininity – good looks, interest in other people, care and compassion – that the new market-driven journalism seems to ask for. Thus, it may seem that simply by being a 'true' woman in traditional terms one is a good new kind of commercially oriented journalist. Being one of the girls, in other words, might simply be enough. For one thing, however, this may, will and has been turned against women also, of course. In the USA, women TV journalists have been fired because, according to their management, they were getting too old to appear on screen (Ellerbee 1986). Whereas this has been successfully fought in court, it is indicative of the patriarchal system in which female journalists work, in commercial journalism too. In the Netherlands recently, one of the older female newsreaders was fired for unclear reasons. The public explanation was given that, as in the theater, you have to change the scenery once in a while. In addition, it is likely that within the market-driven context, the stereotypical views on female journalists and what they can and should do will be as strong as in traditional news journalism, leading again to assigning women to subjects that they are supposedly good at and expecting the human touch of women. For the women working in market-driven journalism this means a similar restriction on their working possibilities as the one experienced by women in traditional news journalism. In fact, it may even be stronger because now it is not only the male boss giving sexist orders, but market forces which may, in the end, be much more difficult to negotiate.

Another problem of the role of women and femininity in market-driven journalism has to do with the status of market-driven journalism. As is clear, most traditional news journalists, women and men alike, despise the consumer orientation and look down on its practitioners with ill-concealed contempt. In this they are in the good company of other political and intellectual élites. Partly, this contempt has good reasons; the increasing popularization of news and information certainly has its problematic aspects and one can indeed wonder – with the critics – what the democratic merits of human interest and sensationalism are. Moreover, female journalists who expressed a need for more 'human interest' and compassion or emotions in the news a decade ago will not in their wildest nightmares have thought it would come to this. On the other hand, it is not only the popularization of news that is on trial in these debates; implicitly it is women and femininity as crucial components of this popularization as well. In our patriarchal societies most things women do and like are not valued very highly, and the contempt for market-driven journalism should surely be seen as part of this general patriarchal scheme.

3

JUVENATION

News, girls and power

John Hartley

'Nobody likes child molesters, except newspaper editors'
(Allen Ginsberg and Joseph Richey)

Paedophilia or paedocracy?

It was because of a crackdown in my home community, which at the time was Western Australia, that I became involved in this topic.[1] A mature student taking a course in my department was arrested (and remained on remand for more than two years before the case was thrown out) on suspicion of child pornography, for taking pictures of her naked pre-pubescent sons as part of a Photomedia project. Simultaneously, the WA Attorney General, Cheryl Edwardes, introduced a Censorship Bill into the State Parliament. Her opposite number on the Labour benches, Diana Warnock, asked me to provide an expert comment on the draft Bill. Among other things, the definition of 'child pornography' was alarmingly wide:

> **'child pornography'** means an article that describes or depicts, in a manner that is likely to cause offence to a reasonable adult, a person who is, or who looks like, a child under 16 years of age (whether the person is engaged in sexual activity or not).
>
> (WA Censorship Bill 1995)

This wording is similar to that contained in Australian federal censorship legislation, and also to the wording in the Protection of Children Act (1978) in the UK, and the Child Sexual Abuse and Pornography Act (1986) in the USA (WA Legislative Assembly, Tuesday 30 April 1996: 1123–30; see also Newnham and Townsend 1996; Ginsberg and Richey 1991). It is drafted to 'capture' any depiction in any medium of any person who is under sixteen *or looks* under sixteen (to whom?), which would offend a 'reasonable adult' (not defined) whether or not the person depicted was engaged in sexual activity. In other words, 'child pornography' can include pictures of adults not engaged in sexual activity, and it can also include *any* image of a 'child' which causes 'offence' to a 'reasonable'

47

adult. In practice this means a police officer, and police in several countries are on record as taking the test of indecency and offence to be nudity alone. Such a definition captures news images of children in Rwandan refugee camps, for these certainly cause offence. It may also cover fashion images, especially from teenage/women's magazines like *Dolly*; indeed a campaign to ban *Dolly* and *Girlfriend* was launched by a Queensland 'moral entrepreneur' during this period. Advertisements for children's clothes from children's fashion magazines like *Studio Bambini* and *Vogue Bambini*, or from clothing catalogues, might fall within the definition; as might works of literature like Nabokov's *Lolita*.

Perhaps more to the point, because more likely to be prosecuted by police, the definition captures parents' photographs of their own children in the bath, on the beach or in the backyard, and in fact arrests have taken place concerning each of these instances. Clearly such a definition might also capture the photographs taken by our student, even though she was working in a well-known tradition of contemporary photographic art, exemplified most readily in this context by the work of Sally Mann (whose most disturbing images are not of *naked* children at all; see Mann 1988, 1992). Suddenly, and not for the first time, since this story has well-documented counterparts in both the UK and the USA, the aesthetico-political judgement of a photo-lab assistant, and the ideological or moral allegiances of the police officers called to the scene, will decide if a mother and photo-media artist is a child pornographer, and hence whether she is judged fit to keep her own children.

At this point, partly because I was pursuing an Australian Research Council-funded project to monitor the Australian media's coverage of indigenous issues, and therefore saw a lot of magazines and newspapers, I began to notice pictures of juvenated sexuality in apparent abundance, and a definite campaign in the news media organised around attempts to police 'under-age' eroticisation (see Pilcher 1996). In a way, the abundance of images came as no surprise since, like others, I have noticed (over several publications) how the democratisation of the public sphere through the popular media was historically not merely *accompanied by* feminisation and sexualisation, but has been *conducted through the media of* feminisation and sexualisation, using this semiotic genre to communicate with the vast, unknowable, but sovereign and comfort-seeking readerships of modernity. Given this history, pictures of attractive, smiling, sexualised young women, and increasingly young men too, are only to be expected. On the other hand the crackdown was also nothing new – media campaigns against young people are a staple genre, whether they're about sex, drugs, rock'n'roll or violence, they are always available to serve for the time being as the immediate signifier of the general need for governability. Too often the news media deal with the tension between their own propensity to communicate via sexualised young people, and their own tendencies to police young people's sexuality, by having their cake and eating it; showing the pictures (communicatively, democratically) while wagging their fingers (truth-seekingly, governmentally).

What was new, on both the 'positive' and the 'negative' sides of the campaign,

Advertisement for Lois Lane Shoes, from *Studio Bambini*, vol.10, no.20, Spring/Summer 1995–6. Courtesy of Lois Lane Shoes.

Advertisement for Red Robin, from *Studio Bambini*, vol.10, no.19, Autumn/Winter 1995. Courtesy of Red Robin Fitwear.

was the age of the subjects; whether sexualised or pathologised, celebrated or criticised, the people featured were literally juvenating – getting younger. The semiotic habits of the daily press, 'quality' and tabloid alike, ensured that there was an appropriate picture accompanying most articles which showed the very images being complained about. So I began to collect them in a haphazard way (so far without being 'captured' by the legislation), as background for the censorship debate in Australia, and subsequently found that the same campaign was in full swing when I arrived in the UK during 1996. At the most evident level, these images and stories show that the campaign is general – it crosses national, media and genre boundaries, and occurs in all taste categories for all the standard audience-demographics. It's certainly a campaign, in the sense that a specific topic is pursued as a running story across multiple media sites, but it is unauthored and directed only by the people who choose to take part in it; an array of journalists, legislators and 'moral entrepreneurs' (the term is from John Wadham of the pressure group Liberty, cited in Newnham and Townsend 1996) – almost never children or young people themselves. While it is clearly gendered, it is not about gender as such; it is a campaign centred on age, about the creation of the image of the asexual child, and the policing of the boundary between this image, for whom sexuality can only mean victimisation, patholo- gisation or a crime of looking, and the adult world, where sexuality is ordinary, if sometimes unruly. At the same time, however, the 'children' who are being placed firmly outside the frontiers of the 'we' community of adults ('parents') in this way, are also available to serve as the very icon of that community, in the communicative, inclusive, 'paedocratic' mode of address (Hartley 1992b) that is necessarily employed by news media in their quest to attract, address and retain readers.

From gender and power to juvenation

I argue that the concept of *readership* is more important in the history of journalism than that of *power*. Indeed, I suggest that a much better model than 'power' already exists to describe cross-demographic communication where there is a clear desire not only to gather and inform but also to influence reader- ships, whether in journalism and the media, or in cultural studies and the academy: the model of *teaching*. Looked at this way, 'influence' may be seen posi- tively, as an activity, where 'power' has negative and categorical connotations. Of course, techniques of teaching can be woeful as well as wonderful, and they can be colonising as well as libertarian. The practice of 'teaching' large reader- ships through media communication is full of examples of both. Taken sympathetically, however, the model of teaching alerts us to more in the relationship between addressers and addressees in modernity than coercion/ oppression, and it puts the analyst in the same boat as the media (we're all teachers). The giant modern institutions of media, government and educa- tion are in fact converging around a desire to influence readerships via cross-demographic communication, and their inter-connections include the same quest to influence the hearts and minds of readers, who themselves are textually imag(in)ed as young.

Throughout the modern period, the construction and maintenance of, and address to, very large readerships has been accompanied by feminisation. In previous work I have tried to demonstrate that the feminisation, sexualisation and suburbanisation of the 'public sphere' of critical debate has been of crucial political importance. It is from the so-called private sphere of personal identity, domestic life and everyday culture that some of the most important contemporary political movements have arisen: the women's, environmental, and peace movements, for instance, and subcultural, ethnic and multicultural politics (Hartley 1992a, 1992b, 1996). Now, organisations from the 'private' sphere attract more support than do political parties. In 1997, for instance, the RSPB (Royal Society for the Protection of Birds) recruited its millionth member – a support-base larger than that of all the British political parties put together (the biggest, New Labour, was said at the same time to enjoy a membership of 400,000). Meanwhile, the 'classic' public domain has taken on more and more of the issues that were once regarded as private, ordinary or unworthy, so that now the front pages of even the most conservative newspapers of record are suffused with feminised images and privatised news.

But lately, a new figure has appeared in this already feminised, privatised, suburbanised and sexualised landscape; the figure of the young girl. Indeed, judging by the daily and periodical press, young girls may at last have entered history – the 'logic of democratic equivalence' has rippled around them, producing subjectivity where once there was only subjection. They're up to their ankles, if not their necks, in public signification, becoming objects of public policy, public debate, the public gaze. This is part of a phenomenon I've called 'juvenation' in the modern media. Juvenation is the creative practice of communicating with a readership via the *medium* of youthfulness. It includes:

- pictures and stories *about* young people or interests, the representation *of* youthfulness, and address *to* young readerships;
- (more importantly) a discursive drive towards juvenating *other* cultural spheres, from sport to economics, and political stories;
- conversely, an equal and opposite discursive drive to patrol (and thereby to produce) the various age-boundaries between child and adult, and to produce evidence of transgressions.

I am arguing three broad points in relation to juvenation.

1   The news media use juvenation *positively* as an indispensable part of their audience- and readership-building strategies. The 'image' of the audience/reader in the text of news (as in advertising, drama, light entertainment and hybrid genres like infotainment) has become younger as well as more

51

female over the twentieth century. Children are the semiotic carrier of visualisations of 'Wedom' (Hartley 1992b: 206–10). Juvenation is a *communicative* strategy designed to oil the works of journalism; helping people to read things they are not otherwise interested in, making journalism as a textual system more appealing to target readerships who have no necessary commitment to it at all.

2   Simultaneously, the news media retain the 'hard' news value of *negativity* in relation to *truth-seeking* stories about juvenation. Children are now increasingly subject to the same tactics of negative reporting as adults in stories featuring unruliness (boys) or sexuality (girls) in particular (although 'unruly' girls are now much more common). Like royals and celebrities, children are 'fair game' as newsworthy targets in ways that were unthinkable just a few years ago. So while they have become more visible in the news as juvenated metaphors for Wedom, children have also been more thoroughly fenced off from it, in a semiotic move that appropriates their *looks* for the requirements of the news media as a textual system, but which excludes their *actions* not just as threatening/vulnerable, but as outside of the boundary of the social altogether. In fact, I suggest that children have become so caught up in a rhetoric of foe-creation in the hard-news media that now they occupy the structural position of a 'Theydom' (Hartley 1992b: 206–10).

3   News stories about children are almost always about something else. The explanation for the intensity of coverage in any particular instance comes from the '*mediasphere*' (Hartley 1996), not from the event (in those cases where any event prior to signification in the news has indeed occurred). The stories with highest prominence tend to focus on issues not of fundamental importance to children (for instance the long and longing interest in 'waif' fashion models), while stories in which the treatment of children is a life-or-death issue tend to be relatively downplayed, for attention is focused on epiphenomena or on demonising 'evil' individuals, rather than on the care and recovery of the children involved. I would go so far as to suggest, in fact, that despite the pervasive appeal to and by means of juvenation in the news media, children are 'powerless' over their own image, presumed incapable of self-representation, not imagined to have a collective interest which needs to be defended in the news, and represented in ways which are comparable to a colonised people; perhaps the West's last colony, in discursive terms (see Franklin and Franklin 1996).

The boundaries of the social

The themes that follow, of juvenated sexuality, policing and death, are not significant for what they tell the analyst about children. But juvenation is the place to look for some of the most intensive *reading practices* of the contemporary semiosphere; the place where meaning-formation is as turbulent and energetic as a sunspot, where the very boundaries of the social universe are being found, fenced, and watch-towered. Just as the media cannot leave the constitutionally anomalous royal family alone (Hartley 1996: 11–13), so they cannot stop fiddling with the last colonised class; those whose real *and* imagined bodies and lives are still outside Wedom. Young girls are the textual mark of the tension between alternative types of journalism; they are used as *teaching aids* in both 'positive' and 'negative' journalistic visualisations of social identity and civic propriety.

It goes without saying that news media have long found youthfulness fascinating, especially in 'soft' genres like sport, fashion, human interest, entertainment, including glamour and pin-up pictures and 'society' gossip. And young people's bodies, habits and preferences have been subject to compulsive coverage (discoverage, uncoverage) for some decades. But what counts as 'youthful' is now much younger; where once the term was used to describe people from the mid-teens to mid-twenties (for instance in educational and civic policy-making in the 1940s and 1950s, and still in ESRC research programme definitions), now it seems to have slipped back by about eight years, to cover people roughly from eight to eighteen, with peri-pubescence as the most intense site of media concern, especially for girls. Contemporary hard-news stories in which juvenation is a primary component cover a widely varied terrain; from the performance of students in public examinations and the success or failure of schools, to teenage pregnancy, so-called kiddie-porn, paedophilia, anorexia and the age of fashion models, recovered/false memory syndrome, and abuse, crime or murder both of and by children. These are semiotic symptoms of a new politicisation of age. Meanwhile, in a positive print of these negatives, juvenation continues to pervade the print and screen media, extending its range (into a burgeoning supply of new magazines for girls and boys, for instance), taking new risks (with sexualisation, for instance), pervading the semiotic environment with juvenation, and feeding back from the entertainment pages to front-page stories both juvenation itself and an often finger-wagging unease about what's going on.

The current frequency of stories and features about these issues – which appear side by side and often cross-fertilise one another – amounts to evidence not of a moral panic as classically described, but of a more profound uncertainty in the textual system of journalism about where the line that defines the boundary of the social should be drawn. An unauthored but pervasive public conversation with some systematic patterns, albeit with diverse and sometimes contradictory voices, provides the 'textual anthropologist' or the 'semio-historian of the ordinary' (like me) with evidence of cultural thinking-out-loud about issues that are at once ephemeral (hard to trace), and profound, going to the heart of a given reading-community's self-understanding. In fact, while juvenation in the news media may not amount to a moral panic, although some stories are cast in that generic form, it does display the signs of a *taboo* as described in structural anthropology (Leach 1972); it attracts compulsive attention, simultaneous attraction and repulsion, alternate over-valuation and under-valuation, ritualisation and denial, and (compulsively repeated) responses ranging from sacralisation to attempted extirpation. For several years during the 1990s it has provided an intense and active semiotic hot-spot in the production and policing of the boundary of the social: inside is 'Wedom'; outside is 'Theydom'; both are juvenated.

For fifty years the major sign of the boundary between 'we' and 'they' identifications in political and journalistic discourse was the binary division of the Cold War; Wedom has known what it is by obsessive negativisation of the imputed/presumed characteristics of Theydom, understood as anything that can be associated with an imagined Soviet Union. Now that 'we' do not have such a clear political binary boundary with an outside, it seems that it may have fallen to previously non-political aspects of 'our' selves to provide the pretext for a public meditation upon the question, 'where do we stop being we, and start being they?' and thence 'who are We; what is Wedom?' One of these 'non-political' aspects of ourselves is religious, and it is clear that on the international scene it is the Islamic world that has begun to attract the adversarial journalism once reserved for the communist world. Within the 'home' community, however, age is prominent among those 'non-political' aspects that decide the question of who 'we' are.

Waifs and strays

The specific effect of juvenation in this context is to produce a more clearly identified, more intensely patrolled, and therefore less easily crossed boundary (by the reader) between child and adult, however defined. As has often been the case in popular media, however, the compliant reader is tutored in where-not-to-stray by newspapers and magazines showing something of the transgressions complained of. Stories about anorexic models or under-age eroticism are invariably illustrated by a large and appealing picture of the symptom under investigation, often trailed in colour on the front page. The 'anorexia' genre was given a boost in the newspapers by a furore that followed the appearance of Annie Morton in *Vogue* in June 1996. Omega watches' brand director threatened to stop advertising in *Vogue*, because, as the *Guardian* reported on its front page (31 May 1996): *Company says 'distasteful' pictures could help push girls into eating disorders.* No evidence was offered on how many girls even read *Vogue*, much less on how they might develop an eating disorder as a result, or how many might, and nothing was said about the fact that Omega watches had featured in the same issue in a photo-set that may well have disappointed the company, since the watches were blurred with the artistic equivalent of camera-shake (though the subsequent publicity certainly took their brand name right around the mediasphere, along with that of *Vogue* itself). While several newspapers printed pictures of an 'anorexic' model from the issue in question, they could not agree on which model was anorexic. The *Guardian* and *Daily Telegraph* printed front-page colour pictures of Trish Goff, while the *Star* used a library shot of Kate Moss (31 May 1996). *The Times* showed Annie Morton, though not from *Vogue*, and quoted her agent as saying that far from being anorexic she 'drinks beer and eats hamburgers' (31 May 1996). The *Independent* ran a feature about the press coverage itself, applauding the idea that 'advertising power could succeed where parents and doctors have failed', despite the fact that by this time Omega's chairman had overruled the threat to withdraw advertising (1 June 1996).

The *Sunday Express* made a big splash of the story (2 June 1996). The front-page heading was 'DIANA'S WAR ON WAIFS', book-ended between a shot of Diana, Princess of Wales, 'during her fight against bulimia', and a shot of Trish Goff from *Vogue*. Inside, it ran two stories: one a double-page spread juxta-posing a *Vogue* shot of Annie Morton with a picture of an anorexic teenager; the other on the Leader page, recycling a previous speech of the Princess of Wales. The 'anorexia' story is headlined 'HOW SCHOOLGIRL'S DEATH COULD CHANGE THE FACE OF FASHION', even though it transpires that the 'schoolgirl'

Independent, 1 June 1996.

in question had died twelve years previously aged twenty-two; while in her own article the Princess of Wales never mentions media images as a 'cause' of eating disorders, although 'on good authority' she does express concern for children with 'low self-esteem' who find a 'way of coping' by 'controlling their bodies'.

The London *Evening Standard* was out on its own, ignoring the 'waif' angle altogether, but still managing to feature a *Vogue* story, showing that *Vogue's* cover-image of Naomi Campbell was – uncannily – wearing a completely different swimsuit from the one shown in the identical photograph on an inside page (17 May 1997).

In all this, it is hard to see what the story was 'about', beyond an appetite for *any* excuse to print colour pictures of fashion models and princesses as front-page news, even in the context of a story about the claimed damage such pictures do to young readers. It did not seem to matter which model was 'causing' the problem, or which 'victim' was identified to illustrate the supposed damage. The coverage *generalises* both 'cause' (*'anorexic'* models) and 'effect' (anorexic *'schoolgirls'*), in the teeth of its own evidence and its own practices. Such journalism therefore proposes a generalised boundary between the 'we' community of readers, who are presumably not expected to 'catch' anorexia from reading these stories (see Bray 1994), and a 'they' community of children, who may die from doing so. It seems to follow that children are not imagined as coming within the community of readers, but that hardened readers may find pictures of juvenated models appealing.

It is routine to find stories about child-abuse illustrated by a model posing for a picture of what the effects of the abuse look like – namely a sad, anxious or troubled expression on a child whose body-image the reader is invited to 'read' both for the bad effect of the abuse and, necessarily, the reason for it, namely juvenated eroticisation. Indeed, something so systematic it amounted to a 'law' operated for a couple of years in daily newspapers (although perhaps the moment has passed because the range of uses for front-page juvenation has widened): if there was a *colour* picture of a young girl on the front page, then this child was either missing or dead. Girl-children entered news as attractive victims. The use of them in this structurally double-edged way serves to make childhood more 'innocent' (especially asexual) than it actually is, and that inno-cence more dangerous than statistics would suggest.

One curious example of the desexualisation of children was a story in the *Express*, headlined 'WHEN YOUR CHILD GROWS UP TOO FAST' (13 August 1996), reporting on something called 'precocious puberty' ('suffered' by 'a far greater number of girls than boys'). '*Young children are suddenly confronted with frightening developments including mood swings, PMT, a sex drive and sexual maturity beyond their years*', proclaims the introduction. A large colour picture of a young girl with a forlorn expression illustrates this 'anxious time' where '*so much shame is attached to early puberty that most people keep the condition secret – even from children them-selves*'.

It is not for me to comment on medical conditions (although deep in the story it transpires that the featured case history 'fell into the extreme of the normal range for the onset of puberty'); but the point is that there is a clear *journalistic* strategy of medicalising a binary distinction between asexual childhood and sexual maturity which, if reached 'too soon' (overwhelmingly by girls), is cause for 'shame' and 'secrecy'. This is the language not of medicine but of taboo.

Children who are destroyed or shamed by their adult-like characteristics mark the boundaries of adulthood, and put children firmly outside of it, but the same children are celebrated as the very essence of Wedom in their attractiveness, which cannot avoid eroticisation, since it seems equally a 'law' that photographs of child-victims receive the widest and most sustained coverage, and are printed in the largest format, when they show the most attractive girls. For instance the case of Caroline Dickinson in the UK, and of JonBenét Ramsey in the USA, became running stories not only because the murders were horrifying and unresolved, but also because both girls had been photographed in a beauty context – one, aged six, as a beauty pageant contestant, the other, aged thirteen, in a 'model' portfolio taken by a family friend. The general point about the sexual ambiguity of such pictures is made in the accompanying copy:

> There was one video that showed JonBenét dancing in flirtatious, even provocative fashion. Pictures also surfaced of her in heavy make-up more suited to a woman at least three times her age. 'It's impossible to look at these photos and not see a terribly exploited little girl'.
>
> (*Who Weekly*, 20 January 1997)

Who Weekly, 20 January 1997.

Any 13-year-old girl is on that uneasy precipice between childhood and womanhood. One minute she's a tomboy climbing trees, the next she's trying on every dress in her own and her sister's wardrobe and boogieing on down to the disco. At one minute she's quite vulnerable, even sucking her thumb or cuddling her teddy bear. Next she's defying her mother and slamming the door. These pictures of Caroline Dickinson show it all too clearly, too poignantly. They show a child on the edge of adulthood, like the ancient god Janus looking both ways. . . . Caroline was a 13-year-old like yours, like mine. . . . There is no knowingness in the look of her eyes. She's no Lolita, no catwalk nymphet.

(*Express*, 21 August 1996)

Once established, the trope of juvenation, sexuality and death can run under its own steam – 'victims' are found who are not in the least dead:

THE TOP IS LOW-CUT, THE LOOK SEDUCTIVE, THE HAIR AND MAKE-UP PERFECT. YET KELLY IS NINE YEARS OLD. WELCOME TO THE DISTURBING AND BIZARRE NEW WORLD OF BRITAIN'S CHILD BEAUTY QUEENS
(Headline for 'Femail' cover story, *Daily Mail*, 5 June 1997)

Pictures of Kelly Wyke, 1996–7 winner of a 'Mini Miss' contest, are used to illustrate just how disturbing this 'new' development is – there is a colour picture of her on the *Daily Mail*'s front-page banner as a teaser to the story, a page-high picture on the cover of the 'Femail' insert, and a large swimsuit pose as part of the double-page story itself. The latter picture is juxtaposed between a photograph of the late JonBenét Ramsey, and one of a mother who is captioned as 'watching out for paedophiles'.

We and they

As well as ever-victimised, the papers have begun to make childhood appear unruly, presenting prominent stories about child murderers and teenage rapists, with an irresistible urge to name and picture the alleged perpetrators, whatever the law says (see Franklin and Petley 1996; Newburn 1996: 69–70), schools and housing estates out of control from the predating of ever-younger hoodlums (e.g. coverage of The Ridings school, Halifax, in all the UK national dailies, 23 October 1996), drug-use by children and under-age prostitution (again, with illustrations often posed by models; e.g. *Guardian* 21 August 1996; *Express* 12 February 1997), inviting a punitive, intolerant attitude towards children and young people which seeks to exclude them, for which the appropriate response is to render them docile, useful, biddable, invisible (like servants).

Significant in Britain as directly political evidence of the pathologisation of children's activities was the New Labour government's proposal of September 1997 to lower the age of criminal responsibility from thirteen years to ten: making children more innocent by making people between ten and thirteen 'not-children'; making youthful unruliness more adult by making it criminal.

An extreme example of this tendency in news stories is this: 'TINY HUGGERS ARE EVIL GANG OF MUGGERS':

> Two sick pensioners have been robbed by a gang of tiny muggers – one aged just FOUR. The kids asked their victims for hugs and kisses then nicked £85 before running off. Last night . . . police warned other OAPs: 'Don't be hugged – you could get mugged'. The angel-faced gang – two little girls and a boy – struck as the couple were shopping. . . . One of the tearaways ran up to them saying: 'We do love you – let us hug you'. The frail husband and wife picked the kids up and gave them affectionate pecks on the cheek. . . . Detectives reckon the thieves – aged only four, seven and nine – have formed a Fagin-style gang and will strike again. The Mayor said . . . 'Children know the difference between right and wrong and it is dreadful that they should be committing this kind of crime . . . '. Shocked cop Sgt Paul Bogaard added: 'It's like something out of Oliver Twist. . . . It is a shocking offence for kids so young and we are very anxious to catch them'.
>
> (*Daily Star*, 27 July 1996)

This story raises questions of its own – how can two 'sick' and 'frail' octogenarians 'pick up' three children? is it advisable to kiss strangers, children or not? how did the police know the uncaught children's ages? can persons so young be held responsible in law (i.e. did a 'crime' or 'offence' even occur)? why would a national paper pick up a routine 'shoppers-threatened-by-gang' story of the type normally associated with low-grade local give-away weeklies? if the gang is 'Fagin-style' who is the Fagin? The story's oddity draws attention to its narrative drive, which is to associate terms from two normally unconnected 'lexical registers' (Fowler 1991):

TINY	EVIL
HUGGED	MUGGED
KISSED	NICKED
ANGEL-FACED	FAGIN-STYLE GANG
CHILDREN	CRIME
KIDS SO YOUNG	SHOCKING OFFENCE

Four-year-old girls as the Artful Dodgers of the 1990s; this is history (of moral panics) repeated as farce. The 'tiny' figures who appear here as 'evil' – under-valued 'they' – are the same ones who are cast as 'innocent' – over-valued 'we' – elsewhere in the same news-context. Indeed, a general effect of

Wedom-defining juvenation is to displace discussions about *other* matters onto stories about children. The posing of questions about 'what kind of country' we want or have, in the form of full-front-page headlines about children, is now a recognisable genre. For instance (all with accompanying pictures, two of them posed by models):

A GIRL OF 11 HAS BEEN A HEROIN ADDICT FOR THREE YEARS. HOW DID BRITAIN COME TO THIS?

(*Express*, 12 February 1997)

'I shed tears of rage and impotence. The lives of these youngsters are trimmed and limited at every turn. I would like to see the children, their parents and our politicians rising up to demand better facilities, better resources and better opportunities for all our children.' A School governor speaks out.

(*South Wales Echo*, 28 May 1996)

SCOTLAND'S CHILD ABUSE SCANDAL: CHARTER FOR OUR CHILDREN BY THE EDITOR

(*Scottish Daily Record and Sunday Mail International*, 4 and 10 March 1996)

HOW CAN ANY CIVILISED SOCIETY LET A GIRL OF 13 INTO A BOXING RING?

(*Daily Mail*, 1 October 1997)

Guilty – OF BEING BRITAIN'S MOST EVIL MOTHER

(*Daily Mirror*, 31 October 96)

MY BABY: THE POIGNANT IMAGE THAT SUMS UP THE CONFUSION FACING BRITAIN TODAY

(*Express*, 29 October 1996)

WORLD PICTURE EXCLUSIVE: THE MUM OF 12 AND HER BABY. This is the picture that shames all Britain. '*I knew it was the baddest thing I'd ever done . . . the worst I'd done before was smoke a cigarette at school*'

(*News of the World*, 6 July 1997).

Mother-love as national shame? Meanwhile, juvenation works positively too: the same Labour party that wants to make criminals out of ten-year-olds issued a manifesto for the 1997 general election that constitutes a good example of celebratory juvenation and feminisation; in its visual design almost every page, every policy, is illustrated by a euphoricised image of juvenation. For New

Labour, 'new Britain' *looks* like the hope and promise associated with smiling girls.

In the news, whatever the editorial stance, the print media display the over- and under-valuing tendencies already described, because a journalistic impera- tive sits exactly astride the boundary in question. While in their *truth-seeking* aspect they may be punitive and disapproving of juvenated unruliness and want to preserve the innocence and separateness of childhood, in their *communicative* aspect they must create an appealing text and address their readerships in warm, inclusive and positive terms. Like so many other popular media, they manage the latter by juvenating the visible text and the imagined reader. This means not only addressing readers who are in fact young, but also carrying characteristics pertaining to youth into adult age-groups, from bodily and personal comport- ment (fashion, fitness) to behaviour, taste, lifestyle and purchasing preferences. In a competitive market, the media juvenate the world they textualise and the readers they desire; but this same world and these same readers are also required to disapprove of juvenation when it is displayed by children themselves.

For Valerie Walkerdine, the contradiction between eroticising little girls and disapproving of the same in the press is 'overwhelmingly a matter of class difference' between the tabloids and the broadsheets, reflecting in discourse a social difference between working-class/tabloid/eroticised and middle-class/ broadsheet/disapproval (Walkerdine 1997: 162). But my own observations suggest that differences between class, press and child-image do not map over each other so readily; the popular and serious papers equally show and denounce the same things, and in this display a marked *convergence* between tabloid and broadsheet journalism. In short, juvenation is no respecter of class, nor of the internal differentiations of readership-demographic in the textual system of journalism. But it does always seem to be caught mid-way between communication and truth-seeking; erotics and pathology; appealing and appalled; 'we' and 'they'.

Modernist and postmodern journalism

The tendencies towards juvenation, together with feminisation, privatisation, sexualisation, domestication and suburbanisation, are part of journalism's modernity, since they constitute a further extension of its democratic reach. Simultaneously they are part of its postmodernity, since they represent a progressive abandonment of the supremacy (though not of the idea) of an 'enlightenment' public sphere. They take the subject of journalistic discourse ever further into the previously 'supplementary' (in the Derridean sense) private sphere in search of sales. The readership of journalism is increasingly imagined both to be made up of women and also to be interested in topics which under the modernist regime would have been understood as feminine, including things to do with family, home, leisure, private (personal) life, fashion, health and the body. Now, in my observation, these issues are routinely covered as front-page news rather than featured as 'women's page' topics. The feminisation, sexualisation, and privatisation of front-page journalism became a matter for international controversy after the death of Diana, Princess of Wales. In her newsworthiness she summed up just how important this kind of journalism has become. In her talent not for thinking and speaking but for touching and hugging; her desire to introduce love into public life; her interest in ordinary people while remaining a glamorous star; in her self-doubt, and in the personal tragedies of a nevertheless beautiful princess, she encapsulated in one person/ image a decisive shift from modernist (investigative, critical) towards post-modern (celebratory, emotional) journalism.

Such postmodern aspects of journalism have joined and frequently displaced the traditional menu of *modernist* political coverage. Modernist news is organised around four narratives:

1 *Conflict* (internal and international security, defence, war)
2 *Progress* (state budgets, national industry, the economy)
3 *Competition* (invidious comparisons from the arts to manufacturing to sport)
4 *Accidents* (anomalies, disasters, novelties, innovations) (Lotman 1990)

Modernist coverage is relative, and often directly oppositional – everything covered is in a negative comparative relation to some assumed norm, and newsworthiness depends on competition as well as deviation: an event is understood not only as up/down on expectations and hence positive/negative, but also more/less like similar events among competitive neighbours. How 'our' children perform at school is contrasted with the educational outcomes of competitor nations, especially the more successful economies such as Japan, Germany, the Asian 'tiger-economies', and the USA.

Postmodern news, by which I mean feminised, privatised and juvenated journalism, tends not to be organised around competitive foe-creation and negative relativities. It tends towards:

1 *Secularized homily*: 'useful knowledge' in the semiotic form of the sermon – teaching personal or ethical qualities for self, home, or social improvement.
2 *Cordiality*: stories promoting what Lotman (1990: 153) calls 'law-formation' rather than 'catalogue of anomalies' or 'accidents'.
3 *Private sphere*: readerships are addressed as consumers/clients seeking entertainment for satisfaction of wants, not as sovereign rational citizens seeking information for political decision-making.
4 *Identity*: it is about lifestyles not threats to them, centred on a 'we' community not on outsiders, confirming identity rather than destabilising it.

Quite a bit of postmodern *journalism* does not count as *news* at all: on TV there is plenty of work for reporters on lifestyle shows, including showbiz, movie, music preview and other entertainment programmes; travel, gardening, home-improvement and other domestic programmes; shopping, clothes, money and other consumer programmes. In the print media there are entire branches of journalism dedicated to the desirable rather than the pathological side of juvenation, especially the fashion press, 'women's' and 'lad' magazines, and the entire 'Diana industry', all of which have sizeable cross-gender readerships, and the rapidly expanding market of magazines aimed at young people themselves, from special-interest titles (especially computers) to fashion magazines for teenage girls (McRobbie 1997; Lumby 1997).

Looked at from within the ideology of modernist journalism, the rise in prominence of a feminised, privatised, juvenated journalism is hard to celebrate, and there is of course a continued need for the 'hardest' of negative/competitive news reporting, as front-line journalists continue to demonstrate in war zones from Bosnia to British backstreets. (However, it has to be said that postmodern journalism can score points here too, as with the Princess of Wales's celebrated trips to Angola and Bosnia, producing political shifts in international land-mine policy and in inter-communal communication respectively.) But from the perspective of the readership, the 'postmodernisation' of journalism appears in far from regrettable form. The image of the readership that has been inherited from modernism is very restricted; it is based on the need for an informed governmental class. While journalism retains a need to address issues of conflict, competition, progress and accident so that democratic will-formation can be exercised in a well-informed, critically astute and reasoned manner by as wide a readership as can be reached, this does not use up the capacity of journalism, nor does it satisfy all of the multiple, overlapping and mutually illuminating aspects of a given population's identity, characteristics and desires. Readers are not only citizens exercising democratic judgements in the virtual agora of the mediasphere; they are, as they have been throughout modernity, capable of being organised around other concepts, including comfort, culture and curiosity. What I am calling 'postmodern' news introduces some of these alternative possibilities into the quotidian routines of collective image-sharing and story-telling. While all journalism has two faces – a truth-seeking orientation to the facts and a communicative orientation to the readership – this kind of journalism emphasises communication more than truth, the reader more than the event, Wedom not Theydom, the mutual cordialisation of social relations not adversarial foe-creation, teaching not avant-gardism. In anthropological terms, 'postmodern' juvenated journalism looks at the category of 'neighbour' to find not 'enemy', but 'marriage-partner' (Leach 1972).

In this context, caught midway between modernist adversarialism and postmodern cordialisation (Hartley 1996: 246; Paine 1792/1937: 189), young girls have entered history; they appear in front-page journalism. They are the marker of the tension between these alternative types of journalism.

'This case involves us all and raises questions': children outside 'wedom'

In the mediasphere, the boundaries of the social are continuously reproduced. Children are increasingly imagined in the press as living somewhere outside those boundaries. Children themselves are the only people it is still legal to assault (by their 'carers'); they are judged incapable of speaking publicly for themselves and thus of any kind of organised self-representation, they are subject to laws they have no hand in making. Discursively, they are a dependent population which is subject to correction, protection, exploitation and development in terms that are both borrowed from and a major contributor to the rationale of the imperial colonisations of the nineteenth century. They are, in semiotic terms, a virtual but colonised 'class'; an 'internal colony', in Michael Hechter's important phrase (Hechter 1975).

Like other 'virtual' communities which can be identified by demographic rather than territorial location (such as women in certain contexts, minority or subject ethnic groups, proletariats, people of non-heterosexual orientation, and others), children are apt to be characterised by 'colonising' discourses of control, which function to represent them as weak, prone to victimisation or unruliness, and incapable of self government. Unlike other virtual communities, children have no decolonising 'liberation movement'; the things that are said about them are widely and passionately believed simply to be true. Indeed, children are the metaphor-of-choice for other colonising rhetorics, which have over the years cast women, indigenous or minority-ethnic, working class, or gay/lesbian people as childish or infantile. However, it seems always to transpire that the journalistic passion to reduce children to a stereotype of ungovernability is reserved for the most 'othered' populations ('street kids' rather than the writer's own children, for instance); the strongest editorial rhetoric of correction and protection follows socio-economic contours, and children are more subject to punitive rhetoric if they themselves are also 'marked' by the same (colonial) characteristics of ethnicity, class, gender or sexual orientation that their image was once used to describe. Now, in other words, it is juvenation of 'othered' populations that is used to police childhood in general, whereas in imperial discourses it was a generalised image of childhood that was used to police subject populations of whatever demographic variety.

Where imperial colonisers 'infantilised' those populations they were sent to govern, children themselves are treated like colonised populations in a period prior to freedom movements and independence; in Laclau and Mouffe's terms (1985), their inequality ('subordination') is not signified (not experienced) as 'oppression'. Whether the intention is benign or not – assimilative or punitive, developmental or exploitative, construing these 'natives' as desirable or threatening – the 'place' of children as a journalistically imagined community is the same. They are *outside* of Wedom. Indeed, because it is based on an appeal to nature, not power, the current insistence that childhood is *innocent* – asexual, non-political, separate and apart from the cares, worries and realities of adult, responsible, productive life – is a politics of *exclusion*; euphemised semiotic apartheid (Lucy 1995: 8–12).

The news media conduct a 'not-in-front-of-the-children' conversation about children, and issues that are said to harm them are discussed in pictorial detail. But at the same time the news media are presumed to be freely accessed by children; indeed, one of the repeated talking points is the supposedly dangerous openness of media to juvenile eyes. Always the most recent and most visual media are thought to be the most risky in this context; the internet, computer games, videos, TV and comics are endlessly fretted about, while print media – in the pursuit of truth rather than entertainment, public interest rather than commercial gain, 'protestant' rationality rather than 'catholic' idolatry of images – are exempt from scrutiny.

A quite extreme example of what can result from the faith in print media, and concomitant suspicion of visual media, was circulating at the same time that the news media were fretting about the harm *Vogue* might be doing to teenagers. Issue 19 of the 'TRUE CRIME' quarterly, *Murder Most Foul*, was largely devoted to the Rose West trial, reporting the circumstances of each of the ten killings for which she was convicted, as described in court by the prosecution. The issue also included a round-up of other extreme sex/murder sprees by couples in the USA, in breathtakingly shocking detail, as well as numerous unrelated murder stories. Printed on cheap newsprint and staple-bound, *Murder Most Foul* was freely available, for £1.80 in contrast to *Vogue*'s £2.80, on the lower shelves of high-street newsagents throughout the UK, for several months from January 1996. This was its editorial caveat:

> There are details in our account of the case which were not widely reported because they were too horrifying. Brace yourself before you read it, for this is as full a picture as the trial jury received.

Fair warning, for this is what *Murder Most Foul* proposed to reveal to its readers, young and old:

> Most newspapers felt unable to report all the details to emerge in court, fearing they were too horrific for family consumption. What couldn't they report fully? Such details as precisely what was done with the vibrator to the young victims, how many lashes one victim received on her genitals with the buckle-end of a belt, or what strength is required to sever a human head. We report here the facts as fully as we are able, however repellent, because this case involves us all and raises questions. How could 10 young girls lie in hidden graves for up to 20 years, half of them not even reported missing?
>
> (*Murder Most Foul*, No. 19, 25 January 1996: 2)

Bearing in mind that more than half of Rosemary West's victims were teenagers and minors, this is another example of the journalistic habit of talking about 'young girls' as if they are not present among the reading public, even though its pricing, style and physical position in the newsagent's repertoire actually make *Murder Most Foul* more likely to attract such readers, in greater numbers, than *Vogue* does. But despite its evident narrative investment in sexualisation, juvenation and death, the questions it raises certainly do 'involve us all' – and it is indeed worth asking why the news media, and the public domain at large, are so squeamish about fashion models, and yet so careless about much more profound problems for children.

Taken without consent

If you attend to the voices, rather than the images, in the diverse and pervasive news coverage of juvenation, it is very much a case of young bodies being seen but not heard. They so rarely speak for themselves that when they do it seems false. A rare exception to prove the rule was a front-page feature in the *Independent on Sunday*'s 'Real Life' section, headlined 'SO WE WANT TO MODEL: WHAT'S WRONG WITH THAT?' (22 June 1997). The introduction contextualises:

> THE USE OF YOUNG MODELS PROVOKED FIERCE CRITICISM FROM THE *CHILD EXPLOITATION AND THE MEDIA* FORUM LAST WEEK. BUT HOW COME NO-ONE EVER ASKS THE GIRLS WHAT THEY THINK? EXCLUSIVELY FOR REAL LIFE, HETTIE JUDAH TALKS TO FIVE TEENAGERS WHO WILL BE THE NEXT NEW FACES.

Young people are rarely accessed like this. A *Guardian* report on the use of thirteen-year-old models by Vivienne Westwood, for instance, interviewed a spokeswoman for Westwood, an agony aunt, a Tory MP and another fashion designer – but none of the girls involved. Instead, even their 'rebelliousness' was spoken for them by their minder:

> A spokeswoman for the designer remained unrepentant yesterday. 'I don't know what all the fuss is about. We want to show that young girls can be sophisticated and chic, and that that is being rebellious. The girls love it. They are stars for a day. Basically, what we hope is that their fathers are going to look at them and think, "Gosh, what a little cracker".'
>
> (*Guardian*, 22 February 1997)

An alternative viewpoint is put on the girls' behalf by agony aunt Claire Rayner: 'I can't imagine any caring parent letting their children do this. You might as well put them down a coal mine'. Naturally, one of the girls (unnamed) does make an appearance, in a three-column photograph that takes

Independent on Sunday, 22 June 1997.

up more space than the story it illustrates. The same story, with the same quotation about 'little crackers', but picturing different models, crossed the world to Australia, turning up as a seven-page cover-feature for *Who Weekly* (12 May 1997) – long enough, and far enough into the genre of postmodern lifestyle journalism, to include some quotations from the teenage models themselves.

Where girls speak up in the 'hard' news media they are likely to get what's coming to them: 'EXPELLED GIRL WHO DARED TO CRITICISE TEACHERS' (*Sun*, 24 July 1997) – the story of a teenager whose critical comments to a local newspaper were 'answered' thus by the head teacher, although some weeks later the expulsion was retracted. This authoritarian approach to inter-age communication has grave consequences for the prospects of mutual understanding and trust between 'Wedom' and those who are fenced out. The papers ridicule sex education: 'COPS PROBE "GROPE" GUIDE FOR KIDS OF 9', 'CLINIC'S LESSON IN GROPING FOR PRE-TEEN GIRLS' (*Daily Mirror, Express*, 31 May 1996); but then they agonise about teenagers with babies:

> This extraordinary picture sums up the confusion at the heart of Britain today. Schoolgirl Sarah Taylor, aged just 13 and one of the most unruly pupils at the now-notorious Ridings School, conceived little Chloe when she was 12.
>
> (*Express*, 29 October 1996)

The punitive attitude is always to hand: 'WAR ON UNDER AGE SEX PARTIES: *Labour crusade against gymslip mums*. SCHOOLS ON A MISSION TO TAME TEAR-AWAY PUPILS WHO ARE SLEEPING AROUND AGE 12: paying the price of our moral decline' (*Express on Sunday*, 5 October 1997 – story by the *political editor*). Even when the papers try to find out more about teenagers by asking them directly, you get the feeling the outcome has been, well, prefabricated: '*THE LUST GENERATION*: TELL US THE TRUTH ABOUT TEEN SEX AND VIRGINITY' (call for readers to take part in a survey in the *Sun*, 11 April 1997). It is a no-win situation for children: small wonder that when asked, their comments are those of people who know they are outsiders: 'HOW THE CLASS OF 96 SWITCHED OFF AT MORALISTIC LECTURES AND DOUBLE TALK'. Seventeen-year-old Amarjit Bangar is quoted as saying: 'Citizenship classes ' "would be a good idea. But it's no good giving them to teenagers because they could already be corrupted by then" ' (*Guardian*, 23 October 1996). This is a far cry from the influence of a democratic mediasphere teaching civic virtue; 'teaching' is regarded as 'corruption', and children who are not dialogic partners with those who would influence them (not only the formal educational system but also the news media) simply 'switch off'.

Children are photographically appropriated and semiotically policed in a media polity which does not admit them to its readership-assembly. They are not regarded as citizens, nor even as readers, of contemporary society. They have no control over their own representation. Indeed, it is my own observation that the news media frequently fail to take seriously enough many stories where a high-visibility media-campaign might do something to reduce the incidence of cruelty, neglect and abuse of children. News priorities (negativity, control), and a more pervasive public climate that does not know the language of cordialisation, lead to a failure to understand the importance of an entire aspect of human activity – the one associated with care, love, dialogue, and openness to others. These, I would say, are the *positive* values associated with teaching, in the best sense (Hoggart 1970: 55). But they are also associated with despised branches of journalism – the communicative, lifestyle, postmodern, 'soft' genres; and with despised public figures – notably the Princess of Wales *before* her death. Diana's 'public policy' of promoting love, meeting and touching ordinary people on their own terms, without any agenda or ideology, and of 'giving people a hug', went uncomprehendingly unpraised (in the broadsheets especially), though not unnoticed. Such stuff was sneered at even as it was reproduced, as witness the Sunday papers on the day of her death (31 August 1997). Modernist news has trouble keeping a straight face on questions of love, so in Diana's case the face it pulled was a long one, the Sunday columnists heaping almost unanimous ridicule on her (air)head: Barbara Gunnell in the *Independent on Sunday* wrote of 'the inane Sloane-ish inarticulacy of a woman with fundamentally nothing to say about anything'; the *Observer* called her a 'woodentop', and the 'Mrs Blair's Diary' column commented on 'the witterings of a woman who, if her IQ were five points lower, would have to be watered daily'. Columnist Bernard Ingham in the *Express on Sunday* suggested she had 'more brass than brains', and Jessica Davies of the *Mail on Sunday* headlined her opinion: 'LOATHE US IF YOU LIKE DIANA, BUT PLEASE ACT YOUR AGE'. People's willingness to queue for half a day to sign the books of condolence, and the mass horticide that literally de-flowered the whole of Europe, as retailers sent to Israel and beyond to keep up with the demand for floral tributes, came as a well-documented surprise to the commentators (see 'TURNCOATS: WHAT THE PAPERS DIDN'T MEAN TO SAY' *Frank* magazine, No. 2, November 1997, 132–5). Diana had clearly connected with public sentiment, but not with public-opinion-leaders. It seems to me that this is evidence of a more structural problem. As the inheritor of 'enlighten-ment' attachments to reason, science, progress and truth, modernist journalism is suspicious of emotion, expressiveness and heart-over-head 'populism'. Such stuff, like Diana, is treated with cynicism and even contempt. Diana's crime was that she operated via sight, touch and talk, not thought, reason and critique.

In this climate, care is not easily dealt with at all as news, although its absence may make headlines. Community fear of child-abuse is news; 'teaching' how to sustain a culture of child-care is not. The consequence is that news rarely reports what may be learned from instances of child-abuse by parents, carers and children themselves. There is no editorial urgency about preventative policies. Several major inquiries into institutional child-abuse in residential homes are current as I write, but the evidence of victims rarely commands media atten-tion, and the press benches in the hearing-rooms are often empty. Similarly, a recent case of horrifying parental sex-abuse barely made it from the regional to the national press, and then only to illustrate other 'truths', such as the 'evils' of the internet or the 'failings' of social workers, not as part of any campaign for a general improvement in parent–child relations (see the *Western Mail*, 11 April 1997, and compare the national dailies for that day). The same papers that were *not* reflecting on prevention were, however, camped outside the front doors of 'convicted paedophiles' and interviewing vigilante neighbours. It seems that where the interests of children are most vitally involved, the modernist media are often muted (it is postmodern, 'Diana' journalism that teaches care); where the news interest in juvenation is most intense, children as such are not really involved.

One of the inevitable consequences of the news media's compulsive fiddling with the hemline of the social is that more meaning is produced than can be policed, and publics are called into being which exceed the purposes of those who wish to command them with their particular truth. In the end, the images of juvenation necessarily escape the policing professionals whose creation and currency they are. In a previous article I have likened the reading practices of contemporary readerships to the vehicular practices of juvenile car thieves – readers take texts where they find them, without consent, and use them as vehicles for their own 'joyreading' trips through the suburbs of semiosis (Hartley 1994). The very discourse of governability, textualized in media campaigns such as the current crackdown on juvenile sexuality, is something quite different, perhaps its own opposite, in the hands of the readerships it both creates and requires. Finding and fencing the boundary of the social, of the sayable and seeable, requires transgressions in order for a visible line to be drawn. And here, as everywhere, learning is not directly related to teaching – what is taken, whether it be offence, mischief, comfort or understanding, is not by any means predictable by what is meant. It follows that crackdowns of this kind must always do what they most deny, fail where they most insist. The reason for this is obvious – in order to show us what 'we' look like, images must be created which show an outside, a 'they', which in this case is the last internally colonised population of modernity, namely children. However, what the readerships, including children (however defined), make of these semiotic manoeuvrings, is not pre-given. There is not only the pleasure of the prohibited, of identification with the outsider, but also the problem that whatever meanings are taken away without consent, the victims are likely to be found well away from the site of the accidents reported in the news. It seems that where children are getting hurt, journalism is often silent, but meanwhile, it seems also that parents and artists, such as the photo-media student I mentioned at the outset, are more likely to get hurt in the struggle for the meaning of juvenation than young people themselves.

Note

1 Thanks are due or, like the writing itself, well overdue to Cynthia Carter for asking me to do this, holding me to it, and being positive, patient and purposeful about getting it finished; and to Mark Gibson, for telling me how awful the first draft was, and then arguing and re-reading it into what I hope is at least respectability. I have tried these ideas out on one or two publics; thanks to the students of Alan McKee's Media and Gender course at Edith Cowan University in Western Australia; to Louise Adler for letting me talk about them on ABC Radio National; and to Geoffrey Graig, Wendy Parkins, Alan McKee, Robyn Quin, Catharine Lumby, McKenzie Wark, Kate Bowles and Brian Shoesmith, as the organisers of and co-participants in the *Continuum* Keynote Panel at the 'In Search of the Public' Cultural Studies Association of Australia conference in Fremantle, December 1996, where I learnt, again, how hard it is for a middle-aged father to get away with an interest in 'girl power'.

4

GENDER, PRIVACY AND PUBLICITY IN 'MEDIA EVENT SPACE'

Lisa McLaughlin

Introduction

On the evening of June 12 1994, two people were stabbed to death outside a condominium in the exclusive Brentwood neighborhood of Los Angeles. From the beginning, Los Angeles Police Department detectives labeled the double murder a 'celebrity case', not because of the renown of the two victims, but because one of them, Nicole Brown Simpson, was the ex-wife of O.J. Simpson, former football star, sports commentator, movie star and Hertz rental car spokesman. Detectives were concerned that the media would arrive at the Bundy crime scene or Simpson's Rockingham estate and create a spectacle. Because no spectacle is complete without an audience, the case did not fully erupt as a media event until several days later, on 17 June, when Simpson attempted to evade the LAPD rather than to turn himself over as the prime suspect in the murders. Police eventually tracked him down via a cellular phone in the now-infamous white Ford Bronco in which he was being chauffeured by his longtime friend, A.C. Cowlings. What has become known as 'the lowspeed chase' was televised for hours, with approximately 100 million viewers watching police cars slowly trailing the Bronco down the freeway to Simpson's mansion as detectives attempted to dissuade the suspect from suicide. The freeway and the street leading to the mansion were lined with crowds of people, cheering, clapping, blowing kisses and holding signs declaring their dedication to the celebrity in the Bronco. Following his arrest that evening, Simpson's mugshot appeared across the world's media channels.

When Simpson was put on trial for the murders, television news anchors rushed to label the event as 'the most celebrated trial in US history', 'the trial of the century', and Simpson 'the most famous murder defendant in US history.' Earlier trials-of-the-century, such as those of accused anarchist-murderers Sacco and Vanzetti and of accused spouse-murderer Dr Sam Sheppard, were brushed aside. More than 100 US and foreign media organizations created 'Camp O.J.', a chaotic structure of news vans, scaffolds and satellite dishes outside of the Los Angeles County Courthouse. On air, CNN anchor Jim Moret efficiently described the coverage of the case as 'a blur of news, entertainment and tabloid-like reporting in a surrounding of circus-like atmosphere.' The public's fervor seemed to match that of the media, with the result that broadcast and cable news and talk programs, tabloid television shows and mass circulation magazines enjoyed a huge payoff for their extensive coverage of the Simpson trial. CNN, the only network to provide live, 'gavel-to-gavel' coverage of the full trial, was attracting 2.2 million viewers at any given time during their 631 hours of direct coverage, and is estimated to have increased its ratings and revenues by nearly fifty percent.[1] Outside of the courthouse, vendors sold O.J. T-shirts, buttons and banners to enthusiastic onlookers, while in Brentwood the Bundy murder scene and the Rockingham mansion became the most popular tourist sites in Los Angeles. In 1994, some of the most popular Halloween costumes in Los Angeles featured the likenesses of O.J. and Nicole: for the former, a mask, fake-blood-spattered Simpson football jersey and a bloodied rubber knife, and for the latter, a long, blonde wig and the creative use of red make-up to simulate stab wounds around the head and neck.

From this account, we may want to conclude that Habermas was correct in arguing, within *The Structural Transformation of the Public Sphere* (1962/1989), that a culture-debating public has degenerated into a culture-consuming public. Around the O.J. Simpson case, there existed something of a 'masscultural' phenomenon. A public body was riveted on spectacular images and descriptions of crime scenes, forensic examinations, jury selection processes and the private lives of parties involved in the case. The courtroom could not maintain a semblance of dignity in the face of this made-for-television trial. Courtroom behavior was exposed as a performance, made more intense by the presence of television cameras. The legitimacy of the news as a social institution was thrown into question as the mass media engaged in competitive, tabloid journalism around the case, with the disclaimer that they were simply responding to alleged consumer tastes for more spectacle. The case seemed to have fully exposed the degeneration of the public sphere to the level of commodified culture, the degradation of public discourse to the level of television entertainment, and the inseparability of politics and spectacle. Despite the common scholarly practice of jettisoning the Frankfurt School assessment of the influence of mass culture on society, the views of Habermas and his early colleagues now appear more prophetic than pessimistic.

Yet, as I suggest in the ensuing pages, the early Habermasian model does not offer an interpretive framework that can adequately account for the role of media spectacles in producing difference *as* a subject of debate. The problem begins with the dependence of the disintegration thesis on the earlier existence and merit of the category of the liberal model of the bourgeois public sphere, which emphasizes the desirability of a discursive space where private citizens might meet to debate issues of public concern and engage in criticism of the government in an environment free of power relations. To become unfettered from power relations required the suspension (not elimination) of differences of status and interest. This, in turn, would allow public opinion to circulate as an expression of the objective, general interest. Habermas's dismay at the structural transformation of the public sphere is due to circumstances in which changes in the economic system had motivated changes in political and cultural institutions in such a way that each sphere was infused with personalized politics. Once differences, in the form of inequalities, enter the public domain, following the breakdown of the categorical opposition between private and public realms, Habermas abandons the possibility of locating any sort of emancipatory quality in the new public sphere.

For an approach to the public sphere that can accommodate an attention to the differences within public space, we must turn to the recent work of feminist scholars. These scholars (Nancy Fraser, Mary Ryan, Joan Landes, Carole Pateman, Seyla Benhabib and Iris Young among them) have attempted to document and redress the exclusions constitutive of the normative and historical dimensions of the public sphere. Through their work, they have introduced a normative basis for particularism into the public sphere as the foundation of democracy, affirming the importance of issues including gender, race, ethnicity, age and sexual preference. Although a significant amount of feminist scholarship has explored the lives of women in the intimate sphere, the feminist project of revising the Habermasian public sphere has often attempted to account for the participation of women in various public spaces and to offer theoretical reconceptualizations that can better accommodate public discourses about the needs and interests of women. This scholarly debt is clearly registered to a common feminist rallying cry: the personal is political.

Feminists have exploded the myth of universal access, upon which the liberal model of the public sphere coheres, by establishing that the very meaning of 'civil society' was constructed through the significant exclusion of women, the proletariat and popular culture (Landes 1988; Fraser 1992; Ryan 1992; Pateman 1988). Yet, we cannot turn to a feminist reconceptualization of the public sphere as an ideal yardstick by which to measure the flaws in Habermas's conception of the public sphere. Most of this feminist scholarship rises to the task of debunking Habermas's normative-constitutive assumptions more effectively than it exposes the limits of actually existing democracy in contemporary capitalist societies. By focusing upon the emancipatory allure to the normative dimensions of the public sphere, feminist scholars tend to overlook the workings of a more contemporarily relevant, less fragile, perhaps even more conceptually material, public space in which differences are predominantly managed today. This might be referred to as 'media event space.' 'Media event space' is filled with groups and interests that require representation through the communications media. They would not seem to exist in the absence of media representation.

Taken alone, neither the disintegration thesis nor the feminist critique of

Habermas is adequate to supporting a complex view of the Simpson case, which was both a 'mass' phenomenon and a spectacle of particularity. In the performance of the Simpson case, bodies and cultural differences, always a constitutive component of the public sphere, were irrepressible, bursting through the seams of the objectivist epistemology that informs the languages of law and journalism. This proliferation of difference added considerable resonance to the literal meaning of *habeas corpus*: you must have the body. There were bodies everywhere in the case. Bodily particularities filled the courtroom during the criminal trial: male, female, matriarchal, patriarchal, Black, Jewish, Asian, Caucasian, celebrity and ordinary. We had grown accustomed to the defendant's body, because he was a football star, a sports commentator, a movie star and a Hertz rental car spokesman – because he had been delivered to us via the electronic media – but, for all the effort that he and his publicists had invested in his 'colorlessness', he now allied himself with a collective Black body fighting for equal justice within a legal system that had conventionally privileged Whites. And, of course, two were dead, the alleged victims of the knife-wielding celebrity. For feminists, allegations that one of them, Simpson's ex-wife Nicole Brown Simpson, had been beaten and terrorized by the murder suspect for the most part of their seventeen-year relationship provided an opening into the publicity surrounding the case on the subject of domestic violence. In symbolically employing the body of Nicole Brown Simpson as the collective, maligned and battered female body, feminists were in a public contest with numerous other groups seeking an awareness that their personal was also political.

Through the Simpson case, feminists attempted to seize a forum for talking about domestic violence, a formerly 'private' concern that has become a topic of public discussion because of the efforts of the women's movement. The price of having traffic with the media would be that the spectacular representation of celebrity power and murder overwhelmed the fact that domestic violence is a profoundly gendered, ongoing form of institutional oppression. Domestic violence was constructed as a couple of events in the life of a woman – a 'trophy wife' made visible only as an accessory to her celebrity spouse – rather than as a persistent form of violence against women. As I suggest in this chapter, coming to an understanding of the Simpson case and other contemporary mediated events requires integrating the concerns of Habermas and his feminist critics in such a way as to bring to the foreground concerns about how differences are produced, circulated and managed through the judging, selecting, ordering and framing practices of the mass media.

Privacy and publicity: Habermas and the feminist critique

In *The Structural Transformation of the Public Sphere* (1962/1989), Habermas tracks the historical emergence and disintegration of a liberal model of the bourgeois public sphere, whose normative dimensions include open access to everyone and the importance of suspending differences of status in the pursuit of common concerns. The concept of the public sphere is set into motion when early capitalist long-distance trade creates a 'traffic in commodities and news' (Habermas 1989: 15). Influenced by early modern capitalism and the economic independence provided by property, a new public had emerged in coffee houses and salons, engaging in critical debate motivated by the circulation of literature and literary criticism. Through the emergence of an independent, market-based press early in the eighteenth-century, rational-critical discourse engaged public interest, as intellectually-based articles were included along with the news, and opinion journals were developed as a new genre of periodical. The literary public sphere, consumed with matters of culture, prefigured a political one, which was oriented toward the discussion of state policy.

The bourgeois public sphere becomes Habermas's prototypical site for the formation of democratic consensus through critical reasoning. Its ascendance is made possible through a fairly strict separation of private and public institutional spheres in early capitalist society. The intimate (family) and economic spheres are private, while the official political (state) and public sphere are public. In later work, Habermas (1987) makes a distinction between 'system' and 'lifeworld', with 'system' designating the state (power) and official economy (money), and 'lifeworld' designating the public sphere and the intimate sphere. These spheres are highly dependent upon one another and share vital relationships of exchange. Yet, the existence of the public sphere is dependent upon its constitution as a discursive arena that is conceptually distinct from the state and from the official economy; its participants assemble to discuss matters of common interest, to criticize the state and make the state accountable to the citizenry, and to act as debaters rather than buyers.

Fundamental to Habermas's description of the public sphere is the necessity to maintain a distinction between the private and the public. Preserving the normative separation between the two proves to be a daunting task, particularly since Habermas's approach is to locate the intersections among them in order to elucidate how changes in the economic system and the political system influence the transformation of cultural institutions as the location for reason-based political debate. One confounding factor is that, through their associations, the bourgeois formed a public sphere that was private. The polemics of the public sphere derived from the relationship between the role of human being and that of property owner (and, by extension, between the private, institutional spheres of the family and the economy) as the basis for sovereign citizenship enacted through rational-critical debate (Habermas 1989: 175–6). One could not be a citizen without fulfilling certain foundational requirements of private autonomy, notably the achievement of human intimacy through the family and the ownership of property. Yet, the public sphere remains 'public' in the sense that it exists only through publicity, the mode through which personal opinions can evolve through rational critical debate of a public into public opinion

75

(Habermas 1989: 219). Following Kant, Habermas links the language of privacy and publicity by suggesting that, through the public sphere, private voices could be converted into public virtues (Habermas 1989: 117).

The criteria for entry into the public sphere required that the typical participant in the public sphere be the 'private man', combining the role of 'owner of commodities' with that of head of the family, that of property owner with that of 'human being' *per se* (Habermas 1989: 28). This, in turn, required the social organization provided by the family. The private realm of the household, as Arendt (1958) suggested prior to Habermas, was a critical dimension of 'being human', as the place where individuals were prepared for their role as citizens. Habermas suggests that the intimate sphere of the 'conjugal family' was imbued with the bourgeois ideal that its activities were intimate and not market-oriented, as persons entered into 'purely human' relations with one another: 'the ideas of freedom, love, and cultivation of the person that grew out of the experiences of the conjugal family's private sphere were surely more than just ideology' (1989: 48). Under the aegis of the family, human beings were required to be 'nothing more than human.' The bourgeois head-of-household depended on the family as a source of nurturance for himself and his sons, as well as for insurance that his property would remain private through distribution among his heirs, who would also inherit the status of citizen.

Clearly, the conflation of 'man', 'private property owner', and 'citizen' produced a social distinction structured by gender, between the 'public man' and the 'private woman' who either remained in the domestic realm or risked violating the norms of 'idealized femininity' through her public presence. Private/public boundaries are associated with a vast chain of polarities that act as cultural codes which assign specific places and roles to different genders (Cohen 1996: 208). These binaries include nature/culture, body/mind, emotion/reason, passion/interest, particular/universal, concrete/abstract, and home/the world of work or politics. These differences are often associated with the notion of separate spheres: 'private woman' and 'public man.' The issue is, rather, one of mobility, however: traditionally, women have been consigned to the intimate sphere of the home and family, while men have been allowed more mobility between spheres of politics, economics, civil society and the intimate sphere. In this configuration, the sole sphere established as the appropriate place for women is one in which social discourses are depoliticized, where matters related to women's lives are conventionally off-limits as topics of public discussion and areas of political intervention (Fraser 1989).

Through their interventions in Habermas's discourse model, feminist scholars of the public sphere have revealed that women's oppression and exploitation are legitimated through the distinction drawn between public and private spheres. The issue at hand is not that lines are drawn between private and public altogether, but rather, that distinctions are drawn which circumscribe women in the private realm and legitimate their oppression and exploitation there. Benhabib (1992: 110) makes a simple but astute observation: 'Any theory of the public, public sphere, and publicity presupposes a distinction between the public and the private.' The feminist objection is against a rigid distinction that seems too impermeable, uncontested, and exact (Honig 1992: 224).

It is not surprising that feminist interest is focused upon the area of domestic privacy which, traditionally, has had extensive structuring significance for women's lives. As Fraser suggests, however, the overprivatization of women's issues as 'personal' or 'domestic' fails to notice that 'gender identity is lived out in all arenas of life: paid work, state administration, citizenship, familial and sexual relations.' Gender helps to structure each of these areas and acts as a 'medium of exchange' between them (Fraser 1989: 127–8). Habermas, she notes, errs in his assumption that the domestic sphere is somehow removed from questions of money and power. In fact, the forms of male dominance that were intrinsic to classical capitalism were premised upon the use of money and power to separate waged labor and the state from childrearing and the household. In the shift from this phase to welfare-state mass democracy, patriarchy is shifted from the home to the state, so that bureaucratization and monetarization become instruments of women's subordination. In the case of spousal battery, relations of gender dominance and subordination are reproduced both when the problem is enclaved within male-headed, restricted families and when the public discourse about this matter is enclaved into specialized publics such as family law, social work, and the sociology and psychology of 'deviancy' (Fraser 1989: 168). Abuse toward women reflects and reinforces other patterns of gender inequality evident in broader power relations and social norms, and, like other women's concerns, extends well beyond familial and sexual relations (Rhode 1989: 244).

Another problem with locating privacy as the sole root of women's oppression is that it suggests that all privacy is bad privacy. As Cohen (1996: 191) observes, legal and political protections of privacy are a necessary precondition for developing and defending different, unique identities that contribute to the plurality of public space. These protections include the right to be left alone, freedom from official regulation or control (decisional privacy), and the right not to have an identity imposed by the state or another third party (the right to inviolate personality). We can then under-stand domestic violence as a matter of both too much and not enough privacy, as a problem at the intersection of relationships between privacy and publicity. There are two senses in which this is true, beginning with the status of domestic violence as a violation of women's legal and political right to private autonomy. Until well into the twentieth century, legal protections existed in the USA that supported the inviolate character of the home on behalf of the private autonomy of the male head-of-household (Rhode 1989: 244). Still today, despite enhanced legal protections for victims of domestic violence, the public authority that the state brings to bear on the matter is compromised by the attitudes and practices of the police and offi-cers of the court, who are more likely to pursue conciliatory approaches to battering than to offer long-term protection from the batterer. Moreover, even if a woman if able to remove herself from the relationship, she faces the absence of adequate welfare, employment opportunities and childcare.

Second, because domestic violence is a form of oppression that has been traditionally hidden, and thus protected, as unpolitical, it is prevented from entering the public sphere as a topic of debate. Therefore, domestic violence represents a violation of both the right to privacy and the right to publicity. In the USA, it was not until the 1970s that the private experiences of battered women became a public concern. Before the efforts of the modern feminist movement, virtually no information was available concerning the frequency or severity of family assaults. The total absence of data contributed to the continuation of the problem (Rhode 1989: 237). Once data is generated, however, its influence is dependent upon the extent of its circulation in the public sphere. In a mass-mediated public sphere, issues of domestic violence do not tend to receive prolonged discussion but, rather, come to the fore as 'soundbites' within the marketing milieu of mass media spectacles. The hold that spectacles have on the media and the public is associated with the private sphere of 'the economic', in which protections exist that allow those with substantial resources of money and power to make a profit by creating consumers and then selling to them. As I describe below, this form of 'bad privacy' is the key to understanding Habermas's description of the demise of the liberal-bourgeois public sphere, and also illuminates the bond between the media and the consumer in the production and consumption of media spectacles today.

The 'bad privacy' of mass culture

According to Habermas (1962/1989), the descent into 'bad privacy' begins as liberal competitive capitalism is supplanted by the organized capitalism of cartels and giant corporations. Concurrently, a public that was once politically involved withdrew into the 'bad privacy' of mass culture.[2] This shift provokes the interpenetration of private and public realms. The specific causes of the dismantling of the distinctions between private and public are many and complex, and can be described here only in brief. First, although the bourgeois model of the public sphere had depended upon class interest as the basis of general interest, the inequalities of late capitalism created class polarization. Many of those who now entered the public sphere could not fulfill the bourgeois requirements for entry, since they were excluded from the franchise and lacked private ownership of the means of production; they lacked the autonomy of 'private men' provided by private property. With the inclusion of non-bourgeois elements into the public sphere, civil society's inequalities could no longer be bracketed and instead became a topic of discussion.

Second, and relatedly, state and society became interlocked in a form of 'welfare-state mass democracy.' The state's accountability to the 'common interest' shifted to a concern with special interests as groups made demands of it, in competition with one another. Various interest groups bypassed the public sphere to make demands of the state for social rights, services and protection, and the state encroached on the private realms of the family and the economy. Third, the public was 'relieved of' the task of rational-critical political debate by institutions that attempted to organize private interests in the form of political agency and parties that were 'above the public whose instruments they once were.' The economic sphere intruded into the public domain as private organi- zations began to assume public power: 'The process of the politically relevant exercise and equilibration of power now takes place directly between the private bureaucracies, special-interest associations, parties, and public adminis- tration' (Habermas 1989: 176).

Finally, the growth of large organizations enabled the separation of the inti- mate sphere from the economic sphere. Work and the family became disconnected, the former becoming a separate sphere between the private and public realms, the latter becoming the site of 'regressive' mass-culture consump- tion. Journalism had become mass media and publicity, in the form of rational-critical discourse, had become public relations. The pseudo-publicity that remains is merely an occasion for the manipulation of popular opinion. The activity of the consumer of organized capitalism is public but uncritical and, therefore, not conducive to publicity in the form of rational debate. Mass media now create moments of identification with the public positions and personas of others, while consumers function in an acclamatory role. Today, public-sphere activity of all kinds is overlayed by what Negt and Kluge (1993) refer to as 'public spheres of production', which derive their force directly from capitalist production. These production realms, which are 'pseudo-public spheres', produce public spectacles originating in the privatized corporate sector and include all of the forms taken by the media of consumer culture. The media of industrial capitalism seek direct access to the private sphere of the individual.

The disintegration thesis that concludes *The Structural Transformation* offers a critical opening into an analysis of advanced capitalism, in which the most public of public debate takes the form of media spectacle; yet, its model of a unilinear collapse of public debate into culture consumption is too simplistic, as Habermas (1992) concedes in reflections on his early work. The liberal model of the bourgeois public sphere, as Habermas and several media scholars have suggested, has limited relevance for contemporary social and political life. It prizes a model of public debate that has its foundation in the circulation of print materials and discussions of them in salons and coffee houses when, now, the public sphere is dominated by technical media of extraordinary scale and complexity. We cannot confront this new 'media cartel', as Negt and Kluge refer to it, with mere nostalgia for the public sphere of the eighteenth-century bour- geoisie. Rather, we are forced to engage with the macro-commodity constituted by large-scale media conglomerates, which taps the needs and consciousness of people as raw material for its products, and fuses a diverse group of media into a collective publicity block (Negt and Kluge 1993: 131).

Habermas wrote *The Structural Transformation* without benefit of foresight, when the legacies of the new social movements were unknown and before the 'postmodern condition' had taken hold of society. Because of this, he could not anticipate the extent to which the media of industrial capitalism would devour both general and particular interests in pursuit of the 'borderless market.' As Hansen observes,

> The global unification of the public sphere through the electronic media and transnational networks of production and consumption goes hand in hand with a diversification of appeals and constituencies, as the media strive to get an ever more 'direct' grasp on the 'raw material' of people's experience.
>
> (Hansen 1993: xii)

Far from promoting a 'new cultural politics of difference', diversification galvanizes the efforts of powerful campaigns to employ mechanisms for thwarting the sort of political activity that might extend beyond subcultural communities and the 'masscultural moment' in order to make a systemic difference. The mass media's appetite for regulated plurality simulates 'the personal is political', a slogan which also circulates as a description of 'feminism.' The slogan has served for the feminist movement as an insight and a mobilization strategy. As an insight, it is based upon a hermeneutics of suspicion in which the supposedly natural, unpolitical domain of intimacy (family and sexuality) is exposed as a construction that inscribes and privatizes women's oppression. In this sense, it expresses rebellion against a social order in which the political dimension of personal life is obscured by an extreme differentiation between public and private spheres. As a mobilization strategy, the slogan also represents a hermeneutics of possibility because it suggests its inverse, the political is personal, which, in turn, suggests that radical action can transform the self and oppressive institutional arrangements within the depoliticized domestic sphere. Attention to the personal, the particular and the private reveals more than the public, political dimensions of issues affecting women. It exposes a construction of 'the political' which is predominantly based on the particularity of white male property interests. In this endeavour, feminist scholars repeat and continue the efforts of second-wave feminism.

There is a danger in idealizing the slogan, which is easily done, given the tendency within all social groupings to romanticize their histories, and given the edge that language always has over material conditions in configuring utopias. We need to remind ourselves, however, that 'the personal is political' is fundamentally a descriptive, not a transformative, axiom, which is not to say that it has no impact as a consciousness-raising strategy toward transformation. Here is the problem for feminists: 'the personal is political' is so ubiquitous today that its meaning within the specific context of a progressive social movement can no longer be taken for granted. The feminist movement wishes the statement to refer to 'our' personal and 'our' political, while simultaneously recognizing the differences within the category of 'women.' Yet, precisely because it is an insight into 'how things really are', 'the personal is political' is a battleground that defies ownership and is potentially and promiscuously compatible with every sphere and every social group.

Cultural hybridity has always been an attribute of the populace but, today, it seems ubiquitous, mobilized by media developments that have created a new kind of public sphere, which appears to include 'people who were not in it before, not visible, not public somehow, but have become so by virtue of their new existence as recognized subjects' (Jameson 1991: 357). Differences exist but are systematically managed in such a way as to preclude a transformative effect upon traditional institutions. The management of difference is, of course, precisely the mode through which the liberal model of the bourgeois public sphere sought to protect itself, despite being founded on a set of differences that produced a particular gender- and class-specific public.

The omnipresent circulation of differences would not pose a problem if the normative form of the feminist reconceptualization of the public sphere were operative at the level of institutions. We might then expect a conception of public which in principle excludes no persons, aspects of persons' lives or topics of discussion, and which encourages aesthetic as well as discursive expression. In such a public, the goal may not always be consensus and sharing, but the recognition and appreciation of differences in the context of confrontation with power (Young 1987: 76).

There are few institutional spaces which do not derive their power relations from a personal that has become politicized or a particular that operates as a universal. Turning to the institutional spheres of contemporary society, we find a situation that defies an orderly normative arrangement separating the domestic from the economic and the political. In every sphere, differences, desires and distinguishing characteristics take center stage. Political offices are in the business of legislating personal rights and administering private lives, as in the question of a woman's right to choose an abortion. Personalized, image-based messages are the driving force behind today's government elections and procedures. The capitalist economic sphere uses the vehicle of advertising in which human particulars are churned out to sell everything from food to clothing to computers to investment opportunities to candidates for office. The mass media are the common spherical denominator. As the Almighty Deity for the 'postmodern condition', they transcend and penetrate all spheres.

The mass-mediated debate around the O.J. Simpson case suggested that 'the personal is political' had found security in the public sphere. The case is extravagant but not singular as a place for the circulation of the particular, the personal and the private. As I suggest in the following section, the Simpson case offers an extraordinary opportunity to analyze how media events may open a forum for the public discussion of formerly 'private' concerns, such as domestic violence while, at the same time, they allow the spectacular representation of celebrity power and murder to act as a shield and a substitute for public debate of the issues.

The Simpson case as forensic spectacle

The O.J. Simpson case unfolded as an exposé; it was itself an exposé of the public of late capitalist society. The murder trial offered a view of intertextuality at its dynamic best. Media organizations advertised the Simpson case, and through this advertised themselves. The attorneys played to the cameras, inside and outside the courtroom, in an attempt to manipulate public opinion. Demonstrators amassed outside of the courthouse, protesting against domestic violence, racism and other social problems, and hoping for an encounter with the media. Many of the participants in the case, including the jurors, attempted to trade their new-found notoriety for celebrity and/or book contracts.[3] Witnesses revealed the centrality of television in our lives through their court testimonies. When asked if he had noticed anything unusual about O.J. Simpson when called to a January 1989 domestic disturbance, prosecution witness Detective John Edwards responded, 'Veins were popping out and pulsating on the upper side of his head . . . I'd never seen anything like that on television or anything.' Another witness helped to set the timeline for the murders by remembering the television programming for the evening. He testified that, as usual, he had watched *The Dick Van Dyke Show* until 10:30 in the evening and had then walked the dog. He found Nicole's dog wandering the neighborhood at 10:55, and returned home by 11:05 to find his wife already watching *The Mary Tyler Moore Show*.

One is tempted to join the chorus in exorcizing the Simpson case as 'mere' spectacle, a proliferation of images marketed to an audience. Yet, this 'media event' is more than a box of cheap goods that the media peddled to an unsuspecting audience. The case produced an audience, but it also produced a public that engaged in discursive activity around that which they consumed. The audience experienced the case through live coverage and an explosion of media products, but also through a fragile union with one another. The term 'forensic spectacle' is better able to capture the sense that mass media institutions and audiences are complicit in the production of media events. The word 'forensic', derived from the Latin, means 'of a forum' or 'public'. The Roman forum, or the Greek agora, was a place of citizenship, 'an open space where public affairs and legal disputes were conducted, and it was also the marketplace, a place where citizens' bodies, words, actions, and produce were all literally on mutual display, and where judgments, decisions and bargains were made' (Hartley 1992b: 29–30). In more contemporary times, 'forensic' relates to adversarial argumentation within legal practices and to the transformation of scientific practices within physics and chemistry into the basis for legal discourses and arguments. As Hartley suggests, however, forensics need not be confined to blood samples and other clues: as material evidence, forensics can be combined with the notion of adversarial argument and applied to the analysis of images. Representative public space is made up of pictures that 'talk' and reveal the public in publicity.

Despite their reputation for manipulation and duplicity, images, as Hartley suggests, are the hard evidence of popular reality, more real than the public domain, which has become an abstraction with no geographic center. In everyday life, the pictures and word images of the mass media, for better or for worse, invite more participation in representational politics than do 'official' politics. Which is to say that, today, public-sphere representation demands media representation. Peters (1993), for example, argues that the representation provided by the modern mass media is not an option but a necessity: 'the only "place" that holds the whole process together is the "no place" of the mass media themselves (media taken in the broadest sense).' To be sure, this view conflicts with Habermas's (1962/1989) concerns regarding 'representative publicity', an inferior precursor to the publicity of the bourgeois public sphere that refers to the 'publicness' of rulers, who display status before the people. In this sense, 'representation' means 'presenting oneself', a staging of personhood rather than a gathering of discoursing participants. Habermas, preferring discourse to spectacle, views this pageantry as an elitist mode of politics that blocks democratic participation. With the demise of the liberal model of the bourgeois public sphere, this concern resurfaces, as Habermas's aversion to spectacle is carried through to his analysis of the mass media in the twentieth century. The degeneration of publicity to public relations invokes the possibility that the public sphere will be 'refeudalized' through the displacement of rational discourse by a parade of propagandistic spectacle.

Although Habermas's criticism appears well-founded, it fails to recognize the blurred boundaries between a culture-debating and a culture-consuming public. As a courtroom media event, the Simpson case illustrates the clash between critically-reasoned debate and spectacle. One of the strongest public debates around the Simpson case did not regard whether the defendant was guilty or innocent, but rather whether the court would be able to adjudicate impartially in the midst of a 'media circus' that compromised the objectivity claimed by both the legal system and the institution of journalism. In many respects, the national unease with the case issues from a set of expectations upon which the institutions of law and journalism are founded. The existence of the political category of civil society must be assumed in order for the epistemologies of objectivity informing traditional notions of the roles of law and journalism to be perceived as legitimate. This normative foundation is thrown into crisis, however, when confronted by an information society that redefines the public as consumers and publicity as public relations.

The objectivist epistemology is equally threatened by the revelation that it can only work effectively by hiding its differences. The media attention to the Simpson murder trial and its aftermath has contributed to the case's dubious distinction as a national embarrassment that has 'divided the nation.' I would not be the first to suggest that the discomfiture with the case has less to do with its creation of divisions than it does with the exposure of the US's already-existing tendencies toward racism, misogyny and celebrity-worship. In short, the nation was humiliated by having been caught with its differences showing in public. As the Simpson case reveals, the mass-mediation of issues in the public sphere accomplishes at least two purposes: it displays difference and bodily particularism as ubiquitous and irrepressible *and* helps to create the mass consumer subject that is both captivated and repelled by the differences that circulate within contemporary publicity.

The liberal model of the public sphere, the discourse of law and the ideals of journalism are based in Enlightenment principles of rationality, universality and accessibility. In order to represent the public, they must rely upon a supposed neutrality that silences difference or, taking difference as irrationality, they must attempt to assimilate difference to a rational framework that struggles for homogeneity, variously, within and among groups. The language of law is based in rational disinterested-ness; the lawmaker is to adjudicate impartially, as Eisenstein states, to balance interests in a fair and neutral manner. From an objectivist standpoint, the law distinguishes between right and wrong; it 'recognizes duality rather than diversity' (Eisenstein 1988: 47–8). As MacKinnon suggests, in law:

> The gender question is a question of difference. There are two options under it. The first option I call the 'male standard': Women can be the same as men. In law, it is called gender neutrality. The other option I call the 'female standard': You can be different from men. In law it is called special protection. . . . You can be the same as men, and then you will be equal, or you can be different from men, and then you will be women.
>
> (MacKinnon 1985: 20–1)

As MacKinnon's observation suggests, the recognition of difference alone cannot remedy universalistic assumptions because the two often work together on behalf of (re)establishing the centrality of the white, masculinist, capitalist norm that is foundational to public institutions. In the Simpson case, the particular attention that the media paid to such details as lead prosecutor Marcia Clark's hair and wardrobe, co-prosecutor Christopher Darden's racial turmoil, Judge Lance Ito's Japanese heritage and Johnnie Cochran's Afro-centrism, distracted attention from the role of white male power in setting institutional standards for journalism and the legal system. In one news special alone, CNN's narrator Art Harris referred to Clark as a 'tough cookie that doesn't crumble', 'no shrinking violet', 'an avenging angel for the dead', a single mother who will 'bond with the jury', and 'a street fighter in high heels', while offering no such personalized commentary on the male principles in the case. One of the moments in the case which caused legal observers to recoil in genteel shock occurred when Clark accused prominent, white establishment attorney F. Lee Bailey of lying about having spoken 'marine to marine' to a witness. Shortly after the two had erupted in a shouting match, Clark objected that a glove that

Bailey displayed in court was much smaller than the bloodied one found at the murder scene and quipped, 'I guess it must be Mr. Bailey's.' Joining in the sexually-inflected repartee, Bailey replied that if Clark thought the glove would fit his hand, 'her eyesight is as bad as her memory.' There appeared to be some symbolic value in that Judge Ito decided to issue a set of 'rules of professional conduct' only after Bailey's integrity and size had been attacked by an unreserved female prosecutor.

The defense's deployment of Bailey to grill Los Angeles detective Mark Fuhrman on his use of the word 'nigger' served to place the responsibility for racism and misogyny on individuals. The demonization of Fuhrman as a 'Nazi' by the defense worked to displace attention to a system of race- and gender-inflected contempt and abuse. After it was revealed that Fuhrman had perjured himself by testifying that he had not used the word 'nigger' in the past ten years, media outlets and talk show callers took an approach that largely supported the prosecution's spin: instead of expressing anger that a racist police detective had compromised the murder case by lying in court, they treated Fuhrman as a character whose part had to be written out of the show (Lipsitz 1997: 22). Fuhrman's racism was considered a personal flaw that could not be generalized to other white Americans or any White-run social institution. Meanwhile, lead attorney Johnnie Cochran was widely criticized for 'playing the race card', and along with much of the rest of Black America, of engaging in 'reverse racism' by suggesting that Simpson was the victim of a racist conspiracy (Lipsitz 1997: 23).

Balibar's observation regarding the relationship between racism and universalism is enlightening in respect to these examples: the introduction of 'divisions and discriminations inside the so-called national community, which more often than not are also institutional inequalities and persecutions . . . reconstitutes the "status groups" ' (Balibar 1994: 194). In the Simpson case, the focus on particularity allowed the white, bourgeois, masculinist norm to appear beyond criticism. Perhaps the most prominent division in the case was that which pitted race against gender, racial solidarity against domestic violence. The confrontation between the marginalization of white women in the private sphere and the policing of black men in the public sphere polarized many black and white women and led to pressure on the former to choose to support either race or gender, despite the fact that the two categories are mutually constitutive (Crenshaw 1997: 152). In the end, race and gender maintained a primary relationship as an ideological vehicle for trafficking in fears that black men pose a specific threat to white women, despite the reality that intra-racial domestic violence is far more common.

As Williams (1997: 277) suggests, the confrontation between race and domestic violence dissuaded inquiry into the possibility that white male misogyny might be implicated by virtue of its instrumentality in national debates about budget cuts that would de-fund battered women's legal and welfare services. Lipsitz, accordingly, notes that the racial subtext of the Simpson case, along with media outlets' preoccupation with telling the story in terms of personal problems and acts of consumption, preempted attention to the broad structural processes and the unequal conditions and opportunities in our society (Lipsitz 1997: 26). On the issue of domestic violence, what went largely unmentioned was that one-quarter to one-half of all women will experience domestic brutality in their lives, that about one-third of all female homicide victims are killed by a male friend or family member, and that the vast majority of these have suffered previous beatings. Also disregarded was the importance of ensuring economic independence as a way of stopping domestic violence, or of providing adequate welfare, alimony and child support in order to make separation practical and possible.

The spectacle of 'O.J. consumerism' that overlays all aspects of the case could not completely erase the issue of domestic abuse, for it was presented within the spectacle itself. The marker of its existence was its suppression within the performance of the event. To locate the reality of domestic violence, one has to read through the text to the subtext. We might begin by noting that, according to a 1982 US Civil Rights Commission report, the odds are one-hundred to one that a spousal abuse case will end up in court.[4] Laws against domestic abuse are commonly understood as offering 'special protection' for women, when, in reality, a woman abused by her partner is less likely to receive protection and recompense than would a man assaulted by another in a tavern brawl or on the street. Despite the iconic stature that Nicole Brown Simpson achieved during the trial as a strikingly beautiful murder victim, her experiences with domestic violence had not been so very different from those of other battered women.

Nine incidents of abuse were reported at the Simpson home, and none of them received the serious attention of the police. Reportedly, the Brown family (Nicole's parents and sisters) refused to take seriously her complaints about O.J. and continued to maintain familial and financial relationships with him even after the separation and divorce. After the murders, the family denied that Nicole had been abused, and one sister, Denise, explained to reporters that she did not consider Nicole to be a victim of domestic violence because she was not battered on a regular basis. Prior to the trial, Denise Brown's perspective changed and, at the trial, she testified that O.J. had been verbally abusive to Nicole since 1977, that in 1985 he had grabbed her crotch in public and said, 'This is where babies come from and this belongs to me.' Brown also recounted that in the late 1980s, O.J. had become enraged and had thrown Nicole against the wall and out of the house. Two of Nicole's former next-door neighbors testified that they had viewed Simpson stalking her after their separation.

Following the beating of Nicole on 1 January 1989, O.J. was arrested, taken to the police station and released. He later called police to apologize for involving them in his 'personal problems.' Nicole tried to have charges dropped. Simpson eventually pleaded no contest and was sentenced to community service and psychiatric counseling to be administered by telephone. His public reputation was barely damaged. Less than two months later, he was signed to an

NBC sportscasting contract. A news conference that followed allowed both NBC and O.J. to engage in damage control, as did a subsequent ESPN interview. In these interviews, he dismissed the importance of the domestic abuse incident and stated that both he and Nicole were at fault. The documentation of O.J.'s celebrity had overwhelmed the only public record of her abuse.

Until Nicole was murdered, the violence was largely shrouded from public view. Several pictures of her bruised and lacerated face were revealed to the public – in court and six years too late. During the trial, the *National Enquirer* even featured a computer enhanced photograph depicting the abuse that Nicole was said to have suffered in 1989. The fact that the photograph was re-created is important because few people in the media or the general public seemed to be able to recount that O.J. Simpson had been convicted of beating Nicole in the past. Despite the particular attention that she received during the trial, there seemed to be a massive public amnesia about domestic abuse in general and the publicized incidents of abuse in this woman's life. In the immediate aftermath of the murders, O.J.'s celebrity continued to occupy center stage. West L.A. detectives who arrived on the murder scene in the early morning hours of 13 June were told that, because of its 'VIP nature', the case would be turned over to detectives in the LAPD's Robbery-Homicide Division.

In the trial and its coverage, the particularities of domestic violence provoked a manifest discomfort. Prosecutors employed the unusual strategy of presenting domestic abuse evidence in the first week, with the intention of presenting additional testimony at the end of the trial. Within days, they began to feel that they were becoming too far removed from the details of the case and, shortly thereafter, shifted to the testimony of police and a biochemist who used a romance analogy to describe DNA strands as 'happier when they're together.' In the face of arduous testimony about domestic disturbance calls from police and the LAPD 911 (emergency) operator, the defense's strategy called for Johnnie Cochran to attack police conduct and ask so many questions about procedures that the testimony began to appear mundane. The trial lasted nearly eight months beyond the presentation of the domestic violence testimony, and prosecutors did not return to this evidence.

Several legal experts employed by CNN contributed to the dilution of domestic violence by treating the trial as a sporting event or by trivializing the most damaging evidence. In commenting on Cochran's cross-examination of Detective John Edwards, defense attorney and legal observer Greta Van Susteren expressed admiration for the attorney's tactics and applauded his ability to counter 'the terrible information that O.J. Simpson is a batterer.' On several occasions, she took pains to point out that the trial was not about Simpson's character, but about his guilt or innocence. Another CNN commentator characterized as 'nuts and bolts' the testimony of Robert Riske, the first police officer to arrive at the murder scene, whose statements were accompanied by graphic photos of the bloodied victims. Following the tearful testimony of Denise Brown, Van Susteren derided Brown's testimony as 'inflammatory', while her co-commentator Roger Cossack complained that prosecutor Christopher Darden was 'feeding (Brown) the lines' in her testimony about O.J.'s abuse of Nicole. Van Susteren volunteered a defense strategy, to use Denise Brown's alcoholism to discredit her testimony. And Cossack described Brown as 'a dead ringer for her sister, except with dark hair', adding that 'It's as close as you're ever going to get to having Nicole testify.'

At one show-stopping point in the trial, Nicole came very close to testifying. The approximately fourteen minute playback of a 911 emergency recording is stunning as the most authentic moment in the trial, the only time that the visual performance of the case was arrested by a piece of audio evidence. Nicole's terror is palpable in this recording, made in October 1993, as she reports that O.J. has arrived at her home and broken down a door. She references past abuse: 'It's O.J. Simpson. I think you know his record.' Throughout the recording, the listener can hear her crying, sighing and begging O.J. to leave. In the background, Simpson's enraged voice can be heard: 'You weren't worried about the kids when you were sucking dick in the livingroom!' The 911 operator asks several questions of Nicole: 'Is he the sportscaster or whatever?', 'Has he threatened you or is he just harassing you?', 'Is he yelling at you for something that you did?' The operator originally specified that the call was 'urgent but not life-threatening.' The call's status was eventually upgraded to 'potentially life-threatening.' The listener can hear Nicole's fear increasing as O.J. continues to shout in the background.

While the tape played, the camera surveyed O.J. Simpson, the defense team and the prosecutors as they fidgeted and scribbled on note pads. CNN shifted through a series of computer-generated graphics in an apparent effort to liven up the proceedings. This interval within the trial was remarkable for its stillness; for the first and only time, no one seemed to know where to look or how to behave. When the silence was broken at the conclusion of the tape, CNN's legal experts acknowledged that it was a 'chilling, haunting piece of evidence' and that, through it, the victim herself was speaking. In no time, however, both the court and the media had moved on to new evidence and developments in the case. Beyond that fourteen-minute span, the female murder victim was represented as little more than a body of evidence to the court and to the television audience – a coroner's report, blood evidence, a collection of photographs and diagrams revealing wound locations, sensational books and articles alleging sexual promiscuity, etc. The disembodied voice on the tape provided the one compelling opening into the matter of domestic violence. The problem that it exposed is that battered women are too often represented in their absence, after they are dead or seriously maimed. As Landes (1988) has suggested, there is a paradox built into one common usage of the expression 'to represent.' To 'represent', or to make present again, implies that something must be absent in order to be re-presented. Women's representation in modern public life appears to require their exclusion, she observes:

This exclusion does not automatically 'depoliticize' women but, rather, transforms them into the political *subjects* par excellence of the modern system of representation. In other words, the system requires the production of a subject who complies in becoming the *object* of an act of political representation.

(Landes 1988: 205, italics in original)

Overcoming the exclusion of women from representational space within the public sphere has long posed a challenge for feminists. The issue of access to the media introduces further complications into the question of representation. Media access is perhaps the greatest obstacle faced by feminist and other progressive social movements in publicizing their needs and interests. When contemporary groups compete for representation through public communication, they do so in the thick of an advanced, industrialized climate in which information processing and dissemination is dominated by large corporations whose relationship with the public is that of seller and consumer, where the right to democracy has metamorphized into the right to protect existing structures of private ownership and production relations in order to maximize profit. While those with money and power will almost invariably secure access to the media, these resources are in short supply for many marginalized groups. Peripheral groups are left to promote their concerns in an opportunistic fashion, by becoming an accessory to an existing media spectacle.[5] In doing so, however, we often settle for too little, too late.

While the Simpson case did raise awareness of the formerly 'private' concern called domestic violence, it was for a fleeting moment in the court, the mass media, and the public at large. Of course it may be argued that the Simpson murder trial was not the appropriate vehicle for the circulation of information regarding domestic violence. If the case is defined as something that happened in a courtroom, this may very well be true. But there were two related Simpson cases: one that took place in the courtroom and the other that took place within the public sphere. The latter provided a forum for the discussion of domestic violence only insofar as the information could be shaped to fit the spectacular format of the media event. The public viewed the most particularistic forms of forensic evidence but did not hear that there is an incident of abuse against women in the USA approximately every sixteen seconds, or that at the root of the problem is a domestic economy that confuses women with property. The differences that are associated with the routinized, everyday nature of domestic abuse do not 'perform well' in court or in a public sphere where spectacles hold powerful sway.

Notes

1 Quoted in Lipsitz (1997), from Steve McClellan, 'All Eyes on O.J.,' *Broadcasting and Cable*, 9 October 1995: 6.

2 Habermas uses the term 'bad privacy' to describe the shift from critically-reasoned debate to culture consumption, in 'Further Reflections on the Public Sphere' (1992: 438).

3 Even those who did not seem particularly interested in the spotlight, as with Simpson's ex-friend Ron Shipp, were suspected of using the Simpson case as a shortcut to stardom. Shipp, who claimed to have come forward because he did not want 'the blood of Nicole Brown Simpson' on his hands, was accused by defense attorney, Carl Douglas, of testifying against Simpson in order to become a star by increasing his worldwide profile.

4 I am indebted to Rhode's *Justice and Gender* (1989) for this information.

5 An alternate route to publicity seems doomed to failure. For example, even with the most carefully planned pre-publicity, feminist organizers of the UN Fourth World Conference on Women, held in Beijing in September 1995, could not provoke mainstream media organizations to employ more than 'othering' practices in covering the conference: speculation on whether Hillary Clinton would attend following the detention of Chinese-American Harry Wu (good US/bad China) and on how favorably the freedom of US women compares to those from Third World countries that practice the rituals of veiling and female circumscision (good US/bad Third World).

5

'MRS KNIGHT *MUST* BE BALANCED'

Methodological problems in researching early British television

Janet Thumim

Punctum

I want to declare at the outset the dual focus informing my research. On the one hand I'm curious about beginnings, about the ways in which new technologies, new communication forms – new opportunities – are understood and operated and developed. On the other hand I am constantly exercised – intrigued, I could say – by the conflict of interests which seems to me to be inherent in the various and often conflicting assumptions about that contentious term, 'the feminine'. I know that there are other moments which might be considered candidates for the 'beginning' of television, but I believe the period 1955–65 to be of particular significance. In the UK, commercial broadcasting began in September 1955. Televisual news, in a form that we would recognise today, only began in the mid-1950s. By the mid-1960s, however, there was a multi-channel operation, schedules and genres had settled into a form not dissimilar to that which we enjoy today, and audiences had come to accept television as primary in the routines of daily life. During this formative period the institution necessarily addressed an audience including women – indeed women were acknowledged to be central to the project of inserting television into domestic spaces and routines[1] – yet at the same time the female presence on screen was carefully contained.

In approaching my material – of which there is both too much and too little, a point to which I shall return – I am sometimes struck by what I will call, following Barthes, a kind of *punctum*.[2] By this I mean a sentence, a remark, possibly an image or an intonation which was innocently offered, but which seems to me to reference assumptions which I find contentious and which, therefore, I understand to have been 'made strange' by the passing of time, by history. The historian's task is to dis-cover, to unearth, sufficient material to allow the object of study to begin to speak for itself so that the historian may begin to form an idea not too determined by his or her own preconceptions. It is a task fraught with difficulties, perhaps an impossible task, but nevertheless one worth attempting.[3] In perusing the various different kinds of materials available to me, I have found that a state of alertness to minor details, attention to the unexpected, as it were, yields fruitful food for thought. By way of entry into my paper, then, I want to present a few such *punctum*, and to prepare my own readers for what may seem an odd narrative structure: the point being that it is not (yet) a narrative, but an enquiry.

' . . . Mrs Knight *must* be balanced' is the closing line in an instruction from the BBC Controller of Programmes, Television, to the editor of *Panorama* in January 1955.[4] We're not talking about small boats here, nor harmony or aesthetics, but about an altogether trickier term: *news value*. It is not clear from the memo whether Mrs Knight, who I presume to be a proposed guest to the programme, held views that were considered too extreme, or whether her manner was overwhelming or her voice too loud or too shrill: it could have been any of these, judging from the kind of memos that fluttered constantly between offices of the embattled BBC early in 1955. The memo also informs me that she was to be 'cross-examined' by an interviewer who should similarly examine a person holding opposing views. In addition to *balance*, the notion of *cross-examination* is of interest, suggesting as it does a courtroom model in which the role of the jury was, perhaps, assigned to the audience. But the memo's emphatic instruction ('must' is underlined) draws attention to the proposed interviewee – could her gender have been an issue in the question of balance?

A November 1957 memo to the *Panorama* team, from Presentation Editor Clive Rawes, confirms my unease about the reasons undermining Mrs Knight's acceptability. He was trying out some male announcers recruited from sound broadcasting and would therefore have little occasion in future to call on the services of three 'freelance actresses' (Polly Elwes, Pauline Tooth, Vera McKechnie) all of whom had been previously employed for this work because, he wrote, 'the television service is moving towards the position where its regular announcing team will comprise 3 or 4 men and probably only one girl'.[5] Apart from the ubiquitous demeaning of adult women, there is a barely concealed unease with the female: *probably, only one*, and no explanation for what clearly seemed a self-evidently appropriate policy decision. Did it seem so clear to Elwes, Tooth and McKechnie, I wonder?

In 1959 a similarly revealing memo was sent to Rex Moorfoot on the *Panorama* team. It concerned the on-going production of cartoon puppets for use as a regular item on *Panorama* – anticipating *Spitting Image* (Central, 1984–96) by twenty-five years – a project which in the event was dropped. Three figures had been completed – De Gaulle, Eisenhower and Kruschev – and two more were in production – Adenauer and Macmillan. Derek Holroyd, responsible for their production, wrote 'thereafter the stock characters to be made would be Nehru, Nasser, Nkrumah and Mao Tse-tung, plus three symbolic characters – John Bull and Uncle Sam and a female figure to represent variously the U.N., Peace, etc.'[6] It is the anonymity and flexibility of the lone female which strikes me, here.

Without wishing to stretch my point unduly, there do seem to be clear traces, in these routine messages, of the disturbances which the advent of mass television certainly caused to mid-1950s preferred conventions of gender so recently, and precariously, re-established – in ideology if not in practice – following the disruptions of the Second World War. This is a disturbance similar to that noted by Pat Holland apropos early twentieth century developments in print journalism.[7] In 1903 the *Daily Mirror*, with an all-female production team, was launched as a paper for women. Though the female team was, in the event, a short-lived experiment, the *Mirror* was re-launched in 1904 as an illustrated paper, justified and sold on the basis that its pictures did not merely illustrate the news but were *in themselves* news. Holland suggests that these interventions concern the perceived nature of news itself, and that, as mass-circulation journalism developed, the conventional relations between the public and the private and between production (writing, reporting) and consumption (reading, looking) were disturbed. Here is a paradox as the private invades the public, requiring as a consequence a redefinition of both terms. This move towards 'soft' news, she argues, indicated a 'feminisation of news' in the print media which was (and still is) deplored by defenders of the myth of 'objective truth'. It is this myth which informed the hierarchies of print journalism at the beginning of the twentieth century and, it would seem, of nascent televisual journalism in the 1950s. The hierarchical scale is expressed through a variety of oppositions such as *hard:soft* and *objective:subjective*, which also map onto the *masculine:feminine* opposition determining language itself. The practical dynamics of this tension, if I may call it that, are explored in Linda Steiner's discussion of gender and the power struggles in the newsroom, derived from the autobiographical accounts of female journalists.[8] Women in this environment, she suggests, had to struggle for their definition as professionals, since their male colleagues defined them *first* as women and only *second* as journalists, typically inviting them to write *as women*. The struggle over women's access to the public sphere, not to mention the consequent re-definition of the latter in mass-circulation journalism was, therefore, not a new one, though its particular dynamic in television has yet to be traced. And in the BBC of the 1950s, just as in the Fleet Street of fifty years earlier, the notion of *balance* which was to constrain Mrs Knight, had no place, it seems, in the construction of the announcing team, nor in the selection of models for the cartoon puppets. Selectivity is at work here selectively, so to speak.

Observations

Left at that, it might be argued, these apparently simple remarks *are* as simple as they seem. They merely reflect what we (think we) already know about the 1950s, that it was a repressive period for women, containing tensions which erupted with the women's movement of the later 1960s. These remarks, which seem to me to signify excessively, in the manner of a Barthesian *punctum*, are particularly interesting because there is plenty of evidence of policy decisions which attempted to raise the profile of women on television. For example, *Panorama* advertised in the *Evening News* for women presenters;[9] annotated lists of *suitable* women as potential talk-show participants were circulated from time to time.[10] (I have yet to come across equivalent lists of *suitable* men.) An Audience Research report in December 1959 floated the question of *Weatherwomen*, noting carefully (and typically) the range and percentage of responses before concluding that, on balance, it seemed an unwelcome idea, though not one that elicited very strong feelings on either side.[11] And, in July 1964, the Drama Group urged that writers be encouraged to write for particular actresses, observing with regret that 'young writers are afraid of women'.[12] So there *was* concern and awareness within the BBC about the visibility of women. There were female producers and programme administrators, not all of them confined to the Women's Programmes Unit. Mary Adams had been 'brought in to deal with Talks' (Briggs 1985: 170) in 1938 and was responsible for establishing the Women's Programme Unit in the early post-war period. She later became an Assistant Controller of Television. Grace Wyndham Goldie, Assistant Head of Talks in the later 1950s, Head of Talks from the early 1960s, was a considerable force in the development of current affairs programming – stronghold of the masculine though this was. Unlike Adams, who had herself brought Goldie in to the BBC as a Talks producer in 1948, Grace Wyndham Goldie was not noted for her encouragement of female entrants to the field (Briggs 1985: 272). Perhaps *because* of her primary commitment to current affairs and to the development of political journalism on television as a significant part of the democratic process, she operated rather like the newsroom journalists in Linda Steiner's account. Certainly she privileged the talented group of young men to whom she offered opportunities in the early development of current affairs broadcasting – who came to be known as 'Grace's boys' – and many of whom went on to occupy illustrious positions in the broadcasting hierarchy of the future.

One way of understanding the concern with the visibility of women which was undeniably evident in the mid-1950s is as a pragmatic response to two aspects of the emergent institution. The economics of broadcast television depended on maximising audiences – this was true of both public service and commercial operations in Britain. Since television was developed as a domestic medium, the support of women thought to control domestic spaces and routines had to be secured. Television broadcasters, therefore, in the competitive and expansive years at the end of the 1950s, were acutely aware of their address to the female audience. Audience Research reports on this issue were commissioned more than once.[13] But at the same time, and also linked to the advent of commercial television and its consequences for the BBC's operation, there was considerable and widespread suspicion about the *effects* of television-watching on various sectors of the population (especially children), as well as in the cultural 'health' of the nation.[14] These suspicions were *overtly* linked to fears about the possible debasement of British culture through excessive US influence both in the content of imported drama series and in the models derived from US examples such as the quiz shows, game shows and sitcoms which quickly and easily won large audiences. The low cultural value ascribed to much broadcast material by the self-appointed arbiters of the day was expressed in such terms as *frivolous, light, distracting, mindless* – terms aligned with 'the feminine' rather than 'the masculine' in the parlance of the day. Though such epithets concerned content, the very habit of viewing was itself the occasion for disquiet. The passivity of the viewer in front of the television screen was regularly deplored. Since, in patriarchal discourse, passivity is considered to be an attribute of 'the feminine' we might speculate that fears about the effects of mass television viewing centred on the potential feminisation, or *emasculation* of viewers, quite apart from their pollution through exposure to material of dubious cultural worth. Such anxiety about the consequences of television *per se* might also account for the perceived importance of maintaining the equation between The News and 'the masculine', each term being called on to buttress the other, as it were, against the dangers of cultural degradation. Hand in hand with the excitement of participating in the development of the institution, it seems, was a fairly pervasive unease about its feminising effect on audiences and therefore, by extension, on the electorate.

This complex matrix was certainly recognised by the eternally self-conscious programme planners and producers working to explore and establish new forms. An almost crusading commitment to securing regular and large audiences for current affairs programmes was seen not only as an antidote to supposedly dubious and anodyne entertainment but also as a positive and crucial contribution to the democratic process itself. As a memo from the Head of Talks, Leonard Miall, in relation to a then-current House of Lords debate noted:

> [Nevertheless] it is vitally important for the informed electorate that the television service should retain important and responsible programmes dealing with current affairs which can be presented in a lively manner to attract a mass audience, for the mass circulation newspapers do not concern themselves much with politics, economics and international affairs.[15]

In soliciting audiences for items concerned to confront the uses and abuses of political power, programme makers thought themselves able to hand power to the citizens of democracy who constituted their audiences. Contemporary discussion about coverage of elections is of interest in this context, as is also the question of the Fortnight Rule, finally abandoned during the Suez crisis of 1956. The Fortnight Rule dated from 1944 when there was 'an informal understanding between the BBC and the Government' that 'precluded the broadcasting of talks, discussions or debates on any issue being discussed in Parliament or for two weeks before such a Parliamentary debate was to take place' (Sendall 1982: 233). It was formalised in a notice from the Postmaster General, Sir Charles Hill, on 27 July 1955 (Briggs 1985: 385) but nevertheless came under increasing attack from broadcasters. Its abandonment just over a year later, in December 1956, marked an important acknowledgement of audiences' and producers' rights to engage 'directly' with issues of the day – to bypass Westminster's formulations. That Westminster's role would indeed be fundamentally affected by the abandonment of the 'Rule' was not lost on the then Prime Minister, Winston Churchill:

> It would be shocking to have debates in this House forestalled time after time by expression of opinion by persons who had not the status or responsibility of Members of Parliament . . . I am quite sure that the bringing of exciting debates in these vast, new robot organisations of television and BBC broadcasting, to take place before a debate in this House, might have very deleterious effects upon our general interests, and that hon. Members should be considering the interests of the House of Commons, to whom we all owe a lot.[16]

This newly won freedom for broadcasters represented a considerable achievement for Grace Wyndham Goldie who, since the first years of the decade, had been attempting to persuade politicians of the central importance television could, and would, play as an extra-parliamentary forum for national debate. I would argue that the abandonment of the Fortnight Rule had the direct effect of enhancing the status of broadcasting as a whole because the range of newsworthy topics able to be handled was suddenly, almost dramatically, extended. The attention of those responsible for the conduct of news and current affairs was, during 1955–7, closely engaged with the import of securing privileges previously only available to elected politicians – that is to intervene directly in the democratic process through public comment and debate. In this context, the 1957 decision to consolidate an announcing team of '3 or 4 men and probably only one girl' takes on a new significance, suggesting that the female voice and image would be thought to detract from the masculine weight considered a necessary adjunct to television's democratic presence.

The suspicion of the visual image itself as a means of delivering the veracity required from broadcast news was still evident in the immediate post-war BBC in which sound broadcasting dominated. This dominance was partly a consequence of radio's war-time centrality to British life, and partly of its national reach: whereas a very few privileged households in the London area could receive television signals in 1950, everyone had access to a radio. However, it is perhaps surprising to recall that until July 1954 the news was broadcast on television *in sound only*, the ten minutes' worth of news being read by an off-screen voice in an 'impersonal, sober and quiet manner': undoubtedly, in the climate I have outlined, sobriety and impersonality would be thought of as masculine virtues.[17] Visual presentation, cautiously introduced in September 1955 in the run-up to the start of commercial broadcasting, was thought likely to compromise the authority of the News, as Vahimagi notes: 'visible news readers were originally forbidden (in case their change of expression threatened their impartiality).[18] Just as the visual image was somehow in itself suspect, since it might detract from the gravitas of the newsroom's spoken truths, so too, it seems, was the female voice. It was Independent Television News, no doubt as part of the competitive innovations by which ITV hoped to lure audiences away from the BBC, which, in 1955, first introduced a woman reading the news. However even this innovation was compromised since Barbara Mandell was only invited to read the lunchtime bulletin and did this against a painted set depicting a domestic kitchen[19]. The BBC did not follow suit until 1960 when, for a short time, Nan Winton read the 9 o'clock news on Sunday evening. She recalls that:

> I didn't realise what a revolutionary thing it was . . . I didn't have any trouble from the press or from the public, it was the editorial staff who were a bit dodgy, men in their middle years who'd come from Fleet St. . . . they certainly were a bit ambivalent about me. They were very, very serious about the News. It was a very serious business.[20]

Stuart Hood, at that time a senior member of the BBC's directorate, also remembered the resistance encountered by this short-lived innovation:

> I thought it would be rather nice to have a woman news reader on television. Now this was greeted with alarm and dismay and resistance by my editors. The thought that a woman could be the conveyor of truth and authority on the television screen was something they just couldn't imagine, couldn't accept.[21]

The failure of imagination to which Hood refers is detectable not only in the editorial resistance of the supposedly permissive 1960s, but much earlier, I think, in the very structure of the developing institution. Though, as Mary Malcolm and Sylvia Peters recalled, there *were* many senior women in the earliest days of the BBC and 'the only thing they wouldn't let us do was read the news',[22] nevertheless questions of veracity, control and the possession of 'appropriate' qualities were always central to those sections whose output was most closely aligned with the news operation. Leonard Miall, Head of Talks from 1954 to 1962, suggested that the Outside Broadcast Department, for example, required special (implicitly masculine) qualities from its personnel:

> A lot of them had been fighter pilots in the RAF before joining the

television service and in some ways you needed the same kind of qualities for a good director of a live television programme.[23]

It was in the permeable boundary between news and current affairs that women found opportunities – or made them, as Mary Adams, Doreen Stephens and Grace Wyndham Goldie did – and for this reason current affairs, in all its generic fluidity, offers a more promising terrain for my questions than that bastion of masculinity, the newsroom itself. The development of serious – which means *hard* – current-affairs programming such as *Panorama* and *Tonight* retained enough of the magazine format with its variety of tone, changes of pace and mixture of items, to secure an heterogeneous audience. Indeed, a memo from Grace Wyndham Goldie to the *Panorama* team in November 1956 at the height of the Suez crisis cautioned against a third successive week devoted exclusively to the crisis since this might alienate the audience, and affirmed the intention to maintain *Panorama*'s mixed diet of items.[24] The generic fluidity implicit here was clearly understood as a positive virtue, one which was further developed in *Tonight* and brought to a head – taken too far some thought – in the celebrated *That Was The Week That Was* (BBC, 1962–3). But it is based in an acknowledgement that television's address – in the days before Channels 2, 4 and 5 – must secure the broadest possible audience for programmes intended to fulfil the informative aspects of the broadcasters' mandate, and that this might be done by utilising a range of forms within the same programme. In addition much current affairs programming aimed, like Grierson's intervention into documentary film in the 1930s, to *present* 'the people' to each other. Documentary series such as *Special Enquiry* (1955) and *Marriage Today* (1964), as well as topical magazine programmes like *Panorama* (1953–) and *Tonight* (1957–65) consciously and overtly concerned themselves with *the state* of Britain *today*. The institution of television itself often figured problematically in such discussions. The unease about television's possible effects on British culture which I detected in my *punctum* marks a considerable uncertainty – perhaps not acknowledged as such – about the 'nature' of the developing institution. I think there's a struggle going on over the gendering of this 'nature', particularly in the domain of news and current affairs where there was an attempt to compensate for the perceived worthlessness of much other programming, and where 'the feminine' posed a threat to the masculinity considered central to this endeavour.

Questions

There are some alluring questions here, all posing problems to the contemporary (1990s) researcher. There is the sheer scale of the output, even in a time when this was limited to fifty hours per week on each of only two channels. There is the uneven access to the archives of public service and commercial broadcasting operations. There is the tantalising absence of the majority of broadcast output before 1960. To ascertain *what* was broadcast is a fairly simple task. Gaining access to production notes, scripts, critical comment and all the paperwork associated with a broadcast programme is trickier, but still it is often possible, though the centrally organised, civil-service based BBC is easier to get at than the variety of commercial companies. This has the effect of privileging public service broadcasting in studies of the period. So though it is a simple matter to know the basic details of any broadcast programme by checking the published schedules, the value structure of the period has determined which production notes, later which programmes, were to be preserved. It is of course *only* these to which we can now have access. Early television, like early cinema, was regarded in its day as ephemeral. And this attitude was compounded by the fact that television was celebrated and sold precisely on the virtue of its immediacy. Its simultaneity with the events depicted was thought to be a guarantor of its truthfulness. The prestige of the male-dominated Outside Broadcasting Department is an indicator of this, as are the several discussions in which the ethics of combining filmed inserts with live material were subject to much earnest soul-searching.

It is a truism that as historical researchers we can only gain access to items which *at the time* were considered sufficiently valuable to be preserved, and that we are thus inevitably subject to the hierarchy of cultural worth which informed the production teams of the day. This still allows considerable scope, of course, but nevertheless renders my questions particularly awkward since what I want to do, precisely, is to uncover these value structures – particularly those implying a hierarchy of gender – and to understand how they might have ordered production and reception practices. In considering the fluidity of emergent generic divisions, for example, I noted the ubiquity of the magazine format and its very interesting development in different sub-sections of the BBC's Talks Department. The longest running magazine programmes in the BBC during the decade 1955–65 were *Panorama*, *Tonight*, and *The Wednesday Magazine* (tx 1958–63). The earliest complete programmes I have been able to view are a *Panorama* from 29 June 1964 and a *Tonight* from 29 August 1960. Of the earlier transmissions all that remains are some filmed inserts used in programmes. These are often fascinating in themselves – Woodrow Wyatt's 26 January 1959 interview with the Egyptian leader Nasser being one example – but it is impossible to do more than guess about how the item might have been nuanced in its studio introduction and closure. The case of *The Wednesday Magazine*, an afternoon programme produced by the Women's Programme Unit, is even worse. It is not even listed in Vahimagi's generally useful guide, *British Television* (1994). Only one date (18 November 1959) is listed in the 1994 NFTVA Catalogue, and this turns out to refer to a seven-minute insert of Spike Milligan: preserved, presumably, because of Milligan's growing reputation rather than because of the programme itself. The BBC's own viewing service has two inserts from a 1962 transmission: a very short and stiff interview of Margaret Rutherford by David Jacobs and a picture-only clip of a child and his drawings. So my tentative suggestions about generic fluidity, about variety of pace, tone and address and about attempts to secure audience loyalty are inevitably based more in my perusal of paperwork than of programmes.

While it is true that I can get a long way with such material, it does not substitute for access to the programmes themselves – as anyone who has managed to see the fascinating TV archive programmes at London's Museum of the Moving Image will surely agree. One thing that struck me, for example, in viewing a programme comprising *Off the Record* (tx 1955), *Six Five Special* (tx 31 August 1957) and *Juke Box Jury* (tx 29 October 1960) was the appalling condition of people's teeth. Dentists must certainly have had a field day in the early 1960s because the same individuals appearing in later programmes had clearly had major work done. I'd never find an observation like that in contemporary production or even critical material simply because it wouldn't have been noticed – it looked 'normal'. I'm sure the same is true of body language, lighting and dress codes, sequencing of items and address to both subjects (interviewees, 'experts', vox pops) and audiences. That this is the case is borne out by the few complete programmes I have so far managed to see.

Evidence

By 1964 *Panorama* was at the height of its reputation as one of the most respected programmes on British television. It had progressed from a fortnightly arts magazine in 1953 to a weekly and then nightly current affairs magazine, maintaining the variety of its succession of items despite the shift from arts to politics. As Michael Peacock recalled in his contribution to the BBC memorial to Richard Dimbleby:

> It was after the 1955 Election Results programme that the idea of a weekly *Panorama* was born. . . . With Richard Dimbleby and with Malcolm Muggeridge, Woodrow Wyatt, Max Robertson and, six months later, with Chris Chataway, we set out to explore the virgin lands of weekly television journalism. . . .
>
> Thinking back now, my memories of *Panorama* during that troubled time are blurred and confused. Nasser, the Suez Canal, Budapest, Refugees, Cyprus, Eden, Eisenhower and Stevenson, Kruschev, the Gaza strip, Port Said, the United Nations . . . our cameras rolled, our voices strained, our typewriters tore into paper, as each Monday Richard Dimbleby reported the continuing crisis in *Panorama*.
>
> (Miall 1966: 96–7).

Though it is true that Dimbleby was identified with the new form of the programme, it was Grace Wyndham Goldie whose efforts were equally instrumental in securing a regular, high-profile spot for television journalism – in advance of the demise of the Fortnight Rule. Typically, though, her efforts did not entail any intervention into the masculinist bias of the Talks Department.

Richard Dimbleby is the secure and confident master of ceremonies in this programme which comprised three distinct items, each subject to multiple forms of presentation. The familiar format offers a proposition, exemplified through a location piece or by means of a studio discussion offering varied points of view. The emphasis is on questions. The first item, a studio discussion about police relations with the public, touched on corruption and its investigation, the second was a filmed report about teenage 'morals' in 'two countries very different from our own' which turn out to be Italy and Sweden. British experience was suggested to fall comfortably in between that of the Italians and the Swedes – a clever demonstration of *balance* in practice, perhaps? The final item, trailing the next day's programme, contained a lengthy compilation of five-year old news footage edited to offer a snapshot account of recent and dramatic events (this is the Congo), followed by a chaired studio discussion about the UN's handling of the conflict. Two Englishmen, a journalist and an ex-member of the Colonial office make clear their fundamental disagreement. Here the programme closed, on a sombre and provocative note, effectively setting an agenda through which audiences might consider the matter until the next day's promised development of the arguments.

This programme too had three substantial and quite different kinds of report. The first concerned the innovative use, in Liverpool, of automated surveillance cameras for crime control. Richard Dimbleby, on location in the Liverpool control room, interviewed the Chief Constable whose idea this was, discovering the technology involved, raising the spectre of the technique's 'Orwellian significance' and asking about the films' status as evidence in court. The Police Chief confessed that he hadn't considered the latter and gave an undertaking that the technique would never be used for anything other than crime and traffic control. He suggested further, and rather lamely, that the film could not be used in court since this would entail revealing the whereabouts of the cameras. From Liverpool, via a close-up of Dimbleby making the link, the programme shifts to another location report, this time from a by-election in Leyton, East London. Patrick Gordon-Walker, Labour Foreign Secretary who had recently lost his Smethwick seat in the general election, was contesting the seat. Both campaigns had been marked by racial conflict, and these scenes from Leyton include a racist fight which broke up the election meeting, the fascist leader Colin Jordan and his supporters with their 'Keep Britain White' cries and banners being much in evidence. The *Panorama* reporter interviewed each of the three main candidates before giving a face-to-camera summary of the campaign – essentially interpreting what had just been 'seen', before returning us to the London studio. The final item was another filmed piece about reporter

Michael Barrat's visit to the Gambarene leper colony in West Africa, run on unconventional lines by the celebrated Albert Schweitzer. Barrat spoke to benefactor Marion Preminger, present for her annual visit to the colony, about Schweitzer's philosophy of reverence for life, extended, as she told him, to the management of the jungle and the farm as well as to medical and other human facilities. She described Schweitzer's idiosyncratic refusal to use available technology such as a local generator, or jeep transport, and his autocratic command of the colony: 'the routine of Gambarene is ordered by the bell'. 'When a sage reaches ninety', she said, 'you don't question him'. In a rather dizzying cut we are returned to the Liverpool control room where Dimbleby asks the duty officer what's been going on, then the credits – separate for each item – roll.

Women on screen, as reporters, studio guests or subject matter, were largely absent from the 1964 programme, except for the teenage victims of poverty, depravity or simple peer group pressure, who dominated the film inserts from Italy and Sweden. In the 1965 programme there is a single plainclothes policewoman who, unlike her male colleagues, says almost nothing; there are a (very) few women at the election meeting – none of whom speak – and there is Marion Preminger in the Schweitzer item. The overwhelming impression given in both programmes is of a confident, diverse and overwhelmingly masculine world. This can partly be accounted for by reference to the question of programme hierarchy in which *news* is dominant, and the declared intention of *Panorama*, along with other BBC current affairs programming, to compensate for what they perceived as the paucity of news in the popular press. But here of course is a self-serving circle – the agenda of public affairs is a male one to which *Panorama* must subscribe in order to demonstrate its seriousness. The record of production meetings regularly listed possible new programme ideas, and earlier in the 1950s these often included 'light' items. Invariably such items concerned women and/or the arts and were, it seems, always expendable if 'serious' news required the space – much in the way that, in the latter part of the decade, the Women's Programme Unit's afternoon output had increasingly to relinquish their place in the schedules for Outside Broadcast special events or for sports coverage.

Summary

The summaries of these two editions of *Panorama* convey, I hope, some of what strikes me in my attempt to explore the formation of some televisual conventions and their relation to the power and value structures in which they developed. There *is* a problem about women. I find in the later 1950s many careful interventions intended to raise the profile of women on television. But more often than not these foundered on the rocks of convention and prejudice, being perceived, in the event, as *unsuitable*, *distracting*, with insufficient *gravitas*. It was not until the advent of *Late Night Line Up* on BBC2 in 1964 that a woman presenter, Joan Bakewell, achieved a routine presence in an arts and current affairs magazine as one of the regular reporting and presenting team.[25]

If there *is* a common thread to be discerned in current affairs programming under the aegis of the BBC's Talks Department I think it must be an underlying anxiety about women – their competencies, their ambitions, the extent to which they could be relied upon to continue to operate in the interests of the dominant group, men. Anxieties about 'the feminine' are not the same, but they are also evident. But here I submit that it is not *the feminine* which is the problem but, perhaps, *the masculine*. Both terms reference attributes associated with the preferred or expected behaviour of men and women, and the notorious elision of the semantic difference between 'the masculine' and men, and 'the feminine' and women, has important consequences for the gendered subject's form of access to the social sphere, particularly for their access to power.

Psychoanalytic theory offers insights into this semantic difference, into both its mechanics and its consequences for the individual subject. Drawing on this theory for a moment we might remember that language and the symbolic order are predicated on a masculine subject and that to be a woman means, first of all, *not* to be a man. It then follows that changes, instabilities in the social consensus about women and hence 'the feminine' (since women are required to exhibit feminine attributes) must threaten the stability of 'the masculine', hence of men. For me this explanation begins to make some sense of another pervasive feature of British culture in the later 1950s and early 1960s, and that is its *misogyny*. Male anxiety, displaced onto the figure of the woman, causes the male subject to fear, mistrust and even loathe that figure because by her very existence she poses an insoluble problem to him. I realise this proposition is very close to the so-called Oedipal scenario, to questions of the castration complex, penis envy and so forth, but I don't think it's the same – mainly because though I have couched my proposition in theoretical terms I hope I have demonstrated that it is a real, feet-on-the-ground Britain in the 1950s and 1960s, empirical matter. And I acknowledge, too, that simply to pull 'misogyny' out of the hat, as it were, does not answer all my different kinds of questions about women on the screen, in the audience and in production. But it does help in accounting for some of the contradictory impulses which I observe in operation, and it does also illuminate the paradoxical co-existence of innovative thought and repressive action which characterises the formative years of the broadcasting institution in the UK. Partly it is a question of different generations, but I think it also fair to suggest that, as television's place in society became more secure and more central, its inherent dangers – frivolity, passivity, feminisation – had to be overcome. It had to be masculinised in order to be tolerable as the hub of national life it was clearly becoming. But above all it is the fluidity of forms and conventions in this period that is so compelling to the historian. There is a real and practical debate occurring whose scale allows dissent to take form as well as consensus. In the shifting balance of these terms, a new language is crystallising. The fragments available to the historian – these memos, surviving televisual images, ordering of schedules and resourcing of production – are 'speckled', to return to Barthes' phrase, with unintentional details whose poignancy can alert us to their provisional place in the developing language of televisual communication.

Notes

1 See Spigel (1992) for a detailed account of this process in the USA. The British experience, though not the same, nevertheless bears many similarities especially in terms of the direct appeal to the female audience.

2 Barthes (1984: 26–7): 'it is this element which rises from the scene, shoots out of it like an arrow, and pierces me. . . . the photographs I am speaking of are in effect punctuated, sometimes even speckled with these sensitive points. . . . a photograph's *punctum* is that accident which pricks me (but also bruises me, is poignant to me)'. It is this combination of the poignant and the accidental, i.e. the *unintentional* in a 'scene', which I borrow from Barthes in using his term. The original scene, I contend, can just as easily be a written memo as a visual snapshot.

3 These difficulties are eloquently explored in Carr (1961).

4 BBC written archives at Caversham, file no. T32/1191/1, 14 January 1955.

5 Ibid., T32/1867/1, 11 November 1957.

6 Ibid., T32/1191/6, 30 April 1959.

7 Pat Holland 'The politics of the smile: "soft news" and the sexualisation of the popular press', Chapter 1 in this volume.

8 Linda Steiner 'Newsroom accounts of power at work', Chapter 8 in this volume.

9 *Evening News*, 27 October 1958.

10 BBC written archives at Caversham, file no. T32/395, undated but probably 1965.

11 Ibid., file no. VR/59/703, 21 December 1959.

12 Ibid., file no. T16/62/3, 17 July 1964: 8.

13 Ibid., file nos. VR/55/516, 2 November 1955 and VR/59/364, 1959. It is interesting to note that a 1949 report, VR/50/1, did not once mention the gender differentiation of its respondents, though it did attend to differentiations by social class and by age.

14 Ibid., T32/395 *Television's Influence on Children*. This 1960 report of the BBC's Teenage Advisory Committee was recirculated in the newly formed Family Programmes Unit in 1965 by Doreen Stephens, who noted in an accompanying memo that 'much of it seems to be as relevant today as when it was prepared'.

15 Ibid., file no. T32/1191/7, June 1960.

16 House of Commons, 23 February 1955, col. 1277, quoted in Sendall (1982: 233).

17 For an account of the early days of news broadcasting in Britain, see Allan (1997a).

18 Vahimagi (1994: 43). BBC Television News was first broadcast at 7.30 p.m. on 5 July 1954, presented by Richard Baker as an 'illustrated summary of the news'. Vahimagi notes that 'even when TV news arrived in its own right, it was a cautious compilation of stills, interviews, maps, and newsreels'.

19 *A Night in with the Girls* produced by Mary Dickinson, BBC2, 15 March 1997.

20 Ibid.

21 Ibid.

22 Ibid.

23 Ibid.

24 BBC written archives at Caversham, file no. T32/1191/3, 13 November 1956.

25 *Late Night Line Up* was broadcast six or seven nights each week from 1964 to 1972, the original presenting team comprising Denis Tuohy, Michael Dean, Nicholas Tresilian and Joan Bakewell.

6

POLITICIZING THE PERSONAL

Women's voices in British television documentaries

Myra Macdonald

> Not every personal event is political, but all personal events certainly
> have the potential to be political.
>
> (Trinh T. Minh-ha)

Introduction

Informational genres on British television are coming under increasing pressure
in the 1990s to locate the popular pulse. News bulletins have responded in part
with an added injection of 'human interest'; documentaries, longer habituated
to giving issues a human face, are defining this as an emphasis on the intimate
or the quirky to catch the scheduler's eye. For feminist critics, greater 'intimiza-
tion' (van Zoonen 1991: 217) and personalization in informational television
have produced a curious ambivalence. Suggestive, on the one hand, of a correc-
tive move beyond a masculinized agenda and discourse, these trends can also be
seen as reinforcing old gendered hierarchies, with rational debate of public
issues still valued (as 'masculine') over affective explorations of personal or social
relationships (deemed 'feminine', and consequently trivialized). Van Zoonen
(1991) traces the roots of this quandary to the masculinization of the public
sphere in the eighteenth century and the corresponding feminization of the
private sphere. The slogan 'the personal is political', successful in epitomizing
the feminist project to dismantle this ideological opposition, nevertheless over-
simplifies the issues. As the epigraph from Trinh T. Minh-ha indicates, the
personal is not universally political. Neither can every inclusion of the personal
in the public space of television be thought to mark a feminist advance.

By focusing on the incorporation of women's stories and women's voices
within mainstream television documentary,[1] this chapter aims to examine the
conditions in which the personal can become political, moving the audience
beyond a fleeting fix of voyeurism to fresh perceptions about the workings of

the contemporary or historical world. While feminist critiques of the Habermasian public sphere confirm that successful politicizing of the personal is not automatically achieved by airing the private in a public space, reworkings of the concept of 'experience' within feminist and cultural theory provide more positive help in identifying how conceptual boundaries between the personal and the political might be eroded. The applicability of these theories to television documentary will be considered in relation to three modes of presenting women's accounts of their own lives, which I classify as the confessional, the case study, and testimony. While each category allows public access to women's personal experiences, I will argue that it is only the last of these that succeeds in challenging journalistic wariness about subjectivity as a form of knowledge. Any undermining of binary oppositions between objectivity and subjectivity, or between evidence and experience, also breaks the habitual temptation to overlay these with sharply gendered values.

Limits of access

Feminist critiques of the Habermasian public sphere and feminist linguistics both pinpoint the limitations of widening access to an informational genre without changing its operational rules. Feminist linguists argue that merely allowing women speaking rights in situations where the modes of speech and interaction have been established according to male priorities marks little progress for women. Equally, feminist critics of Habermas' idealization of the public sphere as an arena, free from commercial pressures, where citizens can openly and freely engage in rational-critical debate, describe this as 'a masculinist ideological notion', dependent for its very formation on the exclusion of women (Fraser 1992: 116). The feminist historian Mary Ryan (1992) has demonstrated that women, far from being absent from public life during the relevant period of the eighteenth and nineteenth centuries, played a major role in political activity and in developing women's rights. If this had been acknowledged, the rules of participation would have had to be rewritten. Rethinking the concept of the public sphere in 1992, Habermas accepts part of this feminist criticism: 'unlike the exclusion of underprivileged men, the exclusion of women had structuring significance' (1992: 428). Habermas differs from his feminist critics, however, in arguing that the challenge posed by feminism has been met by the public sphere's capacity for self-transformation from within (1992: 429–30).

Whether documentary should strictly be included within the Habermasian conceptualization of the public sphere is debatable. Purists who adhere to the Habermasian chronology would dispute its entitlement to be defined in these terms. Documentary belongs, after all, to the period that Habermas (1974, 1989) described as 're-feudalizing' the methods of public communication when 'critical publicity is supplanted by manipulative publicity' (1989: 178). Even when he moderated his earlier dismissal of the possibility of open rational-critical debate in the twentieth-century mass media, his model remained one where 'groups of concerned citizens' could come together to compete with commercially-driven media power to effect changes in social values (1992: 453–5). Documentary rarely allows citizens to exchange views directly with each other, preferring instead a form of serial monoglossia, linked through an intermediary. Yet, as several critics imply (Scannell 1986; Corner 1995), the access to 'ordinary' voices in documentary and its evolving challenge to the *status quo* support its alignment with a Habermasian public sphere, conceived as a normative ideal.

The Habermasian privileging of rational-critical discourse has in any case dominated thought about desired forms of informational television, and has helped to blind critics and producers alike to the partiality of the concept of citizenship that underpins it. If, as Ursula Vogel suggests, women or other marginalized groups are to emerge from their positioning as 'indirect citizens' (1991: 58), 'citizenship, as politics in general, should no longer be located in particular sites, or in relation to spaces occupied by particular institutions' (1991: 79). A dismantling of both the public/private divide and current practices of gendering the political and the personal is necessary to achieve this aim. Methods of including women's stories in the public space of the documentary that leave these boundaries untouched perpetuate the problem.

Rethinking experience

Critical and production discourses on documentary have historically been wary of subjectivity and experience, concepts located on the wrong side of a binary divide that privileges observation, verifiable evidence, and dispassionate reportage. As Bill Nichols observes, 'the prevalence of a criterion of objectivity in documentary has left the exploration of subjectivity underdeveloped' (1991: 120). While welcoming subjectivity's ability 'to convey something of the specificity and uniqueness of a historical moment' (1991: 283, note 25), Nichols adds a cautionary reminder that the concept of experience was vehemently attacked in 1970s' film theory by semiology, psychoanalysis, feminism and poststructuralism (1991: 294, note 25). More recently, feminist theory has been actively reclaiming experience from the poststructuralist wilderness, without reinserting it into an Enlightenment paradigm as an ontological state of being or as a guarantor of authenticity. The terms of this rethinking provide the basis for my analysis of documentary's capacity to politicize the personal.

Despite differences in their formulations, feminist theorists unite in rejecting the Enlightenment model of experience as a fixed point of knowledge, conceptualizing it instead as provisional, situated and constantly subject to contestation. As early as 1984, Teresa de Laurctis depicts subjectivity and experience as permanently in formation:

> For each person . . . subjectivity is an ongoing construction, not a fixed point of departure or arrival from which one then interacts with

the world. On the contrary, it is the effect of that interaction – which I call experience; and thus it is produced not by external ideas, values, or material causes, but by one's personal, subjective, engagement in the practices, discourses, and institutions that lend significance (value, meaning, and effect) to the events of the world.

(De Lauretis 1984: 159)

In the 1990s, this view of experience as a process is echoed in the writings of Elspeth Probyn and Joan Scott. Scott describes experience as fluctuating perpetually between offering an interpretation '*and*' being itself 'in need of interpretation' (1992: 37). Elspeth Probyn argues that even in a poststructuralist age we need to recognize that experience has an ontological feel to it, but for feeling to become knowledge we need to shift gear: 'the ontological must be met with an epistemological analysis . . . I want to stretch my experience beyond the merely personal. . . . In other words, I want to put forward a mode of theorizing that encourages lines of analysis that move from her experience to mine, and mine to hers' (Probyn 1993: 4). Advocating 'a speaking position that entails a defamiliarization of the taken-for-granted', Probyn asserts that this depends on undermining 'any assurance of ontological importance' (1993: 80). Experience sharpens into 'a critical tool to analyse and cut into the specificity of the social formation' (1993: 29) precisely when it recognizes its own ontological limits. Probyn's political objectives are clear: 'to figure ways in which we can use our selves critically in order to trouble the material conditions that literally give rise to "us" ' (1993: 168).

Feminist theory argues that political awareness emerges more productively out of intellectual and emotional discomfort and unease than out of the presumption of an already assured position of certainty. The stimulus of the jarring moment of disturbance recalls Raymond Williams' earlier formulation, acknowledged (if very differently) by both Probyn and Scott:

> I have found that areas which I would call structures of feeling as often as not initially form as a certain kind of disturbance or unease, a partic-ular type of tension. . . . To put it another way, the peculiar location of a structure of feeling is the endless comparison that must occur in the process of consciousness between the articulated and the lived.
>
> (Williams 1981: 167–8)

Williams, typically agonizing over the precision and appropriateness of his terminology, admits that 'blockbuster words like experience' can produce prob-lems in 'mak[ing] a god out of an unexamined subjectivity' (1981: 168), but he argues strongly none the less that we need to avert the possibility, posed by post-structuralist thinking, that the epistemological will 'wholly absorb the ontological' (1981: 167).

None of these theorists considers what happens when experience is mediated through television, but their observations have several implications for that process. For the movement between ontological and epistemological to be textually visible and evident to audiences, a sense of disjuncture or unease between these levels needs to become manifest. Equally, sufficient space needs to be provided for the process of 'speaking the self' (Probyn 1993) to enable this moment to arise. Packaging experience as either a commodity or as a colouring-in of what is already known merely prompts a reversion to earlier Enlightenment formulations. While my discussion focuses on textual manifestations rather than audience responses, feminist theories of experience also prompt work beyond the text. The notion of experience as situated, provisional and open to contestation has already strongly influenced models and methods of media audience research.

In his theorizing of documentary, Bill Nichols' distinction between 'spectacle' and 'vivification' highlights the difference between packaging experience ontologically and deploying it as the spark that ignites epistemological enquiry. Commenting on the gap in terms of impact and scale that opens up between articulated representation and the visceral quality of history, even within film documentary, he suggests that this limitation can, paradoxically, produce an intense 'vivification' effect by 'rendering *felt* what representations only allude to' (Nichols 1991: 234). The failure of representation to contain the magnitude of history projects us into the discovery of knowledge as if for the first time. Parallels exist between this movement and the feminist vision of being propelled into the epistemological by the failure of the ontological to do justice to experience. In a striking rejection of postmodern privileging of sensation, Nichols distinguishes 'vivification' sharply from 'spectacle' which he describes as 'an aborted or foreclosed form of identification where emotional engagement does not even extend as far as concern but instead remains arrested at the level of sensation' (ibid.). In television, where film's 'miniaturizing' process (1991: 230) is inevitably intensified, my category of the confessional most closely mirrors Nichols' 'spectacle', while testimony most closely approaches 'vivification'. My third category, the case study, works to produce identification, but not the visible movement necessary to bring alive the shift of gear between ontological and epistemological.

The confessional

The 'confessional' mode of presenting women's stories refers to the expression of experience (in verbal, paralinguistic or bodily codes) where that experience is configured individualistically and ontologically, and where the viewer is positioned on the outside, looking in. To borrow terms used in a slightly different context by the documentarist and critic Trinh T. Minh-ha, the women doing the confessing are reduced to appearing as 'Someone's private zoo' (1989: 82). The viewer, refused a point of contact with the specimen in the confession box, is forced into a position of voyeurism where the pleasure comes from a position of detachment from the experiences offered to us as spectacle. Whereas individual confessions on a talk show may be contextualized into political significance by the host, the confessional documentary presents a series of instances of an ontological phenomenon (recent examples from British television include what it feels like to be in a marital breakdown; to have recurrent problems with nannies; to be jilted, or betrayed) without a metadiscursive commentary. The confessions are most often presented straight to camera with minimal obtrusion from an invisible interviewer.

As authenticity in the world of public affairs appears increasingly chimera-like, the expression of personal emotion on television provides a substitute fix for those who still want to believe that the screen offers a window on the world. Making its first televisual appearance in US talk shows, the public confessional has a longer heritage in popular print, from the nineteenth-century fabricated 'last-dying confessions' of convicted criminals to the first-person narration of personal dilemmas in women's weekly magazines. Michel Foucault sees the confession as a pervasive mode of truth-seeking in Western societies: 'Western man [sic] has become a confessing animal' (1979: 59). Confessionals now extend far beyond the penitence rituals of the Roman Catholic church to include secular interviews, autobiographies and consultations, but, in Foucault's view, they share with the religious practice in granting more power to the hearer than to the speaker. The listener or reader becomes an 'authority who requires the confession, prescribes and appreciates it, and intervenes in order to judge, punish, forgive, console, and reconcile' (Foucault 1979: 62).

In documentary, television's mediation of the confessional prevents the viewer from intervening directly or even from identifying with the speaker. The detached video-box style and avoidance of close-ups present emotion as spectacle. Far from removing the imbalance of power that Foucault notes, this intensifies the confessional's construction of the participants as ethnographically-observed 'others'. In addition, the focus on individuated reactions dissipates any possibility of developing the fleeting glimpses of political connectedness that these documentaries occasionally offer. A *Cutting Edge* documentary, 'Jilted', (Channel 4, 17 March 1997) presents five confessions from people who failed to go through with their wedding plans. Underlying the stories of several of the women is the unrealistic but seductive fantasy they or their mothers entertain about the romance of the wedding day, but this eludes attention as the documentary concentrates on following each jilted lover through a purely emotional journey from disbelief to devastation.

Equally, 'Quality time', a documentary from the *Modern Times* series (BBC2, 13 March 1996), deals with the problems experienced by three executive mothers trying to find suitable nannies, by concentrating on the women's temperamental foibles, not on the tensions of trying to juggle careers and motherhood. These women invite our moral opprobrium by describing their children as 'the most beautiful presents I've ever had in my life' or as 'still quite a new experience' (after five years), so that the prospect of a nanny's illness conjures up a nightmare vision of being 'left with them for a day or so not knowing what to do with them'. Even when one of the women, Dominique, a clothing manufacturer, tearfully confesses that she feels 'like a failure' because her involvement in a business party at her home has prevented her from spending enough time with her daughter, the grandeur of her *prima donna* lifestyle and the misery of her daughter, extensively documented in the previous scenes, distance us from her dilemma: 'And is it really worthwhile, you know, being at work, having a lovely house? Wouldn't you be better to live in a shed and have your kids all the time? I don't know. I haven't got an answer for it'. The documentary has an answer, but it is one that substitutes moral evaluation for analysis of the connectedness of experience and social structures. The women's experiences remain arrested as spectacle, encouraging voyeuristic consumption but denying investigation of a collective dilemma.

The case study

While the confessional is still a relatively rare phenomenon within British television documentaries, the case study is a staple ingredient of the expository form of the genre. By 'case study' I refer to the use of the experiences of 'ordinary' people to support and exemplify the documentary's central thesis. Although documentary increasingly avoids a strong central commentary, aiming instead for at least the illusion of letting the evidence speak for itself, few television documentaries favour dissonance between competing voices. A dominant discourse is established, with interviewees' stories subordinated to this. Women in this situation are allowed in one sense to speak in their own voices, but these voices are continually interrupted by the authoritative discourse of others (whether commentator, narrator, or experts). The epistemological work of the documentary is not carried forward by the women themselves. At worst, this leads to the women's experiences being translated into an alien rhetoric; at best it prevents experience from breaking out of its illustrative confines to create the unease and tension that might propel fresh insights into relations between the personal and the political.

Suspicions run high in the critical literature about the dangers of allowing interviewees free rein to set their own agenda and determine their own contributions. John Corner, for example, comments that 'it would clearly be a mistake to suppose that the public project of documentary is best served by privileging accessees over any sense of the independent integrity of the topic or of responsibilities to the viewer', although he also recognizes the political merit of 'access documentaries' which grant contributors more extensive speaking rights and 'in which the expression of ordinary and often marginalised experience becomes the primary directorial goal' (Corner 1995: 91). This distinction between documentaries that enable access to the marginalized, and documentaries that have an expository purpose, maintains a dichotomy between subjectivity and objectivity, between empathy and knowledge, that diminishes the political potential of the personal. The possibility of access *as* exposition needs to be explored, and will be pursued in my category of 'testimony' below.[2] The strategy favoured by both critics and documentary-makers has been to set the interviewees' voices within a clear discursive framework. While John Corner recommends that this be of sufficiently light a touch to avoid 'simply "appropriating" the speech of the interviewee for a project grounded elsewhere', he also accepts that 'subordination of interviewees to programme logics is a continuing requirement in documentaries' (Corner 1995: 90, 91). This may require documentary-makers to engage in not merely a tricky but an impossible balancing act.

The problems of appropriation are particularly acute in medical documentaries. Their frequently didactic purpose and their subservience to a symptom-based discourse of medicine mean that human case studies tend to be co-opted for expository purposes, reinforcing a familiar hierarchy of professional knowledge over lay experience. A Channel 4 documentary on schizophrenia, 'Edge of madness' (23 July 1996), interweaves the experiences of four sufferers, two men and two women. The women outstrip the men in articulateness and self-awareness, and in their co-operativeness in performing for the camera. Yet both women become subordinated to the informational point they exemplify. After we are first introduced to Miranda Ryder as a lively and perceptive woman who paints in her spare time, and observe, *vérité* style, her humorous exchanges with her own psychiatrist about her condition, she next appears in a cut-away shot, sitting reading in a garden, while a male psychiatric expert delivers an authoritative account of schizophrenic delusions direct to camera. From being a personality in her own right, Miranda is reduced to being an exemplar or instance. As the documentary proceeds, the voice of this male psychiatrist, objectively discussing 'the patient' and impersonally explaining symptoms of schizophrenia, is established as the dominant point of reference. He is consistently filmed facing the camera, usually in medium close-up, whereas the women sufferers, despite their evident vitality and determination, are filmed periodically in poses or from angles that remind the audience of their lack of control over their own lives. When Miranda speaks of her delusions following the expert's intervention, the camera looks down on her from a high angle, literally diminishing her stature. Later excerpts from Miranda's story suggest a complicated narrative of familial conflict and struggle for personal identity, but her positioning as a victim, and the fragmentary delivery of her own analysis, ensure this remains of secondary importance.

In some documentaries, the echoes established between the narrated experiences of the case-study participants are so strong as to forge their own lines of connection. Cumulatively acquiring the status of a quasi-authorial voice, they assert their authority beyond their illustrative role in the exposition. In 'Love child' (part of the *Witness* series on Channel 4, 24 September 1996), three women who were forced to give up their babies for adoption in the 1960s recount remarkably similar narratives of social prejudice and bigotry, despite being sharply individuated in terms of personality and temperament. Unveiling the flip side of the decade more typically associated with Woodstock and sexual liberation, this documentary combines archive film footage, reminiscences from church figures involved in running mother-and-baby homes, and the recollections of the women themselves, to communicate the contradictoriness of a decade that appeared to encourage sexual self-expression, while simultaneously denying contraceptive advice to many single women and surrounding births to unmarried mothers with intense shame and secrecy. The women's experiences, individually and separately presented, acquire the authority of testimony by establishing 'lines of analysis that move from her experience to mine and mine to hers' (Probyn 1993: 4). Strikingly identical in their accounts of how they were treated by their families, by the mother-and-baby homes, and by midwives, their individual expressions of identical feelings of emotional paralysis as they handed their babies over to strangers rebound powerfully off each other and also trigger fresh epistemological insights into the hypocritical social morality of the period. The achievement of resonance across differing case studies comes close in this instance to forming what Trinh T. Minh-ha applauds as a new form of subjectivity potentially emerging out of autobiography: 'the subjectivity of a non-I/plural I, which is different from the subjectivity of the sovereign I (subjectivism) or the non-subjectivity of the all-knowing I (objectivism)' (1991: 192).

Tensions between the documentary's expository line and the performances of its 'social actors' (Nichols 1991: 42, 120) also threaten at times to disrupt the authority of the dominant discourse. The vitality, openness and articulateness of people, selected on the basis of their credibility as performers as well as exemplars, is often at odds with their construction as victims of the problem being explored.[3] John Corner notes how evolving production practices, such as the elimination of the interviewer from the documentary frame, paradoxically 're-subjectivise' speakers by giving them apparent control over their own discourse (1996b: 169). More significantly for this discussion, the position of these interviewees on society's cutting edge makes them intensely acute witnesses to the interrelatedness of personal experience, social realities and political and economic forces. The ease with which their experience can bubble up to disturb the confines of the documentary's line of argument is illustrated in 'Marie's story' in 'Broken Promises', a Channel 4 documentary (9 June 1996) that formed part of a series of programmes on poverty in contemporary Britain.

Carefully framed in a manner that constructs her as a victim of an inadequate welfare system, Marie is chosen to illustrate the problems encountered by women who find themselves, after a lifetime of caring for others, thrown on the welfare scrap-heap, and dependent on charity for survival. Evocative mise-en-scène, inter-title quotations from 'expert' commentators, and voice-over text construct Marie as demeaned by a transition from welfare entitlement to charity dependency. Her own voice tells a different story. Robustly lacking self-pity, and incisive in her perceptions of the interrelations between benefit changes, loss of social cohesiveness and a personal experience that is plural

rather than singular ('there must be thousands in the world like me'), her reaction to being burgled for the sixth time in a short period quickly moves beyond
predictable expressions of shock and dismay to a trenchant comment on the
decline of neighbourliness and community that allows burglars to work undis-
turbed. By cutting into the complex layers of a wider range of Thatcherite
values than the documentary can hope to cover, Marie momentarily achieves
Elspeth Probyn's aim of finding ways 'in which we can use our selves critically
in order to trouble the material conditions that literally give rise to "us"' (1993:
168). Case studies, in such conditions, can occasionally acquire the authority of
testimony.

Testimony

'Testimony' has been used in critical writing on documentary to include any
evidence given by speakers in their own words. In the distinctions drawn here
between different forms of incorporating women's voices, I reserve 'testimony'
for situations in which the movement between the woman's subjectivity and
social or political circumstances is made textually visible. As feminist theory
suggests, experience, under these circumstances, prompts fresh epistemological
understanding, distinguishing it clearly from its role as spectacle in the confessional, or as an exemplary instance of someone else's narrative in the case study.
Television, in a variety of ways, can make manifest the disturbance or shift
between the ontological and epistemological that feminist theorists see as
quintessential to a politics of experience. The remainder of this chapter explores
four ways in which a demonstration of the interlinking between the personal
and political comes to life. In outline, these consist of ironic juxtaposition;
memory work; reflexivity; and, the most difficult to epitomize, a disruption of
the habitual televisual rhetorics deployed to communicate historical magnitude.

Ironic juxtaposition

The juxtaposing of personal recollection and political evidence is common-
place in documentaries, but often these merely co-exist on different planes. By
bringing them into critical collision with each other, documentaries expose the
limitations of any official or habitual discourse that postures as a singular version
of 'the truth'. In 'Love child', as I described above, the power of the women's
voices is largely achieved through an accumulating resonance, but the
redefining authority of their story is also underlined by its ironic relation to
populist images of the 1960s as the era of the permissive society, free love and
self-indulgence. The programme's final commentary, defining the era as one
intent on suppressing female sexuality, is spoken over images of the Woodstock
festival, placing an ironic distance between this version of 1960s' 'structures of
feeling' and the lived reality of the period.

The twenty-six part series on twentieth-century history, *People's Century*, broadcast by BBC television between 1995 and 1997, also deploys ironic juxta-position to allow personal recollections to interrogate authorized records. '1957 – Skin Deep' (BBC1, 20 October 1996) explores racial issues in the southern states of the USA and in South Africa. Official film commentary on the clear-ance of Sophiatown, a 1950s' black settlement in Johannesburg, as part of the intensification of apartheid, ricochets off the testimony of one of the residents. Christine Hadebe's recollections are intercut with scenes from the archive film of the event, open to varying interpretations when deprived of the 'anchorage' of its own commentary. Hadebe relates how 'they [the authorities] forced us into the trucks at gun-point. There was no choice', as the documentary cuts to film of the events, now relocated by its own soundtrack within an assured colo-nial discourse. A white male voice tells us that the 'rejoicing Bantu' are 'on their way to a new home – Meadowland – where one can breathe freely'.

Memory work

Memory work has been increasingly recognized within feminist cultural and historical studies as a means of making visible 'the web of interconnections' between 'outer and inner, social and personal, historical and psychical' (Kuhn 1995: 4). Most of the published accounts (for example, Kuhn 1995; Steedman 1986) are of individual recollections built around personal and familial autobi-ography. Collective memory work might be yet more productive. The artificiality of separating out witnesses seems particularly acute when the witnesses are women. Writers on gender and discourse have commented extensively on women's preference for interactive, co-operative modes of communication, and the relative neglect of this approach in many high-status forms of exchange.[4] Television practices are no exception, with interaction predominantly consisting of confrontation and contestation. Historians are now beginning to explore the benefits of bringing people who participated in past events or processes together to discuss their recollections in 'witness seminars'. These recognize that reminiscing collectively can trigger long-buried memories, and can also tease out the validity of some of the claims that individual memories offer. Documentary rarely provides such opportunities, but when it does, the movement from the personal to the political becomes palpable as we witness the moment of revelation on the screen.

'Playing to Survive' (BBC2, 30 October 1996) focuses on the experiences of cellist Anita Lasker-Wallfisch, who survived the concentration camps by becoming a member of the women's orchestra at Auschwitz. She shares recol-lections with two friends, Violette and Hélène, who were also members of that orchestra and who later accompanied her to Belsen. From this collective remembering, acutely personalized perceptions emerge that add fresh horror to a historical period in danger of being drained of its power to shock through the clichéd familiarity of its imagery. Violette recalls how the women were asked to play an impromptu concert for Joseph Kramer, the notorious commandant at

Belsen, and, after the recital, were invited back to his house, given a large bowl of rice pudding and left to enjoy it to the strains of a Bach suite on his gramophone. Suddenly Anita, whose recollection of this event has been uncharacteristically hazy, interjects that they were required to eat 'without spoons – I remember we ate like pigs that night'. Whether this is an actual recollection (Violette does not remember this detail) or a projection of the feelings generated by the incident is immaterial to its impact on the viewer, vivifying as it does the sharp contradictoriness of the situation. The freshness and intensity of this memory takes us, like the women themselves, by surprise.

This example illustrates the dramatic and informational potential of collective witnessing on television. If documentary has failed to exploit this possibility, it has also missed opportunities to allow witnesses to comment on archive film of the events or times they lived through. Annette Kuhn (1995) has demonstrated the productivity of this approach in relation to the family photograph album, but the documentarist's conventional separation of historical evidence and personal memory bypasses opportunities of re-interpreting both by allowing them to spark off each other.

Suggestions of what this might achieve are indicated in a documentary on the Dionne quintuplets, born in a remote part of Canada in the 1930s, and brought up as a tourist attraction and virtual freak show ('Miracle babies', part of the *Inside Story* series, BBC1, 24 July 1996). Now suing the Ontario government for compensation for their past exploitation, the three surviving quins are reluctant witnesses to the suffering they endured, inhibited partly by awkwardness with English and partly by an unwillingness to blame individuals. But while watching film footage of themselves, aged eight, wheeled out at a massive public rally in Toronto to raise money for the war effort, their feelings suddenly erupt. The movement from measured responses to spontaneous reaction, and from the ontological to the epistemological, triggered by this piece of film, suddenly tears away the veil of civility and rationality that has obscured the interconnectedness between these women's experiences and the public circumstances that helped to construct them. A technique that produces such powerful television in this specific instance holds wider promise as a means of producing new readings of archive film whose familiarity borders often on visual cliché.

Reflexivity

Postmodern celebrations of reflexivity find only tentative echo among documentary critics. Scepticism centres on its potential pretentiousness, although critics also recognize that at its most penetrating it 'emphasizes epistemological doubt' and can even recreate the processes of feminist consciousness-raising by instigating an interrogation of 'the ground of experience itself' (Nichols 1991: 61, 65). Trinh T. Minh-ha condemns reflexivity when it serves merely to enhance the status of the authorial voice, but her belief that 'meaning can . . . be political only when it does not let itself be easily stabilized' (1991: 41) demands a documentary aesthetic that refuses certainty without abdicating responsibility for analysis.

By drawing attention to the provisionality and locatedness of experience, and the contingent link between investigator and subject, reflexivity shifts the distant ethnographic gaze into the uncomfortable proximity of political contact. A documentary on the Rwandan genocide of 1994 for the *Witness* series on Channel 4 indicates how this can be achieved. Living in that country before and during the genocide, journalist Lindsey Hilsum, the presenter of the programme ('Rwanda: the betrayal', 16 May 1996), becomes a self-reflexive participant in the moral dilemmas that confronted Rwanda's inhabitants at that time. As a result, the initial 'shock' she expresses at evidence of the Catholic church's involvement – however indirectly – in the massacres, many of which took place in churches where the Tutsis were taking refuge, is complicated by her own experiences. By exposing her own positioning in the intensely difficult battle between conscience, will, and political reality, easy moral judgements are undermined.

Shifting between commentator, interviewer and interviewee in the course of the documentary, Hilsum also denies her own voice interpretative authority. Asked, as interviewee, whether she herself had to refuse anyone help during the period of the genocide, she replies:

> In the first few days of the genocide my phone worked and a lot of Tutsis I knew rang me and asked me to come and save them, and I failed to do that because I didn't have any petrol in my car, and because I wasn't sure where they lived, and I didn't think that I could reach them. Now that means that I'm like a lot of Rwandans who might have wanted to save people or protect them but I didn't have the means, or maybe I wasn't brave enough, or I wasn't strong enough, or I wasn't good enough, and I didn't do it.

By putting her own situation into play, Hilsum prevents the viewer from occupying a position of detachment. She also destabilizes the conventional aloofness of the presenter towards her interviewees. Janvière Uwizeye, a Tutsi whose relatives were killed in the church in Kaduha where one of the worst massacres took place in April 1994, is one of these. She was saved by a priest who was simultaneously exploiting his position by selling rice, donated by a Catholic relief agency, to the people who were about to be slaughtered. Chillingly, Hilsum reports that he had allegedly raised the price each day until the eve of the massacre, reducing it then to get rid of his stock. When Hilsum asks her how she now feels about this man, Janvière replies that, although she cannot forgive him, she cannot condemn him either, because he was caught in an impossible situation and could not save everyone. Resonating with Hilsum's diagnosis of her own experience, the ambivalence of Janvière's reaction, which in different circumstances might produce a sense of ethnographic distancing, is transformed into a moment of profound disturbance and unsettling of our security of knowledge about the genocide. Experience in this documentary is truly not a fixed point of departure for knowing and evaluating, but a disconcerting prompt to re-evaluation and involvement. More effectively than the schematic movement of irony, reflexivity is capable of producing intense moments of 'radical defamiliarization' when, as here, 'the "This is so, isn't it?" of hegemonic ideology hesitates and wavers' (Nichols 1991: 266, 263).

Reworking magnitude

Capturing the magnitude of historical experience is problematic on a small screen. Even in *film* documentary, Bill Nichols claims: 'narrative and exposition are always forms of miniaturization that seek to encapsulate a "world" that bears some meaning for us' whereas 'history is what hurts. . . . A magnitude of excess remains' (Nichols 1991: 230, 231). Informational television develops its own rhetorics for communicating scale. When celebration of democratizing processes is called for, such as during the free elections in South Africa or the collapse of the Berlin Wall, scale is painted large in mass scenes of public rapture. In situations of extreme public horror, on the other hand, barbarity and disaster are briefly glimpsed in their mass form, their extensiveness documented statistically, but it is to the personal dimension that the medium turns to manage its embodiment of magnitude. The experiences of witnesses and survivors are deployed to bring the events within the miniaturizing scale that makes them affectively intelligible to viewers. The broad canvas of the public arena has to be abandoned, when codes of taste and decency, or the limits of imagination, dictate a shift into personalized mode. When the habitual expectations of these differently constituted conventions for evoking magnitude are disturbed, relations between personal and political are once more thrown into relief.

Survivors of horror 'vivify' the 'incommensurateness between representation and historical referent, the refusal of containment and closure' (Nichols 1991: 240–1) when personal experience cannot carry the load of political or public trauma. In two of the documentaries already discussed, 'Playing to Survive' and 'Rwanda: the betrayal', there are moments of stasis when the expressivity of verbal and non-verbal language falters. Anita Lasker-Wallfisch, revisiting the site of the music block at Auschwitz, is asked by her daughter whether there were ever moments when the women in the orchestra forgot the situation they were in. Anita pauses before replying that it is impossible to say what she was thinking all that time ago. The camera at the same time draws back to position the two women in long shot at the edge of the frame. More of the magnitude of both experience and historical reality is communicated in the visual and verbal terseness of this static shot than could be achieved by any emotional excess. The impossibility of accurately recollecting or representing the unrepresentable leaves the contradictions of the experience lying rawly open, and prevents any comforting closure for the viewer.

In 'Rwanda: the betrayal', there is a similar sequence towards the end of the programme. Lindsey Hilsum is filmed in a wide-angled shot walking towards the church at Kaduha with Bernadette Uwamariya, whose relatives, like those of Janvière Uwizeye, were massacred there. Bernadette, Hilsum tells us in a voice-over, was previously thinking of becoming a nun, but now she is less sure. Between cut-away shots to the church, already firmly associated with unspeakable bloodshed, presenter and interviewee are filmed standing silently together, side by side, in two static shots, one at medium, the other at long range. Spatially composed to invoke a sense of solidarity between the two women, these shots last over ten seconds each, and are filmed without dialogue. Their temporal awkwardness, in a medium that normally edits out such *longueurs*, powerfully signifies the limits of communicability about a period in Rwandan history that has been slipping out from under the documentary's ability to contain or describe it. The chasm between the expressible and the lived remains unbridged.

'1957 – Skin Deep', in contrast, ends optimistically with the celebration of the first free elections in South Africa in April 1994. Reports of that country's political struggles have long been visually accompanied by crowd scenes, depicted historically in violent confrontation, but more recently in tumultuous rejoicing over liberation and democratic rights. This documentary shifts this customary rhetoric, first on the public scale by using a stunning aerial shot to trace the winding miles of queues of people waiting in the heat of the sun to cast their votes. This is a South African crowd scene with a difference, marked by its unfamiliar orderliness and its awe-inspiring evocation of expectation. Departure from the conventional rhetoric of public celebration is more striking still in this sequence's endeavour to evoke political magnitude at a personal and bodily level. It cuts from the spectacular cinematic aerial shots to the very personal experience of one woman who was voting for the first time. Justina Coha, introduced to us earlier in the documentary as a witness to apartheid whose daughter was caught up in the violence in Soweto in the mid 1970s, graphically enacts the momentousness of the occasion. The excitement she felt on that day is re-created for us, in a verbal and bodily drama that, in its excess of modulation and gestures, breaks through the customary conventions of inter-viewees' 'virtual performance' (Nichols 1991: 122). Bringing the intensity of the political event into play at the level of the personal underlines the artificiality of locating one in the public sphere and the other in the private. This juxtaposition of experiential excess with the spectacular images of the voting queues affirms too that – just occasionally – history does not hurt, but produces moments of intense joy that are felt along the pulse as well as in the mind.

Conclusion

Documentary-makers' concerns about the validity of subjectivity and experience as evidence have centred on issues of reliability and typicality. As one of the producers of the *People's Century* series put it, 'we had to make sure that our interviewees, while giving a highly personal account of a particular event, were in line with the consensus of what most people in their situations were feeling at the time . . . One oddball account could knock the whole narrative out of "true" ' (cited in *Radio Times*, 9–15 September 1995: 24). The discursive framing of this dilemma explains why documentary-makers so often choose to incorporate experience merely as an illustration of an argument developed from other sources. Subjectivity as spectacle produces no such anxieties, since its attention-arresting credentials increase in line with the idiosyncrasy of the confessor's experience.

This chapter has argued that bringing feminist theories of experience into play with documentary aesthetics opens up possibilities both for democratizing human interest and for preventing a stultifying repetition of gendered assumptions about the agenda and discourses of informational television. The personal and the political, access and exposition, do not inevitably exist on separate planes, or possess inherently different claims to legitimation. Documentary-makers, searching for novelty and besieged by the need to increase ratings, may find commodification of experience a tempting option in a medium that already gives prime space on confessional talk shows and self-immolating game shows to those whose experiences are least represented in the informational media. The creative opportunities and rewards of exploring how personal experience might activate the 'radical defamiliarization' (Nichols 1991: 266) that stimulates new forms of political insight could, however, be more exhilarating. As the examples in this chapter demonstrate, forms of testimony that collapse familiar boundaries between the personal and political often provide arresting and inspiring moments within television documentary. They also help to uncover a rich seam of witnesses who are still largely hidden from news and current affairs programming. Hearing more of the testimony of women, and of other groups under-represented in the televisual news agenda, might reconfigure the relation of centre to periphery as well as of the personal to the political. It might even help to reconstitute the public sphere as a democratic space.

Notes

1 Although the video-diary format would repay analysis in the terms of this chapter, it has not been included here.

2 Interestingly, Corner implicitly suggests this himself by citing Connie Field's film *The Life and Times of Rosie the Riveter* (1980), both as an example of 'access' filming (1995: 183, note 11) and as enabling the women's contributions to emerge as 'testimony' (1995: 99; 1996a: 125), producing 'a *process* of reflection-as-self-awareness' that becomes 'the means by which the "personal is made political" ' (1996a: 136).

3 See Winston (1988, 1995) for further discussion of the construction of people as 'victims' in the realist documentary tradition, and Nichols (1991) for a fuller discussion of the 'virtual performance' of 'social actors'.

4 See, for example, Cameron (1990), Coates (1986), Spender (1980) and Swann (1992).

7

(EN)GENDERING THE TRUTH POLITICS OF NEWS DISCOURSE

Stuart Allan

Truth, according to a journalistic dictum, is the news reporter's stock-in-trade.[1] Significantly, however, current research concerned with the ideological features of news discourse often tends to displace the problem of truth, generally preferring to prioritise in its place questions of 'objectivity' and 'bias'. That is to say, debates over whether or not the news media accurately 'reflect' social reality, or the extent to which journalists can produce a 'neutral', 'impartial' news account, typically restrict the discussion to one regarding how best to separate 'facts' from 'values'. As a result, the issue of what constitutes truth is often ignored, or otherwise simply dismissed as a philosophical matter of little consequence when the routine conventions of reporting are under scrutiny. To the degree that this conceptual orthodoxy is reproduced, then, rigid limits will continue to be placed on the types of research problematics which can be formulated.

Feminist researchers committed to recasting this conceptual orthodoxy have sought to intervene in these debates from a variety of different vantage points. A principal point of contention concerns the gendering of the dominant discourses of truth being mobilised by journalists, that is, the extent to which a 'gender bias' is discernible in the ritualised practices of 'objective' news reporting. Here three distinct modes of enquiry may be briefly sketched as follows:

1   For some feminists seeking to uphold 'objectivity' as a journalistic ideal, the problem is one of male norms, values and beliefs being allowed to subjectively distort 'what really took place'. Good reporting, they maintain, is gender-neutral reporting. Advocates of this position call for journalists to observe a rigorous adherence to systematised methods of gathering and processing 'concrete facts' dispassionately so as to ensure that news accounts are strictly 'impartial'. The 'truth' of the 'real world' is to be discovered through these facts; 'biased' journalism can thus be avoided so long as news accounts accurately reflect reality.

2   Other feminists have sought to highlight the gender-specificity of

'objectivity', that is, the essential distinctions between female and male apprehensions of reality derivative of sexual difference. In their view, only women are justified in speaking for women as a social group: personal experience, it follows, stands as the arbiter of 'truth'. Using a language of 'balance', they contend that 'objectivity' is primarily a matter of ensuring that male values are counterpoised by female ones in a given news account (or range thereof). This is to be achieved by news organisations employing equal numbers of male and female journalists, as well as through changes in newswork practices (such as ensuring that a representative selection of female voices are accessed as news sources).

3   A further position adopted by some feminists is marked by a resolve to effectively jettison the concept of 'objectivity' altogether due to its perceived complicity in legitimising patriarchal hegemony. In their view, this concept prefigures a dichotomy between the knower and the known which is untenable: facts cannot be separated out from their ideological, and hence gendered, conditions of production. Moreover, they argue, the imposition of this false dichotomy is further masculinised to the extent that it obviates the experiences of women as being 'outside' the realm of what are proclaimed to be universally valid standards of reason, logic and ratio-nality. What counts as 'truth' in a given instance is determined by who has the power to define reality.

It is evident from these differing positions, situated as they are amongst a myriad of alternative ones, that any attempt to theorise the relationship between discourses of truth and gender relations will be necessarily contingent upon politically-charged epistemological presuppositions. With this and related diffi-culties in mind, it is my aim in this chapter to contribute to current discussions about the gender politics of news 'objectivity' by centring for exploration what may be termed, after Mikhail Bakhtin, 'the dialogics of truth'. I shall attempt to show that a gender-sensitive engagement with Bakhtin's conceptual project (1934–5; 1937–8; 1963; 1973) encourages a sustained reconsideration of many of the ostensibly 'common sensical' precepts underpinning ordinary journalistic procedures for dealing with conflicting truth-claims.

To this end, a number of the imperatives informing different feminist assess-ments of the heuristic value of Bakhtin's writings will be addressed first of all. The focus then shifts to accentuate the basis for a critique of 'monologic' notions of truth and, in so doing, shall seek to identify several points of tension in patriarchal conceptions of knowledge, reason and rationality. This enquiry is followed, in turn, by an attempt to elaborate a Bakhtinian approach to the news account as an (en)gendered site of dialogic interaction, one that is inextricably caught-up in matrices of definitional power. Overall, then, this chapter is intended to help facilitate further efforts to investigate the ideological inflection of truth in news discourse precisely as it appropriates 'the world out there' into an androcentric constellation of 'impartial facts'.

Feminism and Bakhtin

Perhaps an appropriately reflexive way to begin is by posing the question: why initiate this turn to the writings of Mikhail Bakhtin, most of which first appeared in Russia several decades ago?[2] Denise Heikinen (1994), in her provocatively titled essay 'Is Bakhtin a feminist or just another dead white male?', suggests that it is his theory of dialogism which deserves serious attention today. This theory, she observes, 'has been embraced by several feminist critics for its ability to provide a platform for marginalised feminine voices to be heard above the din of the monologic, authoritative, and hegemonic voice' (Heikinen 1994: 114). Still, Heikinen is not alone in pointing out an attendant dilemma, namely that although Bakhtin's approach appears to be, in her words, 'tailor-made for feminist criticism', gender relations fail to receive adequate attention in his theoretical work. It is this paradox which Maroussia Hajdukowski-Ahmed pinpoints when she writes of Bakhtin: 'the great thinker of alterity, whose whole philosophical project argues for respect for the Other, seems to have removed from sight (and mind) the Other par excellence: woman and the feminine' (Hajdukowski-Ahmed 1990: 153).

Not surprisingly, the issue of how best to re-appropriate Bakhtin's work so as to contribute to the advancement of feminist conceptual and strategic agendas has been the subject of much critical discussion in a range of disciplinary contexts (see also Bauer 1988; Díaz-Diocaretz 1989; Glazener 1989; Hajdukowski-Ahmed 1990; Hohne and Wussow 1994; O'Connor 1990; Pearce 1992, 1994; Pollock 1993). Dale Bauer, for example, argues that Bakhtin's method can be 'refashioned' into a feminist dialogics, a point echoed by Karen Hohne and Helen Wussow who write:

> Bakhtin is accessible and valuable to feminism not only in terms of his philosophy, which is specifically directed at celebrating, highlighting, bringing to the fore the vitalising force of dialogism – that is, the incorporation and interweaving of various voices to create a sum far greater and more generative than the parts – but even in terms of his form.
>
> (Hohne and Wussow 1994: viii)

Many feminists consider the insights Bakhtin provides into the fluidly dynamic logics of dialogism to be rich with potential for analyses of masculinised ideologies (as detailed below, dialogue is a category of both power and resistance).[3] Mary Pollock, in describing the importance of a Bakhtinian project for feminism, writes: 'Bakhtin's work is attractive to us because it seems to resonate, more than perhaps any other theory emerging from a masculinist tradition, with our voices, because it seems to critique *from a male perspective* the power-plays deployed in patriarchal language' (Pollock 1993: 231).

Notwithstanding Bakhtin's failure to attend to sexual difference as a distinct matter of concern, then, Myriam Díaz-Diocaretz observes that: 'He was at least aware of *gender differences* occurring at different levels and moments within discursive interaction, and, most importantly, his theoretical foundations can be enlarged and enriched with feminist revisions' (Díaz–Diocaretz 1989: 128–9; see also Pearce 1994). Adopting a similar position, Nancy Glazener maintains that even though Bakhtin's writings are not 'markedly feminist', they appear to be 'hospitable to the inclusion of gender as an additional, significant social and discursive category' (Glazener 1989: 109). This is not to deny, however, that his concepts must first undergo a process of amendment before they can be re-appropriated for feminism. She declares that this effort is warranted, from a feminist point of view, because Bakhtin's project possesses at least two particularly important attractions:

> First, his assertion that [a text] represents a struggle among socio-ideological languages unsettles the patriarchal myth that there could be a language of truth transcending relations of power and desire. Second, Bakhtin's insistence that words and discourses have socially differential significance implies that linguistic and literary forms are necessarily shaped by the gender relations that structure society. . . . The concept of the subjectively-defined utterance ensures that for as long as gender has a share in the social constitution of subjectivity, part of every utterance's social intelligibility will derive from its orientation towards gender.
>
> (Glazener 1989: 110)

Consequently, for feminists such as Glazener, Bakhtin's inattention to the effectivity of gender may be substantively rectified by reworking his conception of the socially situated relations of meaning construction. It follows that each and every text, regardless of its ascribed genre, intermingles discourses which have been conditioned – often in highly contradictory ways – by the interests of patriarchy.

It is along these lines that this chapter's enquiry will develop, with particular attention being directed to the problem of truth in news discourse. As I hope to show in light of this feminist re-appropriation of Bakhtin, the strategies routinely employed by journalists to lend to their accounts a factual status aligned with truthfulness recurrently exhibit an (en)gendered exclusivity of both representation and address.

The gender politics of 'objectivity'

'Truth is not born nor is it to be found inside the head of an individual person', writes Bakhtin; 'it is born *between people* collectively searching for truth, in the process of their dialogic interaction' (Bakhtin 1963: 110). The question of what constitutes truth, he suggests, will always be the subject of dispute between contrary voices, any number of which may be claiming to speak 'reality' in an impartial, value-free manner. An advantageous starting point for our purposes here, therefore, is the Bakhtinian attempt to render problematic the very assumption that 'facts' can be separated from 'values' at the level of discourse. Such a division underpins the journalistic appeal to 'objectivity' and, as will be argued, is premised on a masculinised configuration of truth.[4]

The conviction that journalists, by observing certain professionally-codified methods of reporting, will be able to set aside their individual preconceptions and depict reality 'as it actually is' to their readers prefigures what is, after Bakhtin, a 'monologic' approach to truth. In his book *Problems of Dostoevsky's Poetics* (1963), he advances the thesis that this monologic sense of truth has been consolidated across 'the entire ideological culture of recent times'. Although he does not discuss the origins of monologic truth in any detail, he contends that it found its most precise expression in the 'idealistic philosophy' indicative of the 'unified and exclusive reason' of the Enlightenment. To briefly elaborate upon Bakhtin's claim, what appears to be at issue is an epistemology which asserts that a single and incontrovertible system of true knowledge may be 'uncovered' through formal methods of 'observation' and 'fact gathering'. These methods ensure that this 'innocent' knowledge mirrors the objective, as opposed to subjective, 'external' world which is independent of the dispassionate observer (visibility is equated with veracity). Carefully established factual observations are rational, detached and universal; as a medium of truth they provide direct, immediate and empirically accessible experience of the events which make up this world free from 'bias'.

Journalists choosing to uphold the doctrine of 'objectivity' (even those for whom its desirability is to be distinguished from its attainability) are thus in many ways subscribing to the tenets of a monologic conception of truth. They are endorsing, either explicitly or implicitly, the postulate that true knowledge is grounded in reality and that it may be given expression via a 'transparently neutral' language without becoming tainted by 'personal values'. In such a monologic world, Bakhtin maintains, truth is divorced from personality. Ideas of truth, it follows, belong to *no one*; rather, because they are deprived of any direct power to signify, they can only be either affirmed or repudiated as the unified product of a *single* consciousness (Bakhtin 1963: 79). In other words, this conception of truth is represented as being the only one possible; its tenets assume a position of dominance because of their ostensibly unmediated correlation with an unchanging Real ('the real world'). This monologic principle is embedded in social relations throughout society: 'Monologue', Bakhtin writes, 'pretends to be the *ultimate word*. It closes down the represented world and represented persons' (Bakhtin 1963: 293).[5]

This reference to the 'ultimate word' resonates with a diverse range of feminist critiques of Enlightenment thought in general, and masculinist definitions of truth in particular. The final declaration of truth under relations of patriarchy, many of these critiques contend, is imposed upon women by men as a means to legitimise diverse forms of oppression. The invocation of a monologic truth is

125

masculinised to the extent that (predominantly white, élite) men's orientations to 'the world of facts' are accepted as the most *appropriate* vantage points from which the immutable truth of reality is to be revealed. Taken for granted in this masculinist epistemology is the presupposition that reality may be assumed to be a *given* (it exists 'out there'), and that, as such, it constitutes the standard by which truth and falsity are to be impartially measured. Once it is resolved that there is one, absolute Truth, then the 'search for objectivity' becomes essential if the ideal of abstract, universal knowledge is to be realised. Male hegemony is thus contingent upon the displacement of counter-hegemonic, namely feminist, discourses as being complicit in the 'distortion' or misrepresentation of reality.

A key point of contention for a range of feminist interventions, therefore, has been the (often tacit) masculine/feminine dichotomy prefigured in androcentric definitions of knowledge. More specifically, the gendered basis of this hierarchical dichotomy has been shown to be dependent upon a separation of the knower (subject) from the known (object). This separation naturalises, to varying degrees, a series of dualisms whereby 'masculine' discourses about reality (held to be objective, rational, abstract, coherent, unitary and active) are discursively privileged over 'feminine' ones (posited as subjective, irrational, emotional, partial, fragmented and passive). Implied in this dynamic is the precept that 'feminine knowledge' is to be understood as being inferior to 'masculine truth' and, as such, is to be recognised as constituting its Other. This conflation of the masculine with the rational and the feminine with the irrational serves to sanction the exclusion of women's truth-claims as falling outside the prescribed parameters of reason (reason is deemed to both represent and embody truth). It is only 'logical', on these grounds, that women are to be denied the authoritative status of 'objective knower'.

Accordingly, in my view, efforts aiming to first contest and then subvert the 'rational' appropriations of truth which help to sustain androcentric relations of power and privilege will find a consideration of Bakhtin's writings on the nature of truth to be advantageous. As I shall attempt to show in the remaining portion of this chapter, evident in his work is a conceptual basis to challenge the monologic configuration of truth, and with it the naturalised divisions which underlie any proclaimed pursuit of 'innocent' knowledge. Knowledge, he insists, cannot be separated from the knower; rather, what is to be distinguished as knowledge is socially situated, perspectival and thus politicised. Appeals to 'objective' modes of knowing, and with them the quest for a unitary truth, will therefore be effectively transposed once it is demonstrated that the idea of truth is by its very nature dialogic.

Dialogising truth

The formulation of truth in one discourse, Bakhtin contends, is always conditional upon 'living contact' with alternative truth-claims embodied in the voices of others. That is to say, the 'true realm of the life of an idea' is situated beyond any one person's *isolated* individual consciousness:

> The idea begins to live, that is, to take shape, to develop, to find and renew its verbal expression, to give birth to new ideas, only when it enters into genuine dialogic relationships with other ideas, with the ideas of *others*. . . . The idea is a *live event*, played out at the point of dialogic meeting between two or several consciousnesses. In this sense the idea is similar to the *word*, with which it is dialogically united. Like the word, the idea wants to be heard, understood, and 'answered' by other voices from other positions.
>
> (Bakhtin 1963: 88)

A Bakhtinian critique of news discourse, as I envisage it here, would maintain that the language of news can never be ideologically 'neutral'. Rather, each word of a news account is a 'two-sided act' in that it is continuously *oriented toward an addressee*, that is, it is conditioned by *whose* word it is and *for whom* it is meant (see also Vološinov 1929). The meaning of the word can never be affixed once and for all, as it is actively negotiated through the reciprocal relationship between addresser and addressee.

A dialogical sense of truth, it follows, places a crucial emphasis on the inter-subjective dynamics of representation at the level of the 'double-voiced' word. In Bakhtin's view, each and every truth-claim is to be recognised as a site of dialogic, and thus gendered, interaction; its ontological status will be constantly redefined from one ideological context to another, and not in relation to a totalised invocation of reality. It is this insight into the irreducible plurality of 'unmerged voices', and their 'unceasing and irreconcilable quarrel', which throws into such sharp relief the 'integral position of a personality' in every truth-claim. Any strategy to exercise monologic control over truth rests on the denial of this situational embodiment. Such a disavowal can never succeed entirely, however, for it runs contrary to what Bakhtin terms the 'heteroglossic' or 'polyvocal' nature of all meaning relations. Once this lived mediation is acknowledged, a 'genuine polyphony of voices', previously all but silenced, will be 'heard'.

In this way, a Bakhtinian critique of news discourse brings to the fore the contradictory imperatives of *truthfulness* as they are re-inflected in a news account which implicitly assumes the status of being a factual *translation* of reality. In attempting to prioritise for discussion the 'objective' journalist's claim of referential transparency, this issue of how monologic configurations of truth inform the 'discipline of objectivity' as a seemingly apolitical ('gender-neutral') normative ideal is critical. Such a problematic, I would argue, avoids many of the familiar pitfalls of the 'objectivity' versus 'bias' debate as it has developed in various studies of news discourse. At stake is the need to recentre the problem of truth in a way which overcomes the limitations of those approaches which, on the one hand, consider news language to be 'value-neutral', and those approaches which, on the other hand, treat it as being inescapably determined by patriarchal values. Thus in order to secure a politicised understanding of 'objectivity' as an (en)gendered construction, the intricate ways in which the ontological hierarchies of gender relations shape the journalist's everyday, routine methods of apprehending and assigning value to certain truth-claims at the expense of alternative ones need to be unravelled.

This project of de-naturalising the 'taken-for-granted' rationales of journalistic 'objectivity' may then proceed to identify the procedures by which truth is particularised as being directly accessible via 'professional methods' for 'gathering facts'. The 'impartial' news account posits the news event as an essential entity, the reality of which exists independently 'outside' of socially situated relations of knowledge and power (that is, for Bakhtin (1934–5: 279), the 'living, tension-filled interaction' with the 'already uttered', the 'already known', the 'common opinion' and so forth). The conflicting truth-claims mobilised by news sources seeking to define the reality of the news event must be handled 'dispassionately' by the journalist. Not surprisingly then, the appeal to 'objectivity' becomes a defensive strategy, one which assists the journalist in countering charges of sexism (as well as racism, amongst others) being levelled at specific instances of reporting. A journalism genuinely committed to impartiality, its adherents insist, cannot be sexist. So long as the appropriate procedural rules are followed, 'tangible facts' will be separated out from the values expressed through partisan argument and opinion; indeed, it is the task of the 'good' reporter to ensure that this segregation is achieved.

'Objective' journalism dictates that only those truth-claims forwarded from 'legitimate' news sources, which fulfil professionally approved criteria of 'accuracy' and 'authenticity', are to be presented as 'factual'. The 'common sensical' authority of news values, that is, the informal yet routinised judgements made to justify the processing of certain types of 'voices' over and above others, guide the journalist's orchestration of competing definitions of reality in accordance with a 'will to facticity' (Allan 1995). The alignment of these different news sources as accredited fact makers helps to frame the journalist's preferred inflection of the reality of a news event. It is their 'loyalty to the truth' which purportedly determines routine decisions about who is and who is not a *legitimate* definer of a news event (a similar politics of legitimacy is played out, often in highly competitive ways, between the sources themselves). Care will be taken to select only those voices which can be made to speak within the 'calm and considered' strictures of the news narrative. These statements will then be arranged within a hierarchical sequence based on 'gut feelings' or 'professional instincts' about 'credibility' (most sources, after all, have their own 'agenda' or 'axe to grind') so as to enhance this larger will to facticity proclaimed by the news account.

There can be no guarantee, of course, that the actual reader, listener or viewer of the news account will accept this preferred inflection of reality as being the most truthful one available. In order to stabilise this definition, and in this way enjoin its reaffirmation by the reader, a range of narrational devices will have to be employed (see Ang 1996; Nightingale 1996; Scannell 1996). Once the journalist introduces a news source's voice into the account, the voice's words will undergo a process of re-evaluation in relation to a series of evolving postulates about what readers are likely to ratify as being 'true' in light of their knowledge and experience. Each respective voice will be marshalled to speak to a particular narrative structure in a way which satisfies the frameworks of interpretation being set in motion by the journalist as the author of the account. Only those voices willing and able to satisfy the shifting dictates of validity as they are governed by the will to facticity will have their declarations enter the discursive field. Consequently, the journalist's invocation of 'objectivity' may be analysed as an androcentric instance of definitional power to the extent that it ex-nominates (places beyond 'common sense') those truth-claims which do not adhere to masculinist assumptions about the social world.

Rules of inclusion and exclusion

Whilst critical researchers have succeeded in documenting the means by which journalists organise the voices of these news sources so as to enforce professionalised norms of reportage, insufficient attention has been granted to the question of how gender relations, together with those of class, race, ethnicity, and sexuality amongst others, shape these (largely unspoken) rules of inclusion and exclusion. In what ways, researchers may proceed to ask, do these professional norms centre the predispositions, 'habits of mind' and attitudes of white, middle-class male journalists? In other words, why is it usually the case that these journalists' 'instinctive' judgements about the 'credibility' or 'expertise' of news sources lead, in turn, to such a small portion of the accessed voices being those of women?[6] Moreover, to what extent do they regard female journalists as 'deviating' from these norms in their approaches to validating truth-claims? In the light of questions such as these, then, it is apparent that these rules of inclusion and exclusion need to be contextualised in relation to long-standing institutional power differentials within the journalistic workplace (where they tend to be all-too-readily defended with reference to a work ethos consistent with masculinised 'traditions' and 'customs'). In the words of one male journalist writing for the *Independent*, a British national daily newspaper: 'The way papers are produced may have changed dramatically in the last decade – green screens replacing eyeshades and metal spikes – but a macho culture still reigns in the nation's newsrooms' (Brown 1997: 3).

Studies of British news organisations recurrently show that the vast majority of senior decision-makers are men, most estimates placing the number at higher than eighty per cent (see Christmas 1997; Dougary 1994; Tunstall 1996). As would be anticipated given this situation, and as has been documented by feminist researchers, the interests of female journalists as participants in defining the organisation's news agenda often encounter considerable resistance from male colleagues. This is particularly evident where 'old boys' networks' are in operation within the organisation and, as is often the case, at the level of news sources. Most newsrooms, moreover, appear to be characterised by a gendered division between 'hard' news (such as economics, politics, government and crime) reporters, who tend to be men, and 'features' reporters, who are more likely, at least in relative terms, to be women. This division, far from correlating with the 'natural competencies' of individual male and female reporters ('men are better suited for the cut-and-thrust of hard news'), is frequently indicative of a sexual division of labour in the journalist's own household. Female reporters are more likely to experience a 'double-day' of work, one where they perform a disproportionate share of domestic (especially child care) responsibilities, than do their 'more professionally committed' male colleagues (see Lafky 1993; Lont 1995; van Zoonen 1994; see also Adam 1995). These forms of labour are somewhat easier to manage in relation to the more regularised, structured and predictable hours associated with features reporting.

Some feminists make the additional point that sexualised divisions of news-work are also embedded in the reporting process at the level of narrative modes of address. 'Even when women select the same news content as men', according to Linda Christmas, a journalist with over thirty years of experience in news-paper and televisual news, 'they write it in a different manner'. In her view:

> Women want news that is 'relevant', news you can 'identify with', news that is explained in terms of their lives. Issues therefore are 'person-alised', or 'humanised' in order that the reader understands the relevance. This move recognises: that women prefer to communicate with the reader; they put readers' needs above those of policy-makers and other providers of news; that women tend to be more 'people' oriented rather than issue orientated; that women place greater impor-tance on seeing news 'in context' rather than in isolation; and that women like to explain the consequences of events.
>
> (Christmas 1997: 3)

Still, to maintain that the discourses of 'objectivity' which operate to sustain the norms of 'hard' news reporting have been mobilised, intentionally or not, to justify the entrenchment of patriarchal news values is not to suggest, in turn, that there are essential categories of 'maleness' and 'femaleness' which male and female journalists (or their readers) occupy, respectively.

'The most difficult question for women', writes Jane Arthurs, 'is how to transform [media] institutions in a way that will give a voice to their aspirations and experiences without falling back on an unchanging and undifferentiated definition of what it means to be female' (Arthurs 1994: 83). To avoid a relapse into a further set of reductionistic dualisms, then, I would argue that the cultural-specificities of gender relations need to be addressed in ways which do not reify or essentialise sexual difference as being biologically overdetermined. That is to say, gendered subjectivities need to be conceptually located *vis-à-vis* other determinant affiliations, such as those of age, class, race, ethnicity, sexual orientation and nationality, in a manner which is sensitive to their shared contingency. Notions such as 'male bias' prefigure the possibility of 'non-bias' and with it 'gender-neutrality', and as such are idealistic formulations that are untenable from a dialogical perspective aiming to explicate the lived negotiation of gender relations within contested matrices of power.

Critical analyses, I want to propose, may instead proceed to engage in the difficult task of deconstructing the prevailing norms of newswork so as to pinpoint the ways in which the 'macho culture' of the newsroom (and 'in the field') is reproduced on a day-to-day basis. To be an 'impartial' reporter means being socialised into obeying certain rituals of naming, describing and framing realities, even if 'objectivity' is self-reflexively posited as an ideal never to be entirely realised in practice. Female journalists working in this predominantly male environment, according to much of the available feminist research, are regularly pressured to adopt masculinised forms of reporting which some find to be inconsistent with their own professional identity and thus alienating (there can also be, as Santos (1997: 123) argues, a professionally driven tendency 'to write white').[7] The enduring salience of discourses of 'objectivity', it follows, needs to be understood within these (sometimes hostile) occupational contexts. For it is at the level of the everyday, in the ordinary and often mundane activities of processing 'raw facts', that certain types of 'news values', 'information gathering techniques', and 'styles of presentation' inform not only the construction of truth but also its narration in androcentric terms. Moreover, and as many of these feminist researchers have pointed out, these (en)gendered reporting practices are likely to continue to be upheld long after women have achieved job equality with their male counterparts.

The social boundaries of truth

Is the language of news 'objectivity' inherently laden with sexist values, then? From the vantage point of a Bakhtinian approach, as I am characterising it here, the answer to such a question is 'no'. A dialogical approach to the sexism of news discourse would attend to the news account as a field of struggle, one that is criss-crossed with ideological clashes and conflicts over truth which, being situationally embodied, are gendered but not in an essentialised manner. My reading of British newspaper and broadcast news suggests that invocations of reality asserted by men may be shown to consistently, but not exclusively, command the available discursive terrain over those advanced by women. The boundaries demarcating this terrain are fluid and yet contingent, that is, whilst they undergo constant changes in alignment with the diverse pressures (hegemonic and counter-hegemonic) brought to bear upon them, they will remain hierarchically grounded in conditions of dominance so long as patriarchal truth-claims are deemed to correspond with 'the real world'. Bakhtin's concept of the dialogic, in my view, entails a commitment to exploring the heterogeneous multiplicity of orientations *encouraged*, but not compelled, by a news account's inflection of truth.

This inflection of truth, far from occurring in a wildly indeterminate manner, takes place within what is a discursive economy of Otherness where women's experiences are recurrently effaced, trivialised or marginalised. To extend Bakhtin's mode of enquiry (1963: 195), then, the masculinised narratives of news discourse may be dismantled dialogically to disclose the extent to which they are 'ideologically saturated and stratified' by (en)gendered projections of what the journalist believes the reader will accept to be true. At least as important as what is 'said' in the account is that which is left 'unsaid'. The act of 'hearing' dialogue where an account proclaims only monologue is itself a means of resisting ideological closure around these social boundaries delineating 'what can and should be said' about a given topic. The 'unsaids' of the text, when identified as such, may be re-articulated in such a way as to compromise the inscription of meaning within these normative prohibitions. In other words, this re-insertion of relations of Otherness otherwise 'ruled out' by the preferred meanings in operation propels that which is 'too obvious for words' out into the open where it may be highlighted for purposes of dialogic critique.

These 'unsaids' of news discourse, once 'made to speak' by 'filling in the gaps', can be made to exhibit a multiplicity of traces left behind by the various ideological evaluations performed in and through the journalist's attempt to monologise the social world. The codes of 'objective' reporting dictate, in turn, that such evaluations are not to be directly acknowledged; rather, 'the facts must be allowed to speak for themselves'. Significantly, although the gendered-specificity of these codes must also be stringently denied at the level of textuality, it is all too often apparent in the use of, for example, generic pronouns such as 'he' to refer to both male and female news actors, or in phrases where 'public opinion' is reduced to 'the views of the man on the street'. Further typical examples include the explicit marking of gender when the news actor is female (e.g. 'the female judge' as opposed to 'the judge'), or the use of gendered descriptive terms (a woman's age, physical appearance and marital status are much more likely to be seen as relevant than they will be for men) and male-centred naming strategies ('wife', 'girlfriend', 'mistress'). Due, in part, to these types of codes, women are regularly depicted as passive, and sexualised, agents to be defined in relation to an active male news actor (see also Cameron 1992; Clark 1992; Mills 1995).

Discursive practices such as these invite, to varying degrees, the reader to adopt a textually preferred – that is, masculinised – reading position as being inferentially consistent with 'objectivity'. The oft-repeated dictum that 'hard news requires hard newsmen' simultaneously prefigures a male reader as the projected norm. Crucial questions may therefore be raised regarding the range of presumptions about 'the audience' being operationalised as 'common sense' in the language of the news account (see also Allan 1997b, 1998; Bell 1991; Bell and Garrett (eds) 1998; Corner 1995; Croteau and Hoynes 1992; Gillespie 1995; Hartley 1996; Hobson 1980; Jensen 1994). By asking 'who is the implied reader of this account?', the subtle (or, for the British tabloid press, often not so subtle) interpellative strategies by which the account's assumed audience is situated in gendered (and frequently explicitly racialised) terms may be disrupted. Further questions then emerge as to the extent to which the mode of address of a 'hard' news account is masculinised in relation to its opposite, the feminised one of a 'soft' news or 'human interest' story.

This masculinisation of the news account's mode of address maps onto the implied reader a hierarchical configuration of 'newsworthiness', one that is broadly aligned with the prevailing 'macho culture' in the newsroom discussed above. In the case of British newspaper discourse, for example, a reader typified as male is likely to be positioned as being primarily interested in public affairs (the realms of business, government and sport), whilst the assumed female reader tends to be positioned as being more interested in personally 'private' or domestic concerns, such as health, 'relationships', fashion, 'beauty', and child-care. Evidence to support this line of argument, whilst the subject of much debate amongst journalists, provides a sense of how these dynamics are changing over time, particularly as news organisations (often due to the influence of advertisers) become ever more inclined to attract female readers. It would appear that the rising importance of women as a distinct audience group in demographic terms is helping to dissolve this 'hard' versus 'soft' news dichotomy. So-called 'women's issues', once almost entirely restricted to the 'women's page' or its equivalent, are increasingly finding their way onto the 'hard' news agenda.

The news account's ascription of different attributes and interests to its male and female readers, respectively, thus directly corresponds with the patriarchal (as well as class-specific and ethnocentric) rationales underpinning the 'pursuit of objectivity'. More specifically, the characteristic conventions of these respective modes of address (en)gender different 'horizons of expectations' (Bakhtin 1934–5) for the reader, that is, they speak the social world in ways which affirm distinctive relationships to the issue of truth. 'Hard' news, with its starkly counterpoised truth-claims, typically relies on the 'expert' knowledges of public-sphere institutions to ratify its imperatives. The reader of the 'hard' news account usually encounters an interpretive space where statements have been rendered consonant with the dictates of a monologic conception of truth. In the case of the 'soft' news account, in contrast, truth is not ordinarily cast as residing in quantifiable facts. Rather, it is more likely to be dialogised such that its 'heteroglot' nature is made apparent, if only implicitly, through the account's use of a language of interpretation and explanation. Such differences between 'hard' and 'soft' news with regard to their respective (en)gendering of truth are, of course, only a matter of degree. Nevertheless, it is possible to discern at this level that the means by which 'hard' news is accorded an enhanced 'prestige' status over the 'lighter' items of 'soft' news are linked, in part, to its greater reliance on monologic renderings of (mainly public sphere) news events. Also discernible is the attendant presumption that women's everyday lives (typically located *vis-à-vis* an autonomous, as opposed to structurally co-determining, private sphere) are intrinsically less 'newsworthy' as a result.

How, then, may the disjunctures between monologic expressions of truth and the 'irrational', 'illegitimate' realities they fail to contain be further opened up for interrogation? One possible way forward is for critical analyses to attempt to read the monologic configuration of truth 'against the grain' so as to resist its drive toward closure. Each and every journalistic appeal to a larger, disembodied truth may therefore be seen to be, to use Bakhtin's phrase, 'inhabited by the interpretations of others'. Truth-claims, he argues, are never static; rather, they are perpetually embedded in relations of contestation between centripetal (monologic) and centrifugal (dialogic) forces. It follows that to rethink the news account as an (en)gendered site of dialogic interaction, one which is alive to the larger dispersal of power relations across the social formation, is to recognise that truth-claims cannot be examined in 'isolation' from the conditions of their negotiation. Despite its authoritarian claim to universality, mastery and control over reality, monologic truth is precariously dependent on maintaining the denial of its lived locatedness in the social hierarchies of time, space and place. A gender-sensitive analysis of news discourse may therefore succeed in deconstructing monologic truth by showing how it is inextricably tied to its Other, the dialogic voices it wants to dominate into silence.

'The order of ordinary life'

It has been my aim over the course of this chapter to contribute to the work of critically investigating the discursive strategies routinely employed by journalists to ascribe to their 'purely factual' accounts an ontological status aligned with truthfulness. More specifically, the discussion has centred around the extent to which these strategies underwrite an (en)gendered exclusivity of both representation and address. As I have sought to argue, in part by drawing upon Bakhtin's writings on the dialogics of truth, it is vitally important to recognise that the professionalised formulation of 'objectivity' as the guiding principle of impartial journalism is an impossible accomplishment. In my view, future attempts to elucidate the ways in which gender relations underpin what I have termed the 'will to facticity' will benefit by reconsidering how news discourse politicises what counts as truth in a given instance, and who has the right to define that truth (or, more to the point, who is recurrently not accorded that definitional power), in dialogical terms. Such an approach destabilises the androcentric imperatives of 'objective' news reporting and, in so doing, re-inscribes a basis for an inversion of their authority.

After all, it is at the actual points where this (monologic) language of 'objective' reporting fails, where its 'universal' precepts are identified as being politically perspectival, that analyses may produce new insights into the social disciplines which enable or inhibit the appropriation of truth-claims. This mode of enquiry, in Bakhtin's terms a 'laying bare of conventions', will affirm that truth is not a *natural* property of a particular discourse, and that facts cannot escape bearing the marks of their producers. Rather, truth is a provisional construction sustained (or not) in and through the 'professional norms' governing what shall be deemed to constitute reality in relation to certain institutionally sanctioned criteria of facticity. Truth-claims presuppose ideological commitments; as such, the grounds for anchoring their legitimacy in 'established fact' are undergoing constant erosion. To distinguish the complex intersection of discourses of 'objectivity' with masculinised relations of power and privilege is to problematise the means by which 'impartial' methods of reporting valorise élitist, patriarchal and racialised renderings of reality as 'mirroring' the 'truth of the matter' ('what really happened'). Such frameworks of interpretation, as argued above, invariably work to delimit women's voices, especially when they are feminist voices, to those which are 'manageable' within the tacit rules of inclusion and exclusion held to be indicative of 'newsworthiness'.

Still, as we have seen, although reportorial 'objectivity' tries to monologise the social world by merging a multiplicity of voices with a single impersonal truth, it is always compromised. Its seemingly detached, 'common sensical' verities are situationally embodied and thus contingent upon what Bakhtin refers to as the 'laws, prohibitions, and restrictions that determine the structure and order of ordinary . . . life' (Bakhtin 1963: 122). This emphasis on the 'unfinalisable eventfulness' of discourse underscores the point that monologic truth never has the 'final word'. Its proclaimed authority is neither universal nor permanent but, rather, is continually at risk and, as such, must be ceaselessly renewed in the face of ongoing threats to its hegemony. Consequently, we cannot expect that a monologic conception of truth will always inform the ideals of journalistic practice, for there is no essential reason why this must be so. Indeed, the end of 'objectivity' as a professional ideal for journalists may be already in sight.[8] From a Bakhtinian vantage point, as demarcated here, its demise is to be positively encouraged. Journalists who claim to possess a privileged access to truth are failing to acknowledge that the codified rules of 'objectivity' are helping to lend justification to iniquitous social arrangements of discursive power.

Now is the time, in my view, to engage with journalistic inflections of 'the order of ordinary life' precisely as they seek to reaffirm the patriarchal boundaries of truth within the limits of 'objectively factual reporting'. In closing, then, I wish to suggest that we take up Bakhtin's challenge to refashion our relationships to truth, to generate radically new ways of hearing the multivoicedness of the social world. Such a commitment to dialogicising the abstract universality of monologic truth-claims may succeed in highlighting the parameters of their authority in ways which disrupt their ideological purchase *vis-à-vis* the projections of 'femininity' and 'masculinity' which they actively reinscribe as 'normal' or 'natural'. To recognise that even the 'purest fact' of news discourse is 'permeated with the interpretations of others' is a crucial strategic advance. As such, it may inform the critical work of creating and sustaining spaces beyond the realm of 'objectivity' for those resistant voices routinely dismissed for being 'too emotionally subjective', and thus 'too biased', to warrant inclusion. The ethical stakes associated with this type of intervention could not be more significant as increasing numbers of female journalists struggle to dialogise the 'macho culture' of the newsroom and the androcentric forms of 'objective' reporting it legitimises in the name of 'truth'.

Notes

1   This very dictum was reaffirmed by BBC foreign correspondent Fergal Keane in the 1997 Huw Weldon Memorial Lecture, broadcast on BBC1 on 20 October 1997. In his words: 'The art of the reporter should more than anything else be a celebration of the truth. . . . The reason millions of people watch and listen is because we place the interests of truth above everything else. Trust is our byword. That is the unalterable principle. It is our heritage and our mission, and I would rather sweep the streets of London than compromise on that. . . . The fundamental obligation of the reporter is to the truth. Start messing with that for any reason and you become the moral accomplices of the secret policemen'.

2   Mikhail Bakhtin was born on 16 November 1895 in Orel, south of Moscow. Several recent biographical accounts have traced important events in his life, such as: his work with Valentin Vološinov, Pavel Medvedev and Ivan Ivanovich Kanaev in the 'Bakhtin Circle' (the precise authorship of several of the resultant texts remains a matter of considerable dispute); his arrest in the Stalinist purge of intellectuals in 1929 (his sentence to a death camp was eventually commuted to six years' internal exile); his years as a political exile in Kazakhstan; his research and teaching in Mordovia where, in 1937, he was forced to resign by the Stalinists; his years spent teaching university students following the Second World War; the belated 'rediscovery' of his writings by other scholars (his work created a 'sensation', especially amongst younger intellectuals, in Russia during the 1960s); and his death in Moscow on 7 March 1975. See Clark and Holquist (1984); Dentith (1995); Gardiner (1992); Holquist (1990); Morson and Emerson (1990).

3   Bakhtin argues, in turn, that the internal dialogism of the word is never 'exhausted' as every word is also directed 'toward an *answer* and cannot escape the profound influence of the answering word that it anticipates' (Bakhtin 1934–5: 280; see also Allan (1994) for a discussion of the chronotopic or time-space dynamics of dialogism). In Lynne Pearce's view, this notion of dialogue 'touches the heart of what it means to be a feminist: a concept evocative of sisterhood, of the perpetual negotiation of sameness and difference, of our dealings with men and patriarchal institutions, of our relationship to a language which simultaneously is, and is not, our own' (Pearce 1994: 100).

4   Elsewhere, I have attempted to trace several aspects of the historical emergence of discourses of 'objectivity' in US newspaper journalism, and those of 'impartiality' in the early days of British news broadcasting, in relation to current debates about the public sphere – see Allan (1997a). See also Bromley and O'Malley (eds) (1997); Corner (1995); Hartley (1996); Hardt and Brennen (eds) (1995); Sebba (1994).

5   Bakhtin identifies two constitutive elements of this monologic conception of truth as follows. The first element is the 'separate thought', by which he means that within monologic discourse 'there exist separate thoughts, assertions, propositions that can

by themselves be true or untrue, depending on their relationship to the subject and independent of the carrier to whom they belong' (Bakhtin 1963: 93). These separate thoughts may be removed from their context and still retain their respective 'semantic meaning in an impersonal form'. They are, in effect, 'no-person's thoughts', for they are 'faithful to the referential world' to such a degree that their truth-status is detached from the social relations of their articulation. The second feature of monologic truth is rendered distinct by the means by which these separate thoughts 'gravitate' toward a larger combination. This 'system of thoughts' is typified by a unity of a referential order, that is, 'thought comes into contact with thought and one thought is bound up with another on referential grounds' (1963: 93). The monologic perception of truth is thus systemic in its claim to represent the world accurately. In other words, the truthfulness (or not) of a given discourse is to be determined on the basis of this system of thoughts, as opposed to measuring it in relation to the status of the voice who claims to speak it.

6   This systemic under-representation of women as news actors and as expert sources (as well as their limited appearance as reporters) needs to be contextualised in relation to the patterns of discrimination they encounter across the (mutually determining) 'public' and 'private' spheres. When women's voices are actualised in news accounts, as Patricia Holland (1987: 138–9) points out, they are routinely presented 'either as an anonymous example of uninformed public opinion, as housewife, consumer, neighbour, or as mother, sister, wife of the man in the news, or as victim – of crime, disaster, political policy. Thus not only do they speak less frequently, but they tend to speak as passive reactors and witnesses to public events rather than as participants in those events' (Holland 1987: 138–9). See also Kidd-Hewitt and Osborne (1995); Rakow and Kranich (1991); Sanders (1993).

7   'Objectivity', Mercedes Lynn de Uriarte contends, 'has long been white and largely remains so today' (Uriarte 1997: 144). This point is echoed by John Phillip Santos, who writes: 'The long-hallowed cult of journalistic "objectivity" has too often been a veneer for what is essentially a predominating white male point of view in our news culture'. In his view, the 'overarching challenge is to rid our journalism of any vestige of an "us and them" attitude, of an unspoken regard of any community or group as "others" ' (Santos 1997: 123). See also Campbell (1995); Cottle (1993); Jordan and Weedon (1995); Swenson (1995); van Loon (1997).

8   New questions thus arise as to how journalistic discourses of truth will be transformed should the ideal of 'objectivity' eventually be displaced from its current position of dominance. See also John Hartley's discussion of 'post-truth journalism', where he argues: 'Clearly quite a bit of journalism is post-truth; many stories are lies, and we have 'tabloid' and 'trash' news media that glory in them. . . . This type of journalism . . . doesn't refer to an external world beyond the intertextual semiosphere of contemporary symbolic culture, nor does it invoke a reality which takes precedence over its narrative renditions' (Hartley 1996: 201–2). On the related issues of 'infotainment' and 'tabloidisation' as they pertain to 'reality-based' televisual programming, see also Branston (1993); Dahlgren and Sparks (eds) (1992); Fiske (1987); McGuigan (1992); Sholle (1993).

Part II

THE GENDERED
REALITIES OF NEWS

INTRODUCTION

Debates over the question of how journalists construct the 'world out there' for their audiences need to be recast, as several of the contributions to the previous section's discussion suggested, so as to bring to the fore the problem of how this discursive power is (en)gendered. That is to say, these debates take on a new resonance once we enquire into the issue of precisely who possesses the means to make their definition of the 'reality' of gender relations prevail over alternative definitions. It is a commitment to elaborating upon this complex issue with respect to specific instances of reportage which forms a unifying thread throughout the chapters presented in this section of the book. Each chapter adopts a different conceptual and methodological approach to investigate the means by which gender relations are caught up in ideological struggles over definitional ascendancy. Analyses range from examinations of how these gendered realities are embedded at the level of newswork practices, to their re-inscription as 'common sense' in news narratives, and to their negotiation by listeners, readers or viewers. Overall, then, these chapters share the aim of discerning the often subtle, taken-for-granted strategies in and through which journalists, knowingly or not, routinely define 'what counts as reality' in alignment with patriarchal renderings of the social world.

This exploration of the gendered realities of journalism begins with Linda Steiner's chapter, 'Newsroom accounts of power at work'. Using autobiographies as her primary research resource, she examines the lives of several British and US women who worked for 'mainstream' commercial newspapers in the early and mid-twentieth century. Of particular interest to Steiner are power dynamics in the newsroom, especially questions concerning who is allowed to write about various issues, whose interests are taken seriously, whose ways of doing things have been accepted, and who has the authority to make judgements. Her research finds that women in this period were torn between their identities and loyalties as women, and as professional journalists. More specifically, she argues, their autobiographies address a central paradox: these women were deviant if they refused to uphold definitions of 'femininity' at work, but they were marginalised if they allowed themselves to be treated as 'feminine'. A major issue which Steiner unravels is the rôle of the 'women's beat', for, as she points out, women feared that such an assignment would ghettoise them and undermine their journalistic authority.

The need to extend a historical engagement with the gendered realities of journalism is similarly addressed by Patricia Bradley in her chapter, 'Mass communication and the shaping of US feminism'. She argues that the Second Wave of feminism was largely made possible by the attention it received from mass communication channels, and yet this attention was a 'double-edged sword' in the US context. While the media dispersed the feminist message across a wide spectrum of venues, they also shaped feminism in ways that weakened the possibility that it would become a lever for radical change. She contends that feminism found a place on the media agenda because of a confluence of influences, including new legal opportunities offered by the Federal Communications Commission and the Equal Employment Opportunity Commission. She also appraises the rôle of certain activist women who, being knowledgeable about the media, shaped feminist messages in ways to attract their attention. In considering a range of different wings within the women's movement, she shows how journalistic processes served to lend approval to the inclusive, traditionally liberal vision of that wing represented by Gloria Steinem at the expense of other views. The belief that media attention was necessary for the success of the movement, she argues, dealt a blow to the construction of feminism as a political force.

The issue of how discourses of 'masculinity' are inflected in and through news representations is centred for analysis in ' "Mad cows and Englishmen": Gender implications of news reporting on the British beef crisis', a chapter co-authored by Rod Brookes and Beverley Holbrook. Their study begins with the British Government's public admission in March 1996 that 'mad cow disease' (Bovine Spongiform Encephalopathy, or BSE) could be transmitted to humans through beef consumption. They proceed to document how the subsequent newspaper coverage framed the crisis as a debate between the perspective that a major health problem had been created by 'unnatural' farming methods and exacerbated by political cover-ups, and the view that dismissed public concern as hysteria which could threaten to destroy the British beef industry. They argue that discourses on both sides of the debate were gendered to a significant extent, a thesis they elaborate upon in relation to evidence drawn from the coverage: specifically, modes of address which define women as 'housewives'; the characterisation of public concern as hysteria; the alignment of male actors with scientific authority; and the association of beef consumption with 'masculinity'.

Jenny Kitzinger's chapter, 'The gender-politics of news production: Silenced voices and false memories', analyses the gender-politics which operate in the organisation and practice of media reporting. In particular, it focuses on reporting about 'false memory syndrome' – a condition supposed to affect adults recalling memories of childhood abuse. Kitzinger demonstrates how coverage of 'false memory syndrome' was shaped by anti-feminism, male power and class influence (within both source and news organisations). She also explores the ways in which the reporting was informed by more subtle processes such as the selective privileging of 'masculine' over 'feminine' discourses and 'ways of knowing' (logic versus emotion, science versus intuition), asymmetrical judgements about men's and women's emotions and credibility (e.g. through the notion of 'hysteria') and the gendered operation of formats and genres ('hard' versus 'soft' news). In combination, these gendered elements illustrate the interplay between dominant cultural values, source strategies and the relations between and within source and news organisations. She then concludes by arguing that attention to these gender-politics will help to refine, and sometimes to challenge, existing theories about news production and the operation of different media formats.

This type of agenda is addressed from a complementary perspective in the chapter which immediately follows. Paula Skidmore's 'Gender and the agenda: News reporting of child sexual abuse' examines the 'gender factors' in the production of news about this most sensitive of issues. Drawing, in part, upon findings derived from research carried out in Britain between 1992 and 1995, she assesses the extent to which there is evidence of a gender orientation in journalism. Of particular concern in this discussion is the concept of a 'male' news product (see also van Zoonen 1994). Skidmore argues that it is important to address the idea of news as gendered, particularly given that these processes have been almost completely overlooked in mainstream sociological studies of journalism. Taking as her principal point of focus media coverage of child sex abuse, she suggests that male journalists and editors have a problem in addressing this issue, and that they are reluctant to bring such stories into the news arena. Placing her findings within the context of wider debates about women in journalism and the informal discrimination they experience, Skidmore underscores several reasons why the theoretical category of gender needs to be used with great care in critiques of news reportage.

Several related insights into these gendered processes of reporting are made by Cynthia Carter in her chapter, 'When the extraordinary becomes ordinary: Everyday news of sexual violence'. Focusing on the British tabloid press, she argues that the ways in which male sexual violence against women and girls is being reported on a day-to-day basis is helping to normalise certain preferred ways of understanding such incidents for the reader. In order to address the everydayness of these representations, she presents the findings of a quantitative content analysis of 840 news accounts published over a two-month period. By setting this evidence in relation to police statistics, Carter is able to show, for example, that the news values employed by journalists covering such crimes lead to a disproportionate emphasis being placed on certain types of incidents, such as murder and rape, at the expense of other types, such as domestic violence. Underpinning this dynamic is a related emphasis on those incidents where the male attacker is a stranger to the victim, as opposed to someone she knows (although, interestingly, to a lesser extent than other studies have indicated). Overall, her analysis suggests that there are certain gendered patterns in this coverage which may be, in turn, encouraging readers to consider male sexual violence to be an ordinary, even inevitable feature of everyday life.

A further illustration of the gendering of news coverage of violence is provided by Maggie Wykes in her chapter, 'A family affair: The press, sex and the Wests'. Her case study of a particularly horrific British 'news story' begins in early 1994 when police discovered the bound-and-gagged bodies of several young women. They had been buried in the garden and basement of the home of Fred and Rosemary West in Gloucester, England, dubbed by the media as the 'house of horrors'. In court, Rosemary West pleaded not guilty. She blamed the rape, torture and killing of the dead girls on her husband Fred – but the prosecution claimed that she was a 'willing partner in murder' (*Daily Telegraph* 7 October 1995), and journalists agreed. Wykes proceeds to analyse newspaper coverage of the West trial, seeking as she does to explain and evaluate the press accounts in relation to broader issues of gender, representation and power. In showing how important aspects of the story of the West family were never fully explored, she points out: 'It is hard to see Rose as a victim of the violent abuse of masculine and commercial power, but easy to see her as a scapegoat'.

Finally, the volume draws to a close with C. Kay Weaver's chapter, '*Crimewatch UK*: Keeping women off the streets'. Centring for attention the televisual programme *Crimewatch UK*'s reconstruction of a sexual assault and murder of a young woman hitchhiker, Weaver explicates its representations through a combination of textual and reception research. Drawing upon textual analysis, she demonstrates how the programme's 'public service' warning against hitch-hiking encourages a critical reading of the murder victim. It also illustrates how voyeuristic material entirely superfluous to the crime investigation is included in the report. Weaver's reception study comprised ninety-one women of varying class and ethnic backgrounds, half of whom had experienced acts of male physical violence. As she reports, it found an almost overwhelming acceptance of *Crimewatch*'s warning to women against hitchhiking. Many respondents applauded how this message was dramatised in the reconstruction, though some did question how the crime victim was portrayed. Weaver thus argues that by encouraging women to fear crime and censor their activities accordingly, *Crimewatch* helps to reinforce the powers of gendered hegemony.

8

NEWSROOM ACCOUNTS OF POWER AT WORK

Linda Steiner

Introduction

Some of the oldest clichés circulating in journalism mythology refer to the power of the press. Notions about such power typically rest on assumptions about the impact of messages on people and public opinion. Since media content is thereby said to influence institutions, ideas and places, research into news usually begins with content. Entire research agendas center on how or when news coverage affects public opinion or policy, and who or what is reported as being powerful or powerless. What these projects ignore is how news stories are selected and organized, and whose definitions of power are in effect. Studies of news sources show how people or organizations outside the newsroom manage more and less successfully to manipulate journalistic decisions. Nonetheless, this gives insufficient attention to how journalists, with what experiences and acting by what processes, produce the news. What is proposed here is a study of the work lives of journalists – by examining the conditions and circumstances in which they produce news, with particular attention to how these conditions and circumstances are gendered. This chapter offers some general methodological, philosophical and historical speculations on behalf of that programmatic agenda. These claims are backed up with evidence grounded in autobiographical descriptions from several women who worked for newspapers in Britain and the USA in the early and mid-twentieth century.

The point here is not to produce 'bottom-up' history for its own sake, or to empower otherwise literally and ideologically powerless journalists to rediscover their past and the implications of gender. Rather, the goal is to understand journalists' encounters with worksite power, including both the power to construct people as engendered and to ignore gender dynamics. Since so many experiences turn out to be highly gendered, and given that historical trends usually have different impacts on men and women, when does gender matter in the newsroom? Do reporters' perceptions enter into their work, for example, in their definitions of newsworthiness, choice of assignments, approaches to sources, or ethical decision-making? What have been the power relations operating in the production of newswork? Who has helped whom? Who provided encouragement and mentoring? What are the consequences of working with stubborn colleagues or dictatorial editors? What about sexual harassment in the newsroom? Or being underpaid, or underappreciated, or underutilized? Or being positioned as the token woman on staff?

Implications of objectivity and professionalism

At least two lines of reasoning may explain the resistance to investigating the work experiences of journalists, especially in relation to gender. The first follows from that well-known philosophical (or ideological) development in journalism, the notion of objectivity. Newspapers' concern for objectivity emerged in the late nineteenth century in the context of growing emphases on technology and scientific expertise, as well as from commercial motives.[1] As the profit possibilities of newspaper publishing became increasingly apparent and attractive, newspapers required objectivity on the part of employees. Wanting to attract more advertisers, and therefore reluctant to alienate subscribers, newspaper management insisted that their practitioners were objective and scientific.

According to the standards of objectivity, journalists' professional and personal experiences are irrelevant. Their histories do not enter into their work. Their identities do not matter. Supposedly, journalists transcend the limitations – the peculiarities of angle – that contaminate everyone else. Although the notion that even the best-intentioned professionally-trained journalists can achieve objectivity has been intellectually discredited, it continues to hold popular sway. The celebration of objectivity as a standard for newswriting forces reporters to erase themselves from their stories, distance themselves from their subjects, and proclaim their attempts to adopt a consistent stance of transparent neutrality.

Other newsroom trends contributed to the disempowerment of reporters, including the increasingly hierarchical and bureaucratic nature of the newsroom. Technological innovations made journalists' work even more standardized and mechanized, albeit specialized. Through the early twentieth century, 'reporters continued to be a replaceable cog in the machinery of the modern newspaper' (Salcetti 1995: 73). Solomon (1995) describes the emergence of vertical and horizontal levels of editors, as well as copy editors, who rewrote to produce conformity to the discipline. One of the several tasks absorbed by these layers of bureaucracy was that of facilitating an erasure of the self in the interests of standardization.

Likewise, while professionalism enhanced collective status and offered political cover to groups (as abstractions), it decentered the individual. Bledstein (1978), among others, shows that at the same time that the culture of middle-class professionalism bred submission and passivity in the public (i.e. among clients), its vertical rationality elevated structures and institutions at the expense of the individual, including the individual professional. Bylined or not, the

146

neutral, dispassionate reporter was merely a transmitter of facts, and no longer an active, creative agent. As many reporters noted in books about their careers, the emergence of professionalism did not bring significant improvements in working conditions, compared to the period when journalism was considered a trade or craft. Reporters still endured long hours at low wages. That is, although they were intended to protect the press as an institution, the much-vaunted conventions for objectivity, professionalism and routines of bureaucracy disempowered individual reporters.

The insistence that reporters' identities and experiences can be made irrelevant, and that good reporters manage to be transparent and neutral, changed the standards for all journalists, but these developments had particular implications for women. The demand for disembodied objectivity immediately butted up against the notion that women are inherently embodied. Feminist philosophers have noted that modern political and moral theories depend on a dichotomy between reason and desire, between rationality and emotion (see Young 1990: 92–113). Epistemological subjectivity implies someone's capacity to act as an independent, disinterested impartial observer. This stance, or standard, has been couched in universalized terms, but it effectively involves 'being male and having a male body.' 'The subjectivity attributed to women is not convertible into objectivity, and therefore does not bring with it the attribute of rationality' (Hodge 1988: 166). The alignment of the political, the rational and the public with maleness – and the corollary assignment of the female body to the private, domestic realm – have consequences not merely in philosophy, but in a number of social, political and cultural practices, including writing. According to the prevailing mythology, women are peculiarly unable to transcend their bodies or their personal involvement with others. Therefore, they simply cannot write their way out of their bodies the way that men can (Russ 1983). Clearly, then, this works 'powerfully' in journalism, which is itself a particularly public form and public forum, even more so when its cornerstone is objectivity.[2]

Meanwhile, methodological problems that at some level are connected to objectivity hinder scholarly attempts to investigate how journalists experienced these dramatic changes in their professional practices. As a consequence of attempts to appear 'objective' – especially once content gets filtered through bureaucratically organized gatekeepers – journalists' responses to the conditions of work can no longer be read off from their published work. They have been edited out, if they were ever drafted. Therefore, even the most careful, nuanced readings of articles in commercial newspapers provide no insights into the conflicts and arguments that journalists later describe autobiographically. Reporters have occasionally admitted – or proclaimed – that they have resisted attempts to enforce conformity, and even subverted the system. In 1988, for example, A. Kent MacDougall, a journalism educator who had worked for such bastions of objectivity as the *Wall Street Journal*, announced that for years he had sneaked Marxism into his articles.[3] His former editors vociferously denied that this occurred, adding that editorial processes prevent such attempts. In any event, such a claim is rare. The larger issue is that reporters' political views and their views of the workplace, especially of the institutional workings of power, and the entire editing process itself are covered over well before articles get into print.[4] The product delivered to the front door or newsstand reveals nothing about arguments over assignments, about stories not assigned or not published. Articles are critiqued and altered by many people before publication. Thus, for all the concern with the power of the press, how power works in the newsroom is hidden.

As Brennan (1995) and Hardt (1995) point out, event-oriented communication historians rarely address the conditions of production of artifacts and have failed to problematize the writing process. Media historians equate the labor of media workers, especially journalists, with the media and therefore treat media institutions as representations of media workers. As a result, biographies of journalists – and it is primarily famous ones who rate biographical treatment – celebrate media institutions rather than reflect on editorial processes. Hypothetically, similar suspicions may lurk behind scholars' dismissal of autobiography as a resource for studying power relations in the newsroom. That is, the criticism may be that autobiographies are not necessarily statistically representative of the labor force, that the autobiographers are atypical individuals or are typical only to some unknown extent, and that, in any case, individual stories cannot form the bases for research. The solution, however, is to contextualize these narratives systematically, rather than dismiss them as scientifically irrelevant (Maynes 1992). 'Focusing on life stories does not entail a retreat into methodological individualism or a return to great-man history', as Maynes (1992: 534) explains. Defending narratives that are orally told to someone else, who in turn writes the story, Geiger comments that the accusation that life histories are not representative 'assumes we already have knowledge about the culture in general against which individuals can be evaluated' (Geiger 1986: 337). Of course, as Geiger notes, precisely because traditional social scientists have often failed to consider women's experiences, statistical methods have produced invalid claims.

Fidelity is a second issue. The ways that authors manipulate the events of their lives are covered over in self-narratives, just as the convention-laden selection and organization of events are covered over in news narratives.[5] Ideally, if one followed LaCapra's (1985) call to treat texts as 'events' posing complex problems in interpretation, the social, ideological and rhetorical dimensions of documents themselves would be examined. At a minimum, in order to avoid taking each assertion as true – and to avoid the sentimentality of biography – students of autobiography must check for patterns in what these autobiographers said about themselves, their colleagues and their work, and put all of this in context, that is, by checking this against other available historical data. As it turns out, media historians appear quite willing to accept the autobiographical claims of reporters, who have, after all, often introduced their stories by promising to be honest. Autobiographers do acknowledge that they are constrained by considerations of taste. When writing news stories, reporters use mental scissors to anticipate the responses of their editors. Analogously, in drafting their lives, writers anticipate the concerns of publishing company editors, who in turn are thinking about readers, critics, librarians and so on. In any case, since evidence of self-censorship may itself point to something important, different accounts of events and different accounts of causality should be compared, rather than ignored altogether. Indeed, investigating which women had the toughest time getting their autobiographies published says much about 'powerful' conceptions about gender as well as assumptions about what readers will find plausible and interesting. The assumptions dictating what authors can publish (i.e. what publishing executives find acceptable) are equally powerful and gendered.[6]

No documentary resource is without liabilities. With their problems recognized and taken seriously, however, the 'self-writings' of journalists offer insights, particularly regarding gender politics, not available through other documents. Volumes of memoir, autobiography and personal recollection provide a necessary and important entrée into reporters' relationships with their editors, colleagues, sources, advertisers, mentors, readers. This is not to romanticize the individual or over-dramatize a single author's role in writing news. The extent to which news production is bureaucratic, or at least collaborative, cannot be overestimated. Therefore, studying a single life story, including that of a presumably powerful publisher or editor, provides only anecdotes about newsroom dynamics and gender politics. When the genre is treated collectively, however, autobiographies offer more persuasive testimony about stories changed in anticipation of criticism, stories altered by superiors, stories written but then not submitted, stories investigated but then not written, stories suggested but then not investigated, stories stolen by jealous colleagues. Because, conveniently, the storehouse of journalist autobiographies is huge, and growing, histories of power in/and newsrooms need not rely exclusively on accounts of well-known journalists.[7] Not 'everyone' writes or publishes an autobiography, but famous people have never retained a monopoly on the genre.

Returning briefly to the implications of objectivity, one might speculate about why only a handful of journalists published autobiographies in the nineteenth century. Yet, in the USA, about fifty journalists published autobiographical books between 1900 and 1934, and in the next decade twice that many. Wolseley (1943) says journalists' newly-won professionalism and celebrity-status explain these dramatic increases. A contrasting argument is available: precisely that disempowerment and the disappearance of personal and partisan writing in favor of the information mode encouraged reporters to look to autobiography and memoir as a forum for telling their own stories – including their stories at and of work. Carey (1969) shows how this 'descent into professionalism' among journalists produced a downward conversion. As the conventions and routines of objectivity became codified, the self that increasingly had to be suppressed in newswriting surfaced in autobiography.

Sex and gender in autobiography

If, as autobiographies show, all press workers had to struggle with questions of identity, women were compelled to work extra hard to prove that they could achieve the same degree of tough-minded disembodiedness as men. Simultaneously, they resisted the prevailing but patronizing notion that they had some special dispensation to insert themselves into their stories. Women journalists do not all say the same thing, and inconsistency across their books is undeniable. The authors varied in their degree of bitterness over their treatment in the newsroom. Some were resigned to, while others were even casual about sexism. Nonetheless, women have used autobiography in specific ways, among them to tell their stories as women, to women, about women's powerlessness. What these women journalists vehemently insisted is that they were always and inevitably engaged in a struggle to be treated – by editors and colleagues inside the newsroom as well as by sources and readers outside the newsroom – as professionals. Men insisted on defining women in terms of sex. Ironically, men not only required women to act as females but then punished them for it. A consistent complaint articulated in autobiographies written by women working for mainstream British and US newspapers in the first half of the twentieth century was the difficulty, if not impossibility, of facing down this central paradox: women who refused to be specifically feminine at work were treated as deviant, while women who allowed themselves to be treated as feminine were marginalized. Thus, the most unyielding barrier to success – and otherwise women's terms for success were not unlike men's – was men's power to position them as female.

This double bind has plagued women in a variety of professions. Within journalism, the assumption that femininity is inherently incompatible with authority has produced highly worrisome difficulties for female broadcasters and newsreaders. As Holland notes in an essay included in the aptly-named *Boxed In*: 'Women newsreaders are called on to speak from a carefully constructed position, with the mythical neutrality of the universal voice, and yet, as women, they are defined as outside both the political consensus and the masculine structure of language' (Holland 1987: 148). Print reporters' struggles to achieve professionalism are less consistently and obviously marked than those of broadcasters. Writers are not quite so compelled publicly to walk a narrow tightrope by 'doing' their hair, make-up and clothing 'just right.' (On the other hand, women who worked as foreign correspondents in the mid-century dramatize much more clearly the point of anthropologist Pierre Bourdieu and philosopher Michel Foucault about the body as a practical site of social control.) Nonetheless, print reporters' autobiographies also testify to their conscious attempts to resist gender disciplining already early in the century. Without using the word 'power', the women describing their journalism careers in the 1920s, 1930s and 1940s were very explicit about gender/sex as a site of ongoing struggle.

According to literary scholars, female autobiographers are reluctant to acknowledge any interest in power, ambition or participation in the public sphere. Jelinek (1980) asserts that women's autobiographies de-emphasize the public aspects of their lives, concentrating instead on domestic details, family difficulties, close friends and people who influenced them.[8] She finds that even women famous as professionals refer only obliquely to their careers: 'This emphasis by women on the personal, especially on other people, rather than on their work life, their professional success, or their connectedness to current political or intellectual history clearly contradicts the established criterion about the content of autonomy' (Jelinek 1980: 10).

This pattern is born out in the autobiography of Mary Stott, a British journalist who expressed outrage when someone called her a career woman: 'My work was as much me as being a mother. Being a mother was as much me as being a journalist. I could not have split myself in half' (Stott 1989: 58). Consistent with the literature that predicts that women will define themselves relationally, Stott described herself as 'mutilated' by the death of her husband, an editor for the *News Chronicle* in Manchester, and she pointed to her chapter on widowhood as her most important piece of writing (1989: 7). Aware that her anecdotes might seem to fly in the face of the 'Women's Liberation' movement that she otherwise advocated, Stott mixed a slight embarrassed ruefulness with a stubborn pride in recalling how she and other 'high-powered' women journalists attending a 1971 international meeting spent their time exchanging snapshots of their grandchildren.

The opposite seems true of most women journalists' autobiographies, however. Most of them ruthlessly excised references to their personal or romantic life. Even the married ones said remarkably little about domesticity. Notably, after mentioning a happy marriage and her love for her garden, pets and two sons, the 1944 autobiography of Marie Manning, better known to readers of her advice column as 'Beatrice Fairfax', essentially ignored her home-making period. The implication is that only her journalism experiences would matter to readers or interest them. Stott never named her husband. Florence Kelly, who worked for literally dozens of newspapers across the USA, sermonized extensively on sundry topics, such as the value of college education (Kelly 1939). But her 571-page narrative said nothing about marriage, either in general or her own. Kelly skipped over the death of her first son and only occasionally mentioned her second 'boykin.' Although she listed the many times she followed her husband, also a journalist, from job to job, she allotted one sentence to her husband's death. Nearly all women have been remarkably self-effacing and modest in their autobiographies.[9] At the same time, their autobiographies have focused on ambition and the issues that have interfered with their ability to pursue their careers. They wrote the stories of their lives in the way that men typically have, by concentrating on their work.

Notably, women paid little attention to the sexual tensions in the newsroom. There are a few complaints about sexist incidents involving sources and colleagues. Elizabeth Jordan, who worked for New York newspapers in the early 1900s, recalled several unpleasant experiences, including 'horribly degrading' winks and passes. She said: 'There was a period when I was wretched over them – when I felt that they not only smirched me but that, in a way, I might be responsible for them' (Jordan 1938: 128). Apparently, she stopped blaming herself when she realized that a friend, an editor then in her sixties, endured the same thing. Nonetheless, it has been much more common – well into the 1970s and 1980s – for women journalists to present flirtations or romantic encounters with newsroom colleagues as unproblematic, if they mentioned them at all.[10] Jordan and many other prominent women reporters never married, but a notably large percentage of the married women married fellow journalists.[11]

These narratives emphasize the formidable barriers women have faced in establishing a serious (especially as opposed to a gender-specific) foothold in the newsroom. Those who somehow connived their way into interviews were treated to patronizing sermons by editors on why women cannot succeed in the rough-and-tumble business of the newsroom. If they were hired, they were sidetracked into a single 'beat' reserved for 'the woman' because it was created to attract female readers. Women who managed to achieve higher status and higher profile reporting beats constantly had to defend themselves, to prove themselves, to fight for their professional identity and equal pay. These aspects are fairly predictable. What is interesting is how women made sense of this, how they responded to it, and how they described how such experiences entered their work.

The women's angle

The extent to which the question of the women's angle tends to dominate the lives of women journalists is seen in the life of Mary Stott, who began working as a reporter at the *Leicester Mail* in 1925, when she was seventeen years old. She explained:

> Perhaps I might have made a good hard news reporter if I had been given time, but I wasn't. I was only nineteen when a new editor called me to his room and broke my heart by telling me I was to take over the women's page. I scarcely exaggerate. It *was* a heartbreak, for I thought my chance of becoming a 'real journalist' was finished.
>
> (Stott 1989: 50)

Stott then rationalized the assignment: the women's page turned out to suit her.

Stott made her way to an organization publishing the *Co-operative News* and other organs serving working-class families, women and children. Once she was able to delegate the women's side to others, she enjoyed the job more and more. In 1942 she was denied the position of editor at the *Co-operative News*, although the previous editor told her she would have been appointed had she worn trousers. This time Stott assuaged her bitterness by reminding herself that this was just as well, since she was pregnant. When she again found herself chafing, and since it was 'intolerable' to consider more 'women's work', she got a job as news sub-editor on the *Manchester Evening News*. According to Stott, she got the job both because many qualified men were still serving in the military and because her editor was 'totally devoid of sex prejudice' (Stott 1989: 58). But she attributed her success in Manchester to her mastery of jobs men assumed were beyond women's abilities. She handled 'every kind of story except, thankfully, the most gruesome murders' (1989: 60).

The next time she was denied a promotion because of sexism, she was less willing to rationalize: 'To help to teach boys their job and have them jumped over you to a position where they have to give you instructions is not tolerable' (Stott 1989: 63). After one more unsuccessful attempt to 'escape' women's journalism, she apparently resigned herself to the women's pages. In 1957, she became 'the virtual, though not titular', editor of the women's pages at the *Guardian*. She proudly called her section a 'midwife' to some real reforms, institutions and organizations that helped women. The pages provided a community of interest for readers. Ironically, Stott, who was writing her autobiography in the midst of a women's movement in which she was a participant and leader, expressed considerable dismay that male colleagues took control of the women's section after she retired in 1971. Again expressing both self-deprecation and a feminist consciousness of power at play, she commented: 'Whether or not there was an intention to limit my autonomy it is the fact that I let authority drift out of my hands. I am not a battling woman and very conscious that a battling woman is likely to incur more hostility than a battling man' (1989: 79). She added: 'I felt miserably guilty that I had done so little to fight against the current trend towards appointing men to run women's pages and magazines. I, the lifelong feminist and liberationist!' (1989: 82).[12]

These gender issues are also illustrated in the chronologically-earlier story of US journalist Marie Manning, who in 1898 began writing a column providing common-sense advice to the lovelorn. Manning (1875–1945) said she 'stumbled into the newspaper game' when she met *New York World* editor Arthur Brisbane at a dinner party. Having revered journalists and with her head 'full of the new idea of careers for women', the twenty-year old Manning immediately accepted his invitation to come to New York for an interview. After she scooped colleagues with an interview with ex-President Grover Cleveland, Joseph Pulitzer gave her a $50 bonus and shifted her from space rates to the payroll. In 1897 she followed Brisbane over to Hearst's *New York Evening Journal*. There, along with two other women, she dutifully helped put out the women's page.

Not allowed to have desks in that 'inviolate masculine stronghold', the city room, the three women were consigned to an area known as the Hen Coop. 'It was an amiable little Victorian world that we young women viewed from the Hen Coop, with its treacly sweet interviews given by ladies bent on impressing the public with their domestic urges. Everyone was afraid of stirring up something unpopular. "Home" was a tag women wanted to have attached to their skirts, even if they keep the back-door key in their pockets', Manning said (1944: 28). Male reporters appeared in the Coop only when they were being punished: 'Forcing a man to work in the same room with us was the equivalent of sending a dog to the pound or standing a child in the corner' (1944: 126).

One day Manning's editor brought over some letters from readers, including a frantic mother abandoned by her husband and a suicidal girl forsaken by her lover. Manning proposed a confessional department 'promising unbiased opinions and friendly advice.' Soon the 'Letters from the Lovelorn' column was receiving sacks of mail and 'circulation zoomed like an ascending airplane' (1944: 36). Manning's real satisfaction came from general reporting assignments, but she and the other women had to exercise considerable ingenuity to 'horn in' on interesting assignments: 'The only course open to us to get away from our chores was to invoke that abracadabra, "the Woman's Angle" ' (1944: 71). Manning expressed particularly acute embarrassment when a sister reporter asked a Russian sniper who had earned the Order of Lenin whether she had been wearing make-up while killing over 300 enemies (1944: 219). Yet, Manning acknowledged that journalistic success required a certain kind of subversive collaboration with female subjects. Manning explained: 'As for Mrs. [William Jennings] Bryan, she was a graduate in law, and probably a suffragist. Did this make it easier to interview her than if she were brainless? You could never tell. But I understood perfectly, of course, the silly questions they expected me to ask her' (1944: 80).

Writing about the women's suffrage movement required an additional measure of craft and craftiness on Manning's part. If the paper's big shots did not simply discard even well-written articles about suffragists, they reduced such stories to a sentence. Finally, Manning and O'Hagen realized that the 'masculine hierarchy' found women's suffrage newsworthy when stories included references to in-fighting at meetings. Henceforth, she not only looked for fights, but invented them. 'Doubtless these innocent prevarications never got the movement very far', said Manning, who also published two novels, 'but it helped to keep our spirits up in the Hen Coop, and it mightily amused those splendid old high priestesses of the movement' (1944: 157).

In 1905 Manning married a real estate dealer and moved to Washington, DC. She did not indicate whether she wanted to retire from journalism. She merely said that Washington had few writing folk, and women were restricted to society work. She published fiction in *Harper's Monthly*, and during the First World War she often freelanced for Brisbane. Otherwise, she apparently devoted herself to domesticity for nearly a quarter-century. But Manning begged Brisbane for a job after the 1929 stock-market crash. Brisbane reassigned her to the Beatrice Fairfax column, then carried by 200 newspapers. In a chapter called 'It Seems that at Last Women are Becoming People', Manning said: 'Those two ancient pious frauds, "the woman's angle" and the "teary bit" have mercifully gone into the discard' (1944: 227). The claim may have been premature. Manning, who helped found the Woman's National Press Club, was herself assigned the women's angle for the Hearst-owned International News Service.

Irene Kuhn (1899–1995) expressed less bitterness than Manning about having to ask people silly questions as a way to keep her job. Assigned by the *Syracuse (N.Y.) Herald* editor to ask men whether they wore belts or suspenders (braces), she said: 'I was so enthralled by the importance of being a reporter, so enraptured with the idea that at last I was part of the sacred machinery which found things out first and then told the public dependent upon us for its news, that it never occurred to me to criticize the question for its impertinence' (Kuhn 1938: 100). Kuhn was unapologetic in her 1938 autobiography about how she often manipulated her appearance or used feminine wiles to win a scoop. Given her commitment to journalism, she would apparently have done anything for a good story.

Upon moving up to the newly-founded *New York News*, Kuhn offered a somewhat different reason for not challenging her editor's 'preoccupation with the mid-section of the human anatomy.' She rather casually attributed his concern with sex to the fact that male journalists had lived with death during the war, but now were seizing on life, 'and life meant women and women meant sex' (Kuhn 1938: 73). She was somewhat less tolerant, however, about editors' refusal to assign tough gang stories to women. She was allowed only to deal with 'ladies of virtue, easy and otherwise.' Not surprisingly, she was very unhappy, but self-mocking, when her editor fired her as part of a reduction in staff.

Kuhn worked briefly in Paris for the *Chicago Tribune*, became a reporter for an English-language paper in Shanghai, and then worked for the International News Service in Honolulu. She continued to work through pregnancy and her daughter's birth. Work became even more important after the death of her journalist-husband. In 1926, Irene Kuhn returned with her daughter to New York, where she remained, working for three different papers, except for a brief interlude back with the *Honolulu Star-Bulletin* and two years in Hollywood writing scripts.[13] She voiced few complaints, although at one point she commented that men rarely prefer independent women to ones whose 'helplessness cozens his vanity and makes him seem like a big protecting male' (Kuhn 1938: 409).

Conflicting identities

Female journalists virtually echoed one another in describing conflicts between their identities as reporters and their sensibilities as woman. They wanted to be recognized, respected and rewarded as journalists, but their sense of membership in a female sorority was perceived to undermine professionalism. Elizabeth Banks, who was probably the first woman journalist to publish an autobiography (it appeared in 1902), admitted that her early experiences as a society reporter brought her in contact with a number of snobbish women who treated her quite badly: 'Honesty compels me to say that during those first few months of my journalistic career there were not very many kind hands stretched out to me by the members of my own sex' (Banks 1902: 13). She contrasted the 'thoughtlessness of the womankind' with the kindness of the men who helped her carry out her duties as society editor.

Later, however, Banks described her inner turmoil when an anguished actress, after pouring out her woes to Banks during an interview, suddenly announced that she had confided in Banks as a woman. Banks was to publish nothing about their conversation. Banks first replied: 'I am a working woman, with a hard struggle before me. When my editor tells me to do a thing I have no choice but to obey. The world is very hard on women. I'm sorry for you' (1902: 48). But the actress convinced Banks that no woman should help send another to ruin in a world that was already so hard on woman. 'Promise that you will never for the sake of your own success tread on another woman and try to crush her', the actress said (Banks 1902: 50). Banks reluctantly agreed. Appalled, the editor told Banks: 'As you are a woman, I will say that you have not the journalistic instinct. You will never be able to do big things in journalism. . . . The fact is, you're all woman and no journalist' (Banks 1902: 51). Soon after, Banks went to England, where she did her best work, freelancing for the *London Referee* and other papers, usually under the pen names of 'Enid' or 'Mary Mortimer Maxwell.' Banks investigated the conditions of women in a variety of low-status, low-wage jobs, including maid, flower girl at Piccadilly Circus, laundry worker and dressmaker's apprentice. Each series was based on her own stint on the job, undertaken on false pretenses. For example, in 1894 she assumed the guise of an American heiress trying to buy a pedigree; her series for the *St. James Gazette*, exposing how rich Americans paid aristocrats huge sums of money to present them at Court, led Queen Victoria to rule that only ambassadors could make such introductions.

Ethical dilemmas were not always occasioned by loyalties to women. According to Banks, her editor once assigned her to interview an important diplomat, telling her, 'you are absolutely feminine and . . . haven't got newspaper woman and "interviewer" placarded all over you' (1902: 249). Whether because of Banks' femininity or because the diplomat knew her personally, he spilled some secrets whose publication would allegedly have damaged US interests. Again, Banks agonized: 'Should she govern her womanhood and her honor by her journalistic instinct, or should she govern that journalistic instinct by that honor and that womanhood?' (1902: 256). Ultimately, Banks decided he had talked to her *as a woman*, not a reporter. This time Banks lied, telling her editor that the diplomat had refused to say anything.

Usually it was dealing with another woman as a woman that precipitated the agonizing. Many journalist-autobiographers recalled being asked to withhold either information or an entire story, in order to protect someone, often a woman the journalist construed as already victimized. Again, they all expressed some conflict over this – because they knew that acting as a woman required a certain sacrifice to their personal sense of professionalism and to their public reputation. For journalists, news is about people in power or about public life and institutions; so the audiences that count are powerful people. Therefore, women tried not to be sidetracked in their writing. In particular, women resisted getting derailed as female by avoiding writing for the women's pages. They insisted on this, even though there was also the sense that their personal disparagement of women's pages entailed a contradictory and even troubling distancing of themselves from their 'sex', as Banks and others often put it. Likewise, usually, but not always, women wanted to put their 'human' sympathy for subjects above journalistic sensibility. Yet, they knew that they did so at the risk of undermining their reputation as hard-boiled. A likely consequence of any compromise of journalistic ruthlessness would be that they would betray their femaleness and would be permanently excluded from the masculine realm of hard news.

Women working for mainstream media have not argued for any particular power (re)arrangement in the newsroom, nor does this chapter. Without actually confirming this by research, journalists have long assumed that just as every ship needs its captain, every newsroom needs its editor-in-chief. Even efforts among feminist and alternative media to abandon hierarchical divisions of labor and to minimize status differences have failed in the long run.[14] On the other hand, as newsroom staffs continue to diversify in terms of race, ethnicity, gender and sexual orientation, it seems likely that the distribution of newsroom control will be modified and perhaps even democratized. This is more than a question of critical mass. Energy and emotional space are needed for any experiments with alternative approaches to power and control. Meanwhile, the issue here is consideration of how the very structures and conventions that journalists believe insulate them from bias – including their mental and discursive strategies for dealing with gender – end up producing distortion.

If anything, these autobiographies demonstrate the idea of feminist-standpoint theorists that people forced into an acute awareness of their marginal status, develop insights into the mental habits and behaviors of the dominant class as well as a sensitivity to the problems of being located in a secondary class. Not that these women were globally oppressed. After all, the women working for British and US periodicals in the twentieth century have been white and middle class. They enjoyed all sorts of advantages, including solid educations and friends in high places. Certainly these women, *as reporters*, rejected not only essentialist theories of womanhood but also exceptionalist views of themselves. They do not present themselves as extraordinary. But if these autobiographies do not bespeak a consistently prominent concern for suffering people, they do describe an ongoing struggle over the negotiation of power and especially inequalities of power.

The question for women, then, is whether or how they can exercise their commitment to their profession. Their references to a struggle to define themselves reflect what Fiske (1993) usefully calls local power, as a 'bottom-up' process, as opposed to imperializing power. These women were not trying to

157

extend their authority, but to control their immediate context and conditions. Even this, however, involved never-ending struggle. Indeed, sustaining this process of resisting, complaining and protecting their own locale and self-definition was exhausting.

Women described serious and disquieting ambivalence. On the one hand were their loyalties to women and their own sense of virtue. On the other were their identities as reporters and their obligations to a career in which sympathy and sensitivity were disadvantageous. The autobiographers explicitly and passionately described these contradictions, which caused them no small amount of anxiety and brought them no small amount of trouble. They sensed that these contradictions would always plague them. Meanwhile, maleness was not an issue for men. Men rarely, if ever, understood how women resented men's lack of self-consciousness about gender. Even those women who were not literally consigned to the Hen Coop, as Manning was, chafed at men's assertion that 'real newspapermen' did not choose between professional sensibility and gender sensibility. The point was, according to these women, that men never needed to choose, because men had already defined journalism in male terms. No wonder that men, as males, could be comfortable with their work and their male identities.

As their own autobiographies attest, men also complained about journalists' working conditions. Novels set in the newsroom written by male (and female) journalists likewise depict the dehumanization of newsworkers and commodification of their labor. Indeed, journalists' novels, as Brennan (1995) describes them, provide more devastating critiques of newsworkers' oppression and victimization than do their autobiographies. In contrast to the grim tone of the novels set in early and mid-twentieth century newsrooms, the dominant theme of the autobiographies studied here was hearty confidence in 'the Power of the Press.' They celebrated the newsroom as a site of glamour and meaningfulness. Women were proud to be a part, albeit a ghettoized one, of an institution that could expose wrong-doing and inspire reform. Nonetheless, they recognized how being required to write as females would inevitably, and powerfully, marginalize them. By these accounts, then, women's ambivalence over their recognition that practical journalism excluded idealism and that serious journalism excluded women's journalism, affected their work. Their stories thereby raise important questions, still to be addressed, about the enervating effects of power battles and the constraints on women who try to resist or subvert prevailing definitions of news, of womanhood or femininity, and of women newsworkers. They suggest what kinds of power women are up against when they try to negotiate their own definitions and self-definitions.

Notes

1   See Carey (1969), Schiller (1981), and Schudson (1978). For an excellent account of the history of the demand for objectivity in the US newsroom and the demand for impartiality in the British broadcast studio that puts both in the context of literature

on the public sphere, see Allan (1997a).

2 The larger debate between those who highlight women's ability to be just as rational as men and those who argue that emotion and desire ought to be incorporated into standards of what is logical and reasonable is beyond the scope of this paper. The point here is that men in power in sites such as the newsroom have made decisions for and about women on the basis of an assumption that women were constitutionally unable to meet male standards for rationality.

3 See MacDougall (1988). MacDougall, the son of Curtis MacDougall, who himself was a famous reporter and journalism educator, also worked for the *Los Angeles Times*.

4 With stories created, edited and immediately sent to the print all on the computer, lasting evidence of alterations is lost, thus making research into such processes increasingly difficult.

5 Good (1993) and others who adopt psychological perspectives on autobiography claim they can discern these unconscious processes at work.

6 Conversely, the autobiographies of women forced out of journalism also reveal crucial features of the newsroom's division of labor and distribution of power (Steiner 1997b).

7 For autobiographies by US women journalists in the first half of the twentieth century, see Steiner (1997a).

8 Maynes (1995) finds that class makes as much difference as gender, in terms of an autobiographer's willingness to defy conventions of the genre.

9 This modesty is consistent across the fifty autobiographies I have studied, and is clear even among the most prominent women in journalism. For example, one US reporter who won a Pulitzer Prize for her Korean war reportage emphasized how she overcame her lack of natural talent by working extra hard, but she also credited luck (Higgins 1955). Perhaps the exception that proves the rule is Alice Allison Dunnigan's 673-page boastful account of her achievements and successes as the Washington DC correspondent for a press-association serving African-American newspapers (Dunnigan 1974). A very recent and extreme example of this tradition of self-effacing modesty is Katharine Graham's discussion of her journalism career and then her stewardship of the *Washington Post* (1997).

10 The problems may be so common that they became naturalized and thus unseen – or 'unremarkable.' Perhaps some defining event or special moment is required to make sexual harassment observable. One notes that under five percent of women journalists surveyed in the late 1980s answered that they had experienced sexual harassment in the workplace. Just a couple of years later, in the wake of law professor Anita Hill's allegations that she had been sexually harassed by Supreme Court nominee Clarence Thomas, new data suggested that some two-thirds of US women journalists had been harassed.

11 Of the dozen successful women of 'bygone bylines' Belford studied (beginning with Margaret Fuller, born in 1810), few had happy marriages (Belford 1986: 6).

12 Men have been reluctant to edit the women's sections of newspapers, but until the 1980s, it was common for men to monopolize the top positions at women's magazines.

13 Shortly after her autobiography appeared, she began working for the Mutual Broadcasting Company; she continued to write after retiring from broadcasting in 1950.

14 Organizational structures in broadcast and print newsrooms are significantly understudied, so the potential for making a difference by subverting hierarchy *per se* is unclear. For a historical overview of feminist experiments with different ways of producing and financing media, see Steiner (1992). For specific contemporary examples, see accounts in Allen *et al.* (1996).

9

MASS COMMUNICATION AND THE SHAPING OF US FEMINISM

Patricia Bradley

Introduction

On 26 August 1970, after having just marched down Fifth Avenue in the 'Women's Strike for Equality', the advertising executive Midge Kovacs sat down to watch the television coverage:

> That evening, seated in front of the television set, switching dials to catch the news coverage of the march on all three networks, I received my first taste of media distortion of the women's rights movement. Cameras moved in for tight shots of stringy haired, bra-less women in T-shirts, with angry signs. With my own eyes, I had seen a cross-section of women at the march, including establishment types, career women and many older citizens. But none of these women were represented that evening on TV.
>
> (Kovacs 1972: 73)

Kovacs' response was not surprising. As two early chroniclers of the movement noted, 'Rage would not be too strong a word to describe the emotion felt by large numbers of feminists about the media's coverage of the women's movement' (Hole and Levine 1971: 266).

What is interesting about feminist fury at the news coverage of the re-emergence of feminism in the late 1960s and 1970s is that it did not stop feminists from seeking the attention of the US news media. Betty Friedan, in her first report to the National Organization for Women (NOW), noted, 'Unlike most women's organizations and official spokeswomen, we are not timid about taking our case to the nation through the mass media' (Friedan 1976: 98). News coverage was also sought by at least some part of the women's radical left, particularly the group Women's International Terrorist Conspiracy from Hell, better known as WITCH, which mounted 'actions' solely designed to attract media attention. While both camps were equally enraged by the news coverage

160

afforded their actions, it did not lead to a feminist re-examination of media strategy. Instead, feminists turned to the reform of the US news institution itself. Even as feminists were attempting to use the channels of mass media to spread the feminist message, the reform of news media became a prime objective of feminism's rebirth.

Media representation and political change

Women and media have been an ongoing subject of feminist study since the benchmark 1978 work of Gaye Tuchman and her colleagues. Tuchman's work set out a research agenda with the same trajectory as the period's media activists, both emerging from the assumption that a change in media representation of women was necessary for the achievement of political change. This remains a prominent line of research in US scholarship (Rhode 1995; Cirkensa 1996), although its corollary — that the representation of women in media will change as women come into positions of media influence — is beginning to be doubted (Creedon 1993: 13). Such a transmission model of media, however, has been rejected by Liesbet van Zoonen, who offers a more complicated cultural studies paradigm (van Zoonen 1994). This chapter also rejects the power of the trans- mission view in favor of what might be considered a factory model. I suggest that feminist activists attempted to intervene in the media process at the last stages of production, as if re-shaping the box or bringing in female line supervisors could, at that stage, make essential differences.

The interest here is to examine the decisions made by feminists in the 1960s and 1970s aimed at advancing feminist causes by way of mass media. These choices included the use of mass media vehicles such as the *Feminine Mystique* and *Ms.* to carry a feminist message, the focus on marches and demonstrations to gain media attention, and the use of newly available legislative levers to bring about increased hiring of women in US media.

These prongs — the continuing use of media and the concomitant call for reform of their employment practices — indicated an ultimate faith in mass media as agents of change in the nation. Not sufficiently recognized were the limitations of mass media imposed by the craft traditions of news, nor the undergirding benefit mass media receive from support of the *status quo*. What was also not recognized was how the feminist message would be adapted — unwittingly encouraged by feminists themselves — by industries that seek stability rather than change.

Recognizably in place by the early twentieth century was the tendency of the mass-communication industries to eliminate systemic challenges by means both direct and subtle. In the early part of the century, the feminist notion of the 'New Woman' was re-framed and diminished by powerful US magazines, the dominant national media of the time. In the *Ladies Home Journal*, for example, the 'New Woman' was transformed into the respectable lower middle-class 'Bachelor Girl' (*LHJ* 1898), a helpful characterization in building a cheap female

labor force. By the 1920s, popular culture had trivialized the female empowerment represented by the New Woman into the childlike and hardly formidable
'Flapper', distorting what had been a new ideological strain into a form that
seemed to represent change but did not challenge traditional power relationships. Moreover, the flapper's preoccupation with clothes and entertainment, as
Martin Pumphrey argues, made her a saleswoman for the new service, leisure
and fashion industries (Pumphrey 1987).

What was revolutionary in the 1960s and 1970s was that feminists tried to
take charge of this process by *targeting* mass media for the dispersal of the feminist message. Because of that effort, second-wave feminism found new
audiences to a much greater extent. Women far from centers of radical thought
were able to connect with the movement simply by turning on a television,
picking up a newspaper, or by reading the easily obtainable *Ms.* magazine. These
connections to feminism by way of mass media led to understandings of feminism along its broadest and least radical lines. It is noteworthy that in his *Rules
for Radicals* (1971), Saul Alinsky emphasized the role of the community orga-
nizer, not mass media, as the strategy for the achievement of social change. This
was a view that could have found support in the communication scholarship of
the period, as researchers discounted media 'magic bullet' theories and
concluded, like Alinsky and others who drew upon the organizing traditions of
labor, religious and political parties, that beliefs change as a result of individual
intervention (Patterson and McClure 1976).

But for a generation who had seen the thunderous events of the civil rights
movement unfold on television, these and other warnings could only be minor
keys. As we have learned from the work of Sara Evans, many of the White feminist activists came to the women's movement after work in civil rights,
including the media-saturated 'freedom summer' of 1964 that was designed to
attract the attention of White media (Evans 1979).

The civil rights movement's affect on the women's movement can also be
considered from the standpoint of television viewers, some of them nascent
feminists, who, without an understanding of the organizational and legal
maneuvers that had gone before, saw the successes of the movement in the
simplified terms of its dramatic television moments. Also less well understood
in the heady times of the movement was the media's construction of civil
rights along lines of mainstream acceptability. As observers now point out, civil
rights as presented in mass media became an either–or case of 'decent but
aggrieved blacks who simply wanted to become a part of the American dream,
or as threats to the very notion of citizenship and nation' (Gray 1997: 350). In
hindsight, we see the same pattern was followed in the media construction of
the women's movement. Angela Davis and the Black Panthers had their feminist
counterparts in Kate Millet and WITCH. These constructions had to do with
the US news value of 'balance', interpreted to mean the presentation of opposites. As in civil rights, the framing of some aspects of feminism as logical
outgrowths of US liberalism gave institutional approval to the negative framing

of everything else. As Susan Douglas has written, 'There is no doubt that the news media of the early 1970s played an absolutely central role in turning feminism into a dirty word and stereotyping the feminist as a hairy-legged, karate-chopping commando with a chip on her shoulder the size of China' (Douglas 1994:165).

The Feminine Mystique and the founding of NOW

The tocsin that put feminism on the mass media agenda was the publication of *The Feminist Mystique* in 1963. The feminist movement of the 1970s may have taken a different direction if Betty Friedan's book had not been published by a well-known New York publisher, W. W. Norton, tempted by the possibility that the book would reach a new audience of suburban women (Brockway 1996). Moreover, the work was promoted by a public relations expert, not a usual practice for the time, who booked Friedan on radio and television interviews (Wilkes 1970: 149). Primarily, however, *The Feminist Mystique* is the perfect example of the accommodation that occurs when new ideas are shaped for a mass-media audience.

We have to acknowledge that Friedan consciously dropped her own radicalism in order to make the book appropriate to a commercial press. Daniel Horowitz has spelled out Friedan's radical roots in the labor press. He asks:

> Why did a woman who had spent so much energy advocating political solutions focus in *The Feminine Mystique* largely on adult education and self-realization and turn social problems into psychological ones? How did a woman who had fought to improve the lives of African Americans, Latinas, and working-class women end up writing a book that saw the problems of America in terms of the lives of affluent, suburban white women?
>
> (Horowitz 1996: 22)

Horowitz' answer is partial – saying that the book emerged in a period when Friedan was seeing herself as a professional writer, although if this were entirely the case, it does not seem likely Friedan would have devoted the rest of her life to feminist causes. However it came about, *The Feminine Mystique* avoided overt radical language and its theoretical base became 'the problem that has no name.' The approach of the book was rooted in the anecdotal style of the mass magazines that Friedan had developed as a contributor. Further, thanks to her magazine experience and her husband's involvement in media, Friedan was knowledgeable about the professional world of agents and marketing, essential in the launching of the book as a mass-media product. The paperback edition became the number one bestseller of 1964 (*Publishers Weekly* 1965: 72).

One of Friedan's appearances promoting *The Feminine Mystique* was on Virginia Graham's syndicated 'Girl Talk' (Graham 1978: 106–8), an early daytime talk show that was among the first to utilize contemporary social themes in an entertainment format. Friedan, however, was not skilled in the presentation of the feminist message in broadcast terms, much less in entertainment values, and her appearance on this and other shows set the stage for the mass media's subsequent framing of American feminism as confrontational. Tania Grossinger, Friedan's public relations' representative, recalled in a 1970 interview, 'There were few stations that asked her back because she was a tough interview. I can remember her confronting Virginia Graham on "Girl Talk" and screaming, "If you don't let me have my way, I'm going to say orgasm ten times" ' (Wilkes 1970: 148).

By the time of the Grossinger interview, Friedan was routinely characterized as humorless and aggressive. Forgotten in the retelling of the 'Girl Talk' episode was the show's concept that promoted confrontation. As Graham described it, her guests were 'people who would never meet in life, never sit next to each other at a dinner party, never glare at each other in contempt or purr silken insults at each other' (Graham 1966: 169). Graham's job was to bring out the opposite points of view in a lively, entertaining way while she took on the conservative stance that made the show acceptable to a spectrum of purchasing stations. Friedan appeared on the program in 1964, three years into the show's run when spark by way of opposites was well established, and was paired with the English comic actress, Hermione Gingold. This was clearly an odd match. Gingold's archness could only magnify Friedan's intensity. From Graham's point of view, however, it was good television. In one of her memoirs, she recalled she was delighted when 'Hermione and Betty went after each other tooth and claw.' Not surprisingly, Graham saw the program in terms of its entertainment value – 'one of our funniest shows' (Graham 1966: 172).

Friedan's interest in media (beyond the marketing of the book) was apparent with the founding in 1966 of the National Organization for Women, established to represent women's issues on a national scale in the US. One of its first organizational meetings was on 'image', when Friedan brought together her friend, the actress Betty Furness (Friedan 1976: 84), the ABC reporter, anchor and documentary producer Marlene Sanders (Sanders and Rock 1988: 117), and one of the few female, high-level public relations experts, Muriel Fox (*Who's Who* 1997: 11,392–3), all of whom would play a role in putting the new organization in the national eye beyond a function of building membership. Friedan warned early on that NOW would use every political tactic available:'We don't even exclude the possible of a mass march on Washington' (Hole and Levine 1971: 87), a telling comment in its implication that media attention was the penultimate political tactic.

The notion that mass media were to be utilized as a lever to achieve political aims was soon demonstrated when NOW attempted to activate the US Equal Employment Opportunity Commission on behalf of women. Seeking to have the EEOC find it illegal for newspapers to segregate 'help wanted' advertisements by gender (Hole and Levine 1971: 82–4), NOW members picketed offending newspapers in a tactic sure to draw local television attention. Early the next year, at a well-attended news conference, Friedan announced NOW was considering a suit against the government. The publicity worked, a Congressional hearing was called, and segregated 'help wanted' advertisements were eventually banned (Friedan 1976: 98–9; Freeman 1975: 75–80).

Encouraged by its first success with the EEOC campaign and by members who were media professionals or who had media experience, few NOW goals did not have a media component. The organizers of the action to call attention to the prohibition of women from the Oak Room of New York's Plaza Hotel, for example, included Dolores Alexander, a *Newsday* reporter and NOW member, as well as the indefatigable Muriel Fox (Cohen 1988: 143).

At the Plaza event, Friedan and her colleagues judged correctly that the hotel's refusal to seat a woman and her party in the male enclave would be newsworthy for it easily met many of the needs of a news story – the location was well-known, there was sufficient visual interest for television, the event was scheduled at a time that was helpful to deadlines, and the occasion promised conflict. From the standpoint of the television medium, it was an easy story to tell; from the feminist perspective, the story represented the kinds of exclusion that faced women in all spheres of life.

For many viewers and readers, however, the story was interpreted as having less to do with the secondary position of women in society than the perception of NOW as an organization of upper-class women concerned with upper-class privilege. While Friedan and NOW focused on the scheduling appetites of the media, they had not recognized the class component of potential TV audiences with little sympathy for women excluded from the Oak Room. At the *New York Post*, quite clear about her constituency, the columnist Harriet Van Horne called the Oak Room episode 'The Feminine Mistake' (Cohen 1988:21).

When Friedan stepped down from the NOW presidency in 1970, it was with the announcement of an event that promised to outdo all others, the 'Women's Strike Day for Equality' march scheduled for August in celebration of the fiftieth anniversary of women's suffrage in the US. Recalling her labor past, Friedan's original aim was a work stoppage to protest wage differentials between men and women:

> The women who are doing menial chores in the office as secretaries put the covers on their typewriters and close their notebooks and the telephone operators unplug their switchboards, the waitresses stop waiting, cleaning women stop cleaning and everyone who is doing a job for which a man would be paid more stop.
>
> (Hole and Levine 1971: 92)

The arrival of *Ms.* magazine

But by 1970, feminism was a coat of many colors and not all factions could agree to Friedan's original purpose. In order to present to the nation an image of a united women's movement, in the mode of the civil-rights marches, the work stoppage aspect of the march was de-emphasized in favor of a march demonstrating the widespread support of three 'demands' – 24-hour child-care centers, abortion on demand, and equal opportunities for women in education and employment.

With 50,000 marchers in New York alone, the event was easily defined as justifying considerable news attention. *The New York Times* gave the march front-page coverage and a banner headline (1970a section 1: 1), although marred by an inside-page sidebar that covered Friedan's trip to the hairdresser (1970b section 1: 30). The television networks similarly covered the marches, selectively, as Kovacs and others would charge, and framed by the observations of male correspondents that served to enrage many women (Douglas 1994: 164–5).

After Friedan stepped down, NOW and its chapters continued their emphasis on media, knowing the value of the news release and the news conference, and mounting then-newsworthy street actions. NOW chapters also provided local spokeswomen, accepted by local media because of the recognizability of the national organization no matter how many members in the local base. While left groups often refused to identify leaders, charging that such identification aped male models of political organization, the willingness of NOW and its chapters to identify spokeswomen served to take to the mass media a particular feminist message that may already have been shaped in some degree – e.g. a street protest – in order to meet the demands of the medium.

The 1970 march clearly placed the women's movement on the news agenda and, in a classic example of consensus reporting, movement stories flooded print and broadcast media. As Jo Freeman noted, 'Within the short space of a few months the movement went from a struggling new idea to a national phenomenon' (Freeman 1975: 150).

The surge of public attention not only swelled the ranks of already-formed organizations but, as women applied feminism to particular situations, encouraged the formation of new feminist groups along lines of careers, religion, race and ethnic identification. Although NOW remained the nation's most recognizable feminist group, women in the early 1970s were coming to feminism largely by such specialized groups (Freeman 1975: 151). The specific focus of these groups, however, made them of less interest to mass media unless the specific goal (less tolerance for pornography, for example) was seen to represent widespread interest (as well as fitting other criteria). Even as feminism was evolving into a multi-pronged movement, the media tended to represent feminism in established, either–or terms. In this context, as they sought to find an acceptable mainstream representative against which to pit the 'bra-burners', media fixed on Gloria Steinem.

As early as June 1969, Steinem was a guest on the National Broadcasting Company's late-night talk program, 'The Tonight Show' (*TV Guide* 1969). She clearly represented the values of commercial television. Classically attractive, humorous not 'strident', and possessed of a confident but not confrontational speaking style, Steinem's emergence as a media celebrity was not surprising. Her aviator glasses, straight hair with a becoming 'streak', and simple tops and jeans provided new packaging of traditional standards of beauty. Further, her look never wavered and left no doubt that it was consciously crafted, which, for a nation long familiar with trademarks and celebrity 'types', indicated safety rather than change.

Steinem's emergence as a national figure, coupled with the media's dispersal of a feminist message that covered feminism in broad ways, suggested an environment ready for a mass-circulation feminist magazine. Like Friedan, Steinem and her most important colleague in what would become *Ms.* magazine, Patricia Carbine (Farrell 1991: 37), were experienced practitioners and had the contacts and expertise to launch the magazine as a commercial venture. They also had a basic faith in the ability of mass media to promote a feminist message.

Yet the magazine was faced with the dilemma of reflecting what was, by 1972, the pluralistic nature of the women's movement while still attracting a mass audience. This was accomplished, in the manner of mass media of the period, by finding the broadest possible bottom line; in the case of *Ms.*, gender alone.

To establish an editorial policy that stressed female inclusiveness, the original choice for the name of the magazine was to be 'Sisters.' In a remarkable and perhaps insufficiently noted decision, 'Sisters' was put aside in favor of 'Ms.', which not only eschewed traditional familial relationships as its model but discarded the centuries'-long tradition of basing courtesy titles for women on their married status. In the premiere issue, however, Steinem's article, 'Sisterhood' emphasized the inclusive nature of the magazine's name rather than its radicalism. The article drew attention to 'deep and personal connections' that women made across 'barriers of age, economics, worldly experience, race, culture – all the barriers that, in male or mixed society, seem so impossible to cross' (Steinem 1983: 114). By 1975, the Steinem vision had not dimmed as she observed a 'contagion of feminism is crossing boundaries of space and language' (Steinem 1975: 45).

In its concern with female universality, there seemed no one who was not included in the pages of *Ms.* Housewives, mothers, feminists who sought radical political solutions, feminists who sought radical social restructuring, women of color, women of varied ethnic groups, and poor women were all gathered under the magazine's single roof. Women were women before they were representatives of a race, class, educational background or a political point of view. Inclusiveness was emphasized by Steinem in her speaking tours, which pointedly included a woman of color. Her support of Kate Millet in a famous news conference in which she held Millet's hand after Millet had been 'charged' with lesbianism by *Time* magazine (Cohen 1988: 232–51) was consistent with Steinem's personal point of view that later translated into *Ms.* policy. Indeed,

Steinem's unswerving commitment to women above all other calls seemed to be represented in her personal life, which, for the public's view throughout this period, did not apparently include male sexual companions. Typical of the *Ms.* approach was the June 1973 special issue, 'Women and Money.' Steinem wrote: 'We have also been used as a source of unpaid or underpaid labor – whether in offices or factories or in their own kitchens – women of all races have suffered not only as cheap labor, but as a means of production.'

Here was an opportunity for a critique of the market system, but Steinem's solution was a call for women to alter their views on money. 'It will be a long road. The first step is believing in ourselves; understanding that we are indeed smart, even if we aren't rich. And the second is giving up the myths of power, so that we can see our economic plight as it really is' (Steinem 1973: 37–8). Other articles supported these themes in the personal, anecdotal style of self-help articles that were familiar to readers of women's magazines.

Feminist radicals dismissed *Ms.* as conservative (Willis 1975: 170–4), but by the standards of the US industry there was nothing conservative about the routine inclusion of lesbian writers and covering women of color, women in poverty and women outside the USA – the first time these groups had been regularly reflected in national US media. What made this new content palatable to a mass medium was that it was presented in ways that were consonant with the strains of US liberalism that believed fairness was primarily accomplished by overcoming prejudicial thinking – another familiar theme to those who had come of age in the civil rights movement. This was a theme that seemingly did not require difficult choices but, rather, was a call to a generosity of spirit, as if the inclusion of what had been previously left out was the correction of an oversight. *Ms.* magazine articulated feminism as a logical extension of American life and culture as the US political movement known as the Progressives had positioned social reform a half century before.

Thus, despite its content, there was a traditional comfort about the magazine – from its layout and use of regular 'departments' to the notion that women composed a 'family' and the magazine was to serve the family of women as previous women's magazines aimed to serve traditional family units. The emphasis on the kinship of women on the basis of gender alone led *Ms.* to support the empowerment of all women in whatever realm – all women who ran for office, the sharing of power among women regardless of talent or efficiency, class action suits on behalf of all women, and support of legislation that was broad in sweep. There was room for the feminist radical left in the *Ms.* spectrum, as in the discussion column 'Forum.' But the column really represented another enlargement of the *Ms.* umbrella. As Amy Farrell noted, the column gave the magazine a claim that 'it could speak not only to those women who had no previous ties to the movement, but also to those who had considerable experience as activists, writers, and organizers' (Farrell 1991: 116).

For *Ms.* critics, this slice of the pie only emphasized the marshy ground of *Ms.* ideology. Ellen Willis, a 'Forum' contributor, broke with the magazine because of its 'mushy, sentimental idea of sisterhood designed to obscure political conflicts between women. Anything a woman says or does in the name of feminism is okay; it is unsisterly to criticize or to judge; disparities of power, economic privilege, political allegiance are politely glossed over' (Willis 1975: 170).

Carol Hanisch, like Willis a member of the early radical cultural feminist group the Redstockings, attacked what she viewed as the liberal bias of the magazine.

> Today the women's liberation movement is in the hands of a group of liberal opportunists, and therefore in the hands of the left liberal male establishment. These women – Ms. magazine, some of the Village Voice writers, and the 'women's lib ladies' in communities all over the country – are scrambling frantically after the few crumbs that men have thrown out when we radicals began to expose the truth and demand some changes.
>
> (Hanisch 1975: 163)

Criticism of Ms. also came from women of color. Feminist scholar bell hooks wrote: 'Divisions will not be eliminated by wishful thinking or romantic reverie about common oppression despite the value of highlighting experiences all women share' (hooks 1984: 44). The poet Adrienne Rich was more critical, viewing Ms. as part of a general societal oppression in which mass media participated: 'For many readers the feminist movement is simply what the mass media say it is, whether on the television screen or in the pages of New Yorker, Psychology Today, Mother Jones, or Ms.' (Rich 1979: 14).

The emphasis by Ms. on the commonality of women's experiences might be considered a print version of the televised mass march in which differences were subsumed to the larger image of universality. By subsuming difference Ms., consciously or not, was covering over the differences that were so easily marginalized by mass media. In the 1970s, when the institutional press and the television networks were at their most influential, any detail was routinely interpreted as a representation of a larger issue. For institutional media, seeking 'balance', the 'stringy-haired, bra-less' demonstrator was the detail used to represent the issue of feminist radicalism. Ms. countered the negative judgments implicit in that use by sweeping up all differences into a larger construct, but was nonetheless still trapped by the overall paradigm. Feminism came to seem huge and monolithic to the outside eye and, still under aegis of balance but on a larger scale, invited the media search for a counterweight. This would turn out to be the political right.

It should be noted that the tendency of mass media to use every story as a representation of a larger judgment – every crime story a reminder of the problem of crime in all society, for example – has not always been the mark of US mass media. As any survey of the penny press of Jacksonian America will attest, the newspapers of the 1830s and 1840s were packed with news stories that were topically varied and had no obvious unifying agenda, appropriate for a society that valued independence. By the end of the century, homogeneity had come to characterize the institutional press. In the 1980s the development of cable narrowcasting and the emergence of specialized magazines marked a shift away from the nineteenth-century emphasis on mass appeal. One explanation for *Ms.'* subsequent financial difficulty is its continuing emphasis on universality at a time when media industries were shifting to segmented markets, a shift to which *Ms.* finally adjusted in 1992 with the adoption of a subscriber-based operation.

Equal opportunities and the news

Debates on media representation encouraged moves to reform the gender aspect of media practices, television news in particular. Originating with the United Church of Christ and carried forward by NOW, efforts were launched to reform television news by the use of governmental levers newly in place. As a result of court decisions in the late 1960s, broadcast stations were required to reflect the concerns of their communities or run the risk of losing their licenses. License challenges were fairly simple to lodge, and community-based feminist organizations, sometimes assisted by national NOW, took on big and small stations (Lewis 1986). The petition against WABC in New York cited demeaning coverage of women's issues, lack of hiring of women in the news-room, and lack of programming reflecting the concerns of women. In Los Angeles, a consortium of women's organizations negotiated a settlement with KNBC on the same basis. Other notable settlements were negotiated in Tennessee, Colorado, Pennsylvania and in other parts of California (Beasley and Gibbons 1993: 243–62).

In the print media, the Equal Employment Opportunity Commission became the lever for women's caucuses inside media organizations. It was because of action from inside the organizations utilizing existing governmental protection that *The New York Times*, the Associated Press, *The Washington Post*, *The Philadelphia Inquirer* and other press organizations agreed to widen the opportunities for women journalists and other women in their news organiza-tions. The revolt began in an unlikely place. A group of women conducted an eleven-hour sit-in at the *Ladies Home Journal*, calling for more women in posi-tions of power and providing a mock-up of what the preferred *Ladies Home Journal* should look like, including stories on abortion (Beasley and Gibbons 1993: 210).

But even with the FCC and EEOC on the side of feminism, and a changing cultural climate, the industry response was minimal. At the *Ladies Home Journal*, for example, a former *McCall's* editor, Margaret Cousins, was brought out of retirement to be fiction editor (Bradley 1995). Newspapers that had showcased the civil rights movement were nonetheless grudging about making change for women. The nation's most important newspaper, *The New York Times*, fought the women's EEOC suit for years, and even when it was settled in the women's favor, refused to acknowledge wrongdoing. The women involved in the *Times* suit found their careers shortchanged while the women who had not joined the suit were rewarded (Robertson 1992). The AP and the *Detroit News* suits did not get settled until 1983. The EEOC found *The Washington Post* practiced gender discrimination and, as in other organizations, was required to set up an affirmative action hiring program. These agreements all needed close monitoring (Beasley and Gibbons 1993: 235–41).

The threat of the license challenge brought local television leaders to the table fairly quickly, and thus no licenses were revoked (Lewis 1986). Television stations also began to find benefits to the FCC insistence on more women. As Jessica Savitch had illustrated at KYW-TV in Philadelphia, on-air women could help sell the news (Blair 1988: 174). Women employed in US broadcasting increased significantly between 1971 and 1982, from twenty to thirty-four percent (Weaver 1997: 23). Moreover, women's issues could be interpreted several ways, as in consumer news reporting prompted by the recession of the mid-1970s. In short, television stations maintained their licenses and found new ways to increase profits, to say nothing of the benefits of hand-wringing, a practice that further disguised the fact that power relationships had not changed even as women's visibility increased.

The women hired as a result of such actions found it difficult to challenge entrenched news traditions, even if they wished to. While the addition of women reporters may have blunted the edges of overt discriminatory behavior and language, women found if they wanted to succeed they had to utilize traditional career behaviors. Gains made in female employment during the period stabilized by 1982, and today remain at the 1982 level (Weaver 1997: 23).

Feminists who did not share the view that feminism was about the integration of women into mainstream society quickly found themselves outside of the media frame. 'The radicals have been cut off from media', Kathie Sarachild said in an interview in 1973, 'because there are so many more "respectable" feminists around' (Reisig 1975: 169). Some radical women insisted on media attention and came to be the 'bra burners' of collective memory. Influenced by the left's protests at the 1968 Democratic National Convention the week before, the demonstration against the Miss America contest, was sure to get on the news agenda as were subsequent WITCH-sponsored events, including the occasion when white mice were released among hundreds of young women shopping for bridal wear at New York's Madison Square Garden (Hole and Levine 1971: 127–9; Morgan 1992: 21–9).

None of this encouraged discussion of radical feminism, and the media turned to Steinem as the only sensible choice, prompting the radical feminist group, the Redstockings, to call a press conference in 1975:

> Today all the trappings of the radical upsurge remain, but the content
> and style have been watered down. We have reached a point when the

movement must have a revival of the radical ideas and leadership which marked its early growth and success.

(Heilbrun 1995: 287)

But the Redstockings' point was lost in the accompanying implication that Steinem, who had once worked for a CIA front, was still a CIA operative. Although the press conference had been called at a journalistic conference (or perhaps because of it), the subsequent lack of coverage indicated that Steinem and *Ms.* were considered mainstream enough to warrant consensus protection.

Conclusions

What made the women's left pay attention to the mass media even as they criticized mass media as the tool of the master and utilized a substantive underground press (Allen 1989)? Part of the answer may be that women of the left, like many women in mainstream feminism, were also often involved in communications. Further, the women's left became centered in New York, the nation's news capital, which made media an obvious choice for actions by women knowledgeable about media values. And, despite their ongoing fury at the mass media, many of the young women of the feminist left, if judged by their actions, appeared to share as much basic faith in the mass media to change ideology as did the mainstream feminists.

Given the media preference for the Steinem vision of inclusiveness and the ability of the women's movement to attract media attention, it is not surprising that feminists would launch a renewed campaign for the Equal Rights Amendment, the long-sought amendment to the US Constitution to outlaw discrimination on the basis of gender. A critic blamed its failure on a campaign of 'shallow political strategy' conducted in an atmosphere of incoherence (Kramer 1986: 141). Indeed, the ERA was a logical product of mass-media feminism, put out from above in the general expectation that support would emanate from the grassroots once the story was put on the news agenda.

Although one function of news media, as news organizations would agree, is providing forums for discussion, there is no necessary connection between the availability of a forum and the instigation of a political agenda. While the institutional media premise their news processes on the notion that their forums lead to appropriate change, the history of social reform is one in which public calls for change still have to be accompanied by organizational depth. 'It's the detail work, not the great speech, that creates a movement', NOW President Eleanor Smeal commented after an extension for the ERA campaign had been won (MacLean 1979: 38). Nonetheless, as recounted elsewhere (Berry 1986), the ERA failed, and largely because NOW and supporting organizations came late to the focus of detail work.

It might be instructive to compare the rise and decline of US feminism in the 1960s and 1970s to the rise of the far-right during the same period. From the nomination of Barry Goldwater for President in 1964 to the inauguration of Ronald Reagan in January 1981, the far-right made few adjustments to its conservative agenda. At a time when the National Women's Political Caucus was putting its support behind any woman seeking political office, the right made pro-life its litmus test. The far right also eschewed mass media when the price was to soften its positions, instead choosing to build itself through church organizations, think tanks, wealthy contributors, political action committees, and the development of its own powerful media, as today represented by the Christian Broadcasting Network on cable, the metropolitan newspaper, *Washington Times* and influential magazines such as *American Spectator*. Until the development of talk radio, the right produced no popular talk-show guests, no mass magazines, and few celebrity spokespeople. With less interest in popular image or the distribution of its message through popular channels, the right developed political power while retaining a radical agenda that is now not easily ignored by politicians or the US culture industry.

The USA at the millennium is a nation in which traditional power relationships are more firmly entrenched than ever. The media's use of women and non-white workers (whom the audience may assume are close to non-elite roots) gives the appearance that the interests of gender and underclass are being represented, even as they are not. It is only to be reiterated that the US mass communication industries, operating in contexts of craft traditions, audience desire, and profit concerns, can seldom function as agents of activist reform, let alone revolution.

10

'MAD COWS AND ENGLISHMEN'

Gender implications of news reporting on the British beef crisis

Rod Brookes and Beverley Holbrook

Introduction

'Mad cows and Englishmen'[1] was a pun used in a number of headlines on the British 'mad cow disease' crisis of 1996. It was a phrase used mainly, but not exclusively, in the context of stories about British nationalism and/or relations between Britain and Europe following the ensuing European ban on British beef exports.[2] In this chapter, we argue that the phrase could aptly summarise the gendered character of much of the British national press coverage of the crisis. As we will demonstrate, on the one hand, the Labour shadow health minister – Harriet Harman – was characterised in some newspapers as hysterical, as effectively a 'mad cow'. On the other hand, public and political reaction was often represented as an attack on the natural appetites and pleasures of Englishmen, not just in terms of national identity but also masculinity. Overall a significant number of articles covering mad cow disease were addressed to the 'housewife', a mode of address which had characterised earlier news coverage of food health issues (Fowler 1991; Irwin 1995: 53).[3]

In late March 1996 the issue of 'mad cow disease' exploded in the British national press. The first cases of Bovine Spongiform Encephalopathy (BSE) in cattle had been identified in Britain around 1985–6. BSE is a fatal brain-wasting disease for which there is no live diagnostic test – cases only came to light when affected cows began to stagger about and collapse. The disease is similar to scrapie in sheep, and the explanation most generally offered is that BSE was caused by the feeding of rendered sheep carcasses to cattle as animal protein. By 1990, 290 cases a week in Britain were being reported (Irwin 1995: 22). The crisis was extensively reported in the media, which periodically speculated on the possibility of transmission to humans. When on 20 March 1996 the Conservative Government finally admitted that BSE could be passed to humans in the form of a new variant of a known syndrome called Creutzfeldt-Jakob disease (CJD), the extent of coverage was unprecedented. Headlines like 'Mad Cow Can Kill You' were splashed across the front pages (*Daily Mirror* 20 March 1996). At the time of the announcement, ten cases of the new variant of the CJD were now officially recognised as possibly linked to BSE. At the time of writing (August 1997), twenty-one deaths are believed to have been caused by the disease.[4] The nature of the risk of BSE/CJD is such that it is impossible to forecast future mortality rates.

The British press coverage of this crisis was characterised by frequent use of words such as panic, scare and hysteria. In his critical analysis of the 'science-centred' approach to this issue taken by government and official experts, Irwin has argued that according to this view 'continued public concern after scientifically-based reassurances had been given could only be the product of an emotional and badly informed public' (Irwin 1995: 27). Based on textual analysis of national newspaper articles during the week immediately following the Government's announcement, we argue that news representations of the issue were structured around essential gender difference.[5] Our method of analysis assumes that it is possible to identify internally coherent discourses defining themselves as normative and self-evident. In the case of the BSE crisis the key conflict developed between two 'competing discourses' (Lee 1992; for an application of this concept to a different environmental issue, see Coupland and Coupland 1997). On the one hand, a populist environmental-health discourse emerged whose key themes were that a major health problem had been created by 'unnatural' farming methods and had been exasperated by political incompetence and/or cover-ups. On the other hand, an economic-scientific discourse claimed that the panic and hysteria whipped up by sections of the media had caused a collapse in world-wide consumer confidence in British beef. The nation's economy in general and the beef industry in particular were threatened because of the failure of the public to be reassured by experts and scientists (Brookes forthcoming). However both these conflicting accounts were criss-crossed by a discourse demarcating different gender roles across the public and private spheres.

In our analysis of these reports, we identified a number of conventionally stereotypical themes:

- women are addressed as 'housewives' and mothers
- public concern over BSE is depicted as female hysteria
- conversely, male actors in the crisis are aligned with values of authority and reason
- finally, beef consumption is associated with values of masculinity

The argument of this paper broadly follows these themes. First, we examine the portrayal of women as predominantly housewives and mothers, and how this is legitimised through connotations of nature. Second, we discuss the characterisation of consumer panic as female, in particular through the *Sun*'s vilification of shadow Health Secretary Harriet Harman. Third, we argue that male attitudes to eating beef are represented through quite conventional stereotypes of masculinity.

Yet at the very same time as these conventionally stereotypical themes are clearly visible, signs of change, complexity and even crisis can also be discerned within these accounts. While representations of women's views on the crisis are negatively associated with panic and hysteria, they are positively aligned with the protection of natural values. By contrast, the values of authority and reason associated with male experts are by no means unambiguously positive, as the whole beef crisis was represented in a range of accounts as epitomising the decline of public trust in politicians and scientists (Beck 1996).

Women and 'nature'

Throughout much of the news coverage of the crisis, the beef 'consumer' is routinely represented as the 'housewife' (see also Irwin 1995: 53). In this sense, news coverage reflects (and arguably reinforces) the division of labour within the household – in their review of recent studies of gender roles within families, Bell and Valentine conclude that 'despite the changing nature of gender roles and gender relations . . . it is still usually women who shoulder the responsibility of choosing, shopping for, preparing and cooking "proper meals" for the "family"' (Bell and Valentine 1997: 70). Hence in sources quoted in the *Independent*, the collapse of the beef market is linked directly to the action of female consumers. A senior government official is quoted as saying, 'rightly or wrongly, housewives all over Europe are already turning their backs on beef in the shops. We could be looking at meltdown' (*Independent* 22 March 1996). Moreover, it is the female in the household who is depicted as having stopped buying beef. The owner of the Cock steakhouse in London's Smithfield market is quoted as saying 'We get people coming in here for a steak because their wives won't buy beef anymore because they are scared to do so' (*Independent* 21 March 1996).

Fowler (1991) argues that health scares have gender implications. In his analysis of the salmonella-in-eggs and listeria health scares, he has argued that one discursive strategy employed was to 'blame the consumer, more specifically, the housewife' (Fowler 1991: 181, 186–202). BSE is slightly different from either of these in that it is not possible to eliminate the virus through cooking. But there is an assumption in many of the news stories that it is 'mum' who is ultimately responsible for decisions in regard to beef consumption. This is the case in both positive and negative stories about beef. For example, the *Daily Star* of 26 March 1996 reported the government's reassurance about beef in this way: 'Keep beef on your kids' plates, mums were urged yesterday by Health Minister Stephen Dorrell. He assured them:"there is no reason to remove it from the daily diet" '. By contrast, in the human interest stories on victims, references are often made to the wife or mother's role in the onset of BSE. A story of 'The Loving Husband who became a stranger', in the *Daily Mail* (22 March 1996), reports that the wife of the victim felt guilty that 'she might have fed him diseased beef, she now feels only anger'.

Stereotypical examples of the representation of housewife and mother are often legitimised through discourses of *tradition* and *nature*. On 22 March 1996, the *Daily Mirror* led with a story headlined 'I won't eat burgers', about Health Secretary Stephen Dorrell's mother speaking out about burgers and sausages. 'Farmer's daughter Mrs Dorrell said at her Worcester home: "the whole business of feeding animals other animals' entrails is just disgusting. It certainly wasn't done in my day – beef cattle used to be elegant and grazed in meadows" '. This common-sense view of the natural is legitimised in the story by her status as 'farmer's daughter', as someone who knows something about both farming and motherhood. For the *Daily Mirror*, the news value of the story is that her view of food safety contrasts with that of her son the politician: the inference here seems to be that mother knows best.

A small number of articles involve a critique of scientific rationality in a way which parallels feminist critiques of science (Birke 1986; Harding 1986, 1991; Keller and Longino 1996). In the *Guardian*, John Gray assesses CJD as a symptom of nature's rebellion:

> The public health crisis that may result from the link between Creutzfeldt-Jakob Disease in humans has repercussions as profound as those of Chernobyl. . . . It forces us to reconsider the culture of tech-nological *mastery* of nature from earlier ages. . . . Did it not occur to anyone that feeding animal protein to what nature evolved to be a herbivorous species might be dangerous?
>
> (*Guardian* 26 March 1996)

Nature has emerged as a key signified in the coverage of the beef crisis. As the disease originated in cattle through the feeding of the remains of one species to another, the transformation of herbivores into carnivores has been represented as a crime against nature. As Fiddes has noted 'cows do not *naturally* eat meat' (1991: 139, our emphasis).

There is one article in the *Daily Mail* (26 March 1996) which demonstrates how the positive mobilisation of nature in a critique of male rationality and science can be adopted for traditional, conservative values, and it is worth discussing at length. The feature is sub-headed 'a mother writes an open letter to [Health Secretary] Stephen Dorrell about why she can no longer trust farmers, scientists, politicians and civil servants'. The article begins by reinforcing the position that women are primarily responsible for childcare: 'There cannot be a caring mother in the land whose confidence in her ability to feed her children wisely and responsibly has not been shaken to its foundations'. The article then argues that the practices used by farmers, and defended by officials were *unnatural*:

For years those who warned that turning herbivorous cows into cannibals, by feeding them the intestines of other animals, was not just
indecent but dangerous, were branded cranks by the men from the
ministry. Families who insisted on feeding their children an organic
diet based on simple, freshly-cooked food produced in the old-
fashioned way, without recourse to hormones, pesticides, antibiotics or
irradiation, were deemed over-anxious and slightly dotty.

(*Daily Mail* 26 March 1996)

The article then details some of the farming methods. Arguing that it is 'hard
not to interpret these plagues as nature's revenge', the author discusses the fate
of pigs, who 'under traditional farming methods' lived for ten to twelve years,
now survive for three to four. 'Piglets, which are weaned naturally at ten weeks,
are taken from their mother at between three and four weeks to force her back
into season as early as possible'. She compares the time when she 'was a child we
had chicken on special occasions', when 'it was a treat in a way that today's
watery, insipid flesh never can be'. Finally she argues that 'the lesson is that we
squeeze nature at our peril and that we must be less greedy in the demands that
we make of her'.

What this account implies in references to desirable qualities of food –
'simple, freshly cooked food produced in the old-fashioned way' – is a critique
of frozen, processed 'convenience' or exotic food. The celebration of values
around nature and tradition assumes a critique of modern life: it is not explicit,
but presumably a return to tradition also involves a return to traditional forms of
motherhood, especially given the increased domestic labour that 'freshly-
cooked' foods involve.

Mad Harriet, mad cows and the feminisation of panic

Significantly, the two most visible female commentators on the beef crisis both
highlighted the danger to the public health. Sheila McKechnie, the Director of
the Consumer Association, unambiguously stated 'The only way to avoid the
risk of BSE-infected meat is to stop eating beef' (*Guardian* 26 March 1996).
However, more attention was paid by the media to the speeches in Parliament
by the shadow Health Secretary, Harriet Harman, and the response of other
politicians to her remarks. The *Independent* characterised Harriet Harman as the
'champion of the consumer', and further commented:

her voice took on the querulous timbre of the pushy customer
returning goods to a sleepy shop assistant. Why hadn't this been done?
And what about that? Call this a government, she certainly won't be
shopping here again, and nor would her friends. Throughout her
speech Tory Backbenchers showed her the traditional courtesies
displayed by Englishmen of a certain age to women who argue with

them. 'Stupid Cow', shouted Tony Marlow, as Graham Riddick and others guffawed assent.

(*Independent* 26 March 1996)

In support of Harriet Harman, Labour MP Angela Eagle claimed that the BSE business had 'scared every member of the public' to which Mr Dorrell replied 'I prefer the scientific advice of a former Vice-Chancellor of Oxford to that of the honourable lady'. The *Daily Star* reported that Harriet Harman was branded a 'mad cow' by Tony Marlow (26 March 1996). In a *Sun* editorial on an earlier debate, Harriet Harman's speech was described in the following terms:

MAD HARRIET

Harriet Harman proved yet again why she is a liability to Tony Blair.
  She came close to pushing the panic button over Mad Cow Disease, terrifying parents and putting the multi-billion pound beef industry in peril.
  The Government has acted promptly and responsibly. . . . Douglas Hogg says there is as much chance of catching Mad Cow disease as being hit by the rogue Chinese satellite.
  Let's also remember the massive scares over salmonella in eggs and listeria in yoghurt.
  Neither turned out to be serious long-term threats to our health.
  In the absence of any evidence of Government mistakes or cover-ups, Labour could have used this opportunity to offer statesmanlike reassurance.
  Instead, Harriet played politics and stoked our worst fears.
  Her judgement on this, as on so many other issues, was appalling [emphasis in original, here and below unless otherwise stated].

(*Sun* 21 March 1996)

The *Sun* particularly focused their attack on Harriet Harman, seen as repre-senting Labour's position in the beef crisis. What we would like to suggest here is that this approach is to some extent *gendered*. It is not spelt out, but the impli-cation here is that Harriet Harman is herself a mad cow, pressing the panic button and stoking up fears rather than taking 'the states*man*like approach' [our emphasis].
  In the following week, the *Sun* went more on the offensive along the same lines:

HAS THE WORLD GONE MAD? . . .

It's not the cows who are mad. It's us humans.
  Over the past six days, we've put our brains out to grass.

179

> *Hysteria* has taken over from common sense as we contemplate destroying the beef and dairy industry – and four million cattle – because of yet another food scare . . .
>
> *And that's all it is.* A SCARE . . .
>
> The panic which has gripped the British public has been whipped up by those with an axe to grind. LABOUR'S Harriet Harman has behaved disgracefully. She twists public concern into political point-scoring.
>
> In the Commons yesterday she gave another *wild-eyed* performance. She blamed Tory de-regulation. But farming is one of our most regulated, controlled industries.
>
> Has mad Harriet ever spoken to a farmer . . .
>
> So hands off our cows. Eat British beef . . .
>
> And stop talking bullocks.
>
> (*Sun* 26 March 1996)

The *Sun* likes to present itself to its readers as the paper which supports common sense (Pursehouse 1991). In the above editorial, a common-sense assessment of everyday risk is marked out more clearly by defining it in opposition to madness characterised by hysteria.

Of all the possible parties 'mad Harriet' Harman is singled out as the major panic-monger. Concern for BSE is represented as *hysterical*, juxtaposed against the responsible, measured common-sense assessment of risk personified by the (mainly male) government ministers, health officials and experts. It is of course difficult to generalise about the representation of women politicians from one case simply because there are so few of them. But it is worth noting a similar type of representation taken by the *Daily Star* with Edwina Currie. In an editorial (22 March 1996) it pays her a back-handed compliment: 'It's not often Edwina Currie gets anything right. In fact she's often regarded as being as mad as a BSE infected herd'. Other women prominent in the press at the time are also branded by the *Sun* as mad cows. There was speculation that Sarah Ferguson, Duchess of York, had had a facelift: in a *Sun* cartoon, a mad cow stands in a field while two farmers look on, and the caption reads 'Oi call her Fergie, she's on her way out' (*Sun* 26 March 1996).

Throughout the *Sun* coverage, consumer reaction is characterised in terms of panic, hysteria and fear. 'Hysteria' is an interesting word here because of its feminine association with mental illness. Hysteria (which comes from the Greek word for uterus) in the late-nineteenth century was regarded as an illness experienced by women which was related to their reproductive capacity. The symptom of this illness was extreme emotional outbursts, or screaming and crying. Men, of course, did not suffer from this condition. They were the 'voice of authority', and this was seen as the antithesis of hysteria and panic (Ehrenreich and English 1988). Whilst women are no longer treated for hysteria, the public discourse on the beef crisis indicates that the dichotomy still exists between the male expert and the female subject prone to irrational emotions and fears (Harding 1991; Ussher 1991; Keller 1996). There is little evidence of behaviour which could be described as panic-stricken or hysterical; instead what happened was that a considerable number of consumers decided not to buy beef. This appears to be a perfectly rational response given the government's admittance of the link between BSE and CJD and the uncertainty surrounding the actual risk involved in eating beef.

Englishmen at risk

There are two definitions of masculinity operating in this case study, definitions which are heavily inscribed by class. In the first, the gender identity of male experts and politicians is taken for granted and unquestioned. In the case study it is almost exclusively male politicians and experts who are reported as emphasising the low risk from BSE through recourse to science. For example, on the same double spread as the leading article 'Mad Harriet' discussed above, the *Sun* ran an article reporting the views of 'Britain's top medic' Sir Kenneth Calman (the Government's Chief Medical Officer). He was reported as having 'vowed . . . to keep on eating beef', to have 'insisted British beef was safe and that it would be wrong to panic' ('I'll carry on as beef-ore', *Sun* 21 March 1996). A small head-shot appears alongside this story depicting Calman looking over the top of his spectacles, his facial expression appearing to connote neutrality and authority. The views of male critics of government policy, particularly Professor Richard Lacey, are represented, but relegated to the later paragraphs and not accorded the same authority. Underneath this story there was an article by then-Agriculture Minister Douglas Hogg in which he stated 'I am one of the few people who has looked in detail at the evidence of a possible link . . . *I can assure you I have no intention of giving up my traditional British roast beef*' ('Don't give up roast', *Sun* 21 March 1996). Both these articles contrast with the 'Mad Harriet' editorial, juxtaposing the language of panic and fear with that of expertise and reassurance.

The second definition of masculinity is more visible, and this is clearly related to class. In the popular tabloids, particularly in 'soft' news stories, representations of masculinity are made more explicit. Typical is a *Daily Star* cartoon, which shows an apparently 'puny' football fan ordering from a takeaway van, asking for 'a slice of salmon and broccoli quiche', recalling a humorous book popular in the early 1980s, *Real Men Don't Eat Quiche* (see Fiddes 1991: 146).[6] Underneath this cartoon is a story headlined, 'What's the Risk', which emphasises that the risk is minimal. The inference here seems to be that real men can take the risk, that men who do not eat meat are somehow less masculine. This is reinforced in the presentation of vox pops, readers' letters and telephone polls where it is men who are often quoted as being more in favour of beef consumption.

A limited number of stories purport to depict experiences of male journalists, drawing on images of the male culture of national newspaper journalism.

In a commentary in the *Sun*, the assistant editor describes a supposed shopping trip during which he was subjected to the moral indignation of women as he loaded his trolley with beef:

> Women watched open–mouthed as I took it to the checkout. I know what they were thinking, but I didn't care I just have to have it. . . . Any moment I expected a tap on the shoulder from the food police, 'Excuse me Sir that your beef is it. I'll have to ask you to come with me to Vera's Vegan Pantry where anything you consume can be brought up later.'
>
> (*Sun* 27 March 1996)

Hence the journalist's hunger for beef was contrasted with the moral policing by women. A similar type of article appeared in the *Daily Star*, however this time the perceived problem was not women but Europe. Underneath a photograph of the journalist aggressively brandishing a knife and fork over a huge steak, the copy read:

LET'S KEEP IT ALL JUST FOR OURSELVES

> BRITISH beef is just fang-tastic
> If that bunch of Brit-bashers at the European Commission want to ban our beef, that's their loss.
> It means there will be all the more of that traditional flavoursome flesh for US!
> That's me above, tucking into a sizzling 40oz prime steak yesterday. And I'm still here to tell you: Our Best of British is forking wonderful stuff.
> At the Cock Tavern, in London's Smithfield Meat Market, they boast 'The only mad cows here are the ones who work here'. . . .
> 'Aren't you worried?' I asked one bloke 'Pass the mustard please', he said.
>
> (*Daily Star* 28 March 1996)

Smithfield Meat Market had an almost mythical status throughout the beef crisis. An article in the *Independent* describes how butchers in Smithfield eye up a passing woman while cutting up the carcass of a gutted pig: 'Lovely Legs' observes Reg, a 'shopman' (butcher to you and me) as he cleaves expertly through the hindquarters of a gutted pig.

> 'Not much meat on them' adds Stan (a bummaree or porter) . . . trundling a ton of carcasses past Reg's chopping block.
> The Cockney eyes of the butcher and porter are not studying the limbs of a slaughtered porker; they are following those of an early

morning miniskirted secretary.

Honed to aerobic perfection in a City gym, perhaps those secretarial legs might well look good, sprigged with rosemary and teased with butter on a Cannibals Sunday lunch table [sic]; yet in shopman and bummarees eyes [sic] they are hardly a patch on their brawny thews and haunches to be seen trussed and spreadeagled in their edible thousands. . . . Mad cow disease or no, Reg, Stan and 1,500 brawny colleagues are connoisseurs of edible flesh.

(*Independent* 30 March 1996)

Fiddes has argued that meat-eating has been culturally associated with male virility: 'the larger and juicier the piece of meat, the more red-blooded and virile the consumer should be supposed to be' (Fiddes 1991: 147). These associations are amplified through the juxtaposition of stories about the beef crisis with representations which connote 'normal' male heterosexual desire, epitomised by the *Sun*'s 'Page Three'. As Holland has noted, 'Page Three condenses within itself the newspaper's view of itself and its audience: it declares how the paper wants to be seen, how it should be appreciated, used and enjoyed' (Holland 1983: 93). During the week of this case study, front-page headlines about mad cows were frequently juxtaposed with images of Pamela Anderson (the pretext being the release of her film *Barb Wire*). Similarly as part of a *Sun* double-page spread on the beef crisis, under a Page-Three style photograph and the headline 'ULRIKA: I STILL LOVE MY SAUSAGE', an article reports that Ulrika Jonsson 'vowed not to give up sausages' (*Sun* 22 March 1996). Mercer has argued that the 'dominant discourse' of the tabloid press is the '*sexualisation* of social life' (Mercer 1986: 56). BSE stories are integrated within this sexualised discourse.

In many of these stories reporting how BSE poses a threat to normal male appetites, the implication seems to be that the main threat of the virus is to masculinity, not to public health. Here, perceived threats to masculinity are mapped onto those of national identity:

> If Brussels has the power to stop Britain from selling a product anywhere in the world, then we are no longer an independent sovereign nation with control over our own affairs.
> We are just one of the herd.
> John Bull has been *neutered*.

(*Sun* 27 March 1996)

It is significant to note that national power and sovereignty are linked by the *Sun* with notions of masculinity. Neutering is used as a metaphor to illustrate the effect of the EU ban on the export of British beef. Britain is portrayed as being powerless in the beef crisis and this is likened to male castration.

Such representations in the *Daily Star* and the *Sun* assume a *fixed*, essential masculinity. By contrast recent social theory has argued that identities are

183

contingent and continually in process (Rutherford 1990; Hall 1992). An example of how masculine identities are inflected by economic, social and cultural change was the phenomenon of the 'new man' in the 1980s (Rutherford 1988). There is one article in the *Daily Mirror* that registers such complexities. On the whole the *Daily Mirror* tends to avoid the stereotypical view of male meat consumption that characterises the *Sun* and the *Daily Star*. But this article represents some celebrity sports 'hard men' almost as 'new men'. Commenting on Ian Botham, the headline is: 'Yes, even beefy is giving up his beef'. Alongside a photograph of Ian Botham eating a beefburger, 'MIGHTY Ian Botham won't be as beefy from now on. The former cricket marvel has hit the stuff for six. And soccer hardman Vinnie Jones has also cried foul and booted beef into touch'. However, Ian Botham's wife is highlighted in the article as being responsible for their family's decision not to eat beef – 'when you are a mother you have to take the problem seriously'. The rest of the article lists the reactions of various male and female celebrities to the crisis, but it is the sports stars, not the television presenters and actors, whose decision not to eat beef is seen as most newsworthy. The final paragraphs of the story include a number of British television celebrities committed to continuing to eat beef: comedians Stan Boardman (who claims to eat 'steak four times a week'), Jim Bowen (who refers to himself as a 'steak and chips man') and Bernard Manning, soap star Jonny Briggs (Mike Baldwin in ITV's soap opera *Coronation Street*), and turkey magnate Bernard Matthews. What is interesting about these is that they represent a more traditional form of masculinity which in these instances is explicitly of (mainly) northern working-class origin. By contrast, the way in which Botham and Jones are represented in the lead paragraphs challenges the notion that to give up eating beef is somehow less masculine.

Conclusion

In this chapter, we have argued that British press discourse on the BSE/CJD crisis was to some extent gendered, and that this is important in understanding the symbolic resonances of different perspectives on the issue. On the one hand, science-centred perspectives dismissing public concern as panic could be understood in terms of the superiority of rationality and expertise of (male) experts as against the emotionality and hysteria of (female) consumers. On the other hand, as the discussion of the *Daily Mail* demonstrated, this framework can be turned on its head. From this perspective BSE was represented as a predictable outcome of a transgression of nature. Farmers, scientists and officials pursuing scientific and technological progress are depicted as having lost touch with the interests of women and families which are aligned with nature and tradition. Yet these more 'positive' articulations of gender values occur within a framework characterised by essentialist definitions of gender roles. Further, alongside this struggle between competing economic-scientific and environ-mental-health discourses, was a popular cultural discourse around the pleasures of meat-eating which reproduced quite traditional stereotypes of masculinity. In the analysis of the significance of news coverage of conflicting environmental-health and economic-scientific perspectives on the BSE/CJD issue, it is relevant to understand how these discourses intersect with meanings around gender.

Notes

1 The original was 'Mad dogs and Englishmen', a song written by Noel Coward in 1931.
2 Examples of articles include 'Mad cows and Englishmen' *Financial Times* Leader 4 September 1996; 'Mad cows and Englishmen' *European* Leading Article 23 May 1996; John Lloyd 'Mad cows and Englishmen' *New Statesman* 17 May 1996. See also Miller and Reilly (1996).
3 At the time of writing, academic published research on media coverage of food health issues is scarce, but growing. Fowler (1991) devotes two chapters of *Language in the News* to an analysis of the British salmonella-in-eggs and listeria crisis of 1988–9, and discusses the gender implications of this coverage. Miller and Reilly (1995) analyse the incidence of peaks and troughs in the press reports of salmonella-in-eggs and BSE between 1988 and 1994. Kitzinger and Reilly (1997) discuss BSE/CJD alongside two other case studies of risk reporting (human genetics research and 'false memory syndrome'). They argue that the news media tend to cover risk issues as periodic crises which rise and fall, rather than as threats which require substantial long-term coverage.
4 *Guardian* 5 August 1997.
5 The sample, from the week of 20–28 March 1996, consisted of the *Daily Express*, *Daily Mail*, *Daily Mirror*, *Daily Star*, *Daily Telegraph*, *Guardian*, *Independent*, *Sun*, *The Times*.
6 B. Fierstein (1982) *Real Men Don't Eat Quiche*, London: New English Library.

11

THE GENDER-POLITICS OF NEWS PRODUCTION

Silenced voices and false memories

Jenny Kitzinger

Introduction

Newspaper and television news reports are crucial to defining the important issues of the day. The production of this 'news' is not a neutral or 'objective' process. Analysts highlight the way in which media reporting is structurally circumscribed by patterns of ownership in media industries and influenced by 'news values', 'hierarchies of credibility', 'journalistic routines' and dominant cultural assumptions (Golding and Murdock 1991; Hall *et al.* 1978; Schudson 1989; Tuchman 1978c). It has also been pointed out that the contents of press and television news are a product of competition between diverse sources and struggles within media organisations themselves (Ericson *et al.* 1989; Schlesinger 1978; Miller *et al.* 1998). However, the gender-politics of these processes are routinely ignored. Terms such as 'gender', 'feminism' or 'women' (and indeed 'men') are absent from the indexes of many key mainstream texts about source strategies and the operations of news organisations.[1] At the same time this issue has attracted relatively little feminist theorising. With a few exceptions, such as van Zoonen, feminist academics have tended to focus on 'feminine' genres such as soap opera or magazines. In addition, the most influential feminist work has examined men and women as *subjects* of representation or as *audiences* rather than as initiators or reporters of media events (Herzog 1941; Press 1991; Radway 1985). This has left an important lacuna in understanding the operation of gender-politics in mass communication processes.

This chapter attempts to contribute toward filling this gap. It does so through analysing media reporting about 'false memory syndrome' – a condition which is supposed to affect adults recalling long-forgotten memories of childhood abuse. The ability of the proponents of 'false memory syndrome' to attract supportive media attention was, I argue, intimately intertwined with gender-politics as these operate between and within pressure groups and news organisations. Gender-politics do not tell the *entire* story, but they are an essen-

186

tial part of it. (For discussion of some of the other relevant elements, see Kitzinger and Reilly 1997).

This chapter shows how coverage of 'false memory syndrome' was shaped by anti-feminism, and by male power and class influence (within both source and news organisations). It also explores how the coverage was informed by more subtle processes such as the selective privileging of 'masculine' over 'feminine' discourses and 'ways of knowing' (logic versus emotion, science versus intu-ition), and asymmetrical judgements about men's and women's emotions and credibility (e.g. through the notion of 'hysteria'). In addition, I examine the gendered operation of formats and genres ('hard' versus 'soft' news). In combi-nation these gendered elements illustrate the interplay between dominant cultural values, source strategies and the relations between and within source and news organisations. I attempt to go beyond simplistic statements about the relative positions of male and female media personnel to provide a detailed an-alysis of how an array of gender-politics operated in one case. I conclude by arguing that gender-politics fundamentally shape the production of news and need to be a central consideration for those studying the media. Attention to these politics will help to refine, and sometimes to challenge, existing theories about news production and the operation of different media formats.

The public profile of 'false memory syndrome'

The following discussion draws on an extensive empirical study of the 'false memory' story as it evolved in Britain during the 1990s. My research involved analysis of three years of British coverage and interviews with fifty-eight key actors both within the media and within source organisations. These included journalists who wrote stories about the issue, the press officers of a range of psychological bodies, relevant psychology experts, and those involved with pressure groups, in particular the British False Memory Society.

The proponents of the concept of 'false memory syndrome' (FMS) argue that it is impossible to repress memories of repeated abuse in childhood, and then to recall them accurately as an adult. People who recover such memories, especially in therapy, may come to believe them to be true, but they are, in fact, false. The whole issue is deeply embedded in debates about how memory oper-ates, and about the practice and regulation of therapy. However, the argument involves much more that this – the conflict reaches beyond the 'science' of memory or professional disputes about training and qualifications to address far more fundamental struggles. Above all the false memory debate is intimately intertwined with gender-politics.

For a start, the false memory debate involves a conflict between 'Fathers' and 'Daughters'. I used these words with capitals to indicate their generic structural status and how men and women are largely positioned within the public discourse about FMS.[2] Over and above this, the proponents of FMS often explicitly criticise the women's liberation movement for having allegedly helped to promote a 'victim culture' and encouraged 'ideologically motivated counselling' (see Brown 1996). Recovering memories is seen as a 'popular craze' and a product of 'sexual hysteria' (Ofshe and Watters 1994) encouraged by a 'misalliance' between feminists and the 'recovered memory movement' (Pendergrast 1995).[3] Feminist critics, on the other hand, have argued that FMS is a misleading formulation which automatically discredits all recovered memories and serves as a smokescreen for abusers (see special issue of *Feminism and Psychology* 1997). Feminists, they point out, have attempted to address 'victim culture', the 'popularising' of sexual abuse as a trivialised catch-all cultural explanation, and have long been concerned to document psychiatric abuses against women and to question the manipulative potential of self-help literature and therapeutic practice (Kitzinger 1992; Kitzinger and Perkins 1993). Many, including several of the pioneers in researching the field of sexual violence, have also questioned the growth of the 'child abuse industry' and the focus on the extremes, such as ritual abuse, at the expense of the 'mundane', such as routine incest (Armstrong 1994). However, these are not the challenges which have attracted the media attention – these feminist positions are not the territory on which the false memory debate has been founded.

The concept of 'false memory syndrome' rapidly shot to public prominence during the mid 1990s. The very first mention in the British media appeared in the *Daily Telegraph* of 17 January 1993. The article referenced the debate already raging in the USA, and continuing British media interest was quickly fuelled by personal accounts from an accused father in England (e.g. 'When a Father Wakes up to his Worst Nightmare' *Sunday Telegraph* 7 March 1993). This media attention facilitated accused parents in contacting each other and mobilising into the British False Memory Society (BFMS) which, in turn, fuelled further reporting.

There are four crucial features of the media reporting worth noting. First, the majority of the coverage unequivocally promoted the idea that 'false memory syndrome' was a real and common problem. Almost six out of every ten newspaper articles in my sample were clearly supportive of the BFMS. Less than one in ten were critical of this position. Even in the remaining items that could not be classified as clearly 'pro' or 'anti', there were often subtle ways in which the perspective of the BFMS was privileged. For example, while the notion of false memories was often presented as a scientific concept, the competing idea that it is possible to recover memories from complete amnesia was presented as merely a cultural invention, a 'trendy' idea, flourishing in societies where '[psycho]analysis is not only fashionable but highly politicised' (*Newsnight* 17 February 1994). This theme was reinforced through visual imagery. Thus *Newsnight*, for example, illustrated its coverage of FMS with the image of a plastic skull, cross-sectioned to expose the brain. The image located the debate 'in the head' – as if this were a debate about the workings of the human mind rather than the workings of society. While the notion of being able to repress and then recover memories was often identified as a cultural inven-

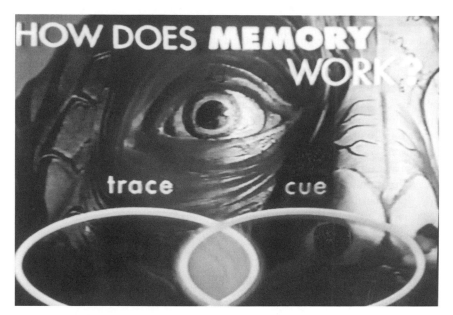

Figure 11.1 A graphic from *Newsnight* coverage of the recovered memory debate – which went on to show the human skull cross-sectioned to expose the brain. Reproduced with kind permission from the BBC.

tion, the notion of false memories was often seen as a purely scientific issue that could be abstracted from all social context.

The second key feature to note about the profile of FMS, is the speed with which the issue attracted media attention. The rapid media response is particularly noticeable if one compares it to other social problems, such as attempts to highlight male violence in the first place. During the 1970s many women's organisations had been working around such issues long before the media became interested (Tierney 1982). By contrast, media attention to FMS was simultaneous and symbiotic with pressure group activity. Media interest rose steadily during 1993, the year that the BFMS was founded and, between 1994 and 1995, there were then a further 125 items about FMS in just three daily and three Sunday papers. The issue was also discussed in chat-shows and documentaries, and was aired on national TV news, including two lengthy discussions on the main BBC news programme *Newsnight* (17 February 1994; 12 January 1995).

The third noteworthy feature of the coverage was the priority given to lay opinion. FMS was not an official psychological diagnosis and there was no major organised professional response to the issue in Britain until 1995.[4] This did not prevent the issue being taken up by the media and much of the early media publicity relied on giving a degree of credibility to lay accounts. Indeed, accused parents were actually more likely to be quoted in the press than professional 'experts' (see Kitzinger and Reilly 1997).

The forth and final point to note about the coverage is the privileging of the

189

voices of those denying abuse (the Fathers) over and above the voices of those recalling abuse (the Daughters). Accused parents were seven times more likely to be quoted than the person recalling the abuse. When the experiences of the Daughters were reported in the press, these were usually based on descriptions by sceptical members of their family who presented them only in order to discredit them. Most strikingly, a leading member of the BFMS has a tape of an answerphone message from his daughter accusing him of abuse. Her angry accusations are played to visiting journalists and the tape has been aired, without her consent, on national television.

How was a small and unofficial organisation able to achieve such remarkable success in defining a new social problem and attracting media attention? Why did journalists seem to disregard their traditional respect for the authority of experts over lay people? How did the Fathers manage to dominate the media coverage – ensuring their own voices were heard, and controlling the voices of their accusers? Male power and broader gender-politics are part of the answer to these questions and I will show how these were reflected both in the strategies adopted by the BFMS and in the media response.

Pressure groups and gendered resources

There were three gender-related factors crucial to the operation of the BFMS as a media source. The first important factor is the gendered nature of the rhetoric surrounding FMS. The terminology of 'false memory syndrome' is itself a good marketing tool. It is a 'catchy' and 'media-friendly' phrase which spotlights and problematises the Daughter's accusation rather than the Father's denials. The use of the term 'syndrome' implies that FMS is a legitimate diagnosis within the medical/psychiatric establishment. It also draws on a long history of psychology dismissing women as suggestible, unstable and prone to hysteria. The addition of one more 'syndrome' to the list of women's peculiarities thus had a plausibility in the context of what the dominant culture already 'knew' about women. The importance of such terminology was recognised early on by parents confronting accusations from their grown-up children. The BFMS was originally called 'Adult Children Accusing Parents', until quickly renaming itself in a way which made it sound more like a learned organisation than a pressure group. In addition, the BFMS constantly allied its perspective with a traditional image of masculine science (hard, objective, providing direct access to truth), and accused opponents of being biased and led by emotion rather than 'facts'. This division inhibited some female psychologists from adopting a high public profile in opposition to the FMS hypothesis. Several commented that it was particularly dangerous for women academics to associate themselves with any position seen as scientifically 'marginal'. They were concerned about being typecast as feminists instead of intellectuals, and damaging promotion prospects.

The second key factor in the success of the BFMS was its practical and social resources. At first glance this pressure group had none of the 'source capital' traditionally associated with influential organisations. This was a small group with no established media contacts and lacking official status or authority. It was not part of journalists' routine beat and had few 'events' to offer as news hooks. By contrast, the professionals who were being challenged by the BFMS had a great deal of status and potential institutional support.

In practice, however, although organisations such as the British Psychological Society were eventually able to use their 'source capital' to challenge the BFMS (see Kitzinger and Reilly 1997) other professional bodies were more reticent. Indeed, some professionals felt gagged, prevented from speaking in a professional capacity. One described her outrage at seeing a client's story totally misrepresented in the press, and the failure of her organisation to support her attempts to challenge this:

> I saw the [newspaper article] and realised it was Jane's case. I couldn't believe it. So we all got together and wrote a letter to the [newspaper] refuting the inaccuracies and giving the true sequence of events. . . . Then I got a call from the press office and one of the Directorate saying the letter could not go off. . . . It was a contentious issue, we had to be careful about attracting publicity. Basically, let's keep our heads down. The other thing they said was you can't write this because of 'confidentiality'. But Jane was saying 'well, I want you to tell my story. Because the story that has been told about me is not true'.

However her organisation would not reconsider its position and this worker concluded:

> If professionals had been allowed to speak the false memory societies wouldn't have got as far as they have with the media. . . . Professional organisations could be so strong. . . . This isn't to say there aren't complications about memory and people who do weird and wacky therapy and all of that. But that's not the argument. The argument here is about whether someone who says they've been sexually abused, when she's defamed, whether that can be responded to. And it can't.

The BFMS had no such institutional processes to inhibit its public declarations. Unlike some of the larger professional institutions, the false memory society was able to respond quickly and effectively to the media and to initiate its own publicity. In fact, although 'resource poor' in traditional terms, the BFMS drew on highly motivated activists and had the support of eminent upper-class and professional allies. The chair of the organisation proved to be an extremely adroit organiser and media spokesman. Described by one accused father as 'the grit that made the pearl' he was seen by both supporters and opponents as: 'a very clever operator', 'a ruthless media manipulator' an...

indefatigable publicist'. The BFMS was also able to draw on accused parents and their friends in order to set up a board of trustees with a wide range of professional experience and contacts. As a representative explained to me:

> The nucleus was accused parents so there was a mother who was accused by her son who herself worked for a charity. There was a solicitor . . . there was a minister [of religion]. . . . There was a peer who'd been accused . . . You name it, we've got it – judges, barristers, solicitors, doctors.

In addition, the BFMS set up a scientific advisory board to advise, and to help give credibility to, the organisation. This board included eight professors (of psychology, psychiatry and psychoanalysis). When I interviewed some of these individuals they emphasised that their motivation for involvement with the BFMS was based on their assessment of the science. They talked about their reservations about the evidential status of repressed memories, concern about the damage done to families and worries about the professional status of psychiatry and psychotherapy. However, one member of the BFMS advisory board also commented on his reactions to the first meeting of the board in the following terms:

> I sat and looked around this table . . . I couldn't help but be struck with what seemed to be the relative ease with which [the BFMS] . . . had gathered this incredibly impressive bunch of academics . . . I think we are very sensitive, males . . . not just me, all of us, I think we're all very sensitive now . . . about the feminist agenda. I can't believe that this assembly of figures of approximately twenty men and one woman isn't something to do with men if you like rushing in to protect their image. . . . I think it's a defensive operation. That is to say recovered memories has as part of its hidden agenda the demonisation of men.

In his view the mobilisation of many eminent professionals in opposition to the 'cult of recovered memories' and in support of the BFMS was also about class identification:

> People who are going into therapy and having these memories after a long interlude are [usually] successful middle class women who of course are the daughters of even more successful, of quite wealthy, [men]. . . . These accused parents . . . these are successful, professional, highly intelligent, well educated, academic people, rather like the eminent professors who sit around [the BFMS] table.

In the event, the scientific advisory board helped to give the BFMS credibility, but it was seldom the deciding factor in attracting media coverage. What proved to be the most important resource of all were the personal accounts of accused parents. The BFMS was acutely aware of the power of such personal stories, not only to provide 'media fodder' but to persuade the journalists of the justice of their case. As a representative of the Society explained: 'with every journalist that comes here we offer to put them in touch with other families and . . . they realise that these are perfectly decent, normal people, and they see that something strange is going on'.

In fact, the personal accounts of accused fathers (and occasionally mothers) were central to the early coverage, and this leads to the third important aspect of the success of the BFMS – the use of emotional, first-person accounts, conveyed through 'soft' outlets. The early coverage of FMS was not predominantly in 'hard news' form. Instead, FMS originally entered the mass media through feature articles, Sunday newspapers, television chat shows, discussion and magazine programmes. These 'soft' formats provided a growing momentum of coverage, leading to increasing interest from the 'hard news' media. The proliferation of such coverage helped to establish the BFMS as a 'key player' in the debate and to force the issue onto the policy agenda. For those critical of the FMS concept it was this 'soft' coverage which was often the most problematic, including some of the coverage on women's pages. One of the very first articles appeared in the right-wing tabloid paper, the *Daily Mail* on 3 March 1993. The headline asked 'Did this man abuse his child?' and declared 'New theories suggest that some women who claim they've been sexually molested by their fathers are, in fact, making it up'. The picture showed a disguised image of an accused father with the caption 'I'm the only one who really knows the truth'. His daughter's knowledge was dismissed as irrelevant. The article was entirely devoted to his challenge to his daughter's perceptions of reality – without any response from her being included. This account ironically appeared on the women's page ('Femail') under the heading 'Femail Testimony'. Clearly *'femail* testimony' can be the antithesis of *'female* testimony'.

The use of 'soft' outlets, formats and styles also highlights an interesting asymmetry in presentations of men's and women's emotions. In their articles and in interviews, journalists routinely referred to men's emotions to signal these men's sincerity. They made comments such as: 'he was so obviously totally bemused and confused' or 'their distress is quite terrible to see'. In one television programme the father himself highlighted the unusual and specific status of men's emotional expressions of distress. He detailed the accusation against him and, expressing his despair, provided his own commentary: 'I've cried and cried and cried, and that, for me, that's an admission I would never have . . . I . . . I can hardly believe I'm saying it' (*Strange Days*, BBC2, 2 June 1996). By contrast, women's expressions of emotion were often used to discredit them. Journalists in interviews (and in their writing) dismissed women's accounts of remembered abuse through descriptions of their 'obvious vulnerability', 'fragility' and 'near hysteria'. This double-standard was highlighted by one woman I interviewed who was extremely angry about the media representation of her case. 'He can use his suicidal thoughts as proof of his innocence' she commented, 'my suicidal thoughts are proof of my guilt'.

The media response

The supportive reporting was partly related to the BFMS's resources and strategies (as outlined above), but it was also related to complementary dynamics within the media at the time. Here I will discuss six issues within the media. These are:

1   The media's 'child abuse fatigue'
2   Capturing the *Zeitgeist* and resisting the matriarchal terror squads
3   Masculine values and newsroom cultures
4   Gendered judgements of source credibility
5   Male-dominated news organisation and gendered identification
6   Legal issues in context

The media's 'child abuse fatigue'

FMS was introduced to the media at a time when media interest in the standard sexual abuse story was waning. Interviews conducted (by Paula Skidmore) for an earlier research project revealed a general feeling among journalists and among press officers that sexual abuse was no longer considered 'news', even as early as 1993 (see Kitzinger and Skidmore 1995). They perceived a declining interest in sexual abuse, pointing to what one reporter called 'child abuse fatigue'[5] (Kitzinger and Skidmore 1995). This 'fatigue' was even more evident a few years later when I was interviewing journalists about FMS. One journalist, interviewed in 1997, commented on the cumulative effect of the media's 'abuse fatigue' on her own efforts to cover the issue:

> It's very hard for a journalist to withstand all the negative stuff – you know, I'm a freelance. I haven't got a million pounds. I earn a modest living . . . I'm extremely judicious about whenever I suggest a child-abuse story . . . because I know that the press are reluctant to take it.

The media's 'fatigue' with sexual abuse was accompanied, according to some journalists, by a desire to challenge old 'established truths' and a feeling that the problem may have been exaggerated. As one journalist pointed out: 'the whole boredom factor on child sexual abuse means that . . . there's a general climate of "let's find out this isn't true" '. A point reinforced by a second journalist who commented that: 'everyone was getting sick with the child-abuse story. They were sick to death of it, every day another celebrity popped up saying they had been abused as a child and people wanted something new'.

The fathers' (and mothers') accounts of being falsely accused were seen to provide a 'new angle' and be a 'hot topic'. Indeed, some journalists saw the story as a new illustration of a growing problem: the threat of political correctness, inappropriate intervention into family life and the power of feminist ideology. FMS was often placed in the context of a history of high-profile events including contested allegations of sexual abuse in Cleveland and Orkney (two notorious cases which resulted in severe criticism of social workers for taking children into care). Some journalists, also used FMS as an illustration of the mood of the times, or *Zeitgeist* – an approach central to the media and of particular importance to column writers.

Capturing the Zeitgeist *and resisting the matriarchal terror squads*

Some of the most uncritically supportive discussions of FMS appeared in columns and commentary sections of newspapers and in television serials such as 'Strange Days', a series of polemical explorations of 'superstitions in the 1990s' (*Strange Days*, BBC2 2 June 1996, Catherine Bennett). FMS was often used to illustrate newspaper or television reporters' general theories about the state of contemporary society. The *Daily Telegraph* informed readers that false memory was a product of a society 'run by vengeful maniacs, who more than condone the explosion of parent abuse in this country' (5 February 1993). In *The Times*, the cultivation of false memories was associated with 'the still blossoming cult of "sexual harassment"' (2 December 1993). The *Sunday Times* 'Comment' section presented FMS as evidence of a 'shift in the collective psyche . . . Stand up the usual suspects: an unstoppable child abuse industry; a feminist agenda that regards all men as bogeymen; a climate in which people are encouraged to see themselves as victims' ('Family Life at risk', *Sunday Times* 17 April 1994). One commentator even declared: 'We live in an age of matriarchal terror squads' and concluded: 'How was it possible, we all asked, for people to watch what was happening in Germany during the 1930s? Open your eyes and look around' ('Memories that surface to destroy us', *Sunday Times* 15 May 1994).

Such articles spell out one perception of the gender-politics of the issue, emphasising the power of 'the child-abuse industry', the 'feminist agenda' and 'matriarchal terror squads'. Other journalists took quite a different view. Some journalists saw false memories as an exaggerated risk, which did not deserve the amount of media attention it received, nor the supportive nature of much of the coverage. Feminist discussions of this sort did occasionally appear, most notably in the *Guardian*. However, journalists who were sceptical about FMS sometimes came into conflict with their newspapers' agenda, the practicalities of news production or the opinions of senior men. It was here that 'newsroom' politics came into play.

Masculine values and newsroom cultures

Some feminist journalists attempted to represent FMS as part of a different type of Zeitgeist involving a male backlash. They were sometimes able to do so, particularly in cases where the journalist was high status or was deliberately permitted 'leeway' because she was employed to add some 'colour' and 'controversy' (see Kitzinger 1996). However, several female journalists described times when senior men discouraged particular approaches to the topic, in ways which the journalists viewed as illogical or discriminatory. For example, some found that their attempts to analyse the BFMS's 'power base' and 'dubious connections' were dismissed as 'simplistic conspiracy theory', others found that prior expertise in the area of sexual abuse could be seen to disqualify them from writing about the issue.

> Whenever I suggest anything on child abuse to my commissioning editor he says the following, 'We don't want [journalists' name] banging on about child abuse, do we?'. You acquire an expertise because you're just following the issue and you then get associated with it and people just think, 'Oh well, you're banging on about the same stuff' – you know. [But] I've written a lot of stuff about housing, which I'm very interested in. I've never ever heard anybody say to me, 'We don't want [you] banging on about housing again. We don't want [journalists' name] banging on about the poor, again'.

At the same time, some journalists were very aware of working within a masculine culture and the ways in which this could influence senior staff's judgement about 'what the reader wants' (see also van Zoonen 1989). One described the 'total glee' with which editorial staff responded to her own article attacking psychotherapy. In their view, she commented, 'therapists are kind of weak-minded and they're in the business of feelings, which in journalism is the bloody last thing that you would ever express in the office'.[6]

Gendered judgements of source credibility

The fourth factor influencing the profile of FMS and, in particular, the dominance of the Fathers' voices, is the issue of 'journalistic intuition'. Journalists emphasised that they relied on a 'sixth sense' and 'instinct' in assessing the validity of their sources' accounts. This journalistic 'nose' for a source's credibility is a valued professional skill which is acknowledged within the newspaper hierarchy. As one journalist, who specialises in feature articles, commented:

> You actually have got to make an assessment quite quickly, do I find this person credible or not? . . . What I'm doing is watching the way they talk, I'm watching their mannerisms, I'm watching the way they construct sentences, what they say and what they leave out. How are they trying to relate to me? . . . Because when you get back to the

196

office what your editor says is, 'well, did you find them credible or not?' and you have to say 'yes' or 'no'.

In documenting the personal account of an accused father (or the woman who is accusing him) journalists make judgements based on their reaction to the protagonist(s). This is key in the false memory debate, given that the credibility of the Fathers proved to be much greater than that attributed to the Daughters.

The FMS debate is characterised by parents (usually fathers) who are white, heterosexual, successful, middle-class professionals (individuals who do not conform to the race, sexuality and class stereotypes associated with child abusers – see Kitzinger and Skidmore 1995). These parents are in conflict with their daughters (and sons) who have often been in therapy and may be defined as 'mentally unstable'. Several journalists emphasised in interview the 'nice' and plausible nature of the BFMS parents. Journalists made comments such as: 'They were a lovely couple . . . my gut reaction was positive' and 'these particular parents, I just believed instantly'. Such positive reactions were contrasted with their (often limited) exposure to those recalling abuse. For example, several journalists were influenced by one father playing them the message left on his answerphone by his daughter – her tone of voice and the nature of her accusations made them feel she was 'clearly disturbed' and 'hysterical'. Women asserting that they have been victims of abuse may also have low credibility, because as one television reporter commented: 'They may have taken drugs, they may have gone into alcohol, they may be slightly unbalanced. So we never quite trust them.'

The importance of such judgements is quite explicit in an article about FMS by Simon Hoggart. 'There is a new witch hunt in Britain: to root out child abusers', he wrote, 'But are some "victims" just having ideas put into their heads?' He went on to describe his visit to a leading member of the BFMS: 'We are in a pleasant middle-class sitting room in Southern England, and Ronald is playing back his daughter's voice from the answer phone'. Hoggart acknowledges that 'of course' the accusations 'may be true' but :

> As one talks to him, a mild-mannered former naval officer, it doesn't seem awfully likely, however, and the less so because the daughter's voice has that quality one associates with the care-in-the-community lunatics sometimes heard in the street or on station platforms: a flat, unchanging aggression which claims to be directed at the outside world, but which is clearly fomented by an inner turmoil.
>
> ('Tricks of memory', *Observer* 27 March 1994)

Male-dominated news organisation and gendered identification

Credibility judgements are not just made by the individual journalist doing the interview; they may also be made by senior editorial staff at a later stage in proceedings. In a few cases journalists actually did manage to meet the daughters of BFMS members, and judged at least some parts of their accounts to be credible. However, this could then lead to conflict with senior staff. Senior staff may counter a journalist's assessment with their own 'common sense' ideas about what is and isn't credible and, therefore, what should, or should not, appear in the paper or on the news broadcast.

There is a gender dimension to all this in that many journalists who specialise in the 'soft' side of reporting, such as feature articles based on personal experiences, are women, and most senior editorial staff are men. This is *not* to argue that the gender-politics can be reduced to the gender of journalists. Indeed, some of the most ardent advocates for the BFMS could be found among women journalists. But these women were not positioned *as women* by senior male colleagues; they were seen to have risen above their potential gender-bias. Rather than adapting a gender-reductionist position, I am arguing that the positions of men and women within media hierarchies interact with gendered values to create particular tendencies in the coverage. One important issue here is not only how journalists assessed their sources, but how they themselves were judged. Although both male and female journalists used their 'gut feelings' in judging source credibility, some female journalists claimed that their 'gut feelings' against alleged abusers were dismissed by male editors as 'subjective' or 'biased' whilst their male colleague's 'gut feelings' in favour of the same man, were seen to constitute 'common sense' or 'professional instinct'.

In the early 1970s, Hoffman argued that female journalists were expected to display greater objectivity and more rigorous standards of sourcing than their male colleagues in order to maintain their professional standing. Over twenty-five years later, similar disparity remains, particularly in relation to reporting involving sexual abuse (and most notably in stories about incest where the father's innocence is in question). Some female journalists commented that, in their view, senior male staff had 'defensive' reactions to the whole question of child sexual abuse. But their resistance to the subject was disguised as 'editorial judgement'. In some cases male journalists also seemed to identify with accused fathers. This was most clearly indicated in an article in the *Sunday Times* of 17 April 1994. Describing his sudden concern about being naked with his young daughter, Richard Caseby wondered whether this moment might be 'unwittingly filed away, just one fragment for a mosaic of repressed memories to be unveiled in all their awful wonder by a psychotherapist 20 years hence'.

Such emotions and identification can work in subtle ways to inform the news-production process. It has been observed that news organisations accord coverage according to a hierarchy of 'social proximity' (Schlesinger 1987: 117) and 'social ranking' (Roshco 1975). Such hierarchies are not just about the ranking of nations or the class position of the individuals involved. They also apply to the ranking of working-class and middle-class, men and women, white and black people, as well as heterosexuals and lesbians or gay men. Coverage will vary depending on the groups' 'social proximity' to the journalists and to their assumed audience. One of the ways in which this influences coverage is in the interpretation and response to legal issues – and it is this which is illustrated in the final section of this chapter.

Legal issues in context

In a key (potential) development in the FMS story in Britain, one journalist gained interviews with two daughters of one of the leading members of the BFMS. This man's story had appeared repeatedly in magazines, newspaper articles and television reports (sometimes accompanied by a playing of his daughters' message on his answerphone). Two of his daughters decided they were prepared to tell their side of the story. As the broadsheet journalist they spoke to explained:

> They had been so infuriated by their lives becoming public property and their friends recognising them, that they actually were interested in talking to a journalist . . . [One of the sisters] said '*Elle* is my magazine and then suddenly there I was, this basket-case daughter in *my* magazine and I couldn't open a newspaper without finding me and my loony sister everywhere I looked.

The two women disputed their father's description both of their childhood and adult relationship with him, and challenged his account of the way in which their memories were recovered. In straight 'news values' terms, interviews with these *particular* women clearly had the potential for 'a good story'. It was a scoop and was 'new' in that it overtly contradicted a series of accounts which had appeared in other newspapers. Their accounts not only provided a different perspective on an individual case of alleged abuse/alleged false memory but also implicitly challenged the validity of the FMS movement. As the journalist concerned commented: 'At its absolute basis people just said "it's a good story and nobody else has got it" '. Indeed, the editor of the women's page who was interviewed in 1994 when this article was first commissioned was excited by its potential. However, even at that point, she anticipated some difficulties in actually getting it into the paper because: 'The features editor . . . doesn't want to know about it, none of us want to know about it, it's too disgusting . . . it's very hard to grasp and I think a lot of men find it really hard to hack. They really just don't want to think about it'.

In the event the story was not published. Although the father's story had repeatedly appeared in the media without any rebuttal from his daughters, the newspaper's lawyers advised against publishing the daughters' accounts, without allowing the father a parallel right of reply in an article of equal length. An interviewer was duly dispatched to provide this 'balance' and that second article was drafted. However, the two sisters refused to have their accounts appear in this way, and the journalist who had originally interviewed them was unable to persuade her paper to compromise. 'Legally we could not persuade the lawyers', she commented:

> And it was really interesting that the whole massed male ranks of the paper were just saying 'well, this guy seems all right . . . what's the matter with him? Yeah, well, this girl has been to see a therapist you know, are you sure she's all right?'

Describing how she and the women's editor were isolated in the dispute, the journalist remarked:

> [We] were totally on our own, totally on our own, totally on our own. . . . [I was] arguing with them until I was blue in the bloody face, getting absolutely nowhere . . . And [the woman's page editor] was saying 'why don't we just go with it, why don't we just run with it and see what happens' . . . I remember just sitting there in the office with this gaggle of suits around me, and they're going: 'you can't run this, you know, seems like a decent chap'.

In this journalist's experience, the sensitivity of senior staff to the threat of legal action is related to the credibility those staff accord to different sources, the protagonists with whom they most closely identify and the extent to which they anticipate a possible breach of the law might be challenged. The legal aspects of the FMS story thus interact with the gendered character of news judgements (source credibility) within the context of a particular newspaper or television newsroom's hierarchy. This point was echoed by another journalist who commented:

> I'm influenced by having worked in Northern Ireland. What I realised there is that you could write the most damaging, scurrilous, speculative reports about the Provisional IRA, and that was OK. But writing about the British Army you had to be ultra careful. What you are allowed to write, what the news desk will accept, depends on who has power and who is the current hate group. So with 'false memory syndrome' you can report the story of someone from the BFMS, and say the most terrible things about their daughter or her therapist, but journalists don't have to find out the other side of the story or ask even the most basic questions like, 'did these women ever *forget* being abused?'.

Conclusion

'False memory syndrome' is clearly fraught with gender power relations and gendered conflict. The gender-politics influencing media attention to FMS varied from the 'masculine' values of the newsroom through to the attempts at resistance and redefinition from feminist journalists and 'experts'. It included struggles over what counted as 'objective' (masculine) science and involved the differential assessment of men and women's anger and distress. Gender-politics were exercised at every level, from the 'gut' reactions of journalists through to their negotiations with senior newspaper staff. It ran through all elements of the story's production: from the resources and strategies of the proponents of FMS through to journalists' gendered judgements about source credibility. Indeed, it would be impossible to tell the story of 'false memory syndrome' without attention to the gender-politics within which it is embedded.

Focused case studies, such as that undertaken here, attempt to offer concrete illustrations of the impact of the hierarchical positioning of men and women (and/or 'masculine' and 'feminine' values) within news media organisations, and to analyse the complex and multi-layered interaction between gender and news production. In this way the chapter seeks to explore the *processes* and the *extent* to which 'the group which dominates newsrooms and managerial positions (i.e. a largely white male group) also dominates news judgements' (Gist 1993: 109).

Attention to gender-politics will complement and sometimes identify factors which *cross-cut* existing theories about media production processes. It will allow for a more nuanced understanding of the operation of source and news organisations. Clearly, for example, gender-politics do not simply operate through structures, but through a whole series of discourses, norms, unspoken assumptions and empathetic identifications. The gender-politics of news production are more complicated than simply saying that the news reproduces the definitions of dominant institutions. Nor is it sufficient simply to celebrate any occasion when lay voices gain precedence over 'the experts'. There are power inequalities among 'lay people' and conflicting interests. Democratising the media should not simply be about 'giving power' to 'the *man* in the street'.

The analysis presented here also raises crucial questions for feminists. In particular, it suggests a need to reflect on changes since the start of second-wave feminism. In the 1970s, Tuchman asked whether women's pages could be a resource for the women's movement (Tuchman 1978b, 1978c). In the 1990s another question may now be equally pertinent: can the women's page, or the 'soft' media format generally, be used against women? The way in which the proponents of FMS accessed 'feminine' formats and used the asymmetrical status of men's emotions to place FMS on the agenda marks a historical shift in the debates around 'experience' and its place in the media, and suggests new areas of research into the operation of gender-politics. It also highlights the problem with 'women's pages' that equate 'women's issues' and 'family issues', especially within particular (right-wing) newspapers which have established agendas where the interests of women, children, men and 'the family' are seen as coterminous.

More generally, there is an urgent need to refine understandings of how 'soft' and 'hard' news operate, especially given the increased 'tabloidisation' and 'feminisation' of news. While mainstream media analysts have often disregarded soft and low-status media formats, it is becoming increasingly evident that these constitute an important site of cultural influence and, as the FMS story highlights, may act as a key point of entry for the emergence of public issues. We also need to consider the changing role of different forms. The usual argument is that 'hard news' will present a more 'masculine' agenda', while 'soft news' may provide a context for coverage of issues of greater importance to women – such childcare, women's health and male violence (e.g. Neverla and Kanzleiter 1984, cited in van Zoonen 1988) Indeed the emphasis the news media places upon 'events' rather than experience has been blamed for its bias against women (Pingree and Hawkins 1978). However, from a feminist perspective the coverage of FMS highlights the dangers of formats which offer raw 'experience' without social analysis, or simply encourage 'a theatre of feeling' (whether that is endless accounts of the trauma of sexual victimisation, or of false accusations).

This chapter began by commenting on the need for increased feminist analysis of news production processes, and I hope that it has illustrated the continuing importance of this area of enquiry for feminists. I also questioned the absence of terms such as 'feminism', 'women' or 'gender' from the indexes of many key texts about media production. Perhaps the most telling examples, however, is from a book in which some material *was* included. Philip Schlesinger's 'seminal' text: *Putting 'Reality' Together: BBC News*, was first published in 1978 and revised in 1987. This does include a reference to women in the index, referring to a useful three-page discussion of women's status in the newsroom. However, the section is somewhat unfortunately entitled: 'A digression – women and the status system'. In my view, women and their place in the news production process should no longer be considered 'a digression'. Not only this, but there is a need to do more than simply take note of the gender of journalists and their place in media hierarchies. Critical analysis of the gender-politics of news production should include unpacking the relationship between 'femininity', 'femaleness' and 'feminism' and, indeed, analysing the operation of men and masculinity as they act upon, and are constructed across, the pages of newspapers and on television. This is an urgent task for all those interested in the operation of media power, and for anyone concerned with the construction and location of women and men in contemporary society.

Notes

1 I could not find any of these terms in the indexes of standard texts such as *Journalists at Work* (Tunstall 1971), *Communicating Politics* (ed. Golding *et al.* 1986), *Sources Close to the Prime-Minister* (Cockerell *et al.* 1984), or *Public Communication – The New Imperatives* (ed. Ferguson 1990).
2 The fact that there are some accused mothers, and some sons recalling abuse, does not undermine the gender-politics of the issue, any more than the existence of Margaret Thatcher means that politics is not male-dominated or the existence of Myra Hindley should be used to obscure the gender-politics of sex murders.

3 Books written by proponents of 'false memory syndrome' highlight the way in which feminist networking and women's influence within the 'therapy industry' have operated to resist the 'discovery' of FMS, yet they routinely ignore the gender-politics of their own stance and power. My research showed that women's networking was, indeed, an important site of resistance to establishing FMS as a bona fide 'diagnosis' (e.g. within psychological bodies). However, such networking was seldom able to challenge the media profile of the issue.

4 In March 1998, after this chapter went to press, the working party of the Royal College of Psychiatrists (RCP) finally reported on the issue. Their findings supported the BFMS position and argued that it was not possible to recover memories. The report was highly controversial within the RCP and was *not* published as an RCP official report. However, it generated a flurry of news stories in 1998 with headlines such as 'Recovered Memory dismissed by doctors', (*Independent* 1 April, 1998) and associated stories such as 'The nightmare psychiatric ordeal of politician's daughter that nearly cost her sanity' (*Daily Mail* 10 March 1998).

5 Thank you to Paula Skidmore for permission to use extracts from her 1993–4 interviews from our joint project on the media coverage of child sexual abuse (Kitzinger and Eldridge, ESRC award no: R000233675). I would like to thank colleagues in the Glasgow Media Group for their helpful comments on a draft of this chapter and the ESRC for research funding which allowed me specifically to examine the false memory debate (grant no. L211252010).

6 This book goes to press in the immediate aftermath of the death of Diana, Princess of Wales. One of the many extraordinary changes displayed in response to this has been the way in which 'the business of feelings' has been reported (see special issue of *Screen* Spring 1998). News presenters and journalists openly describe their own tears (e.g. 'I am crying as I write this . . . I cannot believe Diana is dead', James Whitaker, *Mirror* 1 September 1997). Emotion has become the subject of serious media debate. As Bryan Appleyard noted in the *Sunday Times*, 'Weeping was being debated as earnestly as the poll tax or Scottish devolution. The future of the monarchy seemed to hang on a sob' (7 September 1997).

12

GENDER AND THE AGENDA

News reporting of child sexual abuse

Paula Skidmore

Introduction

'*The women in the office were always so much better at dealing with those things than the men*' [1]

This journalist was talking to me about covering child sexual abuse stories for a quality Sunday paper. Specifically she was addressing the issue of incest, abuse within the home or immediate family circle and the problems for journalists in getting such stories into print. This is precisely the terrain I wish to address in this chapter – the gender factor of the news agenda. The quote is useful because it illustrates two contradictory concerns with respect to the issue, which I wish to tackle. First, it suggests that male journalists have a problem in addressing the complexities of child sexual abuse and are more reluctant to attempt to bring them into the news arena. In other words, there is a gender factor in decision making around the news production process. In itself I do not have a problem with that and I wish to argue strongly that gender is frequently unacknowledged as an aspect of news production, particularly in the sociology of journalism.

However this gives rise to a second concern which I am less comfortable about. Following this path, as I will do below, over the reporting of child sexual abuse, can lead to rather less palatable conclusions about gender and the news. Could it be that, in the words of the journalist above, women are 'so much better' than their male counterparts in dealing journalistically with such topics, that they are forever confined to the 'soft news' agenda? In other words, women journalists are only 'fit' for stories about children, families and related community concerns, because, after all, they do it so much better, don't they? I will conclude by suggesting that we do need to be careful about operationalising the *theoretical* category of 'gender' in order to avoid falling into this trap. After all, as Ginny Dougary (1994) has shown, the 'executive tart' has still got a long way to go towards equality in the newsroom. The fewer obstacles we academics put in her way, the better.

This chapter will examine the gender factors in the news production processes surrounding the reporting of child sexual abuse. It will explore the factors which determine the trends, nuances and emphases within news coverage by outlining the operations of journalists and their sources in relation to this topic. It will assess to what extent these findings support or deny the existence of a gender orientation in journalism and the concept of a 'male' news product (see van Zoonen 1994). Before talking specifically about the reporting of child sex abuse, I will comment on other work in this area of women and the news.[2]

Telling a different story?: Women, news and ideology

Taking these three conceptual strands of women, news and ideology I wish to raise the question, can we bring feminist theories together with the field of media sociology to say something about the significance of the news? I have already rung the alarm bell above about the danger of being over-deterministic in the process of theorisation regarding women and the news media. Nevertheless I wish to argue that it is important to address the idea of the news as 'gendered', particularly given that this possibility has been overlooked almost completely by the mainstream sociology of journalism. It is important to explore the idea through two related avenues which will be returned to in the conclusion; one, news as a *product*, which raises the issue of ideology; and two, news as a *process* which raises the issue of structured inequality.

One of the few academics in the field to address this area in any substantive way is van Zoonen (1994). As well as exploring questions of a 'gender discourse', that is to what extent is there an encoding of gender within media production, she also asks questions about the significance of a 'gendered structure', which she suggests exists at four levels (1994: 49–62). These can be usefully represented as individual, professional, organisational, and institutional (although van Zoonen expresses them differently). This is arguably a very useful framework for analysis, not least because it relates directly to the conceptual terminology of much of the sociology of journalism (see McNair 1994). As van Zoonen argues, it is important to explore how 'the gendered structure of media production extends from micro and meso to macro levels' (van Zoonen 1994: 62). Although it is not possible to represent fully the four levels of the 'gendered structure', they can be summarised with examples from other research on women and journalism to give some context to the argument below.

The individual level

In van Zoonen's (1994) analysis, the significance of gender at the individual level is focused around the issue of women as employees in media organisations. This refers to the gender ratio of men to women in journalism and both the vertical and horizontal segregation which occurs. Although it is important not to over-generalise, it is easy to see van Zoonen's point with an examination of the employment statistics. Gallagher (1979: 47) has already detailed not only the difficulty in obtaining figures on women's participation in mass media but also their exclusion from 'key decision making posts', as well as 'the growth of female ghettos' when she collated statistics. Nearly two decades later it seems the problems remain. As both Dougary (1994) and Christmas (1997) point out, figures are not routinely kept on the proportion of women in journalism or media, the BBC being a notable exception due to its affirmative action policy on women's employment. Dougary collated the figures herself by telephoning all the national newspapers and discovered that across the then twelve tabloids, top editorial jobs were held by sixty-four men and eleven women, whilst the ten broadsheets had sixty-one men and only two women in similar positions.[3] In television it is difficult to obtain precise figures for women in news; however, the general patterns of employment in broadcasting are surely indicative. Back in 1985 the Sims Report for the BBC detailed only six women to 159 men in the top staff grades (cited in Baehr 1996: 15). By 1992 the figures had improved for women to a total of twenty-one, but the ratio was similar, with 199 men now in top executive positions (complied by Women in Television and Film 1993, cited in Dougary 1994: 19). In other words, by the 1990s the largest public broadcasting organisation in Britain still had only ten per cent of its senior positions held by women. The situation is not unsurprisingly mirrored in the ITV network and is only marginally better at Channel Four, where in 1994 top editorial and executive jobs were held by twenty-nine men and eight women (Dougary 1994: 71). Even a recent report on the Independent Television production sector makes grim reading between the lines (Baehr 1996). On the surface not only had the independent sector mushroomed in the 1980s but this has been a place for women to gain gender equity – out of fifty-two companies surveyed in Britain, the total workforce constituted fifty-six per cent men and forty-four per cent women (Baehr 1996: 40). However, scratch the surface and we discover that eighty-eight per cent of the 'low grade' jobs are held by women whilst sixty-three per cent of executive producers and seventy-six per cent of directors are men.

These more recent figures largely confirm van Zoonen's (1994) previous assertion that men dominate the senior levels of media. This horizontal segregation is particularly notable for the British national press. It also indicates that vertical segregation between 'technical' and 'domestic' roles within broadcast media as detailed by van Zoonen is strongest in the national/public networks and marginally weaker in the independent sector. What are the consequences of these statistics?

Following Creedon's (1989) original idea of 'velvet ghettos' it can be seen how even when more women are entering media organisations they are not following male career patterns but, for instance, are entering advertising and PR areas instead. Smith (1980) pointed out how women in British journalism were excluded from serious news outlets and roles, and blocked from the hard news frame – well over ten years later the situation appears alarmingly similar. It is probable that the indirect discrimination van Zoonen (1994) summarises as being behind this is continuing; women trying to combine family and career;

'old boys' networks' and 'informal socialisation' excluding women. These factors combine to discriminate against women's engagement with the 'key learning situations' of career development (Smith 1980).

Women's marginalisation within media employment is not only of concern with regard to a lack of equality between the sexes. It is important to point out that male domination within the workplace has another consequence – it encourages harassment and sexism towards women, and therefore affects their self esteem as employees. This leads us to another level identified by van Zoonen – that of professionalism.

Professionalism and gender

There is very little research on this issue, however, studies which have been done on the professional values and performance of women journalists show that there are no differences between the sexes, as van Zoonen summarises (1994). Nevertheless, there is much anecdotal evidence from women journalists themselves to suggest that male sexism and resistance to women as professionals exists. Dougary (1994) has compiled the most substantive examples of media sexism when she interviewed media women from a range of organisations. One of the most notable inclusions was Eve Pollard, the first woman to edit a mid-market Fleet Street paper, the *Sunday Express* in 1991. She summarised her experiences of male resistance to her success: 'When men hear that I've got a new job they don't think "Good business brain", they think "38D cup" ' (quoted in Dougary 1994: 146)

Elsewhere academics have documented the resistance recounted by prominent women journalists, such as Kate Adie, a very experienced and successful senior news reporter for the BBC. Adie believes that the lack of women in journalism encourages male innuendo, and that she has often had to 'prove' herself a competent reporter as a woman:

> things have changed radically in the last 15 years for women reporters. They are now taken seriously in public at any rate. . . . But most male journalists still believe that you're fluttering your eyelids and that you opened your legs to get the job or story. Or did you use your tits? It's quite amazing.
>
> (quoted in Sebba 1994: 264)

Examples such as these and many others detailed by the same authors build a picture of a hostile, male-dominant environment for women who try to enter into journalism, particularly the hard news field. Anecdotal evidence is that male dominance in journalism has produced a macho culture of newsgathering – aggressive and domineering but also one of male camaraderie and 'bonding' – which excludes women. One senior BBC journalist on Radio 4's *Today* programme has even described the news agenda overall as being 'male'.[4] This sentiment is well exemplified by a comment from the ex-editor of the women's page of the *Guardian*:

> People have this idea that the *Guardian* is full of SNAGS [Sensitive New Age Guys]. But while there may be some men like that . . . the guys at the top are Oxbridge types. . . . en masse, I can feel excluded, particularly when they go on about football and cricket at conference. Usually Georgina [Henry, Media Editor] and I will retaliate by talking about lipstick or periods. They usually get the point.
>
> (quoted in Dougary 1994: 107)

These kind of examples should perhaps lead us not to ask if women journalists have 'different' professional values than their male colleagues but to question the social and cultural expectations of the macho newsroom that women are expected to work within.

The organisational level

At the third level, van Zoonen (1994) suggests that the social and cultural expectations outlined in the previous section build into gender-specific response patterns. Thus journalistic practices and socialisation produce a 'gendered professionalism' through an organisational context. Van Zoonen indicates how the lack of research on this makes it difficult to theorise coherently, and instead raises certain issues and questions related to gender and news organisations. She particularly connects to work on this issue by Neverla, who suggests that 'news professionalism' is predominantly associated with masculine attributes – women journalists are therefore disadvantaged due to their feminine socialisation. Van Zoonen's own work on Dutch journalists showed another aspect of gendered professionalism related to the exclusion of feminist issues from the news agenda.

One woman feature editor from a Sunday broadsheet has described this exclusion in terms of often being the only woman 'at conference' (where the news agenda for the paper/bulletin is decided):

> I was always pointing out the number of dead white males who appeared on the book pages; the number of cricketers who appeared in the big profile; the latest EC directive implications for maternity leave. I got sick to death of having to remind the men that women exist.
>
> (quoted in Dougary 1994: 101)

A clear example of gendered professionalism can be found in the recent Fawcett Society study which monitored two weeks of television news coverage of the 1997 British General Election (see Coles 1997). In the field of political news the study outlined how eighty per cent of the election coverage was by male journalists; only sixteen per cent of people appearing were women; 127 male compared to eight female politicians appeared; twenty-six government spokespersons were interviewed who were all men; seventeen academics were interviewed – all men. One female journalist who did cover the general election wrote despairingly of her experience, not only in terms of the male-dominated output, but the macho culture of the press pack. Writing of the daily male-dominated news conferences she identified:

> an uneasy feeling . . . that such public jousting is largely irrelevant and that many of the questions have more to do with journalistic ego than any real desire for information. Each conference . . . has the air of a boys' public school where a few clever girls have been permitted to enter the 6th Form.
>
> (Coles 1997: 4)

At the organisational level then, women journalists are made to feel that their concerns – feminist or feminine – are not what is required of a true news professional.

Institutional determinants of gender

The fourth and final level of a gendered news structure highlighted by van Zoonen relates to the political-economic determinants of news production. Van Zoonen's most coherent example of this is connected to the increasing representation of gay women in the US mass media as identified by Moritz. She suggests that, however rare, such changing institutional priorities can facilitate the widening of the gender dimensions of media. However, in other respects it can diminish the representation of women's issues, for example over feminist campaigning or the 'women's movement' (see Faludi 1992; van Zoonen 1992). This is an under-researched area in terms of gender, but points to the important issue of the limits set to news production by economic and power relations of media industries. Research on the reporting of violent and sexual crimes has suggested, for instance, that increasing competition and tabloidisation of the news has influenced the content of such coverage (Soothill and Walby 1991; Meyers 1997).

The next section will explore in what ways these aspects of gendered structure are supported by the production research conducted on child sex abuse in the media. It is important to explore what relevance any of this has to the wider concept of gender discourse. This can only be done by addressing the concept of ideology and examining to what degree gender affects news as a product. It will be suggested below that it is instructive to do this by examining the news agenda as it relates to sexual violence, and in this instance specifically the sexual exploitation of children. By examining the production processes around such news stories it will become clear that this area is subtle and theoretically complex.

Reporting the sexual abuse of children

It is only possible to outline briefly the context of the research conducted into child sexual abuse in the media which informs some of the examples cited here. The project was an examination of the emergence of child sex abuse (CSA) as a social problem, and the importance of the media in relation to this.[5] The specific area of work which relates to this paper was an examination of the media production processes surrounding CSA as a social problem. This included the news, press and broadcast, documentaries and fictional television, and involved primary interviews with media personnel – journalists, editors, producers – as well as those who act as sources of information about CSA – children's charities, social services, pressure groups and similar. Through this process some key factors concerning the structure, organisation and ideological influences of media production on CSA were identified. Following standard approaches in media sociology, these findings can be summarised into three areas: the structure of reporting CSA; source–journalist relations within this structure; and news values and production issues (see, for example, Schlesinger and Tumber 1994) . Some findings from the content analysis of the way that news reports the abuse of children will be given first.

The content of news reporting on CSA

The project cited here also completed a content analysis of news coverage of CSA, comprised of a detailed sample of all press and television from 1991, press coverage from 1986 and an overview of more than ten years of *The Times*.[6] Our key findings from this analysis were that most news coverage focused on one particular incident or set of allegations rather than on areas of general concern. For instance, over eighty per cent of TV news coverage for 1991 was case based, whilst the biggest single category of coverage, twenty-seven per cent for press, was the alleged organised abuse in the Orkney Islands (see Asquith 1993 for a discussion of the case). This case-dominance was in stark contrast to issues such as the causes or prevention of CSA – the latter only attracted four per cent of press coverage and twelve per cent of TV for instance. Child sex abuse as an issue in the news also has a very distinct pattern over time – its prominence rose dramatically in the early 1980s, peaking in 1987 with the Cleveland case and never achieving as much attention again in the news media. From the project's content sample it was possible to chart a kind of 'glass ceiling' on the amount of news from 1989 to 1994, characterised by periodic 'new angles' appearing in the coverage, such as 'ritual' abuse, children in care, female abusers and false memory debates. There was a clear shift away from covering issues about preventing CSA, to a focus on intervention and professional responses to abuse allegations which was closely connected to the nature of the cases being reported, such as Rochdale. When prevention issues were raised, the focus was on abuse outside the home or by carers – in 1991 for example the press coverage contained forty-seven such items, with only two items discussing 'incest-prevention' (see Kitzinger and Skidmore 1995).

The structure of reporting

On the journalists' side, covering the issue of CSA was characterised by a lack of specialist knowledge, by the predominance of general reporters who drafted almost eighty per cent of news items in 1991 and a kind of formulaic reporting. This was focused around the dominance of case coverage mentioned above – reporting incidents, usually scandals alleging social-work errors, notably the Orkney, Rochdale and Beck (institutional abuse) cases in our samples from the 1990s, for instance. General news imperatives of immediacy, dramatisation and sensationalism therefore informed the majority of reports concerning CSA. There is no such thing as a 'child abuse specialist', only journalists who have developed deeper understanding of the issue through prolonged involvement in news coverage, usually as a social-services correspondent or similar.

Although a range of sources were used for information, reports were dominated by the use of 'official' agencies such as court reports and the police, complemented by personal social services and children's charities. Some lay groups received considerable attention from the media however – in 1991, accused parents or their representatives in the Orkney case were used twice as much as social services for instance. Others, such as feminist campaign groups, were significantly marginalised. Source organisations were very reactive in their dealings with journalists and relied heavily on the use of 'off the record'. Specialist journalists in particular relied on off-the-record briefings to understand the complexities of particular cases and get round problems of confidentiality which might prevent social services going 'on record'. For the majority of reporters from the general newsdesk, this resulted in a kind of 'information vacuum' which they were able to 'fill' in specific cases by accused parent pressure groups, such as PAIN (Parents Against Injustice).

Source–journalist relations

The most important issue within the production process was the negative relationship between the social work profession and the media, described as a 'trench mentality' from both sides. The second most important was the relationship with parents' pressure groups which in contrast was characterised by good, efficient news management. As one specialist journalist commented: '*The problem with child sex abuse now is that parents and lawyers have started speaking to the media and it is much easier to carry an emotive story than just a straightforward news story*'. This was particularly evident in the Orkney case, for example, where general reporters were faced with the 'trench mentality' of the social work department and simultaneously offered unlimited access to parent's accounts of the removal of their children into care. One reporter from a Scottish broadsheet explained it as follows:

> *If you're the news editor, you're sitting with a story that one reporter's given you about the parents saying 'Oh it was awful, the social workers came at dawn and whipped the children from my arms and they were crying and the animals were all barking and it was just the most awful moment of my life', and your social affairs correspondent is saying 'yeah but the social workers have got this great story about how they prepared everything and they gave juice to the children and some toys' – it doesn't really sit.*

News values and CSA

It is not unsurprising to find that within the structural and organisational arrangements given above, there are issues which cut across the news production process. The drama of 'ritual' abuse allegations, child-abuse fatigue, personal ideologies of journalists and gender issues all seemed to have a significant impact on the production of news stories about CSA.

The impact of case coverage, particularly Orkney, had been to raise doubts about allegations of abuse and social work competence to intervene, especially in organised and 'ritual' abuse cases. Journalists who tried to make sense of these issues had to assess the 'credibility' of sources and decide who were the 'experts'. Aldridge (1994) has termed this a 'template of scepticism' which now exists around such cases. Journalists with good social work contacts and more specialist knowledge felt that there was a general 'disbelief' about organised ritual sex abuse, especially familial abuse, among colleagues, and most importantly on the newsdesk. Related to this was increasing 'child-abuse fatigue' in the newsroom – editors were reluctant to do more stories on the topic and uncertain of how much their readers/viewers could take.

When disputes and arguments arose about these issues, the personal ideologies of journalists and editors became significant. Notably these were debates shot-through with the gender dynamics of the newsroom. It has been briefly indicated above how a clear pattern emerged in CSA cases around the difficulty of ascertaining 'hard news facts'. In the absence of hard facts, personal ideologies fill the decision-making space concerning the news agenda. When cases emerged, part of the process of news production involved matching available sources' accounts against individual 'common sense' – about whether or not abuse could have happened. The production process then becomes intertwined with the attitude of the journalists, editors and other personnel within the media organisation as to how widespread child sex abuse is, if it can be 'ritual' and/or organised, the frequency of familial abuse, the likelihood of social-work error and, crucially, if these 'type of people', in this particular case, could be abusers.

The term 'common sense' was used widely and repeatedly in interviewees' accounts of news production on CSA. It is at this point that gender factors became very significant – in the assessment of the 'newsworthiness' of child sexual abuse stories. To what extent women and men's 'common sense' differs around the issue of sexual violence is at the centre of the final section on gender and the news agenda.

Gender and the news agenda

As was seen above, the content analysis of stories about CSA reveals an emphasis on scandals where authorities are called into question over their actions to protect children. Cases of 'disputed' allegations dominated the news, and parents who denied abuse were given prominence. I have briefly indicated some of the reasons for this and what lies behind the media reluctance to acknowledge that children are abused in the majority by adults who know them. However, the gender dynamics of the newsroom were also significant – interviewees suggested that the 'male agenda' was part of this process and that decision making around news stories was affected by gender.

The Orkney case was one in which interviewees believed gender was a strong factor in newsroom debates. One broadsheet specialist suggested:

> *I think it's difficult enough being a woman reporter in a male environment because there are very few women news reporters . . . it was frustrating on a number of levels in that you're the one that's breaking a story, it suddenly becomes so big they decide to 'send in the troops'– but also you're seen as not quite reliable on a story, I think because you're a woman . . . you're definitely seen as not quite reliable in editorial discussions*

She went on to describe how this conflictual situation worked out for her:

> *I would have constant arguments in the office with reporters that just think – well, male reporters probably don't want to think about child sex abuse . . . I would sit in the office and come out with these arguments in a very matter of fact way, because I was always desperately trying not to get angry – there was one particular occasion where I was saying all of this and the <u>chief reporter</u> was being hysterical about it all and <u>I</u> was told that <u>I</u> was probably too involved with the case!* (Interviewee's own emphasis.)

Another freelance journalist who worked on the same paper described the gender dimension of this story: '*I have never known the whole office to be so divided along gender lines as over that issue – it was so totally, y'know, <u>men</u> and <u>women</u>* [makes parting motion with hands]'. The gender division included other women who worked at the paper, but not in the field of 'hard' news. This reporter used to discuss the case with other women in the toilets when having a cigarette: '*I* *would gather with the other women feature writers . . . and there was always a more balanced view by the women about child sex abuse and what you could say and how you should be reporting it'.*

Interviewees across press and television often commented on the gender dynamics of the news production sphere and how the imperatives of 'hard news' were male dominated. One male senior press officer for social services put it this way:

> *I think the press generally are fairly sceptical about it, particularly organised abuse . . . So you might, if you wish to, see it as a male power sort of thing, that the media is largely controlled by men and people are feeling uncomfortable about it.*

Some male journalists, particularly those who were parents, expressed to me their discomfort in repeatedly tackling news items on CSA and how they eventually felt they 'needed a break from it' as a story. Some male specialist journalists also expressed a belief that the negative image of social work was 'used' to underpin a reluctance to accept widespread familial abuse – in other words, the idea that social work was at fault was a more palatable explanation in specific cases of alleged CSA. Clearly the issues raised in the previous section over 'common sense' take on a particular relevance in terms of this male ideology informing the news agenda. It often appeared to be women journalists who fought for more news items on CSA to appear, especially since the impact of 'child-abuse fatigue'. As one broadsheet specialist pointed out, she was always trying to 'think of a way' to get a CSA story included in her paper without the issue becoming too much for readers.

Gender also appeared as significant in source accounts. One press officer from a children's charity commented about the problem of salacious language with journalists:

> *With all this glut of court case calls, sometimes I get uneasy if it's a male jour-nalist and they are reading out a court report with something approaching relish and they insist on reading out the whole thing . . . one in twenty of those calls I think well, why don't you just ring up the Samaritans and make an obscene phone call, rather than ringing up a female press officer and reading all this out? It really is unnecessary.*

This reveals one way in which the 'macho male journalist' operates when report-ing sexual violence stories. There was also a gender dimension operating within source contacts when feminist organisations were available for information. One feminist-influenced research group identified the dangers of being marginalised as a potential source:

There are some cases where our input has actually fundamentally changed the tone or the content or the line that a piece has taken . . . and there are other times when you feel it's shifted something a bit but not really. And then there are other times when you think 'why did I bother' because there are none of the qualifications or the complexity that you wanted them to think about and I think . . . there are times when we talk to journalists and it's very clear they haven't liked what we said so they've ignored it totally, so we don't even appear in the piece at all.

This has been identified by other sources interviewed from the voluntary sector as 'wilful neglect', when the information being offered does not 'fit' with a news line or agenda already established for an issue. In this way it can be seen how it is very simple to marginalise feminist accounts or specialist knowledge rather than extend the news agenda to incorporate diverse information.

To summarise then, it is useful to return to the starting point of this chapter and the 'gendered news structure' already explored (van Zoonen 1994). The illustrations given above on the reporting of CSA fit most clearly with the individual and professional levels previously outlined. It can be seen that there is a male peer resistance to CSA getting on the hard news agenda and women journalists are undermined in their attempts to place it there. The personal ideologies of journalists are frequently split along gender lines, and the social and cultural expectations of the newsroom do not facilitate broad contextualised reporting of CSA. Other than in cases of disputed allegations, the topic appears to be associated with 'soft news' and consequently 'screened out' editorially from the hard news agenda.

At the organisational and institutional levels, gender is less explicit in its effect. However journalists and sources did believe that source orientation is affected and the erosion of specialist journalism, combined with the dominance of tabloid-style reporting, fuels this. Feminist voices appear to be particularly undesirable in this framework of information collation. Concerns about their (male) readership clearly influenced the predominantly male editorial decision-making teams; one 'agony aunt' from a national tabloid believed her editor's dislike of child-abuse items was because 'there's a huge emotional resistance to running a feature which implies that incest might be an issue amongst [our] readers, because none of 'us' are like that' as she put it.[7] Overall it was suggested from many interviewees that male dominance, especially at editorial and proprietorial level, mitigated against more fully contextualised coverage of the sexual abuse of children.

Conclusion

What has been illustrated above is the complex intertwining of gender dimensions into other determinants of news production around one specific issue, the reporting of child sexual abuse. Using van Zoonen's (1994) four 'levels' of understanding gendered news structure, I have identified some of the individual, professional, organisational and institutional factors which operated negatively around this topic. So what can we make of all this?

It is useful to focus on the idea of 'gender and process' as distinct from 'gender and product' (see van Zoonen 1994). In this way it can be seen above how the structured inequality between men and women in journalism produces what has been termed 'gendered practices' in the social policy field (Pascall 1996). Gradually recognition is being afforded to this, both within journalism itself and in wider academic commentaries. It is important to emphasise that how we utilise the theoretical concept of gender in relation to news should carefully acknowledge the separate levels at which it can operate. This has been previously indicated by Steeves and Smith in their content analysis of class and gender on US prime-time television:

> while more empirical work is needed, we assume that the inaccurate and disturbing class and gender representations we have observed are significant in contributing to and perpetuating ideologies of oppression. We have not offered an explanation of the process. Nor have we theorised the relationship between ideological processes and notions of gender and class oppression in socialist feminist theory. These also remain important areas for further research.
>
> (Steeves and Smith 1987: 58)

I hope I have taken a step towards the 'explanation of the process' above. I have attempted to give one examination of this as it applies to the specific issue of covering news stories about child sex abuse. It does not take much mental effort to realise that these gendered processes will be operating around other types of news coverage on sexual violence: rape, sex assault, sex harassment and 'domestic' violence, for instance. It is possible to suggest this because these types of crime share with child sex abuse the fact that in the majority such incidents are perpetrated by adults (men) known to their (female) victims (see Kelly 1988; Stanko 1990; Dobash and Dobash 1992).

A similar point has been made previously by media researchers on sexual violence such as Soothill and Walby (1991), and more recently Meyers (1997). As such we can argue that gender is at the heart of such crimes – in their perpetration and their subsequent reporting by the media. What this then brings us back to is the importance of gender in relation to the news as a product. It begins to suggest a way we can conceptualise the linkage between gendered processes (such as male domination at editorial level within journalism) and gendered products (such as the lack of reporting incest within the news).

In the case of child sex abuse, gendered practices have proved very damaging in the longer term, clearly exemplified by the findings in Jenny Kitzinger's later work on the reporting of 'false memory syndrome' (see Kitzinger, Chapter 11 of this volume). I believe it is therefore important to raise gender as significant in news production specifically as it relates to news 'objectivity' and the hard news agenda. However, to do so is not straightforward – we cannot simply adopt a male/female split in the newsroom because of the clear dangers of reductionism. Male domination in journalism is important and, I would argue, particularly so over the reporting of sexual violence. However, it is not 'complete', nor is news production a homogeneous process. For example not all my interviewees were women – there were male journalists, editors and sources who acknowledged that a resistance existed amongst their colleagues to covering incest and familial abuse, and that this was particularly strong at the editorial level. Equally not all women journalists would recognise the descriptions I have given of newsroom experiences or agree with them. In as much we should be wary of presuming that these issues only apply to 'men' or 'women' within journalism. If we start to presume only women can report such issues we fall into the very trap that the patriarchal news media has set – women cannot be 'real' hard news journalists after all!

On a serious note, unless we do address these issues at a production level, we are unlikely to address the connected issue of the news 'product' and the gender representations and ideological nuances that prevail – where feminist analyses of the world barely get a look in and children are only ever abused by the 'bogeyman in the street'. What I would argue from the above analysis is that rather than always seeing gender as a 'problem' related to 'women and journalism', or 'feminisation of the media', academics should start to focus attention on *men* and news production. To borrow a phrase from Croteau and Hoynes (1992), questioning 'the male presence and its effect' should be at the heart of future questions about gender and the news.

Notes

1 All quotes in italics, unless otherwise stated, are taken from interviews with media and source personnel in the context of the 'Child Sexual Abuse and the Media' project (1992–5). The research project was entitled 'Child Sexual Abuse and the Media; the emergence of a public issue' and was funded by the ESRC (Award No R000233675) The grant holders were Prof. J.E.T. Eldridge and J. Kitzinger, Dept of Sociology, University of Glasgow.

2 At this point I often feel like reflecting on the 'where did I start?' question. It is probably useful to point out that I have come at this area of theory from the 'back door', so to speak. My own interest in journalism and media production was sparked through working on several research projects where interviewing media personnel was a prerequisite. Working on different projects over a long period of time, roughly ten years, I have been struck by how gender has been paramount to my interviewees' way of understanding things whilst the academic literature on journalism has stubbornly ignored it!

3 These figures were for 1994 and included daily and Sunday versions of all national newspapers then available. See Dougary (1994:116–20) for the breakdown, paper by paper.

4 Sue McGregor, public address to the 'Voice of the Listener and Viewer', Annual Conference, 1992, Overseas House, London.
5 Full details of the background, method, sample and objectives of the project are given in the final report to the ESRC – see Kitzinger and Skidmore (1996); Skidmore (1995).
6 Fuller statistics from the content sample are given in Skidmore (1995).
7 From evidence given to the National Commission of Inquiry into the Prevention of Child Abuse, February 1995, Glasgow.

13

WHEN THE 'EXTRAORDINARY' BECOMES 'ORDINARY'

Everyday news of sexual violence

Cynthia Carter

Introduction

In 1989, a man by the name of Marc Lépine walked into the Engineering Department of the Ecole Polytechnique in Montréal, Quebec armed with a gun. Entering a classroom, Lépine demanded that the women stand on one side of the room and the men on the other. Turning his gun on the women and shouting 'feministes', he then began to shoot. He killed fourteen women that day, and wounded several other women and men who tried to stop him. In much of the subsequent press and broadcast news coverage, journalists referred to Lépine as a 'monster'. Responding to this type of characterisation, several feminists challenged media portrayals of him as inhuman and abnormal. As they were quick to point out, news interviews with a number of Lépine's acquaintances and neighbours revealed that he was widely regarded as a quiet, polite and ordinary man. Commenting on these feminists' interventions, Brian Massumi suggests:

> What was remarkable from their [feminists'] point of view was not that the ordinary could conceal the extraordinary, but that the extraordinary had *become* the ordinary. There is only a difference of degree, they argued, between the spectacular deaths of the women at the Ecole Polytechnique and the less newsworthy deaths and injuries suffered by thousands of women who are mentally and physically abused each year by men.
> (Massumi 1993: 5)

It is this ideological shift in news coverage of sexual violence whereby the 'extraordinary' is normalised into the 'ordinary' that is at the centre of this chapter's discussion.

Critical news researchers have long sought to analyse the ways in which journalists report on crimes of sexual violence.[1] Several studies have confirmed that since 1945 there has been a substantial increase in the quantity of sex-crime news items in the British tabloid press (Lees 1995; Soothill and Walby 1991; Walby, Hay and Soothill 1983) as well as in North America (Cuklanz 1996; McCormick 1995;Voumvakis and Ericson 1984).[2] In Britain, the most significant changes in the news reporting of sexual violence occurred during the 1970s, a time when tabloid newspaper content, in general, became more openly 'sexualised'. By the 1990s, at least one sensational case per week was being reported in the daily tabloid press, regardless of the political affiliation, class or gender of their 'target audience' (see Carter forthcoming). Besides observing a marked increase in the quantity of 'sex crime' news stories, this research has also confirmed that the style of reporting sexual violence has become more explicit and lurid in detail over the past few decades, sometimes inducing 'moral panics' amongst news audiences (see also Voumvakis and Ericson 1984). Investigations have also sought to highlight the extent to which such news reports encourage readers to blame female victims for men's violence (Benedict 1992; Caputi 1987; Clark 1992; Cuklanz 1996; Kitzinger and Skidmore 1995; Meyers 1994, 1997; Nava 1988; Skidmore 1995).[3]

Examining variations in rape-trial reporting in Britain between 1951 and 1971, Keith Soothill and Sylvia Walby (1991: 19) discovered that the *News of the World*, a Sunday newspaper, covered more rape cases than any other title. For much of this time, they suggest, it was unique in its use of a 'distinctively titillating' style to report these types of crime, although it was eventually overshadowed by the launch of the tabloid-format *Sun* in 1969. Sir Larry Lamb, the first editor of the new tabloid, remarks in his book *Sunrise: The Remarkable Rise and Rise of the Best-Selling Soaraway Sun* that:

> This outspoken new newspaper, unlike its predecessor, genuinely born of the age we live in [what he refers to as the 'permissive society'], was staffed entirely by people who remembered a time when it wasn't done to mention in a newspaper such topics as contraception and abortion. When even the prettiest girl did not have a bosom. When the word 'rape' was among the four-letter words banned by most newspapers. But these are issues of considerable interest and importance. And the pages of a popular newspaper are a perfectly proper place in which to raise them – not least because very often people who most need to be informed read nothing else.
>
> (Lamb 1989: 139–40)

Soothill and Walby (1991: 19) claim that the new *Sun* linked reports of sexual violence to both sexual gossip and the 'Page Three' girl photographs as part of a sales strategy to boost circulation. This sexualised *Sun* was clearly popular with increasing numbers of readers – in the first six months after its relaunch as a tabloid it more than doubled its daily sales from 650,000 copies to over 1,500,000. By the end of the 1970s, the figure had risen to 3.8 million (see Lamb 1989: 23–30, 62). Still, the *Sun* faced strong criticism for the inclusion of reports concerning sexual violence on page three. In Lamb's words: 'Occasionally, when by accident [sic] a story of rape or other male violence towards women appeared on the same page, there were those who suggested that such juxtaposition was not a good idea – and they were usually right' (Lamb 1989: 117).

Today, reports of sex crimes have become a seemingly ordinary, everyday feature in the news for a large section of the British population (see Chibnall 1977; Ericson, Baranek and Chan 1991; Kidd-Hewitt and Osborne 1995; Roshier 1984; Schlesinger and Tumber 1994; Skidmore 1995; Soothill 1995; Soothill and Walby 1991). In this chapter, I will argue that the ways in which male sexual violence against women and girls is being reported in the tabloid newspaper press on a day-to-day basis is helping to normalise certain preferred ways of understanding such incidents for the reader. In order to address the everydayness of these representations, this chapter will proceed as follows. First, I will consider several pertinent studies which have sought to explore the ways in which news media reports of sexual violence contribute to the 'normalisation' of the violence being portrayed. Next, I shall present the preliminary findings of a quantitative content analysis of 840 news accounts published over a two-month period. By setting this evidence in relation to police statistics, I will show, for example, that the news values employed by journalists covering such crimes lead to a disproportionate emphasis being placed on certain types of incidents, such as murder and rape, at the expense of other types, such as domestic violence. Underpinning this dynamic, I will argue, is a corresponding emphasis on those incidents where the male attacker is a stranger to the victim, as opposed to someone she knows – in the case of the latter, according to related research, journalists usually tend to view such incidents as being too 'ordinary' to be deserving of coverage. Overall, then, this analysis suggests that there are certain gendered patterns in this news coverage which may be, in turn, encouraging readers to accept certain ideological justifications for male sexual violence as a typical, even inevitable feature of everyday life.

The 'normalcy' of everyday violence

In her book entitled *Everyday Violence*, Elizabeth Stanko (1990) asserts that there is a general social denial of the extent to which male violence happens in private. Even when it is publicly acknowledged (i.e. in the news media), violence in the domestic sphere is somehow seen to be 'ordinary', although not acceptable. Many people view private violence, she suggests, as an almost 'inevitable' part of 'normal' heterosexual relationships. As researchers like Stanko have pointed out, however, so-called 'real violence' is generally equivocated with the public sphere (often between men, but also involving male strangers and female victims). This when police, governmental and academic research reports in Britain (see Dobash and Dobash 1988; Hearn 1996; Lloyd, Farrell, and Pease 1994; Morley and Mullender 1994; National Board for Crime Prevention 1994; L.J.F. Smith 1989), and North America (see Bart and Geil Moran 1993; DeKeseredy and Hinch 1991; Dobash and Dobash 1988), consistently confirm that most women's experiences of male violence is much more likely to occur in private (more often than not perpetuated by men they know within the context of familial and personal relationships).

Significantly, much of the current research also suggests that public discussions in the news media consistently alert women to be particularly fearful of violence from men who are strangers to them (see Benedict 1992; Carter and Thompson 1997; Connelly 1994; Finn 1989–90; Hanmer and Saunders 1993; Meyers 1994, 1997; Schlesinger *et al.* 1992; Stanko 1990). Along with the family and the education system, Stanko (1991) argues, the news media perform a crucial rôle in teaching women and girls about potential dangers of sexual violence, primarily from male strangers, and how best to try to keep themselves 'safe' from such men. Stanko maintains that 'sexual safety is so fragile for women it can be shattered each time the media spotlight a tragedy of random violence against women. We are constantly surrounded by daily news stories of other women's misfortunes' (Stanko 1990: 100).

If it is true that the news media tend to place particular emphasis on reporting what are, statistically speaking, the most extraordinary forms of sexual violence (e.g. murder, attempted murder and rape by a male stranger), that is, those forms which are not 'typical' of the actual types of sexual crime reported to the police, the same may be said for most investigations of sex-crime news. In my view, insufficient attention has been paid to analysing the day-to-day range of sexual violence news reports as they appear on a routine basis. Here, Peter Dahlgren's (1989) study of crime news reporting in Swedish newspapers is helpful in redirecting our thinking to consider alternative approaches to studying news coverage of sexual violence. Briefly, his research indicates that the most typical kind of crime reported in the press involves some form of violence (thirty per cent of all crime news) and that, typically, these accounts are very brief (over half of his sample news accounts contain fewer than twenty column centimetres or 300 words). Such reports, he argues, can only offer a limited explanation of the crime, such that: 'it is the criminal acts themselves which prevail. . . . The actors – the suspected criminals – as well as the recipients of the acts – the 'victims' – are largely left as stock characters' (Dahlgren 1989: 193). Reporters, it follows, are therefore reduced to relaying often complex situations via a 'predictable repertoire of categories'.

'Routine crime news', as David Pritchard and Karen D. Hughes (1997: 49) observe, 'is easy to overlook because it is so familiar and mundane'. Drawing upon a comprehensive investigation of homicides in Milwaukee, USA, and how they were covered by two daily newspapers, as well as on data gathered from interviews with journalists, their study makes a number of points relevant to this discussion. Specifically, in examining certain factors which lead news-paper journalists to report incidents of murder more than other types of crime, the authors found that the salience of a homicide 'is enhanced when Whites are suspects or victims, males are suspects, and victims are females, chil-dren, or senior citizens' (Pritchard and Hughes 1997: 49). As females are actually less likely to be victims of homicide than males, journalists tend to view their deaths as more 'newsworthy'. Pritchard and Hughes maintain that: 'females' cultural roles as mother and nurturer suggest that killing a female has a higher degree of newsworthiness-enhancing cultural deviance than killing a male' (1997: 53).[4] However, their research also shows that despite the fact that homicides in which there was a close relationship between the suspect and victim are 'evidence of greater sickness or perversion than killing a non-intimate', these stories tend to figure less prominently in the news than those in which the suspect is a stranger (1997: 54; see also Wykes 1995). To explain this anomaly, Pritchard and Hughes argue:

> The more complex social aspect of a homicide, such as the nature of the victim's relationship with the suspect and whether a victim was involved in drugs, gambling, prostitution, or gangs, generally take longer to emerge [than other types of information about a given crime]. As a result, reporters tend to judge newsworthiness on the basis of the first facts they get (e.g., race, gender, and age, especially of the victim). Thus, despite the theoretical and very human interest in whether a victim put him- or herself at risk, and in whether the killer and victim had a close relationship, it is not surprising that this study found them unrelated to newsworthiness. Reporters typically do not have the time to wait for such information, so they make their evalua-tions on the basis of the verified facts they have on hand.
>
> (Pritchard and Hughes 1997: 63)

A similar line of investigation informs Marian Meyers' study *News Coverage of Violence Against Women: Engendering Blame* (1997). Specifically, her interviews with crime reporters in Atlanta, Georgia confirm that because news organisa-tions cannot possibly report on each and every crime taking place every day, journalists have developed a 'hierarchy of crime' in which murder is considered to be the most serious offence, and therefore the most important to cover. However, not all murders are deemed to be equally 'newsworthy'. One televi-sion reporter interviewed claimed that 'If someone gets shot on a street corner and it turns out to be a domestic argument, the chances of that making the air are slim' (Meyers 1997: 90). In Atlanta, it seems, 'domestic violence' is viewed by many of the journalists Meyers interviewed as being so common that even when it results in murder it is often not considered to be significant enough to warrant a reporter's attention. In general, Meyers contends, 'women who . . . are battered, raped or even murdered appear to be journalistically unimportant unless they are white and middle class – or if they can serve as a warning to other women' (Meyers 1997: 98).[5]

As detailed below, a preliminary reading of my news sample supports the claim made by other news researchers that journalists recurrently consider homicide, which in Britain is one of the rarer forms of recorded violent crime, as being the most 'newsworthy'.[6] Other types of violent crime, in contrast, are systematically under-represented compared to police records. Given this anomaly in reporting, a range of important questions arises concerning the means by which readers are encouraged to understand what constitutes 'normal' sexual violence within changing parameters of newsworthiness.

Quantitative profile of news reports of sexual violence

In the remaining section of this chapter, I will offer a brief report of several key findings taken from a quantitative content analysis of 840 news accounts of sexual violence drawn from six British daily tabloid newspapers as they appeared between 15 November 1993 and 15 January 1994.[7] The aim of this summary is to provide an overview of some of the patterned characteristics of tabloid news coverage of sexual violence as they relate to the issue of normalisation. Each of the accounts was coded to record: its subgenre ('news report', 'news brief', 'feature', 'backgrounder', 'opinion column', 'editorial', 'letter to the editor', and 'soft' news); any accompanying photographs and graphic images; word and paragraph length; placement within the newspaper (page number and specific placement on the page); headline style (height, width and font style); production and news sources; type of sexual violence; type of victim (woman or girl); and the relationship of the offender to the victim. A full report on these findings, as well as a discussion of the attendant conceptual and methodological issues, is presented in Carter (forthcoming).

Length of news items

The most typical story of sexual violence found in my sample is very brief, with the majority being fewer than 300 words in length. Whilst this result might not seem terribly surprising given the fact that tabloid stories of all types are characteristically short, it is nevertheless important, in my view, to document that the tabloid press typically affords few words in which to explain often very complex incidents. More specifically:

• Almost one quarter of all accounts of sexual violence are presented in 100 words or less, nearly half in fewer than 200 words, and about two thirds in fewer than 300.

These results may also be presented in the following form:

Word length	Valid %	Cumulative %
0–99	24.5	24.5
100–99	19.9	44.4
200–99	21.2	65.6
300–99	18.1	83.7
400+	16.3	100.0

This finding generally concurs with the results of Dahlgren's (1989) analysis of Swedish press coverage of crime news, as noted above. I would agree with his assessment that such short stories are largely incapable of offering the reader more than a severely limited description of the crime. In my view, one of the key consequences of reporting sexual violence in this fashion is that ever more spectacular forms of sexual violence, which tend to be given much more space and prominence within the newspaper (including photographs of the offender, victim and location of violence, the use of large headlines, and so forth), stand out as truly 'extraordinary'. As Dahlgren suggests, it is the daily supply of short, ostensibly mundane crime stories which serves as a background against which a sense of the 'normal' and the exceptional are entrenched. In his words:

> In any case, while sensationalist crime coverage figures large in the popular consciousness and in the debates about news, it is important to distinguish it from the short routine articles which comprise the ongoing, daily chronicle of crime. In terms of the relationship between the two, one could hypothesise that this pedestrian and prosaic prose serves to throw the more spectacular coverage into relief, and that the contrast helps to organise reader expectation. A sense of the 'normal' and the exceptional is established – as an experiential domain of news-reading, not necessarily as knowledge about crime in society.
>
> (Dahlgren 1989: 195)

Placement

British tabloid newspaper editors have often been criticised for the invidious inclusion of news of sexual violence alongside pictures of 'topless' female models (see Lamb 1989; Tunks and Hutchinson 1991). Examining instances of this type of juxtaposition, preliminary results drawn from the sample appear to confirm that, despite assurances made by various tabloid editors, such placement is still taking place. Nevertheless, it is possible to speculate from these results that such occurrences may be declining in frequency. An analysis of the placement of sex crime news shows that:

- Virtually every day, the *Sun* ('Page Three' girl) and the *Daily Star* ('Starbird') feature pictures of 'topless' women on page three. Other tabloids also include pictures of semi-nude women (particularly fashion models who are often featured in sheer clothing or lingerie), although not as regularly as these two titles. Whilst each of the tabloid newspapers included at least one story of sexual violence on page three during the sample period, the greatest proportion of sexual violence reports are found from page twelve onwards. The tabloid newspaper which provides more reports of sexual violence on page three than all of the others is the *Mirror*, although it only represents slightly over 5 percent of its total sex crime news reporting.

	Today	Sun	Star	Express	Mail	Mirror
Page		% in paper				
1	6.1	3.3	6.8	5.3	5.3	6.8
2	5.4	4.6	10.5	8.3	8.0	.8
3	.7	1.3	3.7	2.3	.9	5.3
4	9.5	11.3	8.0	3.0	–	8.3
5	5.4	5.3	14.8	3.0	9.7	7.6
6	1.4	1.3	2.5	.8	3.5	3.8
7	2.7	10.6	10.5	10.6	6.2	6.1
8	.7	1.3	2.5	1.5	2.7	2.3
9	8.1	4.0	7.4	1.5	–	9.1
10	1.4	.7	1.9	9.1	1.8	2.3
11	10.8	5.3	9.9	–	5.3	9.1
12+	48.0	51.0	21.6	54.5	56.6	38.6

It is notable that a significantly higher number of sex-crime news stories occur just immediately prior to and after page three than on the page itself. The cumulative overall percentage of sex-crime stories found on pages two through five is highest for the *Daily Star* (thirty-eight per cent of its total sex crime news), followed by the *Sun* (twenty-two point five per cent). Here I would suggest that in considering the ways in which readers are encouraged to make sense of sex-crime news, it is significant that the 'Starbird' and 'Page Three' girl are positioned at the centre of this concentration of sex-crime news within the two newspapers.

Related to this last finding, my reading of the coverage indicates that news of sexual violence tends to show up more frequently on odd-numbered pages (excluding page one). Paul Nicholas has argued that these pages routinely contain 'interesting but not important' news, that is, a higher percentage of 'human interest' news stories, 'celebrity gossip', 'scandal' stories and sexualised photographs of women (personal interview, 1997). In contrast, even-numbered pages, in Nicholas' view, contain 'important but not interesting' news items, such as reports on politics, business and international affairs.

News sources

Turning to an examination of the particular kinds of sources used for news stories about sexual violence, a familiar pattern emerges in the sample. In all categories, male sources significantly outnumber female. As Hartley asserts, 'news is not only about and by men, it is overwhelmingly seen through men' (Hartley 1982: 146). Studies have recurrently shown that news organisations tend to rely overwhelmingly on male news sources, particularly 'authoritative' ones such as representatives of the courts (judges, lawyers, court officials), the police (detectives, officers, inspectors), 'experts' in respected institutions (psychologists, scientists, corporate officials), and so forth (see Bridge 1995; Croteau and Hoynes 1992; Cuklanz 1996; Ericson, Baranek and Chan 1989). Furthermore, these legitimised sources are usually employed to set the news lead in the opening paragraphs of an account, thereby framing how readers are to make sense of what is being reported (see Hall *et al.* 1978). Female news sources, researchers have argued, are more likely to be regarded by journalists as less credible or reliable, and typically show up as sources when they are the victims of crime, or a relative, friend or neighbour of a victim or offender, or as 'passive reactors' to news events which feature a man as the primary news actor (see Beasley 1993; Holland 1987; Rakow and Kranich 1991). Studies in this area have also illustrated how female news sources are often included only towards the end of a news account, at a point when the reader has already been encouraged to comprehend the issues it has raised via the frameworks of 'authoritative' male news sources (Croteau and Hoynes 1992; see also Holland 1987; van Zoonen 1994; Tuchman 1978a).

The preliminary study presented here reaffirms these lines of argument through its documentation of the limited use of female news sources. There are far fewer female sources included in news reports of sexual violence contained in the sample than those which are male, particularly in terms of sources who are designated by journalists as 'authorised' (active) voices of 'expert opinion'. My analysis of the coverage also confirms that female news sources tend to be viewed by journalists as 'unauthorised' (passive) voices, usually appearing when they are needed to present an 'emotional' or 'familial' viewpoint. Specifically, my reading of the news sample indicates that:

- The three most frequently cited news sources for all types of sexual violence across the entire sample are court officials, police and a range of institutional 'experts' (psychologists, social workers, prison officials etc.). In the first category, 'court officials', sixty per cent of the news sources utilised to explain or frame incidents of sexual violence are male, five per cent female and thirty-five per cent where the gender of the source is unclear. The gender breakdown of police sources is thirty-five percent male, three per cent female and sixty-two percent where the gender is unclear. The number alters slightly with reference to 'experts', because at times official statements are included from women's support groups (e.g. Rape Crisis). The figure here consists of sixty-one per cent male sources, fourteen per cent female and twenty-five per cent where the gender is unclear. As past research has suggested, women appear most frequently as news sources when they are the victim of sexual violence (eighteen per cent of all news sources in the sample), as the relative of a victim (eight per cent of all news sources), and as a friend, neighbour, acquaintance or colleague of either the victim or the offender (eight per cent of all news sources).

Categories of sexual violence

Turning to an examination of the types of sexual violence covered in the tabloid press during this period, this study appears to confirm a repeated finding in crime news research that murder is substantially over-represented compared to its recorded occurrence with the police. In 1995, of the 5.1 million notifiable criminal offences taking place in England and Wales, 4.7 million were crimes against property. Violent crimes recorded by the police amounted to 311,000 offences, out of which the largest proportion (sixty-two per cent) are defined as 'less serious wounding', followed by 'robbery' at twenty-two per cent, 'other sexual offences' at eight per cent, 'homicide and acts of endanger life' at six per cent and, finally, rape at two per cent (see Home Office 1996).

In the news sample, distinctly gendered patterns of newsworthiness emerge in the reporting of sexual violence:

• By far the most heavily featured single category of violence is 'femicide' (the murder of females) representing forty-two per cent of all news of sexual violence in the sample. The next most recurrent category is 'rape' at eighteen per cent of all news accounts, broken down via the sub-categories of 'stranger rape' representing eight per cent of all stories, followed by acquaintance rape' at four per cent, 'incest' at three per cent and 'marital rape' at three per cent. This is closely followed by 'battering' at seventeen per cent of all sex crime news, 'sexual assault' at fourteen per cent, and, finally, 'sexual harassment' at nine per cent.

Examined in relation to the official crime records presented in *Criminal Statistics, England and Wales 1995* (Home Office 1996), homicide and attempted homicide constituted six per cent of all recorded instances of violent crime. Out of the 754 deaths that occurred in that year, thirty-two per cent of the victims were female. Males, the report indicates, are much more likely to become victims of homicide than females (over two thirds of all victims are male). By far, females are most likely to suffer sexual violence which falls into the report's category 'less serious wounding', constituting sixty-two per cent of all violent crime. However, the news sample establishes that only thirty per cent of sex-crime news falls into this category.[8] Tabloid reports of incidents of rape also do not correlate with recorded crime of this type. Around fifteen per cent of sex crime news in the sample features accounts of rape, whilst out of all recorded violent crime it accounts for two per cent.[9]

Whilst my findings largely substantiate those of other studies which have examined the tendencies of the press to over-represent recorded incidents of murder and rape, accounts of 'battering' also feature quite significantly in the sample. News of 'battering' significantly outnumbers reports of 'stranger rape' which past news media research has suggested constitutes another of the most over-represented sex crimes in relation to its recorded occurrence (see Benedict 1992; Cuklanz 1996; Meyers 1997; Soothill and Walby 1991; Voumvakis and Ericson 1984). Moreover, 'battering' and 'sexual harassment' are crimes which often take place between men and women who are at least acquainted with each other, such as partners and other close relatives, friends, bosses and colleagues. Several news studies have insisted that these types of sexual violence, which crime records indicate to be amongst the most common forms of sexual violence, are rarely reported in the press (see Finn 1989–90; McCormick 1995; Meyers 1994; Connelly 1994; see also Kramarae 1992). This claim is not wholly substantiated by the study reported on in this chapter. Nevertheless, the relatively high number of news stories featuring these types of violence does not necessarily constitute a conscious effort to provide female readers with a clearer view of their most likely risks of sexual violence. As one reporter indicated to Meyers (1997: 91), 'domestic violence' is usually reported only when journalists think that something about the incident has rendered it truly extraordinary.

Philip Schlesinger and Howard Tumber (1994) suggest, on the basis of their interviews with British newspaper crime reporters and correspondents, that the (over)reporting of murder in relation to police records can be traced to journalists' own understanding of what constitutes 'newsworthy' crime. Newspaper readers are 'fed up with the everyday murders', claims John Weekes, crime correspondent for the *Daily Telegraph*, in his interview with the authors. According to Weekes, readers want murder stories, particularly those which are seen to be extraordinary (Schlesinger and Tumber 1994: 145). *Daily Express* crime reporter, George Hollenberry, substantiates this point with Schlesinger and Tumber and adds that increased tabloid concentration on crime news during the 1990s has helped to shape daily reader interest and appetites (demand) for particular kinds of crime news – those which both journalists and readers view as 'unusual' or 'bizarre' (Schlesinger and Tumber 1994: 144). Over time, the journalist argues, readers demand increasingly extraordinary crime stories if they are to remain interested in this genre of news reporting.

A desire for the 'unusual' has led to increasingly sensational forms of sex crime reporting (Benedict 1992; Caputi 1987; McCormick 1995; Soothill and Walby 1991; Soothill 1995). Moreover, it has encouraged journalists to seek out 'new' crimes which 'become predominant in the news media until the level of saturation reaches a point where future events are deemed to be of no further

interest to the public unless they exhibit some unusual characteristic'
(Schlesinger and Tumber 1994: 146). Significantly, the 'new' crimes Schlesinger
and Tumber describe in their study in the early 1990s, such as rape in marriage
and child sexual abuse, are now not generally viewed to be unusual by reporters.
Many journalists seem to have grown tired of reporting them and moved on to
direct their attention to other 'breaking' types of crime (see Kitzinger and
Skidmore, Chapters 11 and 12 respectively in this volume, for a discussion of
journalists' 'child-abuse fatigue'). There is a danger, of course, that when journalists cease to report certain types of crime, an impression might be created
amongst readers that they are no longer a cause for concern.

Relationship of offender to victim of sexual violence

Examining precisely who is identified as the offender in reported cases of sexual
violence yields a rather unexpected result. The findings suggest that tabloid press
coverage may be more closely aligned with how most women and girls experience sexual violence than past research has tended to suggest (see Benedict
1992; Caputi 1987; Clark 1992; Finn 1989–90; McCormick 1995; Stanko 1991;
Soothill and Walby 1991; Soothill 1995; Voumvakis and Ericson 1984). Whilst
the investigation confirms that there is still a marked tendency to over-represent
the threat posed by the male stranger, when added together over half the
incidents of sexual violence reported in the tabloid press during this period are
linked to males known by their female victims. More specifically, the sample
shows that:

- The single most frequently featured offender is the male stranger, who represents forty-three per cent of all male suspects in reports of sexual violence,
  followed at some distance by 'husband' at eleven per cent and 'male
  acquaintance' at ten per cent. However, adding up all of the categories of
  offenders where the victim at least marginally knew her attacker results in
  a figure of fifty-two per cent of all male suspects in the news sample.[10]

Recorded crime statistics for homicide confirm that, in most cases, the main
suspect was known to the victim (fifty-four per cent of male victims and
seventy-three per cent of female victims). Out of the total number of female
victims of homicide or attempted homicide, forty per cent were killed by
current or former partners or lovers, sixteen per cent by family members, and
only thirteen per cent were killed by strangers. This compares with male victims
who are equally at risk from friends or acquaintances and strangers (thirty-four
per cent in each category), followed by a spouse or lover at thirteen per cent
and, finally, a family member at eight per cent. Although it might be reasonably
assumed that a similar pattern exists for female victims in other categories of
violent crime, at present such figures are not included in official crime reports
(see Home Office 1996).

230

Conclusions

This chapter has attempted to establish how the gendering of the ostensibly mundane character of sex-crime news in British tabloid newspapers is contributing to its wider cultural normalisation. It has also tried to show how such reports invite readers to accept that sexual violence is a 'natural', seemingly inevitable feature in the daily lives of women and girls. Furthermore, it has been suggested that the routine character of much of this news provides a background upon which it is taking increasingly spectacular incidents of male violence to stand out as being truly exceptional.

The relative over-representation of femicide in the tabloid press compared to its actual occurrence encourages (if not guarantees) female readers to infer that the risk of them becoming a victim is high, and that should they become the victim of sexual violence it is most likely to result in their death or rape. Moreover, females are directed to view male strangers as the men and boys whom they should most fear, although, interestingly, to a lesser extent than other studies have indicated. This daily diet of representations of the most brutal forms of sexual violence constructs the world outside as well as inside the front door as highly dangerous places for women and girls, one in which sex crimes have become an ordinary, taken-for-granted feature of everyday life. Consequently, I wish to conclude with a call for the development of new feminist strategies of intervention committed to resisting the ways in which tabloid news discourses reproduce hierarchical (and at times brutal) forms of gender difference as being consistent with a woman's *proper* place in society.

Notes

1 The term 'sexual violence' is utilised here to designate the categories 'femicide' (the murder of women and girls), 'battering', 'emotional abuse', 'sexual assault', 'sexual harassment', 'date' 'martial' and 'stranger rape', and 'incest'. For Soothill and Walby (1991: 17), 'sex crime' primarily refers to rape, but also includes 'murders where there is a clear sexual element, and some other forms of sexual assault and crime'. In Benedict (1992), examples of 'sex crimes' are marital, gang and acquaintance rape, murder and battering.

2 The term 'tabloid' refers to both 'popular' and 'mid-market' tabloid format newspapers. 'Popular' papers (the *Sun, Daily Star, Mirror*) are produced to attract largely working-class readerships, whereas 'mid-market' tabloids (*Today, Daily Mail, Daily Express*) target the 'skilled working class' and middle-class audiences. Approximately 12 million tabloid newspapers are sold in Britain on a daily basis.

3 For some feminists, the term 'victim' is best represented in quotation marks in order to acknowledge what they perceive to be its disempowering connotations. Owen (1995: 247), for example, follows this format, arguing that this strategy calls attention to the fact that 'victim' does not represent a fixed identity and its meaning should therefore not be taken for granted.

4 Pritchard and Hughes identify four forms of 'deviance' underlying everyday journalistic decision-making process. Statistical deviance, described as a 'classic news value', is 'the extent to which something is unusual. . . . The greater the statistical deviance of an event, the more prominent the news coverage of the event'. Second,

newsworthiness is measured against 'status deviance', which is 'the extent to which a person or group is different, using the well-established benchmarks of high status in US society. As a group, wealthy, White males have high status, and, thus, a low level of status deviance. . . . The greater the status deviance of the participants in a crime, the less news coverage the crime will receive'. Next is 'cultural deviance', which is 'the extent to which an act is considered to be unhealthy, unclean, or perverted. . . . News reports of crime help audience members define the moral centres of their cultures which suggests that the greater a crime's cultural deviance, the more news-worthy the crime'. And, finally, stories are rated by journalists for their 'normative deviance', which 'exists when an act violates formal norms. A fundamental way for societies to define normative deviance is by establishing criminal law, the violation of which is an office against the public. . . . The greater the normative deviance of an event, the more prominent the news coverage of the event' (Pritchard and Hughes 1997: 51–2).

5 The everyday patterns which emerge across news reports of sexual violence also might be partly attributable to journalistic discourses of 'objectivity' which help to protect journalists from charges of 'bias'. As a professional ideology, objectivity is also employed by reporters to sustain the claim that they simply report 'the facts', as opposed to subjectively engaging in a construction of reality (see Allan 1995, 1997a; 1998; Hartley 1996; Lichtenberg 1996; Tuchman 1972, 1978c; van Zoonen 1988, 1994). Additionally, objectivity is based on the premise that there are always 'two sides' to every story and that all statements and acts must be presented in a 'balanced' and 'fair' manner. Thus, when reporting sexual violence, journalists are likely to presume that there are two 'legitimate' and equally weighted views explaining it, which raises the question of whether reporters should always try to provide 'balanced' accounts of sexual violence. 'Attempting to do so', Meyers claims, 'denies the seriousness of violence against women and raises questions about the woman's behaviour in provoking the attack' (1997: 122).

6 This category is used in Home Office (1996) crime statistics. Less serious violent crimes include 'less serious wounding', 'rape', 'robbery' and 'other sexual offences' which include things like 'buggery', 'indecent assault on a male', 'indecency between males', 'indecent assault on a female', 'unlawful sexual intercourse with girl under 13', 'unlawful sexual intercourse with girl under 16', 'incest', 'procuration', 'abduction', 'bigamy' and 'gross indecency with a child'.

7 During the sample period under scrutiny there were six daily tabloid newspapers published in Britain, each of which was included in the study, as follows: *Daily Star*, the *Sun*, *Mirror*, *Today*, *Daily Express*, and the *Daily Mail*. Since then, *Today* has ceased to publish. All statistical figures presented here are rounded to the next whole number; see Carter (forthcoming) for further details.

8 The *Criminal Statistics, England and Wales 1995* (Home Office 1996) report indicates that 'victim surveys', such as the *British Crime Survey*, estimate that only twenty-four per cent of all types of violent crime are recorded in any given year. Thus, recorded crime statistics do not provide a full account of actual incidents of all types of crime occurring annually in the country.

9 Overall in the news sample, three per cent of the sex crime items concern incest. Official crime figures (Home Office 1996) do not classify incest in its category of 'rape', electing instead to include it in the category of 'other sexual offences'.

10 Those categories include 'husband', 'ex-husband', 'common-law partner', 'ex-common-law partner', 'boyfriend', 'ex-boyfriend', 'father', 'step-father', 'brother', 'uncle', 'friend', 'colleague', 'boss', 'acquaintance'.

14

A FAMILY AFFAIR
The British press, sex and the Wests

Maggie Wykes

Introduction

The media dubbed 25 Cromwell Street the 'house of horrors'. Now demolished and replaced by a garden, number 25 was a modest, semi-detached Victorian villa, typical of the kind of home found in respectable, middle class, suburban streets all over Britain. The rear garden backed onto college grounds; there was a well; a DIY patio; wrought iron gates; cellars and a range of rooms on three floors. 'Gulls from Gloucester docks' (Sounes 1995) perched on the roof. It was home to Fred and Rose West, their children and many lodgers for more than twenty years. On Saturday 26 February 1994 police began to search the property. By the end of the following fortnight 'The bones of nine young women had been discovered at 25 Cromwell St. Some had clearly been buried for many years, and apart from three the police had no idea of the victims' identities' (ibid.: 257). A tenth body was found at a previous address. She was Charmaine, Fred West's eldest daughter by his previous marriage to Rena. The bodies of Rena and Anna Mcphail (a babysitter who was heavily pregnant by Fred at the time she died) were found in a field. As police continued to search for more bodies; the media circus took over Gloucester.

The press, sex and violence

Sex and violence are newsworthy, fitting the value criteria identified by Galtung and Ruge (1965) as underpinning a good story; so the media circus was to be expected. Journalists broadly comply with a dominant profile – white, male, heterosexual and middle-class. Tunstall identifies an elite group of 200 journalists whose 'incomes are in the national top one per cent; most of them are men. Most are university graduates' (Tunstall 1996: 151). Christmas notes 'female decision makers in national newspapers hovered at 20 percent' in 1995 in a 'mature industry' where 'male norms have prevailed for more than 200 years' (Christmas 1997: 8). The masculinity of the profession in terms of its history, ideology and practices embeds it in patriarchy, where masculine power largely depends on feminine passivity, family and marriage. Traditional gender norms and values are collapsed in a case like the Wests, placing the obligation to report and the topic in contradiction, even conflict (the needs of commerce versus the needs of patriarchy). Husband (1984) suggested such conflict could provide a useful point of access for the analyst in that it strains the consensual 'umbrella' causing gaps, which reveal the process of hegemony.

Coverage of the West case renewed my interest in press accounts of gendered violence, which tend to devote more space and more blame to women involved in violence, whether as victims or perpetrators (Wykes 1994). The case also fitted within a continuum, identifiable from the late 1980s, of a news focus on issues of gender relations and family.[1] That continuum was commensurate with a broader ideological 'claw-back' of feminist 'gains' and a drive, recognisable in policy and popular culture, towards the re-instatement of traditional models of family organisation and femininity (Faludi 1992). The West case raised many questions – not least in relation to criminal justice and press freedom[2] – which need to be addressed. In this chapter, my particular aim is to show that the media hype over the case continued and was symptomatic of a broader political agenda foregrounding and extolling traditional, conservative family and gender relations throughout Thatcherism/Majorism, even though the Wests' family and marriage were sites of violence, sexual abuse and murder.

Family matters

Number 25 Cromwell Street no longer exists, but its history is a catalogue of horror – gagging, bondage, sado-masochism, necrophilia, mutilation and pornography. Yet the children went to school; neighbours came for tea; lodgers moved in and out; family members visited; babies were born; punters called for sex and the police knew the house. The press reports of the case documented many police visits – linked to stolen goods, complaints about noise and soft drugs. No charges resulted.

Ann-Marie (Fred and his first wife's second daughter) testified at trial that she was being sexually assaulted by Fred and Rose from the age of eight in 1972.[3] From twelve years of age, she was regularly prostituted to West Indian clients and Fred's workmates; Fred would watch through a spyhole. He also raped her systematically and became obsessive about reproducing a perfect child. He successfully impregnated a lodger, Shirley Robinson. Rose's jealousy of this last project led to Shirley's murder – nobody reported her missing and Rose even claimed the maternity benefit for the dead mother and child. No checks were made at the Department of Social Security.

Ann-Marie had an abortion at fourteen – there was a home visit from welfare officers but no action resulted. 'The authorities were fooled by Fred's chatty bonhomie and Rose's "cup-of-tea and slippers" air' (*Observer* 26 November 1995). Ann-Marie ran away leaving Heather, the eldest of Fred and

Rose's own children. (A second family consisted of Rose's children from prostitution.[4]) Heather became the focus of Fred's attention, whilst Rose turned
towards their son, Stephen. Heather began to talk about home whilst she sat
examinations in 1986. She left school and disappeared. Nobody investigated.

The Wests' lives were settled and outwardly 'normal' until in 1992 an under-
age girl claimed that Fred had sexually abused her. The police were brought in
led by DC Hazel Swaze. Both Wests were charged with abuse, and pornographic
material was seized from Cromwell Street. The case fell apart and never reached
court. A fateful consequence was that police destroyed the seized material.

During that process Ann-Marie was interviewed. She told police about her
experiences and informed them that Charmaine, Rena and Heather had disappeared. Fred was held in prison; the younger children were taken into care and
Rose attempted suicide. Yet again Fred was not prosecuted and he returned to
Cromwell Street. Rose had her sterilisation reversed so they could start a new
family. Early in 1994 one of the West children in care claimed that Heather
was buried beneath the patio. Police began a search of the West home and on
24 February Fred confessed and detailed the sites of burials. Overnight
Gloucester filled to the brim with journalists and sightseers. Fred insisted that
Rose knew nothing, but as the bodies were found over the next fortnight the
likelihood of Rose's innocence diminished. They were charged in July – Rose
on nine counts of murder and Fred on twelve. DC Hazel Swaze was made an
MBE in the New Year's Honours list. On New Year's Day 1995 Fred was found
hanging in his cell at Winson Green prison. Rose was left to stand trial alone.

One explanation for the lack of intervention in the Wests' 'affairs' is the
powerful mythology surrounding the family in our culture and social organisation. During the later nineteenth century, sexuality was moved into the home;
licensed by marriage; legitimated by reproduction; controlled by legislation and
conventionalised through culture (Foucault 1979). Marriage and family
continue to underpin British society 100 years later. The Victorian period
underwrote this cultural shift through a specific reconstruction of the feminine
as passive, maternal, married, monogamous and well-mannered – respectable
woman. Concurrently, husbanding and fatherhood 'tamed' masculinity (Collier
1994).

As the family was instituted as the appropriate site of adult sexuality, childhood was constructed as innocent; subject to parental control; supervised by
medicine and educated by the state. Marriage and family became pivotal but
conflictful sites of social/sexual control.[5] Today, these institutions are readily
reified in the press, usually through the castigation of any 'other' manifestations
of sexuality or reproduction, which are readily seen as causal of family and
consequently of social 'problems'. Hence the furore over 'single mothers' as
housing queue jumpers (Wykes and Woodcock 1996) and *delinquent breeders*
(Campbell 1991) let alone the fury over *lesbian parenting* (Rantzen BBC2
10 February 1996). Difference is readily constructed as deviance by causal association with crime.

Under this barrage of traditionalism, explanations for 'problem' families have tended to relate to unconventional sexual organisation. Poverty is rarely cited as causal above and beyond parenting; nor is there any popular discussion of the family as often a site of crisis for many battered women or abused children. Most significantly missing is the question of the father, even though in real families, he is systematically absent, feckless or abusive. In 1991 Stanko argued that most 'professionals' would be shocked at the levels of violence in the home, nearly all attributable to men, yet home and family are still promoted as the desirable norm. Bea Campbell (1988) noted that in press accounts of the Cleveland child-abuse cases the focus was on over-zealous *feminist doctors, inept liberal social workers* or *colluding mothers* rather than on men in the rôle of fathers systematically raping very small boys and girls. Later accounts continued to avoid the 'problem' by contextualising abuse in Satanism. Child-abuse court proceedings, which anyway regularly fail to convict, were further problematised with an added level of mystification and obfuscation – especially as 'Satanism is not a criminal offence' (*Guardian* 20 February 1991).

Instead of analysing the dangerousness of families, journalists tend to adopt a strategy of deflection. This shifts discussion of family problems into discourses where all but the actual causes are addressed. Lesbianism, feminism, Satanism, feminine promiscuity and psychosis take preference over any account of male, heterosexual husbandry and fathering as dysfunctional at best, terminal at worst. In its place, feminine transgression from the still resonant Victorian ideal is foregrounded as causal of familial/marital chaos, even when women are victims of violence (Wykes 1994). If men are explored as 'dangerous' this is done through personalisation, pathologisation or 'Faustianism'. Such men are unique, damaged or in league with the devil; they are thus excluded from masculinity per se and often rendered as beasts, monsters (Clark 1992) or evil. Most commonly men are barely addressed at all.

There appears to be a clash between the real and the represented: Women commit little crime, minimal violence; men commit virtually all violence and crime, yet the media focus is on the feminine. That clash suggests a construction of social/sexual identity, commensurate with the needs of power – male (patriarchal) and economic (capitalism). The representation of crime, 'normally', fails to address masculinity whilst perpetuating models of femininity that support Heidensohn's (1986) claim that, in our culture, women are represented as either *good and placed on pedestals or bad and given their just deserts*, and my addition 'women are responsible for men's badness'.[6] So good women are represented as wives, mothers and homemakers and the reality that for women and children that ideal family can be a dangerous place when it includes a father/husband figure is rarely addressed outside of feminist academia. Such representations merit concern because, in reality, the sense of self and understanding of society is articulated through language.

Feminists have tried to address the problem of male violence in the home (Dobash and Dobash 1992; Stanko 1990; Lees 1989; Hanmer *et al.* 1989) but much of this work has focused on the victims in terms of support, safe houses, therapy and legal defences. Any tangential criticisms of family men in policy – such as the recognition by local authorities that women applying for re-housing as *homeless* may be fleeing violence, and the 1991 legal recognition of rape in marriage – have led to vigorous refutation and resistance from new men's groups like *Families need Fathers* and the *Cheltenham Men's Group*. In a range of social arenas, struggles on behalf of women have been curtailed by a pretence of feminist success – post-feminism – when in reality the most entrenched and oppressive sites of patriarchy have barely been defined – male heterosexuality and paternity. Partly, perhaps, because they are barely represented. The media generally comply with this, and have been termed backlash collaborators (Faludi 1992). In the West case, the press invoked a range of discourses that obscured, reduced, deflected or obliterated criticism of generic masculine values and power.

Trial by jury and by media

In the press accounts of the first and last days of the West trial, (7 October and 23 November 1995) that lack of criticism of masculinity can be identified as working in modes, fields and sites of discourse.[7] The modes of focus are the individual subjects: Fred and Rose; small groups such as the children and the victims and institutions–social services; the police; the criminal justice service and others. The primary fields of discourse are legal and sexual. The sites are the court and the home – 25 Cromwell Street.

Through a focus on the subjects, Fred and Rose, the press accounting process attributed blame specifically to individuals. This enabled a personalisation of the crimes and pathologisation of the causes. Pre-trial press restrictions and Fred's suicide tipped the weight of this mode of account onto Rose. The invocation of the law by the press was relatively straightforward, although problematic for criminal justice. The resolutions (guilty verdicts) were pre-empted by headlines at the opening of the trial. For example: '*Rosemary West helped husband to kill 10 women after appalling and depraved violence; "Willing partner in murder"*' (*Daily Telegraph* 7 October 1995) and '*Their last moments on earth were as objects of the sexual depravity of this woman*' (*Daily Mirror* 7 October 1995). As these headlines appeared to close the criminal case so they also opened the discussion of sexuality. Post-verdict reports in the tabloids almost ignored the legal framework altogether and plunged into a construction of Rose's sexuality as depraved, illegal, violent, evil and 'perverted'. The headlines on 23 November 1995 included: '*Burn in Hell*' (*Sun*), and '*Hand in hand with Hindley*' (*Daily Mail*).

The tabloid account replicated other accounts of gendered violence (Wykes 1994, 1995; A. Young 1988; I.M. Young 1990) in that it focused almost exclusively on the feminine in a largely denigratory manner and sustained a highly conservative set of gender norms and values. Even the descriptions of the Wests' victims managed to offer negative detail. They were from children's homes;

lesbian; illegitimate; runaways; fostered; students; picked up on the 'streets' or hitchhikers. There was virtually nothing in all the coverage about the male clients who bought sex at Cromwell Street; readers were told some were West Indian but not that others were white, British and heterosexual. Few men seem to have been called as witnesses even though many policemen were familiar with the house, family and case. In fact most of the men featuring in the press coverage were members of the legal profession. The effect was to place femininity in the dock – tried by icons of traditional masculinity.

Fred as the protagonist effectively removed himself from the account through suicide. The *Sunday Mirror* reporter, Howard Sounes, described Fred's youth. He was one of the lads, 'boorish' but seen as 'one of the best looking boys around town' (Sounes 1995: 23). A motorbike accident that left Fred unconscious for seven days (with a steel plate on his fractured skull and a crushed leg and limp), combined with a later fall from a fire escape, wrought a change in Fred. 'The family began to wonder whether he had suffered brain damage' (ibid.: 29). (In the case of the Yorkshire Ripper, Peter Sutcliffe's father offered virtually the same explanation for his son's 'excesses'.) By constructing Fred as 'damaged'; his behaviour becomes pathological and personal. With this explanation, there was no need to relate his actions to either natural maleness or a culture of masculinity. Fred's torture, rape and murder of females were due to an 'accident'.

In both broadsheet and tabloid press accounts of the trial, Fred was made tangential to events. It was always Fred and Rose – or Fred was portrayed as an accomplice as, 'Frederick West is alleged to have been primarily responsible for the dismemberment and burial of the victims' (*Daily Telegraph* 7 October 1995). Such syntax, which suggests someone else killed the young women, was on the front page on the first day of Rose's trial.

Some of the references to Fred seemed inappropriately respectful. The *Daily Mirror* stated that he had an 'affair' with Shirley Robinson; the *Daily Telegraph* that he had 'sexual intercourse' with Miss X (who brought a charge of rape). The *Guardian* offered a ten-line biography of Rose and the comment that Fred 'worked as a builder'. The *Daily Star* reported that he worked long hours, whilst the *Sun* provided us with 'sex-craved housewife and her husband'. It was also curious that Fred's status as husband/father/handyman seems to have made it difficult for journalists to apply the usual non-human/non-male/abnormal terms of 'beast', 'animal' (Clark 1992), 'evil' or 'mad'. Instead the inference was that Fred was driven by a 'mad and terrible love'. Sounes told readers that Fred 'assured Rose he would take all the blame and that her everlasting love was payment enough':

> For Rose, Fred had been a good husband, a reliable provider who allowed her to have the large family she craved. He had also encouraged and condoned her passion for violent lesbian sex and been willing in crude terms to clear up afterwards.
>
> (Sounes 1995: 348)

The facts that he had already killed at least twice before they met, collected home-made pornography, had a prison sentence, had been a pimp and picked up Rose when she was fifteen and he twenty-eight could only be teased out by reading 'between the lines' of the news. Even then the information was often juxtaposed with deflecting material, such as the *Sun* informing us: 'Fred was introduced to sex by his mother' (23 November 1995). In this attribution, neither he nor the worst excesses of masculinity was responsible for the acts of brutality and perversion; they were his mother's fault. One of the dominating headlines was '*He claimed: "I was only the undertaker"* ' (*Sun* 23 November 1995), intimating that Rose was the sexual killer. In both instances Fred's behaviour was blamed on women – an abusive mother or sadistic, lesbian wife. Women are responsible for men's badness.

Rose was never 'normal'. Nicknamed dozy Rosie, she was 'backward at School, overweight and a bully who became fascinated with sex as she entered puberty' (Sounes 1995: 51). Rose was constructed as the anti-woman by the press corps, incidentally promoting a particular model of normal woman through comparison (see Derrida 1968 on '*differance*'). Rose was described in the newspapers in the following ways: *depraved; lesbian; aggressive; violent; menacing; bisexual; likes black men; likes oral sex; kinky; seductive; a prostitute; over-sexed; a child abuser; nymphomaniac; sordid; monster; she had a four poster bed with the word c**t* [sic] *carved on the head board; posed topless; exhibitionist; never wore any knickers; liked sex toys; incestuous; who shed tears in silence 'no sobs, no sound at all'.* At puberty she, allegedly, developed an obsession for sex and 'Fred confided', 'When Rose was pregnant her lesbian tendencies were at their strongest. I had to go out and get her a girl. She gets urges that have to be satisfied' (*Sun* 23 November 1995). Such a commentary links to the bio-explanations for women's violence found in accounts of so-called pre-menstrual and post-puerperal killing, and maintains a model of femininity always close to *mad* (Young 1988). In the same accounting vein, the *Daily Mail* of 23 November 1995 paralleled the case with that of Hindley with the information that 'Rose West and Myra Hindley have formed a macabre friendship in jail . . . the two most evil women in Britain, both openly bi-sexual – have been seen holding hands in Durham prison'.

It may be that Rose West killed all the victims, or that she only killed Charmaine (when Rose was seventeen with a new baby and two small stepchildren in a one-bedroom flat). It may be that she colluded with or even instigated sexual violence. It may be that she performed sexually for money (and/or for others) at Fred's behest; she certainly advertised for clients. These possible truths are less my concern than how and for whose benefit such matters were reported: partly for the impact that may have had directly or indirectly on criminal justice, partly for the effect it may have had on *us*, the public, and specifically on women.

The accounts of Fred and Rose were personalised, but qualitatively and quantitatively different – this was not narrative of male sexual violence but of female inadequacy (as mother) and perversion (as wife). It was also a story about what happens to feckless girls who leave home young and/or take lifts from strangers on city streets. This was the gender-conservative account the tabloids offered and some twelve million newspaper buyers read daily, for several weeks.

Of course the quality, broadsheet press eschewed such overtly sexualised and sexist agenda (at least some of the time) and there was evidence of less salacious detail, but in many ways the net effect was broadly complementary. The tabloids offered a recognisable calling to consensus around sexuality ('none of this would have happened if women involved had been good mothers – monogamous and respectable'); the broadsheet agenda focused more around the home and family or, rather, focused on diverting the critical discussion from home and family. The quality papers did this by turning their (and our) attention to the various institutions, which could be found culpable of neglect; impropriety; ineptitude and mismanagement of information. Their liberal attribution of blame closely paralleled the earlier coverage of child abuse.

The broadsheets discussed a range of agency failures *to intervene* (yet when doctors and social workers did intervene in Cleveland they were dubbed liberal/feminist and anti-family). In Gloucester there was a 'communications failure' between schools, hospital, NSPCC, social services and the police. These are predominantly staffed by women, with the exception of the police-force, which is minimally castigated. The *Guardian* (23 November 1995) lists nineteen of these instances on the front page, by decade. Examples are:

1960s Seven of the ten victims had been in care at any one time between 1965 and 1979, as had two of the main three survivors, but Social Services had no record of 25 Cromwell Street being where they were sent.

1970s The West family had thirty-one treatments at accident and emergency between 1972 and 1992. These included many injuries for which different and unconvincing explanations were given.

1980s In 1987 Fred West did tell a teacher he had 'laid Stephen out'. The teacher did not feel it merited a child protection order.

Neither the tabloid/conservative nor the broadsheet/liberal news offered a radical[8] account, which might have questioned the social relations that enabled such atrocities. Nor did either address masculinity as a problem; the conservative model minimally interrogated Fred as a phenomenon but not as a man, whilst the liberal agenda was to divert the debate from a failure of family to a failure of institutional services.

Home is where the hurt/heart is

One explanation for such an interrogative gap is that the case goes against the grain of everyday understandings about home/family: understandings, which can be construed as symbolically central to British subjectivity and socio-culture

(Weedon 1987). For most of us, home is a taken-for-granted concept about place, identity, privacy and security. It is closely linked to personal relations with others (sexual and familial) yet is also a site of intervention and information for public bureaucracy. Local authorities, health administration, police records, utility providers, education, financial services and demographers monitor our movement and status via our homes. In the reports of the West case the 'house of horrors' works as a trope for a range of representation, allusion and attribution. As readers, the deep familiarity with the concept of home adds potency and clarity to the interpretation. For women that may be especially intense because women's sense of self and respectability is 'endlessly defined in culture' McRobbie (1993), around sexual norms and values.

Central to those values are the concepts of wife and mother, which are often marked with a move from the home/house of our childhood to the new marital, family home/house.[9] Home is belonging; home is safe; home is where the heart is. Yet our fictional culture is steeped with less welcoming versions of homes (Wykes and Jones 1994). The threatening, imprisoning, ambivalent, isolated or secretive house pervades not only a long, gothic, literary tradition but also more contemporary culture in a series of popular films such as *Psycho* (1960), *Rosemary's Baby* (1968), *Poltergeist* (1982), *Wars of the Roses* (1989) and *Pacific Heights* (1990). In fantastic representation, houses are often sites of terror; spaces where the worst excesses of human behaviour and human nightmare are played out. In contrast, in realistic texts such as policy documents and advertising, houses are portrayed as good investments, Englishmen's castles, love nests or IKEA-style templates – good places to raise a family. The evidence is increasingly that many women and children's experience of house and home is closer to the ghastly fantasy than the realism, yet the mythic pervasiveness of that fantastic popular culture removes our interpretation to Gothic twilight rather than enlightening us about the culture of suburban England. Domestic violence and child abuse 'can't be real'.

We now know that women suffer violence in large numbers in their own homes (Dobash and Dobash 1992); that most murdered children are killed by parents (Wilczynski 1995) and that sexual and physical child-abuse within families is more common-place than many can bear to accept (Campbell 1988). Yet the confused dynamic between the realistic/fantastic versions of home seems to generate a symbolic barrier across the threshold of the house which problematises research on the family as causal of such violence. It is as if there is a mythic wall, as well as real bricks and mortar, shielding private lives from the public gaze and distorting our view of the family towards the realist models offered by commerce, the state, the church and welfare organisations. Generally, we simply do not know what goes on behind closed doors because to enter another's house uninvited requires the sanction of the law. Moreover, because we are all so dependent on home/family myths for our sense of self, reluctance to critically explore behind closed doors is utterly understandable. To deal with our worst nightmares of house and home as general, everyday truth is perhaps conceptually untenable, massively inhibiting theory, let alone practice.

Theorising and analysing cultural representations and values, associated with gendered violence, can offer insights into the failure of criminal justice to effectively intercede prior to disaster (and even after it in some cases) and the tenor of most of the public-domain accounts of the West case. Our everyday notion of the family, and perhaps more crucially the role of heterosexual, paternal masculinity within the family, is seen, over and over and inter-factual-textually, as unproblematic, even when the evidence is of systematic human devastation through generations. Male violence is secure in the family, in the home, behind closed doors, because it is invisible – symbolically and physically. If manifest, it is disguised – blame is shifted readily into attributes such as deviant femininity, psychopathology and stranger danger. Historic patriarchal power, is contained within walls – literally – and disguised by walls – metaphorically. Male abuse is secured by the myth of home and family, sustained in language through institutions and popular culture.

A familiar Story

Both Fred and Rose came from large families, which in 'back to basics' terms appear normal, if allegedly dominated by an overbearing father in each case. Few of the press accounts offer much detail on either childhood in reports prior to or during the trial.[10] The Sounes book, published soon after the case, reveals that Fred and Rose :

> Had a stable home where they lived for many years and where they intended to stay, a mortgage, which they worked hard to pay off and a large family. They were the people next door, who waved a cheery hello to neighbours as they walked down the street. Their home was the centre of an English city, just yards from a shopping centre and a police station, a street where hundreds of people passed by every week.
>
> (Sounes 1995: 333)

Their public image complied with a conventional model of British family life – heterosexual couple; children; mortgage; hardworking; neighbourly. Nothing in this adult life seems causal of sexual violence, incest and murder or even suggestive of it; at least nothing that has been made public.

The biographies offered by Sounes hint at sexually deviant childhood experiences but it is clear that the evidence for these was usually suspect. It was gossip, titillation and innuendo: 'If Fred was abused by his own mother that may have had something to with his attitude to sex, but this is only hearsay' (1995: 335); 'It was understood by members of the West family at 25 Cromwell St that Rose had been sexually abused by her father' (1995: 56). Rose's family led a semi-urban life; her father was employed in a factory whilst Fred's worked the land and led a rural and poor existence in circumstances Sounes hints made 'it possible they became closer than natural' (1995: 19). Such a hint was later given weight by Channel 4 *Dispatches* (November 1995) when a retired police officer claimed that incest was/is rife in Gloucestershire. He commented: *why go outside the family when it's available free within?*

It may be that Fred and Rose had childhood experiences which promoted sexual relations between siblings and/or parent and child as acceptable; such biographies are often thought to underwrite adult in-family abusers (Campbell 1988). But neither Fred nor Rose, even on the basis of unsubstantiated rumour, seems to have grown up familiar with kidnap, torture or murder linked to sexuality. Nor do their histories point to a future of prostitution, pimping or procurement and the production of pornographic video material.

The link between sexuality, violence and commerce has no family history in the West case – what it does have is socio-economic context. The criminal commerciality of the West's activities was barely discussed throughout the press accounts; instead explanation focuses on pop-psycho-sexual babble. It may be of course that Fred and Rose never charged for sexual favours; never sold videos; never took room rental from voyeurs and never procured their own and other children to satisfy customers' sexual appetites. Alternatively, all the extremes of their sexual sadism were purely a personal indulgence – sometimes overstepping the mark and leaving Fred 'the undertaker' with a corpse to dispose of. It may be right to explain the awful events at Cromwell Street as pathologies – peculiar; individual; traumatic and dramatic – but such an explanation leaves too much intact at Cromwell Street. How could a family go so awry in the first place? Such a question necessitates taking a critical view of family life, difficult to initiate let alone to sustain in a political and cultural climate that is almost universally pro-family.

To suggest that 'family' may provide a haven, or even the impetus, for child abuse and sexual perversion is controversial. The *Sun* never came out with the headline '*Dad buggers his baby son*' during the Cleveland child abuse case, even though that was the news event, whilst the *Guardian* misinformed readers with the headline: '*Cleveland: the doctors were wrong*'.[11] Criticism of the institution of the family and the power it confers on adults (especially on heterosexual men as husbands and fathers), even the concession that masculinity is dangerous, let alone dangerous and hidden by family, would pose an enormous threat to our value system. This lack of media critique is important because, in a kind of dominant group-think, the press can confirm and/or excite broader explicatory models offered by medicine, the law, social work and popular culture. These other discourses pick up on the personalisation central to news values[12] so crime is often psycho-pathologised, leaving the socio-sexual foundations of the broader social order intact.

Critiquing the individuals, usually (often by default) the woman,[13] was much favoured by the popular press during the trial in Gloucester. Media castigation of women's behaviour, in terms of non-compliance with normal expectations of femininity, often focuses on maternity[14] and sexuality, and the tabloids complied in the West case. In the title to 'Naggers, whores and libbers: driving men to murder' (1989), Sue Lees neatly summed up the classic value labels which construct women as to blame for family collapse, their children's abuse and even their own death.[15] For the tabloids, 25 Cromwell Street was a site of feminine transgression.

Less inclined to personification and gender conservatism than the tabloids, the broadsheets replicated the debates on the roles of social workers so tiresomely repeated each time a child suffers either at its parents' hands (Jasmine Beckford case, 1985), or a child is removed from its natural family (the Orkneys, 1991). Such debates rarely discuss the family as problematic, only the mechanisms for maintaining it as effective or not. The liberal, broadsheet thesis deflected attention from masculinity and family towards bureaucratic failure, very often called 'communications breakdown'.

The implications of such signification are several: masculine violence is seen as women's responsibility; masculinity is barely analysed; Victorian models of femininity are constantly reaffirmed; the family is under-researched and psycho-sexual knowledge paradigms are given explanatory precedence over political economy or feminist social accounts. Characterising both accounting models is a systematic lack of (admitted) awareness of masculinity as a problem.

Critical comments

Journalists, lawyers, police officers, social workers, criminologists and psychologists seemed unaware of the terminal (often literally ending life) patriarchy at the heart of Cromwell Street: it was present in Rose's family (the Letts); the West family[16]; Fred's behaviour; the punters at Cromwell Street; the buyers of the porn movies and amongst the experts and authorities. Such unawareness was not due to ignorance but because masculine values and interests are so much part of cultural hegemony that they appear natural – so natural that it requires an act of will (political will) to objectify them – to make them other. To place dominance under the analytic gaze is awkward and uncomfortable because it means questioning our own subjectivity, so heavily dependent on the families within which we are constituted and the language of our community, both of which are steeped in masculine ideology. Such a process necessitates consciousness-raising and a commitment to change – it certainly means many men critically considering their own identity and the benefits offered by everyday masculinity. Brownmiller's (1975) controversial claim that all men are rapists was never intended to be literal – but it did suggest that all men gain sexual power from the one rapist's sexual violence which through language and the media keeps women in fear and in convention[17] and it is useful here. The masculine model of home and family is self-perpetuating because it renders alternative models – gay parents, single parents, communal living – denigrate or deviant.

Masculine interest and values underpin journalistic ideology and practices, which are still imbued with the model of the macho-hack or Oxbridge (Tunstall 1996). A recent survey (Christmas 1997) uncovered sexist attitudes and practices both in products and processes. Policing also has its own set of problems – not least of which are several high-profile sexual harassment cases, as in D.C. Dina Fleming's charges against Lincolnshire police (local TV News, 18.30, BBC1 9 May 1997). The prevalence of patriarchal ideology also informs the epistemology of explanatory sciences like psychology, which ignore masculinity as a genus – favouring individual analysis. The same argument applies to criminology, which as Maureen Cain (1990) suggested has yet to recognise the *masculinism at the heart of its project*, not least in crimino-genesis. In universities only three per cent of professors are women, and publishing and research in media and cultural studies are dominated by, what a young colleague recently termed, the 'middle-aged, middle-class, male, media Mafia'. Knowledge is power and power is patriarchal.

Work on discourses of representation and explanation offers some insights into the nature of accounts of the Wests – in terms of what is present, lacking, why and with what implications – and of course a direction for more adequate investigation. The 'cultural turn' of work in media analysis, Stuart Hall argues, means primacy is often given to understanding the 'production and exchange of meanings' rather than to the contextualisation of those processes within powerfully directive political and economic institutions and relations (Hall 1997: 2). Such contextualisation offers up another possible explanation for the diversions, obfuscations and closing downs in these accounts.

The *Daily Mail* (23 November 1995) offered a headline once, which appeared nowhere else: '*Rose's home was police brothel*'. 'A Police Complaints Authority investigation has cleared Gloucester police' (*Star* 26 September 1996) of that accusation but nowhere has there been there any denial that 'the cellar at 25 Cromwell Street was not just an abattoir, it was a child brothel' (*Observer* 26 November 1995). The Wests were known to sell sex. Yet no prosecutions were ever brought either for soliciting or possession of obscene material. Why were Fred's videos destroyed when the earlier assault case was dropped? Why were so many videos made?[18] Did he sell them? If so, who to? (According to the press, local video stores claimed they had been offered home-made porn by Fred, but none admitted buying). Were they snuff movies? Who was featured – Fred, Rose, the murdered young women, other victims, other punters? Why were social services records of missing girls mislaid or partial?

Much of the activity at Cromwell Street suggests more than personal depravity. Fred had previous convictions and the *Observer* claimed 'police knew of other attacks on women' (26 November 1995) but there were no prosecutions. Many of the Wests' victims had links to nearby Jordan's Brook children's home. Fred and Rose offered company and sanctuary to frequent escapees, until police took them 'home'. 'Yet the home had no record of any connection between its children and 25 Cromwell St.'.

Events at Cromwell Street, Gloucester, suggest a wider implication than Fred and Rose – many men moved through the house unscathed; many organisations held information about the family, yet many questions about paedophilia, pornography, procurement and profit from immoral earnings were never asked – let alone answered.

In Cheshire recently, 'three senior social workers, from NCH action for children, have been jailed for physical and sexual attacks on children at Danesford community home . . . 13 paedophiles have been convicted and more than 500 complaints have been made' (*Observer* 9 March 1997). Whilst discoveries in Belgium – '*Police search for children's bodies amid fears of international sex ring*' (*Guardian* 19 August 1996) – support the existence of widespread, powerful groups of paedophiles – kidnapping, sexually abusing, imprisoning, killing young girls and selling images of the process. '*Hi-tech sex*' (*Marie Claire* April 1993) discusses cyber-porn on the internet – practically beyond policy and policing, and readily available down the telephone line. Child sexual services and pornography are multi-million dollar businesses. Men who produce, use and trade this material are secretive and powerful. A British diplomat was jailed for three years (2 September 1996) for importing child pornography – he thought his luggage would be shipped straight to Madrid where he would be protected from customs by diplomatic immunity. It seems to me to make sense to place Cromwell Street in this wider context – in which case the story is only partly told and the sentencing/resolution pre-emptive and restricted.

Even if these last concerns can only be speculative, the skewedness of the accounts offers a clear interpretation. Whether through conspiracy or hegemony, many aspects of the story of the West family were never fully explored or explained. It is hard to see Rose as a victim of the violent abuse of masculine and commercial power, but easy to see her as a scapegoat.

Notes

1 Previously the press had preferred class 'violence' as epitomised by the Miners' strike of 1984–5, and prior to that racial tension as evidenced by the inner city disturbances 1981–5. The turn to the family and gender can be traced to the coverage of child-abuse cases in 1986–7, specifically to the Cleveland case.

2 Lord Taylor warned that the cheque book journalism which characterised press activity during the West case 'could put justice at risk'. Government is putting pressure on the Press Complaints Commission to regulate because '19 witnesses signed media contracts' during the West case (*Guardian* 30 October 1996). If the new Code of Practice is agreed, editors could face jail for payments to witnesses..

3 1972 is the year Caroline Owens brought a charge of rape against the Wests. She refused to testify and the Wests were fined for sexual assault.

4 Four of the West children were still in care in Spring 1996. Social workers were having to fight 'to protect their legal rights to the estate of their parents' (*County News* February 1996, vol. 88) in light of various media deals.

5 However this control works in sometimes contradictory ways. Foucault (1979) refutes the repressive hypothesis. He claims rather than contain sexual activity it drew focus to it leading to a proliferation of alternative/perverse practices and pleasures. In the 1990s these are evident in the rampant commodification of sex; recently

blamed for youth rape (*Observer* 11 May 1997). What we are instructed to reject through discourses of normal sexuality we are tempted to indulge in through the needs of the market place. Such contradictions leave the area of sexuality a site of struggle, riddled with ideological gaps, which provide glimpses of the exercise of power and only by knowing how power works can we struggle for change (Hartsock 1990).

6 See Wykes (1994). When women are victims they are often blamed for their own demise in ways which suggest they let down the men who kill them, and so are responsible for men's violence.

7 See Foucault (1980) for a full account of these concepts.

8 This is not surprising given the difficulties encountered by the only recent attempt to provide radical accounts in a newspaper, 'News on Sunday' (Wykes 1991).

9 I use wife/husband and marriage to generically include 'significant heterosexual others' and 'living together' on the basis that our roles and values often remain similar in the more modern construct (monogamy; commitment; loyalty; family etc.) even if the labels and processes have changed

10 Hearsay suggested that journalists were anxious at the time of the trial that Rose should not be offered sympathy by disclosure of any hint of abuse within her family. The same source also suggested to me that further cases of child abuse were likely to be forthcoming involving the West family, and therefore some evidence was being withheld; see note 16.

11 For a more detailed discussion see Campbell (1988), which claims only some twenty of the 120 children diagnosed as abused by use of the anal dilation technique were ever returned to their intact, original families.

12 See Galtung and Ruge (1965) for the seminal and still-valid account of news values.

13 There is a certain irony that this is also true in the West case. Once Fred had removed himself from the accounting-from through suicide, all the attention was directed towards Rose's deviance.

14 When mountaineer Alison Hargreaves died on Mount Everest in 1996, leaving two small children, she was lambasted throughout the media as a bad mother. The paternal role is never part of the discourse around male adventure.

15 Wykes (1995); Wykes and Jones (1994) offers more on this area

16 Fred's brother, John, hung himself on 29 November 1996 rather than face the verdict of the jury in a trial where he was accused by his niece of systematic rape. 'The two brothers were close in the seventies when John took part in sexual activities at Cromwell St. He and Rosemary had sex on a number of occasions' (*Guardian* 30 November 1996).

17 Often rape is blamed on the woman – for dressing immodestly, being out late, flirting or hitch-hiking (Wykes 1995). See also Benedict (1992), Clark (1992), Stanko (1990), Lees (1989), Brownmiller (1975). The underlying message is 'stay home; stay modest; stay pure'.

18 The *Sun* (22 November 1995) claimed Rose and Fred had a library of 200 porn videos, gathered since the original collection was destroyed by police in 1992, but there is no mention of these being offered as evidence, their nature, or their subsequent whereabouts.

15

CRIMEWATCH UK

Keeping women off the streets

C. Kay Weaver

Introduction

Through an examination of *Crimewatch UK*'s reporting of a sexual assault and murder of a young woman, this analysis discusses how such news programmes mediate messages to women about the need for self-regulation if they are to avoid becoming the victim of violent crimes. Drawing on a combination of both textual and reception research, the investigation illustrates how crime reconstructions help promote the power of a gendered hegemony by reinforcing women's fears for their safety in public spaces.

Television programmes showing reconstructions of real-life crime are a regular and popular feature of the British television schedules. *Crimewatch UK*, broadcast since 1984 on BBC1, a public service broadcasting channel, was the first of such programmes transmitted in the UK. It has since been followed by two sister productions *Crimewatch Unlimited* and *Crimewatch File*, also broadcast on BBC1, and on commercial television by ITV's *Crimestoppers*, *Crime Story* and Michael Winner's *True Crimes* series, and London Weekend Television's *Crime Monthly*.

Transmitted nationally once a month ten times a year (with a break over the summer months), *Crimewatch UK* is made by the BBC documentary features department with extensive co-operation from the police. In relation to the BBC's public service remit, this programme functions to 'seek help and information from its audience in the solution of major crimes' (*BBC Annual Report and Handbook 1986*: 9). With each edition watched by up to 12 million viewers, *Crimewatch* also serves the BBC's need to attract audiences. The types of crimes featured in the programme and their reporting methods play a crucial role in attracting and holding these viewers. As Schlesinger *et al.* detail, 'the programme team select their crime stories from the popular end of the market, with murder, armed robbery with violence and sexual crime as the staple items of coverage' (1991: 408). Denying that this constitutes a concentration on the reporting of sensational crime, Anne Morrison, Executive Producer in charge of BBC crime programmes, has argued that *Crimewatch* simply 'appeals on the most serious cases which have happened, which very often are murders, rapes and so on' (interviewed on *Biteback*, BBC1 5 December 1993).

Yet, crime reconstruction programmes such as *Crimewatch UK* have been surrounded by controversy. The moral justification of their presenting real-life crime as entertainment has been questioned (Hebert 1988, 1993; Minogue 1990; Sweeney 1992), and they are accused of creating a public fear of crime, or even capitalising on that fear (Hebert 1993; Moore 1993; Osborne 1995; Sweeney 1992). Further, they have been described as voyeuristic (Culf 1993; Hebert 1993) and sensationalist (Moore 1993).[1] Research also demonstrates that these programmes have particular consequences for women in terms of increasing their fear of crime and/or concern about their personal safety (BBC Broadcasting Research 1988: 18; Schlesinger *et al.* 1992: ch. 3; Wober and Gunter 1990: ii).

The fact that crime-reconstruction programmes can increase women's fear of crime could be considered an effect of violent sex crimes against women forming part of their staple menu for coverage. However, this increased fear needs also to be considered in relation to *how* these type of crimes are recon-structed, given that crime reconstructions stretch the category of 'factual reportage' and involve a 'blurring' of fact and fiction by drawing on narrative techniques very similar to those of crime-fiction (Kilborn 1994: 63). More accurately described as '*dramatised* reconstructions', these often show events entirely incidental to the crimes and which are included purely to increase viewer involvement in the programme.

The manner in which violent sex crimes against women are represented in crime reconstruction programmes can also be considered in relation to claims made by the Annenberg School of Communication's Cultural Indicators Project. The Annenberg researchers assert that media representations of violence constitute a means of social control in that they 'vividly dramatise the preferred power relations and cultivate fear, dependence on authority, and the desire for security rather than social change' (White 1983: 287). They also argue that television's repeated portrayal of certain groups as victims represents a symbolic expression of the social impotence of those victim types (Gerbner and Gross 1976: 82). In terms of the audience, such symbolic imagery is theorised as cultivating social conceptions about 'who are the aggressors and who are the victims' where 'there is a relationship between the roles of the violent and the victim. Both roles are there to be learned by viewers' (Gerbner *et al.* 1979: 180). As is argued below in the investigation of *Crimewatch UK*, there are considerable grounds to claim that this programme does indeed contribute to this type of learning for women viewers.

The analysis focuses on a *Crimewatch* reconstruction concerning the sexual assault and murder of a seventeen-year-old female hitchhiker. The first part of the investigation examines how viewers are encouraged to engage with and read this presentation through the reporting and narrativisation of the crime, and the characterisation of its victim. The second part presents the findings of reception research into women's readings of the reconstruction. The reception analysis draws on data originally gathered for the book *Women Viewing Violence*, the aim of which was to investigate 'What . . . women *make* of the violence that they see in the media . . . to try to probe what representations of violence against women *mean* in their lives' (Schlesinger *et al.* 1992: 3, original emphasis). In examining this, *Women Viewing Violence* concentrated on assessing how the social, cultural and material experiences of women interviewees affected responses to portrayals of violence. It did not consider how the *texts* themselves may have encouraged certain interpretations and understandings of that violence. Yet it is significant that the project concluded that:

> for the most part, the violence on television portrayed in this study was not defined as 'exciting' or 'entertaining', but rather as 'educational' or 'relevant', while at the same time as 'disturbing' and sometimes 'offensive'. Thus the importance attributed to what was viewed was not in terms of pleasure, escape or fantasy but in terms of relevance and social importance.
>
> (Schlesinger *et al.* 1992: 169)

Here, it is this question of how women thought that this crime report was of *educational relevance* and *social importance* which is of central concern. Thus, it is what women believed they *learnt* from the depiction which is at issue.[2]

The reception study comprised ninety-one women formed into fourteen groups. Half of these women had experienced physical violence of a domestic and/or sexual nature, whilst the other half had no such physical experience of violence. Groups varied further in terms of nationality, class and ethnic background. In Scotland, six groups were interviewed: one white working-class group, one white middle-class group and an Asian group, all with no experience of violence; and two groups of white women and a group of Asian women all with experience of violence. In England, similarly constituted groups were interviewed as in Scotland, with the addition of one Afro-Caribbean group of women with experience of violence and one with no such experience.

Textual analysis of the reconstruction

This reconstruction was presented in a style typical of all *Crimewatch* reconstructions, in that actors play the roles of crime victims, witnesses and suspects (though in this particular reconstruction the murder suspect does not figure, as nothing was known about this individual), and a presenter's voice-over narrates events surrounding the crime. In this instance the regular male presenter, Nick Ross, provided this voice-over and, in-studio, introduced the reconstruction thus:

The last of this month's reconstructions is yet another that highlights the dangers of hitchhiking. Now young people, and especially young women of course, know the risks of hitchhiking. But the truth is, if you don't have a bike or a car and there are no buses where you want to go when you want to go, the temptation to hitch is overwhelming.

Over a photograph of a young white woman with long dark hair, dressed in jeans and a cardigan, Ross's voice-over continues: 'Rachael Partridge took that risk. She was seventeen years old'. This introduction immediately and explicitly suggests that Rachael was a victim of crime *because* she went hitchhiking. It implies that no sensible young person, and especially a *woman*, would hitch-hike without considerable concern for their safety. Hitchhiking is then described as a 'temptation' – one Rachael evidently succumbed to. Focusing entirely on the victim of this crime, Ross's introduction encourages audiences to view the reconstruction as a critical examination of a young woman who acted without prudence. Therefore, it is presented as having, among other functions, a didactic role, where viewers are alerted to the folly of hitchhiking. This is further emphasised by the calm, matter-of-fact tone of Nick Ross's voice-over, the intonation of which remains constant throughout the reconstruction, up until the point where details of the discovery of Rachael's body are presented. At that point the voice-over takes on a sombreness which tends to reinforce a reading of the reconstruction as a moral tale about the fatal consequences of a young woman's lack of vigilance. This is especially so given that practically no evidence on who the perpetrator of the crime might be is contained in the crime's reporting.

As the reconstruction begins, visuals and verbal information are presented which locate the area in which the crime was committed. These enable viewers to consider whether this locality is known to them, and whether there is a chance they may be able to assist the crime investigation. Yet it is also notable that this establishing of the geographical context for the crime story bears considerable similarity to the sort of early narrative scene-setting which occurs in crime fiction.

Scenes two and three, again conforming to accepted conventions of fiction 'storytelling', introduce the 'character' at the centre of the real-life drama, Rachael. These scenes are among a number contained in the reconstruction which are entirely superfluous to the needs of providing information which might help solve the crime. In scene two, Rachael is shown working at a dental laboratory and Ross's voice-over states that her employers were very impressed with her. In scene three, over the same photograph of Rachael used in the introduction to the reconstruction, Ross explains that Rachael was the youngest of three sisters and that she lived with her parents in the countryside. With this comes the potential to consider the family as perhaps affluent and middle-class. The fact that Rachael succumbed to the 'temptation' to hitchhike might then be regarded as surprising. Her intelligence, and *possible* privileged and 'respectable' upbringing, could be viewed as providing her with the resources to know better than to hitchhike, as well as the financial means to pay for trans-portation home – assuming such transportation was available.

Scenes four, five and six continue to portray Rachael in contexts superfluous to the murder investigation, further develop her characterisation and promote a sense of identification with her, and also introduce her boyfriend, Steven. In scene four, Rachael and Steven are seen sitting together on a large settee laughing at each other's passports. They are described as having been together for some time and about to embark on a first holiday together in Italy. Thus, an additional tragedy surrounding Rachael's death is introduced. Though clearly fond of each other, there is no indication that the couple have indulged in sexual activity, as only limited physical contact occurs between them. As scene four continues, Rachael appears thoughtful in not wanting to detain her mother who arrives in a car to take her home. With scene five, showing Rachael's mother in the car outside Steven's house, it can be further extrapolated that Rachael was not in the habit of staying overnight with Steven, an interpretation supported by the voice-over stating that Rachael simply visited him 'most *evenings*'. In terms of classic narrativisation techniques, scenes four and five thus show a 'happy situation', and an evidently innocent and 'respectable' one, which is about to be disrupted.

Scene six of the reconstruction offers indications of the motivations for Rachael's later hitchhiking and sets the central narrative plot in motion. As Rachael and her mother drive down a country road in the car, Ross's voice-over states that 'though Rachael's mother had specially driven down to the village to bring her home, Rachael announced that she had other plans that night'. Rachael then asks her mother to take her to a girl friend Alex's house so she can use a sunbed. Although her mother says that she cannot as her father needs the car, Ross's voice-over explains that:

> Rachael couldn't be persuaded. She didn't want to go home and there wasn't time to take her to her friend's in Thame. So her mother turned around and, at Rachael's request, left her back in the village. Once there, Rachael met a colleague from work and cadged a lift to Thame to use her friend's sunbed.

Here, what could be considered an adolescent insistence on going to Alex's contrasts with the earlier characterisation of Rachael as a responsible and thoughtful young women: in this scene she makes impossible demands on her mother in selfishly asserting that her needs are more important than her father's need for the car. Further, with the voice-over stating that Rachael '*cadged* a lift to Thame', there comes an invitation to perceive her in a critical light in relation to an evident willingness to impose on the good nature of a colleague. At this point then, Rachael's respectability can be brought into doubt.

An example of how *Crimewatch* reconstructions tend toward voyeurism comes with scene seven. Again, this scene is of no relevance to the pursuit of

Rachael's killer. Alex is shown switching on a sunbed and telling Rachael to use it for ten minutes only. In medium close-up, Rachael lies on the sunbed in a white bra and eye protectors. She protests, saying she doesn't want to be 'all white and horrible on the beach'. Alex says she risks being 'all red and horrible'. Rachael giggles. The voice-over states, 'after using the sunbed Rachael had the problem of getting home'. In terms of a dramatic plot function, this scene illustrates that it was Rachael's wanting to use the sunbed that caused her to hitchhike home. Yet Rachael's partial nakedness and giggling on the bed could be considered titillating, particularly as this is shot from above, with the point-of-view being one bearing down on her. Further, this scene could imply a lack of responsibility and common sense on Rachael's part through a vain desire to remain on the sunbed for longer than is wise. Such an interpretation is enhanced if Rachael's attitude is compared with that of Alex, who emphasises the dangers. Thus, the portrayal links notions of feminine vanity and the wish for a desirable body designed to solicit public attention, with notions of risk-taking behaviour and, therefore, notions of culpability.

A critical perception of Rachael could also be achieved if her lack of concern about getting home is compared with her boyfriend's attitude in scene eight. In temporal terms this scene illustrates what other characters were doing while Rachael was with Alex. It consists of an image of Steven riding a motorbike with Ross's voice-over stating 'Her boyfriend had heard she was somewhere in Thame and knew there were no buses back, so he went to look for her. Ironically he drove right past the road where Rachael was'. Steven thus demonstrates a sense of foresight totally lacking in Rachael who, in scene nine, is seen leaving Alex's house with the voice-over explaining that 'Rachael had no way home now except to hitch a lift'. A caption reading 8.40 p.m. appears at the bottom of the frame as Rachael walks down the pavement waving goodbye to Alex. Additionally, this scene again provides the potential to view Rachael as middle-class given her association with Alex, who lives in an obviously expensive house.

It is only when scenes ten and eleven are reached that the reconstruction begins to portray Rachael in contexts which might help bring forth evidence from viewers about when she was last seen alive, who was responsible for her death, and at what time she met that person. The initial image of her in scene ten is designed to resemble that reported by individuals who saw her as she attempted to hitchhike. At this point the voice-over states that witnesses had seen Rachael hitchhiking, and that she was seen talking to the driver of a white van. Accompanying visuals show a figure standing beside a white van in the distance. Scene eleven then depicts Rachael in long shot on another section of road, where she had also been sighted, looking nervously at passing cars. The voice-over commentary explains that 'this is the outskirts of Thame. Beyond this point there are no street lights. Rachael was frightened of the dark and there was six miles of black country lanes between Rachael and her home at Chinnor Hill'.

With scenes twelve and thirteen, the reconstruction again turns to presenting events which serve dramatic needs rather than informational ones in depicting what was occurring 'elsewhere' at the time Rachael was hitchhiking, and again feature Steven. First he is portrayed in mid-close up making phone calls in a worried effort to locate Rachael. He is then shown outside a local pub on his motorbike, but it is explained that on not finding Rachael, at 11 o'clock he gave up looking for her. This portrayal of Steven's search for Rachael clearly invites the audience to identify with a concern for her well-being.

The final two scenes of the reconstruction detail how, and where, Rachael's body was found. The voice-over explains that she was discovered by two farm workers in a barn just off a farm track, that her body was naked with blood around the head and neck. Accompanying visuals first show two men, in extreme long-shot, jumping from a tractor and running towards a barn. With the scene-change, this same barn is then seen again in extreme long-shot surrounded by police personnel and vehicles. Finally, over the same photograph of Rachael featured earlier, Ross's voice-over states in sombre tone, that 'Rachael had been struck heavily on the face, sexually assaulted and asphyxiated'. Such information might function to further persuade viewers of the need to come forward with information relating to the crime and/or assist in the identification and capture Rachael's killer. However, this detailing of Rachael's death also caters to a desire to know exactly what was involved in her murder, a desire encouraged by the enigmatic nature of the story presented in the reconstruction. In terms of classic narrative conventions, the point has been reached where the happy social equilibrium of Rachael's life depicted in the early scenes of the reconstruction is now revealed as tragically and terminally violated.

Whilst the ending of this reconstruction serves to report on the crime committed against Rachael, it also demonstrates what can happen to those who are tempted to hitchhike. If viewers adopt this reading of the reconstruction as a message against hitchhiking, as they are clearly encouraged to, then with this would very likely come a critical reading of Rachael as she functions to illustrate what can happen to women who fail to protect their own safety. As Gordon and Riger argue, 'blame acts as a cautionary warning to other women not to do the same' (1989: 122).

The reception analysis

Having explored how the crime presentation about the sexual assault and murder was constructed and mediated by the makers of *Crimewatch*, we now turn to examine how women viewers read and engaged with this reconstruction. Though the above analysis argues that the reconstruction contains a preferred reading which warns against hitchhiking, and one which implies that it was largely Rachael's irresponsible behaviour that led to her demise, it cannot be assumed that *all* women would accept and/or concur with this reading. Therefore, the intention of the reception analysis is to identify whether, and to what extent, if at all, the groups of women interviewees did indeed adopt this reading, and to examine how the reconstruction might contribute to their understandings of how and why women are subjected to male violence.

Reading the reconstruction as a warning against hitchhiking

Interviewees engaged with this text on a range of levels. Broadly speaking, the reconstruction was universally perceived as intended to develop an *awareness* of this type of violent sex crime and how it could be avoided. There was comparatively much less discussion of *Crimewatch's* intention to help solve the crime. This might be a consequence of this murder having been committed in a locality unfamiliar to the respondents. Yet it could also be considered an effect of Nick Ross's statement that this reconstruction was '*highlighting the dangers of hitchhiking*'. In all of the groups, respondents viewed the reconstruction as an illustration of this danger, and as a warning to those who might be tempted to hitchhike. For example:

> People have got to be made aware. Some seventeen year old lassie could have watched it and said 'Well if I'm in the same situation I'd better not do that'.
> (Scottish white working-class woman, with no experience of violence)

> That's the type of thing I would have done at that age myself [hitch-hiking]. But then you didn't have *Crimewatch* and you weren't aware of crimes.
> (Scottish white middle-class woman, with no experience of violence)

Very evident in the responses were widely expressed beliefs that women are vulnerable to attack in public places. This is demonstrated in comments made by many of the women who considered *Crimewatch* to be performing a valuable role in stressing that women should be extremely vigilant in relation to their personal safety. For example:

> It says you [should] be careful – more aware. Don't just walk along the street. . . . I don't see anything wrong with walking at night and looking around you all the time, because that's the way you've got to be these days.
> (Scottish Asian woman, with experience of violence)

> I watch it and I hope that it's highlighted that particular risk area. This woman has been murdered and hopefully somebody has learnt something from it.
> (English Afro-Caribbean woman, with experience of violence)

Such readings demonstrate how this reconstruction worked to promote understandings of gendered power relations which call for women to censor their
activities and, in Jane Caputi's words, 'internalise the threat and message of
sexual terrorism' (1987: 118).

Given the prevalence of beliefs that women need to be vigilant about
personal safety, it is worth considering how the respondents' judged the representation of Rachael given her supposed *lack* of vigilance. By far the
commonest view was that Rachael's actions reflected her age and an ignorance
of the 'appropriate fears' of adult womanhood. For example:

> I remember when I was seventeen, I wasn't scared of nothing and
> nobody.
>> (English Afro-Caribbean woman, with no experience of violence)

> A bit young and foolish.
>> (English white woman, with experience of violence)

However, Rachael's decision to hitchhike rather than walk home was understood by some interviewees, since the country road was unlit and potentially
dangerous. Her reconstructed fear of the dark led to such readings as:

> She was frightened of walking down a dark road. She would feel a bit
> safer in a car. You never know what's behind the trees or the risk,
> things like that. So it's the lesser of two evils.
>> (Scottish white woman, with experience of violence)

Though the reconstruction did not suggest that Rachael might have contem-
plated walking home, the mention of her being afraid of the dark was used by a
number of interviewees to explain why she did not do so. In the process, they
reveal their own sense of enormous unease about being alone at night on a dark
country road, an unease which has significant impact on their understanding of
Rachael's decisions. Nevertheless, several groups believed that Rachael still
failed to identify alternative ways of securing her safety. For example, given that
Rachael's boyfriend Steven had a motorbike and was available to search for her,
many interviewees could not understand why she did not telephone him to
arrange a lift:

> He was a respectable person, so I can't imagine why she couldn't phone
> him up and say 'Look, I'm stranded, could you give me a lift?'
>> (Scottish white middle-class woman, with no experience of violence)

Many respondents believed they would have thought of options which Rachael
did not think of, and thereby present themselves as being different from her, and
not prone to the same fatal mistakes. Yet there were variances in how respon-

dents distanced themselves from an identification with Rachael. A proportion of Asian and Afro-Caribbean women identified her hitchhiking as something white women are more likely to do. Several Asian interviewees explained that the constraints placed on women in their culture prevented them from doing this and made them less vulnerable to attack. For example:

Respondent 1:   I think Asian women are more careful than white ones. Especially late [at] night, we don't go out alone.
Respondent 2:   We are not allowed that's why.
Respondent 3:   Yes we are brought up like that and that's why we can't go alone. . . . [If] we should go [there are] two women, and sometimes a man and a woman go, sometimes son and mothers go. We can't go alone after eight o'clock. . . . You [white women] are not brought [up] like that.You always go [out] alone.
                   (Scottish Asian women, with no experience of violence)

Similar comments were presented in the three other Asian groups. Clearly, for these women, Asian culture is perceived as bringing certain benefits in terms of their safety, benefits which women are not afforded in more Westernised cultures due to their greater independence.

Some Afro-Caribbean women with experience of violence argued that hitchhiking brought particular dangers for black women, as illustrated in this response:

I feel that it is mainly something that a lot of white women would do. They've got the confidence to go out there and do that kind of thing. Whereas we know, as black women, there's nothing out there protecting us and we can't all put our fingers out to stop a white man in his car. Because for one he'd go 'Fucking black bastards, you're not getting in my car', . . . [or] 'Oh there's a piece of erotica. I'll stop and pick her up'. That kind of thing.
                   (English Afro-Caribbean woman, with experience of violence)

This indicates that for Afro-Caribbean women, assessments of risk are not only based on a belief in women's vulnerability to attack, but also on beliefs that black women (as a consequence of white racism and the way in which black women are sexualised in white hegemonic discourses) are especially vulnerable.

Yet, some interviewees did question the way in which the reconstruction invited viewers to understand Rachael's murder. One group of English white women with experience of violence showed a marked resistance to the implied suggestion that women hitchhikers are themselves to blame for this form of crime:

What they actually said about hitchhiking was wrong. . . . The first thing they said is 'this is what happens when you hitchhike' basically.

257

Why should we be the ones to stop hitchhiking? They should be catching the people that are murdering these people. . . . it's not us that are at fault because we hitchhike. . . . They made you think that you shouldn't hitchhike, because this is what will happen to you.

(English white woman, with experience of violence)

In the group of Scottish Asian women with experience of violence, one women argued that *Crimewatch* was operating with a gendered agenda which sought to control women:

Why should women be restricted? . . . Men − they're privileged. They're privileged to walk about wherever they like, at whatever time of the night, at any time it doesn't matter. Nobody says he shouldn't be doing it if anything happens to him.

(Scottish Asian woman, with experience of violence)

Such critical responses to the reconstruction were not, however, commonly expressed and on only one occasion were similar criticisms of the programme's message found among women with no experience of violence. This was in the Scottish white working-class group of women, where one interviewee remarked 'Does it mean all women are not allowed to go [hitchhiking] because somebody might come along and murder them?'

Engaging with the reconstruction as drama

The readings of the reconstruction about the sexual assault and murder presented above concentrate on responses to the *message* about the dangers of hitchhiking. However, the way in which this message was dramatised through techniques of narrativisation and characterisation was also significant in terms of how women engaged with the reconstruction.

Women with no experience of violence appeared to value the illustrative *dramatisation* provided by the reconstruction of how a young woman might come to place herself in a vulnerable situation:

I thought it helped you to identify with this person; what she was doing, where she worked, that she was a responsible young girl, hard working. She had her love life. Everything [was] really going for her. And then she was murdered. I think that was the whole point of the first part of the reconstruction, to make you care somewhat about this individual.

(Scottish white middle-class woman, with no experience of violence)

This comments reveals how the reconstruction created a sense of identification with Rachael, one which many women with no experience of violence appear to have found some pleasure in as it enhanced their engagement with the crime 'story'.

Conversely, there is some evidence to show that, for women with experience of violence, an intimate knowledge of how Rachael may have suffered meant that they found little pleasure in engaging with the reconstruction as drama. In two such groups, interviewees indicated being greatly disturbed at being able to imagine how Rachael met her death. For example, one woman remarked:

> It's like watching a film with no ending. You [create] your [own] end[ing], that girl was either unconscious or she was conscious, you don't know. They haven't said. That girl could've gone through hell, so your mind, if it's going to upset you, is going to think what that girl went through.
>
> (English white woman, with experience of violence)

In terms of how Rachael herself was characterised, interviewees generally perceived this characterisation as intended to show that she was not a particularly unusual young woman, but rather one who embodied the qualities of many a seventeen-year-old in both thoughts and actions. For example:

> I think that's probably just to portray she was like in the norm. Yes, happy and in love. It's like having the kind of stereotype of the normal girl.
>
> (English Asian woman, with no experience of violence)

From some English women with experience of violence, there was an expressed understanding that *Crimewatch* constructed an impression of Rachael as very respectable. It is as though they were particularly sensitive to assumptions that 'promiscuity' might – however indirectly – explain violent attacks against women. Yet these responses can also be considered in terms of a cynical perception of *Crimewatch* foregrounding the reporting of crimes against citizens of the (so-called) 'respectable' classes:

> One thing they did make sure [of] in that programme was that they didn't actually show any physical contact between her and her boyfriend – so that she didn't look like 'Oh well, get your clothes off'. She didn't look like she was asking for anything. They'd obviously done that.
>
> (English white woman, with experience of violence)

Respondent 1: It showed a positive image of her, that's she's not sort of a loose girl didn't it?

Respondent 2: Yes. Showing that she's not one of them girls that go out and sit on the corner and doss.

Respondent 1: And that she's very twee and middle-class and very nice.

Respondent 2: Yes. If she'd had that much sense she wouldn't have been hitch-hiking. . . . She'd already know the dangers.
(English Afro-Caribbean women, with experience of violence)

However, whilst some women did believe that the makers of *Crimewatch* were careful in how they characterised Rachael, in a number of the interview groups women expressed concerns about how and why she was depicted on the sunbed. This was the one scene which a number of women argued *should not* have been included in the reconstruction. Scottish white working-class women with no experience of violence, for example, objected to its being superfluous to the need to bring forward witnesses to Rachael's hitchhiking:

Respondent 1: I don't think they should have put in the bit about she wanted to sunbathe and that, because who else would be there? Her friend and that would have been it. Plus she was wearing her top – you don't wear a top on a sunbed.
Respondent 2: I know, that's stupid isn't it?
Respondent 3: She went to a sunbed at her friend's so only her and her friend must have been there.
(Scottish white working-class women, with no experience of violence)

This group was the only one to criticise the lack of *relevance* of the scene to the murder investigation. In other groups, however, this scene was at times also read as tasteless and in several groups, particularly among English women with experience of violence, there was an uneasy suspicion of *Crimewatch* as portraying Rachael in this context *because* the crime committed against her was a sexual one, a fact which was being played upon:

I think that was a bit of titillation which you don't need – the sexual context for a sexual murder.
(English white middle-class woman, with no experience of violence)

Respondent 1: They could just have said she'd been to her friend's sunbed, there was no need to actually show her lying on it.
Respondent 2: Well, it all depends if they were trying to show a sexual part of it doesn't it?
(English white women, with experience of violence)

These readings reveal a certain sensitivity to the way in which Rachael was sexualised in the reconstruction. They indicate a critical reading of the portrayal in terms of its allowing a link to be made between Rachael as a sexually desirable women and the fact she was the victim of a sexual attack.

There were, however, many interviewees who did not criticise the inclusion of the sunbed scene, even in those groups where scepticism about it was expressed.

A number of women with no experience of violence valued this scene as integral to the *dramatisation* of a warning against hitchhiking. For example:

> I could say 'I'm going down my friend's for a bit of sunbed'. . . . You're just thinking 'I'm going to do this, I'm going to do that' and you've forgotten about how you're going to get back home. So it just makes you more aware again.
> (English Afro-Caribbean woman, with no experience of violence)

Again, then, the findings demonstrate how *Crimewatch* and its reporting methods are valued *because* they encourage women to identify the need to constantly think about their personal safety and forms of activity which might put them 'at risk'.

Those scenes which portrayed Rachael hitchhiking and those revealing where her body was found were also perceived as being of importance by the interviewees. On the one hand, these were identified as performing the vital function of prompting witnesses to come forward, as is demonstrated by the following responses:

Respondent 1: It is to jog memories of drivers who were in the area.
Respondent 2: I think it was to shake people's memories to [make them] think 'Did I pass her?'
(Scottish white woman, with experience of violence)

On the other hand, the portrayal of Rachael by the roadside was considered a final viewing of this woman prior to the (inevitable) revelation of the details of her death. Indeed, for most other interviewees, seeing Rachael hitchhiking symbolised the closing of the drama:

Researcher: What about when she was hitching?
Respondent 1: You knew she was finished.
Respondent 2: Oh, she was that.
Respondent 3: You know it's stupid for her to be doing that.
(English Afro-Caribbean women, with no experience of violence)

> Everything just fell in place then what was going to happen. . . . Murdered or raped.
> (English Asian woman, with no experience of violence)

Such readings are to be expected given that Nick Ross had signalled that this reconstruction highlighted 'the dangers of hitchhiking'. In relation to this, the actual image of Rachael hitchhiking appears to have functioned to further illustrate an activity which women must refrain from if they wish to avoid putting their bodies at risk.

Concluding remarks

Combining textual and reception research in this analysis of *Crimewatch UK* has demonstrated that the manner in which crimes against women are reported and reconstructed can indeed reinforce and further encourage women's fear of crime. This fear may be a reasonable one given that horrific crimes of sexual violence against women do happen. Yet what becomes very evident in this analysis is the manner in which women are taught to believe that it is their individual responsibility to restrict and censure their activities so as to avoid becoming the victim of this form of crime. In the example of the *Crimewatch* reconstruction, viewers were not provided with any alternative means of imagining how violent attacks upon women could be prevented. The findings of the reception research reveal that while some women did question the message that it is women's responsibility to ensure that these crimes do not occur, such critical readings were expressed by only a handful of interviewees and these were exclusively women with experience of violence. This would suggest that the majority of women 'accept a special burden of self protection . . . that women must live and move about in fear and can never expect to achieve the personal freedom, independence and self assurance of men' (Brownmiller 1975: 400). Moreover, this serves as an illustration of how 'the masculine–male derives power from the censure of all other sex/gender identities, and that (the fear of) rape and sexual assault are important factors in the management of that hegemony' (Roberts 1993: 174). In relation to this, the fact that crime reconstruction programmes such as *Crimewatch UK* present crimes against women in dramatised forms, designed to evoke the pleasures of entertainment, also has to be considered. As is detailed above, several women with experience of violence did not find the dramatised reconstruction pleasurable, as a consequence of imagining what the crime victim might have suffered. Additionally, a number of women criticised the way in which the victim was depicted in scenes superfluous to the murder investigation. Yet the reception research does demonstrate how *many* respondents valued the reconstruction as a drama because it *increased* their engagement with its message. In this way, the power of that message and its calling women to fear crime and curtail their use of public spaces becomes all the more persuasive.

Notes

1 As a consequence of critical concern about crime reconstruction programmes, ITV stopped broadcasting Michael Winner's *True Crimes* series in 1994. This decision, it was said, 'represent[ed] a significant shift in the attitudes of broadcasters towards the depiction of real-life crime cases' (Culf 1994). Given the deregulation of British television and the need to maximise audiences, one might remain sceptical of just how significant this 'shift' will ultimately prove to be.
2 A more detailed textual and reception analysis of *Crimewatch UK* is presented in Weaver (1995), which also contains analysis of other audio-visual representations of violence against women investigated through the same methodologies.

BIBLIOGRAPHY

Adam, B. (1995) *Timewatch: The Social Analysis of Time*, Cambridge: Polity Press.

Adam, B. and Allan, S. (1995) *Theorizing Culture: An Interdisciplinary Critique After Postmodernism*, London: UCL Press, and New York: NYU Press.

Aldridge, M. (1994) *Making Social Work News*, London: Routledge.

Alinsky, S.D. (1971) *Rules for Radicals: A Practical Primer for Realistic Radicals*, New York: Random House.

Allan, S. (1994) ' "When discourse is torn from reality": Bakhtin and the principle of chronotopicity', *Time and Society* 3 (2): 193–218.

Allan, S. (1995) 'News, truth and postmodernity: Unravelling the will to facticity', in B. Adam and S. Allan (eds) *Theorizing Culture: An Interdisciplinary Critique After Postmodernism*, London: UCL Press, and New York: NYU Press, 129–44.

Allan, S. (1997a) 'News and the public sphere: Towards a history of objectivity and impartiality', in M. Bromley and T. O'Malley (eds) *A Journalism Reader*, London: Routledge, 296–329.

Allan, S. (1997b) 'Raymond Williams and the culture of televisual flow', in J. Wallace, R. Jones and S. Nield (eds) *Raymond Williams Now: Knowledge, Limits and the Future*, London: Macmillan, 115–44.

Allan, S. (1998) 'News from NowHere: televisual news discourse and the construction of hegemony', in A. Bell and P. Garrett (eds) *Approaches to Media Discourse*, Oxford: Blackwell, 105–41.

Allen, D., Rush, R. and Kaufman, S. (1996) *Women Transforming Communications: Global Intersections*, Thousand Oaks, CA: Sage.

Allen, M.L. (1989) 'The development of communication networks among women 1973–1983', unpublished Ph.D. dissertation, University of Michigan.

Allen, R. and Frost, J. (1981) *Daily Mirror*, Cambridge: Patrick Stephens Ltd.

Ang, I. (1996) *Living Room Wars: Rethinking Audiences for a Postmodern World*, London: Routledge.

Arendt, H. (1958/1989) *The Human Condition*, Chicago, IL: University of Chicago Press.

Armstrong, L. (1994) *Rocking the Cradle of Sexual Politics: What Happened When Women Said Incest*, New York: Addison Wesley.

Arnold, M. (1887) 'Up to Easter', *Nineteenth Century* 21: 638–9.

Arthurs, J. (1994) 'Women and television', in S. Hood (ed.) *Behind the Screens*, London: Lawrence & Wishart, 82–101.

Asquith, S. (1993) *Protecting Children; Cleveland to Orkney – More Lessons to Learn?*, Edinburgh: Children in Scotland/HMSO.

Baehr, H. (ed.) (1980) *Women and Media*, London: Pergamon.

Baehr, H. (1996) *Women in Television*, London: University of Westminster Press.

Baehr, H. and Spindler-Brown, A. (1987) 'Firing a broadside: A feminist intervention into mainstream TV', in H. Baehr and G. Dyer (eds) *Boxed In: Women and Television*, London: Pandora.

Bakhtin, M. (1934–5/1981) 'Discourse in the novel', trans. C. Emerson and M. Holquist, in M. Holquist (ed.) *The Dialogic Imagination: Four Essays by M.M. Bakhtin*, Austin, TX: University of Texas Press, 259–422.

Bakhtin, M. (1937–8/1981) 'Forms of time and of the chronotope in the novel', trans. C. Emerson and M. Holquist, in M. Holquist (ed.) *The Dialogic Imagination: Four Essays by M.M. Bakhtin*, Austin, TX: University of Texas Press, 84–242.

Bakhtin, M. (1963/1984) *Problems of Dostoevsky's Poetics*, ed. and trans. C. Emerson, Manchester: Manchester University Press.

Bakhtin, M. (1973/1981) 'Concluding remarks', trans. C. Emerson and M. Holquist, in M. Holquist (ed.) *The Dialogic Imagination: Four Essays by M.M. Bakhtin*, Austin, TX: University of Texas Press, 243–58.

Balibar, E. (1994) *Masses, Classes, Ideas: Studies on Politics and Philosophy Before and After Marx*, New York: Routledge.

Banks, E.L. (1902) *The Autobiography of a 'Newspaper Girl'*, New York: Dodd, Mead.

Barr, P. (1977) 'Newspapers', in J. King and M. Stott (eds) *Is This Your Life?: Images of Women in the Media*, London: Virago, 67–81.

Bart, P.B. and Geil Moran, E. (1993) *Violence Against Women: The Bloody Footprints*, Newbury Park, CA: Sage.

Barthes, R. (1984) *Camera Lucida*, London: Flamingo.

Bateson, M. (ed.) (1895) *Professional Women Upon Their Profession*, London: W.H. Cox.

Bauer, D.M. (1988) *Feminist Dialogics: A Theory of Failed Community*, Albany, NY: State University of New York Press.

BBC Annual Report and Handbook 1986, London: BBC.

BBC Broadcasting Research (1988) *Crimewatch UK*, London: BBC Special Projects Report.

BBC Community Programmes Unit (1987) *Open Space: The Page Three Debate*, May.

Beasley, M.H. (1985) *The New Majority: A Look at What the Preponderance of Women in Journalism Education means to the Schools and to the Professions*, College Park, MD: University of Maryland.

Beasley, M.H. (1993) 'Is there a new majority defining the news?', in P. Creedon (ed.) *Women in Mass Communication*, Newbury Park, CA, London and Delhi: Sage, 118–33.

Beasley, M.H. and Gibbons, S.J. (1993) *Taking Their Place: A Documentary History of Women and Journalism*, Washington, DC: American University Press and Women's Institute for Freedom of the Press.

Beck, U. (1996) 'When experiments go wrong', *Independent* 26 March: 15.

Beetham, M. (1996) *A Magazine of Her Own?: Domesticity and Desire in the Woman's Magazine, 1800–1914*, London and New York: Routledge.

Belford, B. (1986) *Brilliant Bylines*, New York: Columbia University Press.

Bell, A. (1991) *The Language of News Media*, Oxford: Blackwell.

Bell, A. and Garrett, P. (eds) (1998) *Approaches to Media Discourse*, Oxford: Blackwell.

Bell, D. and Valentine, G. (1997) *Consuming Geographies*, London: Routledge.

Benedict, H. (1992) *Virgin or Vamp: How the Press Covers Sex Crimes*, New York and Oxford: Oxford University Press.

Benhabib, S. (1992) *Situating the Self: Gender, Community and Postmodernism in Contemporary Ethics*, New York: Routledge.

Benhabib, S. (1994) 'Models of public space: Hannah Arendt, the liberal tradition and Jürgen Habermas', in C. Calhoun (ed.) *Habermas and the Public Sphere*, Boston, MA: Massachusetts Institute of Technology.

Berry, M. (1986) *Why ERA Failed*, Bloomington, IN: Indiana University Press.

Bird, S.E. (1997) 'What a story!: Understanding the audience for scandal', in J. Lull and S. Hinerman (eds) *Media Scandals*, Cambridge: Polity Press, 99–121.

Birke, L. (1986) *Women, Feminism and Biology: The Feminist Challenge*, Brighton: Harvester Wheatsheaf.

Biteback (1993) BBC1, 5 December.

Bjondeberg, I. (1996) 'Public discourse/private fascination; hybridization in 'true-life story genres', *Media, Culture and Society* 18 (1): 27–46.

Black, P. (1972) *The Mirror in the Corner – People's Television*, London: Hutchinson.

Blair, G. (1988) *Almost Golden: Jessica Savitch and the Selling of Television News*, New York: Simon & Schuster.

Bledstein, B.J. (1978) *The Culture of Professionalism: The Middle Class and the Development of Higher Education in America*, New York: W.W. Norton.

Bradley, P. (1995) 'Media leaders and personal ideology: Margaret Cousins and the women's service magazines', *Journalism History* 21 (2): 79–87.

Brake, L. (1994) *Subjugated Knowledges: Journalism, Gender and Literature in the Nineteenth Century*, London: Macmillan.

Branston, G. (1993) 'Infotainment: A Twilight Zone', *Innovation in Social Sciences Research* 6 (3): 351–8.

Bray, A. (1994) 'The "Edible Woman": Reading/eating disorders and femininity', *Media Information Australia* 72: 4–10.

Brennan, B. (1995) 'Cultural discourse of journalists: The material conditions of newsroom labor', in H. Hardt and B. Brennan (eds) *Newsworkers. Toward a History of the Rank and File*, Minneapolis, MN: University of Minnesota Press, 75–109.

Bridge, J.M. (1995) 'What's news?', in C. Lont (ed.) *Women and Media: Content/Careers/Criticism*, Belmont, CA: Wadsworth, 15–28.

Briggs, A. (1985) *The BBC: The First Fifty Years*, Oxford: Oxford University Press.

Brockway, G.P. (1996) Personal interview, 29 September; 12 October.

Bromley, M. and O'Malley, T. (eds) (1997) *A Journalism Reader*, London and New York: Routledge.

Brookes, R. (forthcoming) 'Newspapers and national identity: The BSE/CJD crisis and the British press', *Media, Culture and Society*.

Brown, L. (1996) 'Politics of memory, politics of incest: Doing therapy and politics that really matter', *Women and Therapy* 19 (1): 5–18.

Brown, R. (1997) Untitled Opinion Column, *Independent* 6 October, inner section: 3.

Brownmiller, S. (1975) *Against Our Will: Men, Women and Rape*, Auckland, Middlesex, New York, Ontario and Victoria: Penguin Books.

Brunsdon, C. and Morley, D. (1978) *Everyday Television: 'Nationwide'*, London: BFI.

Buresh, B. (1984) 'Critical Mass', *Quill* (September): 14–20.

Butler, J. (1993) *Bodies That Matter: On the Discursive Limits of 'Sex'*, London: Routledge.

Butler, J. (1997) *Merely Cultural*, talk given at the Institute of Contemporary Arts, London (May).

Cain, M. (1990) 'Towards transgression: New directions in feminist criminology', *International Journal of Sociology of Law* 18: 1–18.

Calhoun, C. (ed.) (1992) *Habermas and the Public Sphere*, Cambridge, MA: MIT Press.

Cameron, D. (1990) *The Feminist Critique of Language*, London: Routledge.

Cameron, D. (1992) *Feminism and Linguistic Theory*, 2nd edn, London: Macmillan.

Campbell, B. (1988) *Unofficial Secrets*, London: Virago.

Campbell, B. (1991) 'Kings of the road', *Marxism Today* December.

Campbell, C.P. (1995) *Race, Myth and the News*, London: Sage.

Caputi, J. (1987) *The Age of Sex Crime*, London: The Women's Press.

Carey, J.W. (1969) 'The communications revolution and the professional communicator', *The Sociological Review Monograph* 13: 23–8.

Carpenter, I. (1946) *No Woman's World*, Boston, MA: Hougton Mifflin.

Carr, E.H. (1961) *What is History*, Reading: Penguin.

Carter, C. (forthcoming) 'News accounts of violence against women and girls in the British, daily national press', unpublished Ph.D. dissertation, School of Journalism, Media and Cultural Studies, University of Wales, Cardiff.

Carter, C. and Thompson, A. (1997) 'Negotiating the "crisis" around masculinity: A historical analysis of discourses of patriarchal violence in the *Western Mail*, 1896', in M. Bromley and T. O'Malley (eds) *A Journalism Reader*, London: Routledge, 28–49.

Chibnall, S. (1977) *Law and Order News: An Analysis of Crime Reporting in the British Press*, London: Tavistock.

Chippendale, P. and Horrie, C. (1990/1992) *Stick it Up Your Punter: The Rise and Fall of The Sun,* London: Mandarin.

Christmas, L. (1997) *Chaps of Both Sexes? Women Decision-Makers in Newspapers: Do They Make a Difference?*, London: BT Forum/Women in Journalism.

Cirkensa, K. (1996) 'Feminism after ferment: Ten years of gendered scholarship in communications', in D. Allen, R. Rush and S. Kaufman (eds) *Women Transforming Communications Global Intersections*, Thousand Oaks, CA: Sage.

Cirkensa, K. and Cuklanz, L. (1992) 'Male is to female as —— is to ——: A guided tour of five feminist frameworks for communication studies', in L. Rakow (ed.) *Women Making Meaning: New Directions in Communication*, London and New York: Routledge, 18–44.

Clark, K. (1992) 'The linguistics of blame: Representations of women in *The Sun's* reporting of crimes of sexual violence', in M. Toolan (ed.) *Language, Text and Context: Essays in Stylistics*, London and New York: Routledge, 208–24.

Clark, K. and Holquist, M. (1984) *Mikhail Bakhtin*, Cambridge, MA: Harvard University Press.

Coates, J. (1986) *Women, Men and Language*, London: Longman.

Cockerell, M., Hennessy, P. and Walker, D. (1984) *Sources Close to the Prime-Minister: Inside the Hidden World of the News Manipulators*, London: Macmillan.

Cohen, J. (1996) Democracy, difference and the right to privacy', in S. Benhabib (ed.) *Democracy and Difference: Contesting the Boundaries of the Political*, Princeton, NJ: Princeton University Press, 187–217.

Cohen, M. (1988) *The Sisterhood: The True Story of the Women Who Changed the World*, New York: Simon & Schuster.

Coles, J. (1997) 'Boy zone story', *Guardian* 28 April, Media Guardian: 4.

Collier R. (1994) 'Waiting 'til father gets home: Family values and the reconstruction of fatherhood in law', *Socio-legal Studies*.

Connelly, R. (1994) 'Domestic violence and the press', *Editor & Publisher* September 3: 48.

Corner, J. (1995) *Television Form and Public Address*, London: Edward Arnold.

Corner, J. (1996a) *The Art of Record: A Critical Introduction to Documentary*, Manchester: Manchester University Press.

Corner, J. (1996b) 'Mediating the ordinary: The "access" idea and television form', in J. Corner and S. Harvey (eds) *Television Times: A Reader*, London: Edward Arnold.

Corner, J. and Harvey, S. (eds) (1996) *Television Times: A Reader*, London: Edward Arnold.

Cottle, S. (1993) *TV News, Urban Conflict and the Inner City*, Leicester: Leicester University Press.

Coupland, N. and Coupland, J. (1997) 'Bodies, beaches and burn-times: "Environmentalism" and its discursive competitors', *Discourse and Society* 8 (1): 7–25.

Coward, R. (1984) *Female Desire: Women's Sexuality Today*, London: Paladin.

Cramer, J.A. (1993) 'Radio: A woman's place is on the air', in P. Creedon (ed.) *Women in Mass Communication*, Newbury Park, CA, London and Delhi: Sage, 154–66.

Creedon, P. (1989) (ed.) *Women in Mass Communication: Challenging Gender Values*, Newbury Park, CA, London and Delhi: Sage.

Creedon, P. (1993) 'The challenge of re-visioning gender values', in P. Creedon (ed.) *Women in Mass Communication*, 2nd edn, Newbury Park, CA, London and Delhi: Sage, 3–23.

Crenshaw, K.W. (1997) 'Color-blind dreams and racial nightmares: Reconfiguring racism in the post-civil rights era', in T. Morrison and C. Brodsky Lacour (eds) *Birth of a Nation 'hood': Gaze, Script and Spectacle in the O.J. Simpson Case*, New York: Pantheon Books, 97–168.

Crewe, I. and Gosschalk, B. (1995) (eds) *Political Communications: The General Election Campaign of 1992*, Cambridge: CUP.

Croteau, D. and Hoynes, W. (1992) 'Men and the news media: The male presence and its effect', in S. Craig (ed.) *Men, Masculinity and the Media*, London: Sage, 154–84.

Cuklanz, L.M. (1996) *Rape on Trial: How the Mass Media Construct Legal Reform and Social Change*, Philadelphia, PA: University of Pennsylvania Press.

Culf, A. (1993) 'BBC defends "voyeuristic" crime series', *Guardian* 23 June: 6.

Culf, A. (1994) 'ITV axes Winner true crime series', *Guardian* 30 August: 18.

Curran, J. (1991a) 'Rethinking the media as a public sphere', in P. Dahlgren and C. Sparks (eds) *Communication and Citizenship*, London: Routledge.

Curran, J. (1991b) 'Mass media and democracy, a reappraisal', in J. Curran and M. Gurevitch (eds) *Mass Media and Society*, London: Edward Arnold.

Curran, J. and Seaton, J. (1991) *Power Without Responsibility*, 4th edn, London: Routledge.

Curran, J. and Sparks, C. (1991) 'Press and popular culture', *Media, Culture and Society* 13: 215–37.

Curran, J; Douglas, A. and Whannel, G. (1980) 'The political economy of the human interest story', in A. Smith (ed.) *Newspapers and Democracy: International Essays on a Changing Medium*, Cambridge, MA: MIT Press.

Dahlgren, P. (1989) 'Crime news: The fascination of the mundane', *Media, Culture and Society* 3: 189–206.

Dahlgren, P. and Sparks. C. (eds) (1992) *Journalism and Popular Culture*, London: Sage.

Davies, K., Dickey, J. and Stratford, T. (eds) (1987) *Out of Focus: Writings on Women and the Media*, London: The Women's Press.

De Lauretis, T. (1984) *Alice Doesn't: Feminism, Semiotics, Cinema*, London: Macmillan.

Deacon, D. and Golding, P. (1994) *Taxation and Representation: The Media, Political Communication and the Poll Tax*, London: John Libbey.

Deakin, P. (1984) *Press On: An Account of the Women's Press Club of London*, London: Henry E. Walter.

DeKeseredy, W.S. and Hinch, R. (1991) *Woman Abuse: Sociological Perspectives*, Toronto: Thompson Educational Publishing.

Dentith, S. (1995) *Bakhtinian Thought*, London: Routledge.

Derrida, J. (1968) 'From differance' in A. Easthope and K. McGowan (eds) (1992) *A Critical and Cultural Theory Reader*, Buckingham: Open University Press.

Díaz-Diocaretz, M. (1989) 'Bakhtin, discourse and feminist theories', *Critical Studies* 1 (2): 121–39.

Diekerhoff, E. *et al.* (1985) *Voor zover plaats aan de perstafel*, Amsterdam: Meulenhoff.

Dines, G. and Humez, J.M. (1995) 'Home, home on the remote', in G. Dines and J.M. Humez (eds) *Gender, Race and Class in Media*, Thousand Oaks, CA, London and Delhi: Sage, 262–366.

Dobash, R.E. and Dobash, R.P. (1988) 'Research as social action: The struggle for battered women', in K. Yllö and M. Bograd (eds) *Feminist Perspectives on Wife Abuse*, Newbury Park, CA: Sage.

Dobash, R.E. and Dobash, R. (1992) *Women, Violence and Social Change*, London and New York: Routledge.

Domhoff, G.W. (1978) 'The woman's page as a window on the ruling class', in G. Tuchman, A. Daniels and J. Benét (eds) *Hearth and Home: Images of Women in the Mass Media*, New York: Oxford University Press, 161–75.

Dougary, G. (1994) *The Executive Tart and Other Myths*, London: Virago.

Douglas, S. (1994) *Where the Girls Are: Growing Up Female with the Mass Media*, New York: Random House.

Dunnigan, A.A. (1974) *A Black Woman's Experience – From Schoolhouse to White House*, Philadelphia, PA: Dorrance & Company.

Ehrenreich, B. and English, D. (1988) *For Her Own Good: 150 Years of the Experts' Advice to Women*, London: Pluto.

Eisenstein, Z. (1988) *The Female Body and the Law*, Berkeley, CA: University of California Press.

Eliasoph, N. (1997) 'Routines and the making of oppositional news', in D. Berkowitz (ed.) *Source Meanings of News*, Thousand Oaks, CA and London: Sage, 230–53.

Ellerbee, L. (1986) *And So it Goes: Adventures in Television*, New York: Berkeley Books.

Elwood-Akers, V. (1988) *Women War Correspondents in the Vietnam War, 1961–65*, New Jersey and London: The Scarecrow Press.

Engel, M. (1996) *Tickle the Public: One Hundred Years of the Popular Press*, London: Indigo.

Epstein, C.F. (1978) 'The women's movement and the women's pages', in G. Tuchman,

A. Daniels and J. Benét (eds) *Hearth and Home: Images of Women in the Mass Media*, New York: Oxford University Press, 216–21.

Epstein, L.K. (ed.) (1978) *Women and the News*, New York: Hastings House.

Ericson, R., Baranek, P. and Chan, J. (1989) *Negotiating Control: A Study of News Sources*, Milton Keynes: Open University Press, and Toronto: University of Toronto Press.

Ericson, R., Baranek, P. and Chan, J. (1991) *Representing Order: Crime, Law and Justice in the News Media*, Toronto: University of Toronto Press.

Evans, S. (1979) *Personal Politics: The Roots of Women's Liberation in the Civil Rights Movement and the New Left*, New York: Knopf.

Faludi, S. (1992) *Backlash: The Undeclared War Against Women*, London: Chatto and Vintage Books.

Farrell, A. (1991) 'Feminism in the mass media: *Ms* magazine, 1972–1989', unpublished Ph.D. Dissertation, University of Minnesota.

Feminism and Psychology (1997) *Special Issue on Retrieved Memories* 7 (1).

Ferguson, M. (1990) *Public Communication – the New Imperatives: Future Directions for Media Research*, London: Sage.

Fiddes, N. (1991) *Meat. A Natural Symbol*, London: Routledge.

Finn, G. (1989–90) 'Taking gender into account in the 'theatre of terror':Violence, media and the maintenance of male dominance', *Canadian Journal of Women and the Law* 3 (2): 375–94.

Fiske, J. (1987) *Television Culture*, London: Methuen.

Fiske, J. (1993) *Power Plays Power Works*, London:Verso.

Foote, J.S. (1995) 'Women correspondents and the evening news', in C. Lont (ed.) *Women and Media: Content/Careers/Criticism*, Belmont, CA: Wadsworth, 229–38.

Foucault, M. (1979) *The History of Sexuality, Volume One: An Introduction*, London: Allen Lane.

Foucault, M. (1980) *Power/Knowledge: Selected Interviews and Other Writings*, New York Pantheon.

Fowler, R. (1991) *Language in the News*, London: Routledge.

Franklin, A. and Franklin, B. (1996) 'Growing pains: The developing children's rights movement in the UK', in J. Pilcher and S. Wagg (eds) *Thatcher's Children? Politics, Childhood and Society in the 1980s and 1990s*, London: Falmer Press, 94–113.

Franklin, B. and Petley, J. (1996) 'Killing the age of innocence: Newspaper reporting of the death of James Bulger', in J. Pilcher and S. Wagg (eds) *Thatcher's Children? Politics, Childhood and Society in the 1980s and 1990s*, London: Falmer Press, 134–54.

Fraser, N. (1989) *Unruly Practices: Power, Discourse and Gender in Contemporary Social Theory*, Minneapolis, MN: University of Minnesota Press.

Fraser, N. (1992) 'Rethinking the public sphere: A contribution to the critique of actually existing democracy', in C. Calhoun (ed.) *Habermas and the Public Sphere*, Cambridge, MA: MIT Press.

Freeman, J. (1975) *The Politics of Women's Liberation*, New York: David McKay.

Friedan, B. (1963) *The Feminine Mystique*, New York:W.W. Norton.

Friedan, B. (1976) ' "The first year": President's report to NOW, Washington, D.C., 1967', in *It Changed My Life: Writings on the Women's Movement*, New York: Random House.

Fritz, S. (1979) 'A change in style', *Nieman Reports: Special Issue on Women and Journalism*, 24–5.

Fry, R.A. (1929) *Emily Hobhouse: A Memoir*, London: Jonathan Cape.

Furman, B. (1949) *Washington By-Line: The Personal History of a Newspaperwoman*, New York: Knopf.

Gallagher, M. (1979) *The Portrayal and Participation of Women in the Media*, Paris: UNESCO.

Gallagher, M. (1981) *Unequal Opportunities: The Case of Women and the Media*, Paris: UNESCO.

Gallagher, M. (1995) *An Unfinished Story: Gender Patterns in Media Employment*, Paris: UNESCO Reports on Mass Communication, 110.

Galtung, J. and Ruge, M. (1965/1982) 'Structuring and selecting news', in S. Cohen and J. Young (eds) *The Manufacture of News: Deviance, Social Problems and the Mass Media*, London: Constable.

Ganguly, K. (1992) 'Accounting for others: Feminism and representation', in L. Rakow (ed.) *Women Making Meaning: New Directions in Communication*, London and New York: Routledge, 60–79.

Gardiner, M. (1992) *The Dialogics of Critique: M.M. Bakhtin and the Theory of Ideology*, London: Routledge.

Geiger, S.N.G. (1986) 'Women's life histories: Method and content', *Signs* 11: 334–51.

Gerbner, G. and Gross, L. (1976) 'Living with television: The violence profile', *Journal of Communication* 26 (2): 173–99.

Gerbner, G., Gross, L., Signorielli, N., Morgan, M. and Jackson-Beeck, M. (1979) 'The demonstration of power: Violence profile no. 10', *Journal of Communication* 29 (3): 177–96.

Gill, R. (1993) 'Ideology, gender and popular radio: A discourse analytic approach', *Innovation in Social Science Research* 6: 323–39.

Gillespie, M. (1995) *Television, Ethnicity and Cultural Change*, London: Routledge.

Ginsberg, A. and Richey, J. (1991) 'The right to depict children in the nude', *Aperture* ('The Body in Question issue') 42–5.

Gist, M. (1993) 'Through the looking glass: Diversity and reflected appraisals of self in mass media', in P. Creedon (ed.) *Women in Mass Communication*, Newbury Park, CA, London and Delhi: Sage, 104–17.

Glazener, N. (1989) 'Dialogic subversion: Bakhtin, the novel and Gertrude Stein', in K. Hirschkop, and D. Shepherd (eds) *Bakhtin and Cultural Theory*, Manchester: Manchester University Press, 109–29.

Goldie, G.W. (1977) *Facing the Nation*, London: Bodley Head.

Golding, P. and Murdock, G. (1991) 'Culture, communication and political economy', in J. Curran, and M. Gurevitch (eds) *Mass Media and Society*, London: Edward Arnold.

Golding, P., Murdock, G. and Schlesinger, P. (1986) *Communicating Politics*, Leicester: Leicester University Press.

Good, H. (1993) *The Journalist as Autobiographer*, Metuchen, NJ: Scarecrow Press.

Gordon, M.T. and Riger, S. (1989) *The Female Fear*, London and New York: The Free Press.

Graham, K. (1997) *Personal History*, New York: Knopf.

Graham, V. (1966) *There Goes What's Her Name: The Continuing Saga of Virginia Graham*, New York: Avon Books.

Graham, V. (1978) *If I Made It, So Can You*, New York: Bantam Books.

Gray, A. (1992) *Video Playtime: The Gendering of a Leisure Technology*, London and New York: Routledge.

Gray, A. (1996) 'Behind closed doors: Video recorders in the home', in H. Baehr and A. Gray (eds) *Turning it On: A Reader in Women and Media*, London: Arnold, 118–29.

Gray, H. (1997) 'Remembering civil rights: Television, memory and the 1960s', in L. Siegel and M. Curtin (eds.) *The Revolution Wasn't Televised: Sixties Television and Social Conflict*, New York: Routledge.

Grieve, M. (1964) *Millions Made My Story*, London: Victor Gollancz.

Griffiths, D. (ed.) (1992) *The Encyclopaedia of the British Press, 1422–1992*, London: Macmillan.

Grindstaff, L. (1997) 'Producing trash, class, and the money shot: A behind-the-scenes account of daytime TV talk shows', in J. Lull and S. Hinerman (eds) *Media Scandals*, Cambridge: Polity Press, 164–202.

Grist, Cunningham L. (1984) 'We've Come a Long Way, Baby', *Editor & Publisher* 52.

Grose, R. (1989) *The Sun-sation*, London: Angus & Robertson.

Habermas, J. (1974) 'The public sphere: An encyclopaedia article (1964)', *New German Critique* 3: 49–55.

Habermas, J. (1987) *The Theory of Communicative Action, 2, Lifeworld and System: A Critique of Functionalist Reason*, trans. T. McCarthy, Boston, MA: Beacon Press.

Habermas, J. (1989) *The Structural Transformation of the Public Sphere: An Inquiry Into a Category of Bourgeois Society*, trans. T. Burger with the assistance of F. Lawrence, Cambridge: Polity Press, and Cambridge, MA: MIT Press, (first published in German in 1962 as *Strukturwandel der öffentlichkeit*).

Habermas, J. (1992) 'Further reflections on the public sphere', in C. Calhoun (ed.) *Habermas and the Public Sphere*, Cambridge, MA: MIT Press, 421–79.

Hajdukowski-Ahmed, M. (1990) 'Bakhtin and feminism: Two solitudes?', *Critical Studies* 2 (1–2): 153–63.

Hall, S. (1992) 'The question of cultural identity', in S. Hall, D. Held and T. McGrew (eds) *Modernity and Its Futures*, London: Polity Press.

Hall, S. (ed.) (1997) *Representations: Cultural Representations and Signifying Practices*, London: Sage.

Hall, S., Critcher, C., Jefferson, T., Clarke, J. and Roberts, B. (1978) *Policing the Crisis: Mugging, the State and Law and Order*, London: Macmillan.

Hallin, D. (1996) 'Commercialism and professionalism in the American news media', in J. Curran and M. Gurevitch (eds) *Mass Media and Society*, London: Edward Arnold.

Hanisch, C. (1975) 'The Liberal takeover of women's liberation', *Feminist Revolution: An Abridged Edition with Additional Writings*, New York: Random House.

Hanmer J., Radford J. and Stanko B. (1989) *Women, Policing and Male Violence*, London: Routledge.

Hanmer, J. and Saunders, S. (1993) *Women, Violence and Crime Prevention*, Aldershot: Avebury.

Hansen, M. (1993) 'Foreword' to *Public Sphere and Experience: Toward an Analysis of the Bourgeois and Proletarian Public Sphere* by O. Negt, A. Kluge, P. Labanyi, J.O. Daniel and trans. A. Oksiloff, Minneapolis, MN: University of Minnesota Press, ix–xix.

Harding, S. (1986) *The Science Question in Feminism*, Milton Keynes: Open University Press.

Harding, S. (1991) *Whose Science? Whose Knowledge? Thinking from Women's Lives*, Milton Keynes: Open University Press.

Hardt, H. (1995) 'Without the rank and file: journalism history: Media workers and problems of representation', in H. Hardt and B. Brennan (eds) *Newsworkers. Toward a History of the Rank and File*, Minneapolis, MN: University of Minnesota Press, 1–29.

Hardt, H. and Brennen, B. (eds) (1995) *Newsworkers: Toward a History of the Rank and File*, Minneapolis, MN: University of Minnesota Press.

Hartley, J. (1982) *Understanding News*, London: Methuen.

Hartley, J. (1992a) *Tele-ology: Studies in Television*, London and New York: Routledge.

Hartley, J. (1992b) *The Politics of Pictures: The Creation of the Public in the Age of Popular Media*, London and New York: Routledge.

Hartley, J. (1994) 'Twoccing and joyreading', *Textual Practice* 8 (3): 399–413.

Hartley, J. (1996) *Popular Reality: Journalism, Modernity, Popular Culture*, London: Edward Arnold.

Hartsock, N. (1990) 'Foucault on power; A theory for women?', in J. Nicholson (ed.) *Feminism/Post-modernism*, London: Routledge.

Head, A.M. (1939) *It Could Never Have Happened*, London: William Heinemann.

Hearn, J. (1996) 'Men and men's violence to known women: The "lur" and "lack" of cultural studies approaches', paper presented to the 'Crossroads in cultural studies conference', Tampere, Finland (1–4 July).

Hebert, H. (1988) 'The nightmare of nark's corner', *Guardian* 2 June: 21.

Hebert, H. (1993) 'The people's peep show', *Guardian* 23 November: 6.

Hechter, M. (1975) *Internal Colonialism: The Celtic Fringe in British National Development, 1536–1966*, London: Routledge & Kegan Paul.

Heidensohn, F. (1986) *Women and Crime*, London: Macmillan.

Heikinen, D. (1994) 'Is Bakhtin a feminist or just another dead White male?: A celebration of feminist possibilities in Manuel Puig's *Kiss of the Spider Woman*', in K. Hohne and H. Wussow (eds) *A Dialogue of Voices: Feminist Literary Theory and Bakhtin*, Minneapolis, MN: University of Minnesota Press, 114–27.

Heilbrun, C. (1995) *The Education of a Woman: The Life of Gloria Steinem*, New York: Dial Press.

Henry, S. (1993) 'Changing media history through women's history', in P. Creedon (ed.) *Women in Mass Communication*, Newbury Park, CA, London and Delhi: Sage, 341–62.

Herzog, H. (1941) 'On borrowed experience – An analysis of listening to daytime sketches', *Studies in Philosophy and Social Science* 9: 65–95.

Higgins, M. (1955) *News is a Singular Thing*, Garden City, NY: Doubleday.

Higgins, M.M. (1997) 'The social construction of journalist ideals – Gender in journalism education', paper presented at 'Journalists for the new century', conference on the education and training of the new generation, London College of Printing, School of Media (24 April).

Hobson, D. (1978) 'Housewives: Isolation as oppression', in Women's Studies Groups, University of Birmingham (eds) *Women Take Issue: Aspects of Women's Subordination*, London: Hutchinson, 79–95.

Hobson, D. (1980) 'Housewives and the mass media', in S. Hall *et al.* (eds) *Culture, Media, Language*, London: Hutchinson, 105–14.

Hobson, D. (1990) 'Women audiences and the workplace', in M.E. Brown (ed.) *Television and Women's Culture: The Politics of the Popular*, London, Newbury Park, CA, and Delhi: Sage, 61–71.

Hodge, J. (1988) 'Subject, body and the exclusion of women from philosophy', in M. Griffiths and M. Whitford (eds) *Feminist Perspectives in Philosophy*, Bloomington, IN: Indiana University Press, 152–68.

Hoffman, E. (1970–1) 'Women in the newsroom', *Columbia Journalism Review* (Winter): 53–5.

Hoggart, R. (1970) *Speaking to Each Other, Volume Two: About Literature*, Harmondsworth: Penguin Books.

Hohne, K. and Wussow, H. (1994) 'Introduction', in K. Hohne and H. Wussow (eds) *A Dialogue of Voices: Feminist Literary Theory and Bakhtin*, Minneapolis, MN: University of Minnesota Press, vii–xxiii.

Hole, J. and Levine, E. (1971) *Rebirth of Feminism*, New York: Quadrangle Books.

Holland, P. (1983) 'The 'Page Three Girl' speaks to women, too', *Screen* 24 (3): 84–102.

Holland, P. (1987) 'When a woman reads the news', in H. Baehr and G. Dyer (eds) *Boxed In: Women and Television*, London: Pandora, 133–49.

Holland, P. (1997a) ' "Sweet it is to scan": Personal photographs and popular photography', in L. Wells (ed.) *Photography: A Critical Introduction*, London: Routledge.

Holland, P. (1997b) 'The direct appeal to the eye? Photography and the twentieth century press', in A. Briggs and P. Cobley (eds) *Introduction to the Media*, Harlow: Addison Wesley Longman.

Holquist, M. (1990) *Dialogism: Bakhtin and his World*, London: Routledge.

Home Office (1996) *Criminal Statistics, England and Wales 1995*, London: HMSO.

Honig, B. (1992) 'Toward an agonistic feminism: Hannah Arendt and the politics of identity', in J. Butler and J.W. Scott (eds) *Feminists Theorize the Political*, New York: Routledge, 215–35.

hooks, b. (1984) *Feminist Theory: From Margin to Center*, Boston, MA: South End Press.

Horowitz, D. (1996) 'Rethinking Betty Friedan and *The Feminine Mystique*: Labor union radicalism and feminism in Cold War America', *American Quarterly* 48 (1): 1–42.

Houston, M. (1992) 'The politics of difference: Race, class, and women's communication', in L. Rakow (ed.) *Women Making Meaning: New Directions in Communication*, London and New York: Routledge, 45–59.

Hunter, F. (1991) 'The society of women journalists', in G. Cevaso (ed.) *The Eighteen Nineties: Encyclopaedia of British Literature, Arts and Culture*, New York: Garland.

Hunter, F. (1992) 'Women in British journalism', in D. Griffiths (ed.) *The Encyclopaedia of the British Press, 1422–1992*, London: Macmillan.

Husband, C. (1984) 'Social identity and race', in *E3542 5–6 Open University Course*.

Huyssen, A. (1986) 'Mass culture as woman', *After the Great Divide*, London: Macmillan.

Irwin, A. (1995) *Citizen Science*, London: Routledge.

Jallov, B. (1996) 'Women on the air: Community radio as a tool for feminist messages', in H. Baehr and A. Gray (eds) *Turning it On: A Reader in Women and Media*, London: Edward Arnold, 201–10.

Jameson, F. (1991) *Postmodernism: Or, the Cultural Logic of Late Capitalism*, Durham, NC: Duke University Press.

Jelinek, E. C. (1980) 'Introduction: Women's autobiography and the male tradition', in E.C. Jelinek (ed.) *Women's Autobiography: Essays in Criticism*, Bloomington, IN: Indiana University Press.

Jensen, K.B. (1994) 'Reception as flow: The "new television viewer" revisited', *Cultural Studies* 8 (2): 293–305.

Jordan, E. (1938) *Three Rousing Cheers*, New York: D. Appleton–Century.

Jordan, G. and Weedon, C. (1995) *Cultural Politics: Class, Gender, Race and the Postmodern World*, Oxford: Blackwell.

Joseph, A. and Kalpana, S. (eds) (1994) *Whose News?: The Media and Women's Issues*, New Delhi and Thousand Oaks, CA: Sage.

Kaufman, S.J. (1995) 'Jennifer Schulze: From window dressing on the set to WGN-TV news director – a 15-year odyssey', in C. Lont (ed.) *Women and Media: Content/Careers/Criticism*, Belmont, CA: Wadsworth, 239–50.

Keller, E.F. (1996) 'Feminism and science', in E.F. Keller and H. Longino (eds) *Feminism in Science*, Oxford: Oxford University Press.

Keller, E.F. and Longino, H. (eds) (1996) *Feminism in Science*, Oxford: Oxford University Press.

Kelly, F.F. (1939) *Flowing Stream. The Story of Fifty-Six Years in American Newspaper Life*, New York: E.P. Dutton.

Kelly, L. (1988) *Surviving Sexual Violence*, Cambridge: Polity Press.

Kidd-Hewitt, D. and Osborne, R. (eds) (1995) *Crime and Media: The Post-Modern Spectacle*, London: Pluto.

Kilborn, R. (1994) 'Drama over Lockerbie: A new look at television drama-documentaries', *Historical Journal of Film, Radio and Television* 14 (1): 59–76.

King, J. and Stott, M. (eds) (1977) *Is This Your Life?: Images of Women in the Media*, London: Virago.

Kitzinger, C. and Perkins, R. (1993) *Changing Our Minds*, London: Onlywoman press.

Kitzinger, J. (1992) 'Sexual violence and compulsory heterosexuality', *Feminism and Psychology* 2 (3): 399–418.

Kitzinger, J. (1996) 'Media representations of sexual abuse risks', *Child Abuse Review* 5: 319–33.

Kitzinger, J. (1998) 'The moving power of the moving image: media constructions of Diana's death', *Screen* 39 (1).

Kitzinger, J. and Reilly, J. (1997) 'The rise and fall of risk reporting', *European Journal of Communication* 12 (3): 319–50.

Kitzinger, J. and Skidmore, P. (1995) 'Playing safe: Media coverage of child sexual abuse prevention strategies', *Child Abuse Review* 4: 47–56.

Kitzinger, J. and Skidmore, P. (1996) *Child Sexual Abuse and the Media: Summary Report to the ESRC*, University of Glasgow: Glasgow Media Group.

Knight, M. (1937) 'Girl reporter in Paris', in E. Lyons (ed.) *We Cover the World*, London: George G. Harrap & Company, 269–95.

Koerber, C. (1977) 'Television', in J. King and M. Stott (eds) *Is This Your Life?: Images of Women in the Media*, London: Virago, 123–42.

Kovacs, M. (1972) 'Women's rights drive gets off the ground', *Advertising Age* 25 September.

Kramarae, C. (1992) 'Harassment and everyday life', in L. Rakow (ed.) *Women Making Meaning: New Directions in Communication*, London and New York: Routledge, 100–20.

Kramer, R. (1986) 'The third wave', *Wilson Quarterly* 10 (4): 110–29.

Kuhn, A. (1995) *Family Secrets: Acts of Memory and Imagination*, London: Verso.

Kuhn, I. (1938) *Assigned to Adventure*, New York: J.B. Lippincott Company.

LaCapra, D. (1985) *History and Criticism*, Ithaca, NY: Cornell University Press.

Laclau, E. and Mouffe, C. (1985) *Hegemony and Socialist Strategy: Towards a Radical Democratic Politics*, trans. W. Moore and P. Cammack, London: Verso.

Lafky, S.A. (1993) 'The progress of women and people of color in the US journalistic workforce', in P. Creedon (ed.) *Women in Mass Communication*, 2nd edn, Newbury Park, CA, London and Delhi: Sage, 87–103.

Lafky, S.A. (1995) 'Women in broadcast news: More than window dresssing on the set, less than equal with men', C. Lont (ed.) *Women and Media: Content / Careers / Criticism*, Belmont, CA: Wadsworth, 251–60.

Lamb, L. (1989) *Sunrise: The Remarkable Rise and Rise of the Best-selling Soaraway* Sun, London: Papermac.

Landes, J. (1988) *Women and the Public Sphere in the Age of the French Revolution*, Ithaca, NY: Cornell University Press.

Lang, G.E. (1978) 'The most admired woman: Image-making in the news', in G. Tuchman, A. Daniels and J. Benét (eds) *Hearth and Home: Images of Women in the Mass Media*, New York: Oxford University Press, 147–60.

Lazier, L. and Kendrick, A.G. (1993) 'Women in advertisements: Sizing up the images, roles and functions', in P. Creedon (ed.) *Women in Mass Communication*, 2nd edn, Newbury Park, CA, London and New Delhi: Sage, 199–219.

Leach, E. (1972/1964) 'Anthropological aspects of language: Animal categories and verbal abuse', in P. Miranda (ed.) *Mythology: Selected Readings*, Harmondsworth: Penguin Education, 39–67.

Lee, D. (1992) *Competing Discourses*, London: Longman.

Lees, S. (1989) 'Naggers, whores and libbers: Driving men to murder', paper presented to the British Sociological Association Annual Conference, Plymouth, England.

Lees, S. (1995) 'Media reporting of rape: The 1993 British "date rape" controversy', in D. Kidd-Hewitt and R. Osborne (eds) *Crime and Media: The Post-Modern Spectacle*, London: Pluto, 107–30.

Leslie, H. (1943) *More Ha'pence Than Kicks: Being Some Things Remembered*, London: Macdonald & Company.

Lewis, C. (1986) 'Television license renewal challenges by women's groups', unpublished Ph.D. Dissertation, University of Minnesota.

LHJ (1898) 'The Bachelor Girl', *The Ladies' Home Journal*, April.

Lichtenberg, J. (1996) 'In defence of objectivity revisited', in J. Curran and M. Gurevitch (eds) *Mass Media and Society*, 2nd edn, London: Edward Arnold, 225–42.

Lipsitz, G. (1997) 'The greatest story ever sold: Marketing and the O.J. Simpson trial', in T. Morrison and C. Brodsky Lacour (eds) *Birth of a Nation 'hood': Gaze, Script and Spectacle in the O.J. Simpson Case*, New York: Pantheon Books, 3–29.

Lloyd, S., Farrell, G. and Pease, K. (1994) *Preventing Repeated Domestic Violence: A Demonstration Project on Merseyside*, Police Research Group, Crime Prevention Unit Series, London: Home Office Police Department.

Lont, C.M. (ed.) (1995) *Women and Media: Content/Careers/Criticism*, Belmont, CA: Wadsworth.

Lotman, Y. (1990) *The Universe of the Mind: A Semiotic Theory of Culture*, trans. A. Shukman, Bloomington and Indianapolis, IN: Indiana University Press, 153.

Lucy, N. (1995) *Debating Derrida*, Melbourne: Melbourne University Press.

Luebke, B. (1989) 'Out of focus: Images of women and men in newspaper photographs', *Sex Roles* 20 (3–4): 121–33.

Lull, J. (1990) *Inside Family Viewing: Ethnographic Research on Television's Audiences*, London and New York: Routledge.

Lumby, C. (1997) *Bad Girls: The Media, Sex and Feminism in the 90s*, Sydney: Allen & Unwin.

Macdonald, M. (1995) *Representing Women: Myths of Femininity in the Popular Media*, London: Edward Arnold.

MacDougall, A. Kent (1988) 'Boring from within the bourgeois press', *Socialist Review* (November/December).

MacKinnon, C. (1985) 'Feminist discourse, moral values and the law: A Conversation', *Buffalo Law Review* 34 (Winter): 20–1.

MacLean, J. (1979) 'Women fight back', *The Progressive*, February.

Makins, P. (1975) *The Evelyn Home Story*, London: Collins.

Mann, S. (1988) *At Twelve: Portraits of Young Women*, New York: Aperture.

Mann, S. (1992) *Immediate Family*, New York: Aperture.

Manning, M. (Beatrice Fairfax) (1944) *Ladies Now and Then*, New York: E.P. Dutton.

Martin, P. (1997) 'The sad tale of Mr Fox', *Observer Life* 16 February.

Marzolf, M. (1977) *Up From the Footnote: A History of Women Journalists*, New York: Hastings House.

Massumi, B. (1993) 'Everywhere you want to be: An introduction to fear', in B. Massumi (ed.) *The Politics of Everyday Fear*, Minneapolis, MN and London: University of Minnesota Press, 3–37.

Mata, M. (1994) 'Being women in the popular radio', in P. Riaño. (ed.) *Women in Grassroots Communication: Furthering Social Change*, London: Sage.

Mattelart, M. (1986) *Women, Media, Crisis: Femininity and Disorder*, London: Comedia.

Maynes, M.J. (1992) 'Autobiography and class formation in nineteenth-century Europe: Methodological considerations', *Social Science History* 16: 517–37.

Maynes, M.J. (1995) *Taking the Hard Road*, Chapel Hill, NC: The University of North Carolina Press.

McClellan, S. (1995) 'All eyes on O.J.', *Broadcasting and Cable* (9 October): 6.

McCormick, C. (1995) 'Domestic terrorism: The news as an incomplete record of violence against women', *Constructing Danger: The Mis/representation of Crime in the News*, Halifax, Nova Scotia: Fernwood Publishing, 56–73.

McGuigan, J. (1992) *Cultural Populism*, London: Routledge.

McNair, B. (1994) *News and Journalism in the UK: A Textbook*, London: Routledge.

McNeill, S. (1996) 'Getting away with murder', *Trouble & Strife* 33 (Summer): 3–7.

McRobbie, A. (1993) 'Feminism, postmodernism and the real me', *Theory, Culture and Society* 10: 127–42.

McRobbie, A. (1997) '*More!* New sexualities in girls' and women's magazines', in A. McRobbie (ed.) *Back to Reality: Social Experience and Cultural Studies*, Manchester: Manchester University Press, 190–209.

Mellencamp, P. (ed.) (1990) *Logics of Television*, London: BFI/Indiana University Press.

Mercer, C. (1986) 'Complicit pleasures', in T. Bennett, C. Mercer and J. Woollacott (eds) *Popular Culture and Social Relations*, Milton Keynes: Open University Press.

Meyers, M. (1994) 'News of battering', *Journal of Communication* 44 (2): 47–63.

Meyers, M. (1997) *News Coverage of Violence Against Women: Engendering Blame*, Thousand Oaks, CA, London, and New Delhi: Sage.

Miall, L. (ed.) (1966) *Richard Dimbleby, Broadcaster*, London: BBC.

Miller, D. and Reilly, J. (1995) 'Making an issue of public safety: The media, pressure groups and the public sphere', in D. Sobal and J. Sobal (eds) *Eating Agendas: Food and Nutrition as Social Problems*, New York: Aldine de Gruyter.

Miller, D. and Reilly, J. (1996) 'Mad cows and Englishmen', *Planet* (June–July), 117: 118–19.

Miller, D., Kitzinger, J., Williams, K. and Beharrell, P. (1998) *The Circuit of Mass Communication*, London: Sage.

Mills, K. (1990) *A Place in the News: From the Women's Pages to the Front Page*, New York: Columbia University Press.

Mills, K. (1997) 'What difference do women journalists make?', in P. Norris (ed.) *Women, Media and Politics*, New York: Oxford University Press.

Mills, S. (1995) *Feminist Stylistics*, London: Routledge.

Minogue, T. (1990) 'Putting real crime in the picture', *Guardian* 3 September: 23.

Molotch, H.L. (1978) 'The news of women and the work of men', in G. Tuchman, A. Daniels and J. Benét (eds) *Hearth and Home: Images of Women in the Mass Media*, New York: Oxford University Press, 176–85.

Moore, S. (1993) 'On crime and crime reporting', *Observer Magazine* 16 May: 5.

Moore, S. (1997) 'Kirsty or Kirsty, you can choose: The new definition of news', *Independent*, 7 November: 21.

Morgan, R. (1992) *The Word of a Woman: Feminist Dispatches 1968–1992*, New York: W.W. Norton.

Morley, D. (1980) *The Nationwide Audience*, London: British Film Institute.

Morley, D. (1986) *Family Television: Cultural Power and Domestic Leisure*, London: Comedia.

Morley, R. and Mullender, A. (1994) *Preventing Domestic Violence to Women*, Police Research Group, Crime Prevention Unit Series, London: Home Office Police Department, 48.

Morson, G.S. and Emerson, C. (1990) *Mikhail Bakhtin: Creation of a Prosaics*, Stanford, CA: Stanford University Press.

Mulvey, L. (1979/1989) 'Visual pleasure and narrative cinema', *Visual and Other Pleasures*, London: Macmillan.

National Board for Crime Prevention (1994) *Wise After the Event: Tackling Repeat Victimisation*, London: Home Office.

Nava, M. (1988) 'Cleveland and the press: Outrage and anxiety in the reporting of child sexual abuse', *Feminist Review* 28: 103–21.

Negt, O. and Kluge, A. (1993) *Public Sphere and Experience: Toward an Analysis of the Bourgeois and Proletariat Public Sphere*, trans. P. Labanyi, J.O. Daniel and A. Oksiloff, Minneapolis, MN: University of Minnesota Press.

Neverla, G. and Kanzleiter, I. (1984) *Journalistinnen Frankfurt*, Frankfurt: Campus Verlag.

New York Times (1970a) 'Women march down Fifth in equality drive', 27 August.

New York Times (1970b) 'Leading feminist puts hairdo before strike', 27 August.

Newburn, T. (1996) 'Back to the future? Youth crime, youth justice and the rediscovery of 'Authoritarian Populism', in J. Pilcher and S. Wagg (eds) *Thatcher's Children? Politics, Childhood and Society in the 1980s and 1990s*, London: Falmer Press, 61–76.

Newcomb, H. (ed.) (1994) *Television: The Critical View*, Oxford: Oxford University Press.

Newnham, D. and Townsend, C. (1996) 'Pictures of innocence', *Guardian*, Weekend Edition, 13 January: 12.

Nicholas, P. (1997) Personal interview (Assistant Editor, *News of the World*), February 24.

Nichols, B. (1991) *Representing Reality: Issues and Concepts in Documentary*, Bloomington and Indianapolis, IN: Indiana University Press.

Nightingale, V. (1990) 'Women as audiences', in M.E. Brown (ed.) *Television and Women's Culture: The Politics of the Popular*, London, Newbury Park, CA, and Delhi: Sage, 25–36.

Nightingale, V. (1996) *Studying Audiences: The Shock of the Real*, London: Routledge.

Norris, P. (ed.) (1997) *Women, Media and Politics*, New York: Oxford University Press.

NOS (1987) *Het NOS Journaal*, Hilversum: Kijk en Luisteronderzoek.

O'Connor, M. (1990) 'Chronotopes for women under capital: An investigation into the relation of women to objects', *Critical Studies* 2 (1–2): 137–51.

Ofshe, R. and Watters, E. (1994) *Making Monsters: False Memories, Psychotherapy and Sexual Hysteria*, New York: Scribners.

Osborne, R. (1995) 'Crime and the media: From media studies to post-modernism', in D. Kidd-Hewitt and R. Osborne (eds) *Crime and the Media: The Post-modern Spectacle*, London: Pluto Press.

Owen, J.M. (1995) 'Women-talk and men-talk: Defining and Resisting Victim Status', in R.E. Dobash, R.P. Dobash and L. Noakes (eds) *Gender and Crime*, Cardiff: University of Wales Press, 246–68.

Paine, T. (1792/1937) *Rights of Man*, ed. H.B. Bonner, London: Watts.

Parker, R. and Pollock, G. (1981) *Old Mistresses: Women, Art and Ideology*, London: Routledge & Kegan Paul.

Parr, M. (1997) 'August Sander: A personal perspective', Talk given at the National Portrait Gallery, London (March).

Pascall, G. (1996) *Social Policy: A Feminist Analysis*, 2nd edn, London: Routledge.

Pateman, C. (1988) *The Sexual Contract*, Cambridge: Polity Press.

Patterson, T.K. and McClure, R.D. (1976) *The Unseeing Eye: The Myth of Television Power in National Elections*, New York: Putnam.

Peacocke, E.H. (1936) *Writing for Women*, London: A & C. Black.

Pearce, L. (1992) 'Dialogic theory and writing', in H. Hinds, A. Phoenix and J. Stacey (eds) *Working Out: New Directions for Women's Studies*, London: Falmer, 184–93.

Pearce, L. (1994) *Reading Dialogics*, London: Edward Arnold.

Pendergrast, M. (1995) *Victims of Memory*, Vermont: Upper Access.

Peters, J.D. (1993) 'Distrust of representation: Habermas on the public sphere', *Media, Culture and Society* 15 (4): 541–71.

Phillips, A. (1991) *Engendering Democracy*, Cambridge: Polity Press.

Philo, G. (1990) *Seeing and Believing: The Influence of Television*, London and New York: Routledge.

Pilcher, J. (1996) 'Gillick and after: Children and sex in the 1980s and 1990s', in J. Pilcher and S. Wagg (eds) *Thatcher's Children? Politics, Childhood and Society in the 1980s and 1990s*, London: Falmer Press, 77–93.

Pilcher, J. and Wagg, S. (eds) (1996) *Thatcher's Children? Politics, Childhood and Society in the 1980s and 1990s*, London: Falmer Press.

Pingree, S. and Hawkins, R. (1978) 'News definitions and their effects on women', in L.K. Epstein (ed.) *Women and the News*, New York: Hastings House.

Pollock, M.S. (1993) 'What is left out: Bakhtin, feminism and the culture of boundaries', *Critical Studies* 3 (2): 229–41.

Postman, N. (1985) *Amusing Ourselves to Death*, London: Methuen.

Press, A. (1991) *Women Watching Television*, Philadelphia, PA: University of Pennsylvania Press.

Pritchard, D. and Hughes, K.H. (1997) 'Patterns of deviance in crime news', *Journal of Communication* 47 (3): 49–67.

Probyn, E. (1993) *Sexing the Self: Gendered Positions in Cultural Studies*, London: Routledge.

Publishers Weekly (1965) '1964 paperback best sellers in the bookstores', 18 January.

Pumphrey, M. (1987) 'The Flapper, the housewife and the making of modernity', *Cultural Studies* 1: 186.

Pursehouse, M. (1991) 'Looking at *The Sun*: Into the 90s with a tabloid and its readers', *Cultural Studies from Birmingham* 1: 88–133.

Radway, J. (1985) *Reading the Romance*, Chapel Hill: University of North Carolina Press.

Rakow, L. (ed.) (1992) *Women Making Meaning: New Feminist Directions in Communication*, London and New York: Routledge.

Rakow, L. and Kranich, K. (1991) 'Woman as sign in television news', *Journal of Communication* 41 (1): 8–23.

Rapping, E. (1995) 'Daytime enquiries', in G. Dines and J.M. Humez (eds) *Gender, Race and Class in Media*, Thousand Oaks, CA, London and Delhi: Sage, 377–82.

Reid, E.C. (1989) 'Viewdata: The television viewing habits of young Black women in London', *Screen* 30: 114–21.

Reisig, R. (1975) 'MS.: Politics and editing: An interview', *Feminist Revolution: An Abridged Edition with Additional Writings*, New York: Random House.

Rhode, D. (1989) *Justice and Gender*, Cambridge, MA: Harvard University Press.

Rhode, D. (1995) 'Media images, feminist issues', *Signs: Journal of Women in Culture and Society* 20 (3): 678–710.

Rhodes, J. (1992) 'Mary Ann Shadd Car and the legacy of African-American women journalists', in L. Rakow (ed.) *Women Making Meaning*, London and New York: Routledge, 210–24.

Rhodes, J. (1995) 'Activism through journalism: The story of Ida B. Wells-Barnett', in C. Lont (ed.) *Women and Media: Content / Careers / Criticism*, Belmont, CA: Wadsworth, 29–40.

Riaño, P. (ed.) (1994) *Women in Grassroots Communication: Furthering Social Change*, London: Sage.

Rich, A. (1979) *On Lies, Secrets and Silences*, New York: W.W. Norton.

Roberts, P. (1993) 'Social control and censure(s) of sex', *Crime, Law and Social Change* 19 (2): 171–86.

Robertson, N. (1992) *The Girls in the Balcony: Women, Men and the* New York Times, New York: Random House.

Robinson, G.J. (1978) 'Women, media access and social control', in L.K. Epstein (ed.) *Women and the News*, New York: Hastings House, 87–108.

Root, J. (1986) *Open the Box*, London: Comedia.

Roshco, B. (1975) *Newsmaking*, Chicago, IL: University of Chicago Press.

Roshier, B. (1984) 'The selection of crime news by the press', in S. Cohen and J. Young (eds) *The Manufacture of News: Social Problems, Deviance and the Mass Media*, London: Constable, 40–51.

Ross, I. (1936) *Ladies of the Press*, New York: Harper.

Ross, M. (1977) 'Radio', in J. King and M. Stott (eds) *Is This Your Life?: Images of Women in the Media*, London: Virago, 9–35.

Rupp, C.M. (1980) 'Improvements are sought in covering women's news', *Editor and Publisher*, 38–9.

Russ, J. (1983) *How to Suppress Women's Writing*, Austin, TX: University of Texas Press.

Rutherford, J. (ed.) (1988) *Male Order*, London: Lawrence & Wishart.

Rutherford, J. (1990) *Identity*, London: Lawrence & Wishart.

Ryan, D. (1996) 'All the world and her husband: The Daily Mail and women readers', Paper given at Institute of Contemporary British History Conference (September).

Ryan, M. (1992) 'Gender and public access: Women's politics in nineteenth-century America', in C. Calhoun, (ed.) *Habermas and the Public Sphere*, Cambridge, MA: MIT Press.

Salcetti, M. (1995) 'The emergence of the reporter: Mechanization and the devaluation of editorial workers', in H. Hardt and B. Brennan (eds) *Newsworkers. Toward a History of the Rank and File*, Minneapolis, MN: University of Minnesota Press, 48–74.

Sanders, M. (1993) 'Television: The face of the network news is male', in P. Creedon (ed.) *Women in Mass Communication*, Newbury Park, CA, London and Delhi: Sage, 167–71.

Sanders, M. and Rock, M. (1988) *Waiting for Prime Time, The Women of Television News*, Urbana: University of Illinois Press.

Santos, J.P. (1997) '(Re)Imagining America', in E.E. Dennis and E.C. Pease (eds) *The Media in Black and White*, New Brunswick, NJ: Transaction Publishers, 121–7.

Scannell, P. (1986) ' "The stuff of radio": Developments in radio features and documentaries before the war', in J. Corner (ed.) *Documentary and the Mass Media*, London: Edward Arnold.

Scannell, P. (1996) *Radio, Television and Modern Life*, Oxford: Blackwell.

Schiller, D. (1981) *Objectivity and the News: The Public and the Rise of Commercial Journalism*, Philadelphia, PA: University of Pennsylvania Press.

Schlesinger, P. (1978) *Putting 'Reality' Together: BBC News*, London: Methuen.

Schlesinger, P. (1987) *Putting 'Reality' Together: BBC News*, 2nd edn, London: Methuen.

Schlesinger, P., Dobash, R. Emerson, Dobash, R.P. and Weaver, C. K. (1992) *Women Viewing Violence*, London: BFI.

Schlesinger, P., Tumber H. and Murdock, G. (1991) 'The media politics of crime and criminal justice', *British Journal of Sociology* 42 (3): 397–420.

Schlesinger, P. and Tumber, H. (1994) *Reporting Crime: The Media Politics of Criminal Justice*, Oxford: Clarendon.

Schlipp, M.G. and Murphy, S.M. (1983) *Great Women of the Press*, Carbondale: Southern Illinois University Press.

Schudson, M. (1978) *Discovering the News: A Social History of American Newspapers*, New York: Basic Books.

Schudson, M. (1989) 'The sociology of news production', *Media, Culture and Society* 11 (3): 263–82.

Schulman, N.M. (1995) 'Wrinkling the fabric of the press: Newspaper opinion columns in a different voice', in C. Lont (ed.) *Women and Media: Content/Careers/Criticism*, Belmont, CA: Wadsworth, 55–67.

Schultz-Brooks, T. (1984) 'Getting there: Women in the newsroom', *The Columbia Journalism Review* 25–31.

Scott, J. W. (1992) 'Experience', in J. Butler and J.W. Scott (eds) *Feminists Theorize the Political*, London: Routledge.

Sebba, A. (1994) *Battling for News: The Rise of the Woman Reporter*, London: Sceptre.

Sendall, B. (1982) *Independent Television in Britain: Vol. 1, Origin and Foundation 1946–62*, London: Macmillan.

Sendall, B. (1983) *Independent Television in Britain: Vol. 2, Expansion and Change 1958–68*, London: Macmillan.

Seymour-Ure, C. (1995) 'Characters and assassinations: Portrayals of John Major and Neil Kinnock in the *Daily Mirror* and the *Sun*', in I. Crewe and B. Gosschalk (eds) *Political Communications: The General Election Campaign 1992*, Cambridge and New York: Cambridge University Press, 137–59.

Shevelow, K. (1989) *Women and Print Culture: The Construction of Femininity in the Early Periodical*, London and New York: Routledge.

Sholle, D. (1993) 'Buy our news: Tabloid television and commodification', *Journal of Communication Inquiry* 17 (1): 56–72.

Shuttac, J. (1997) *The Talking Cure: TV Shows and Women*, London and New York: Routledge.

Silverstone, R. (1996) *Television and Everyday Life*, London and New York: Routledge.

Simonton, A.J. (1995) 'Women for Sale', in C.M. Lont (ed.) *Women and Media: Content/Careers/Criticism*, Belmont, CA: Wadsworth, 143–64.

Simpson, P. (1979) 'Covering the women's movement', *Nieman Reports*, Special Issue on Women and Journalism: 20.

Skard, T. (1989) 'Norway: Two-edged (s)words for women journalists', in R. Rush and D. Allen (eds) *Communications at the Crossroads*, Norwood, NJ: Ablex.

Skidmore, P. (1995) ' Telling tales: Media power, ideology and the reporting of child sexual abuse', in D. Kidd-Hewitt and R. Osborne (eds) *Crime and Media: the Postmodern Spectacle*, London: Pluto Press, 78–106.

Smith, A. (1974) *British Broadcasting*, London: David & Charles.

Smith, B. (1989) 'A press of our own: Kitchen Table: Women of color press', in R.Rush and D. Allen (eds) *Communications at the Crossroads: The Gender Gap Connection*, Norwood, NJ: Ablex.

Smith, C., Fredin, E.S. and Nardone, C.A.F. (1993) 'Television: The nature of sex discrimination in local television news shops', in P. Creedon (ed.) *Women in Mass Communication*, Newbury Park, CA, London and Delhi: Sage, 172–82.

Smith, L.J.F. (1989) *Domestic Violence: An Overview of the Literature*, A Home Office Research and Planning Unit Report, Study 107, London: Her Majesty's Stationery Office.

Smith, R. (1980) 'Images and equality: Women and the national press', in H. Christian (ed.) *The Sociology of Journalism and the Press*, London: Routledge & Kegan Paul.

Snoddy, R. (1992) *The Good, the Bad and the Unacceptable*, London: Faber & Faber.

Solomon, W.S. (1995) 'The site of newsroom labor: The division of editorial practices', in H. Hardt and B. Brennan (eds) *Newsworkers: Toward a History of the Rank and File*, Minneapolis, MN: University of Minnesota Press, 110–34.

Soothill, K. (1995) 'Sex crime news from abroad', in R.E. Dobash, R.P. Dobash and L. Noakes (eds) *Gender and Crime*, Cardiff: University of Wales Press, 96–114.

Soothill, K. and Walby, S. (1991) *Sex Crime in the News*, London: Routledge.

Sounes, H. (1995) *Fred and Rose*, London: Warner Books.

Sparks, C. (1991) 'Goodbye Hildy Johnson: the vanishing serious press', in P. Dahlgren and C. Sparks (eds) *Communication and Citizenship*, London: Routledge.

Spence, J. and Holland, P. (eds) (1991) *Family Snaps: The Meanings of Domestic Photography*, London: Virago.

Spender, D. (1980) *Man Made Language*, London: Routledge & Kegan Paul.

Spigel, L. (1992) *Make Room For TV*, Chicago, IL: University of Chicago Press.

Squires, C. (1997) 'Empowering women?: The Oprah Winfrey Show', in C. Brunsdon, J.D. D'Acci, and L. Spigel (eds) *Feminist Television Criticism: A Reader*, Oxford: Clarendon Press, 98–113.

Stanko, E. (1990) *Everyday Violence: How Men and Women Experience Sexual and Physical Danger*, London: Pandora.

Stanko, E. (1991) *Guardian*, 2 October.

Steedman, C. (1986) *Landscape for a Good Woman: A Story of Two Lives*, London: Virago.

Steenland, S. (1995). 'Content analysis of the image of women on television', in C. Lont (ed.) *Women and Media: Content/Careers/Criticism*, Belmont, CA: Wadsworth, 179–90.

Steeves, H.L. (1987) 'Feminist theories and media studies', *Critical Studies in Mass Communication* 4 (2): 95–135.

Steeves, H.L. and Smith, M.C. (1987) 'Class and gender in prime-time television entertainment', *Journal of Communication Inquiry* 11 (1): 43–63.

Steinem, G. (1973) 'If we're so smart, why aren't we rich?', *Ms.* June.

Steinem, G. (1975) 'It's your year', *Ms.* January.

Steinem, G. (1983) 'Sisterhood', in *Outrageous Acts and Everyday Rebellions*, New York: Holt, Rinehart & Winston.

Steiner, L. (1992) 'The history and structure of women's alternative media', in L. Rakow (ed.) *Women Making Meaning: New Feminist Directions in Communication*, London and New York: Routledge.

Steiner, L. (1997a) 'An annotated bibliography of autobiographies of women journalists', *Journalism History* 23: 13–15.

Steiner, L. (1997b) 'Why women reporters quit the newsroom: Stories of quitting', paper presented to the Association for Education in Journalism and Mass Communication, Chicago (August).

Steiner, L. and Gray, S. (1985) 'Genevieve Forbes Herrick: A front page reporter "pleased to write about women"', *Journalism History* 12: 8–16.

Stott, M. (1989) *Forgetting's No Excuse*, London: Virago (first published 1973).

Stratford, T. (1987) 'Page 3 – Dream or nightmare?', in K. Davies, J. Dickey and T. Stratford (eds) *Out of Focus: Writings on Women and the Media*, London: The Women's Press, 57–61.

Swann, J. (1992) 'Ways of speaking', in F. Bonner *et al.* (eds) *Imagining Women: Cultural Representations and Gender*, Cambridge: Polity Press.

Sweeney, J. (1992) 'Where fear and loathing stalk the set', *Observer* 10 May: 48.

Swenson, J.D. (1995) 'Rodney King, Reginald Denny and TV news: Cultural (re)construction of racism', *Journal of Communication Inquiry* 19 (1): 75–88.

Thompson, J.B. (1995) 'The theory of the public sphere', in O. Boyd-Barrett and C. Newbold (eds) *Approaches to Media: A Reader*, London: Edward Arnold.

Thumim, J. (1995) 'A live commercial for icing sugar', *Screen* 36: 1.

Tierney, K. (1982) 'The battered women movement and the creation of the wife-beating problem', *Social Problems* 29 (3): 207–20.

Tolson, A. (1977) *The Limits of Masculinity*, London: Tavistock.

Trinh, T.M. (1991) *When the Moon Waxes Red: Representation, Gender and Cultural Politics*, London: Routledge.

Trinh, T.M. (1989) *Woman, Native, Other: Writing Postcoloniality and Feminism*, Bloomington and Indianapolis, IN: Indiana University Press.

Tuchman, G. (1972) 'Objectivity as strategic ritual', *American Journal of Sociology* 77: 660–79.

Tuchman, G. (1978a) 'Introduction: The symbolic annihilation of women by the mass media', in G. Tuchman, A. Daniels, and J. Benét (eds) *Hearth and Home: Images of Women in the Mass Media*, New York: Oxford University Press.

Tuchman, G. (1978b) 'The newspaper as a social movement's resource', in G. Tuchman, A. Daniels, and J. Benét (eds) *Hearth and Home: Images of Women in the Mass Media*, New York: Oxford University Press, 186–215.

Tuchman, G. (1978c) *Making News: A Study of the Construction of Reality*, New York: Free Press.

Tuchman, G., Daniels, A. and Benét, J. (eds) (1978d) *Hearth and Home: Images of Women in the Mass Media*, New York: Oxford University Press.

Tunks, K. and Hutchinson, D. (1991) *Dear Clare . . . This is What Women Feel about Page Three*, London: Radius.

Tunstall, J. (1971) *Journalists at Work*, London: Constable.

Tunstall, J. (1996) *Newspaper Power: The New National Press in Britain*, Oxford: Clarendon Press.

TV Guide (1969) Monday 23 June.

UNESCO (1987) *Women and Decision Making: The Invisible Barriers*, Paris: UNESCO.

Uriarte, M.L. de (1997) 'Exploring (and exploding) the US media prism', in E.E. Dennis and E.C. Pease (eds) *The Media in Black and White*, New Brunswick, NJ: Transaction Publishers, 139–49.

Ussher, J. (1991) *Women's Madness: Misogyny or Mental Illness*, Brighton: Harvester Wheatsheaf.

Vahimagi, T. (ed.) (1994) *British Television*, Oxford: BFI/Oxford University Press.

Valdivia, A.N. (1992) 'Women's revolutionary place', in L. Rakow (ed.) *Women Making Meaning*, London and New York: Routledge, 167–87.

van den Wijngaard, R. (1992) 'Women as journalists: Incompatibility of roles?', *Africa Media Review* 6 (2): 47–56.

van Loon, J. (1997) 'Chronotopes: Of/in the televisualization of the 1992 Los Angeles riots', *Theory, Culture and Society* 14 (2): 89–104.

van Zoonen, L. (1988) 'Rethinking women and the news', *European Journal of Communication* 3: 335–53.

van Zoonen, L. (1989) 'Professional socialization of feminist journalists in the Netherlands', *Women's Studies in Communication* 12 (3): 1–23.

van Zoonen, L. (1991) 'A tyranny of intimacy? Women, femininity and television news', in P. Dahlgren and C. Sparks (eds) *Communication and Citizenship*, London: Routledge.

van Zoonen, L. (1992) 'The women's movement and the media: Constructing a public identity', *European Journal of Communication* 7 (4): 453–76.

van Zoonen, L. (1994) *Feminist Media Studies*, London and Thousand Oaks, CA: Sage.

van Zoonen, L. (1996) 'Feminist perspectives on the media', in J. Curran and M. Gurevitch (eds) *Mass Media and Society*, 2nd edn, London: Edward Arnold, 31–52.

van Zoonen, L. (1998) 'A heroic, unreliable, professional marionet: Structure, agency and subjectivity in contemporary journalisms', *European Journal of Cultural Studies* 1 (1).

van Zoonen, L. and Donsbach, W. (1988) 'Professional values and gender in British and German journalism', paper presented at the 38th Annual Conference of the International Communications Association, New Orleans (May).

Vogel, U. (1991) 'Is citizenship gender-specific?', in U. Vogel and M. Moran (eds) *The Frontiers of Citizenship*, London: Macmillan.

Vološinov, V.N. (1929/1986) *Marxism and the Philosophy of Language*, trans. L. Matejka and I.R. Titunik, Cambridge, MA: Harvard University Press.

Voumvakis, S. and Ericson, R.V. (1984) 'News accounts of attacks on women: A comparison of three Toronto newspapers', Research Report of the Centre of Criminology, Toronto: University of Toronto Press.

Walby, S., Hay, A. and Soothill, K. (1983) 'The social construction of rape', *Theory, Culture and Society* 2 (1): 86–98.

Walkerdine, V. (1997) *Daddy's Girl: Young Girls and Popular Culture*, Basingstoke: Macmillan.

Walkowitz, R.L. (1993) 'Reproducing reality: Murphy Brown and illegitimate politics', in M. Grabber, J. Mattock and R. Walkowitz (eds) *Media Spectacles*, London and New York: Routledge, 40–56.

Warner, M. (1987) *Monuments and Maidens: The Allegory of the Female Form*, London: Picador.

Wasko, J. (1996) 'Understanding the Disney universe', in J. Curran and M. Gurevitch (eds) *Mass Media and Society*, London: Edward Arnold, 348–68.

Weaver, C.K. (1995) 'Representations of men's violence against women: audio–visual texts and their reception', unpublished D.Phil. thesis, University of Stirling.

Weaver, D. (1997) 'Women as journalists', in P. Norris (ed.) *Women, Media and Politics*, New York: Oxford University Press.

Weedon, C. (1987/1994) 'Feminism and the principles of post-structuralism', in J. Storey (ed.) *Cultural Theory and Popular Culture*, London: Harvester Wheatsheaf, 170–82.

Weedon, C. (1997) *Feminist Practice and Poststructuralist Theory*, 2nd edn, Oxford and Cambridge, MA: Blackwell.

White, R.A. (1983) 'Mass communication and culture: Transition to a new paradigm', *Journal of Communication* 'Ferment in the Field' issue, 33 (3): 279–301.

Who's Who in America (1997) 51st edn, Providence, NJ: Marquis Who's Who, 2 vols.

Wigmore, N. (1986) 'The Page Three connection', *Guardian* 27 March.

Wilczynski, A. (1995) 'Child killing by parents: Social, legal and gender issues', in R.E. Dobash, R.P. Dobash and L. Noakes (eds) *Gender and Crime*, Cardiff: University of Wales Press.

Wilkes, P. (1970) 'Mother Superior to Women's Lib', *New York Times Magazine* 29 November.

Williams, P.J. (1997) 'American Kabuki', in T. Morrison and C.B. Lacour (eds) *Birth of a Nation 'hood': Gaze, Script and Spectacle in the O.J. Simpson Case*, New York: Pantheon Books, 273–92.

Williams, R. (1981) *Politics and Letters: Interviews with 'New Left Review'*, London: Verso.

Williams, V. (1994) *Who's Looking at the Family?*, London: Barbican Art Gallery.

Willis, E. (1975) 'The conservatism of *Ms.*', in *Feminist Revolution: An Abridged Edition with Additional Writings*, New York: Random House.

Winston, B. (1988) 'The tradition of the victim in Griersonian documentary', in A. Rosenthal (ed.) *New Challenges for Documentary*, Berkeley, CA: University of California Press.

Winston, B. (1995) *Claiming the Real: The Documentary Film Revisited*, London: BFI.

Wober, M. and Gunter, B. (1990) *Crime Reconstruction Programmes: Viewing Experiences in Three Regions, Linked with Perceptions of and Reactions to Crime*, London: IBA Research Paper.

Wolseley, R.W. (1943) 'The journalist as autobiographer', *South Atlantic Quarterly* 42: 38–44.

Wombell, P. (1986) 'Face to face with themselves: Photography and the First World War', in P. Holland, J. Spence and S. Watney (eds) *Photography Politics Two*, London: Comedia.

Women's Studies Group, University of Birmingham, Centre for Contemporary Cultural Studies (1978) *Women Take Issue: Aspects of Women's Subordination*, London: Hutchinson.

Wykes, M. (1991) 'Alternative reporting: How new was 'News on Sunday'?', *Culture Matters Paper*, Sheffield Hallam University.

Wykes, M. (1994) 'Accounting for intimate killing: the press, violence and gender', unpublished Ph.D. dissertation, University of Sheffield.

Wykes, M. (1995) 'Passion, marriage and murder: Analysing the press discourse', in R.E. Dobash, R.P. Dobash and L. Noakes (eds) *Gender and Crime*, Cardiff: University of Wales Press, 49–76.

Wykes, M. and Jones, K. (1994) 'Danger, desire and identity', *Language and Discourse* 2 (September): 62–77.

Wykes, M. and Woodcock, R. (1996) *Representations of Homelessness*, TASC/Shelter.

Young, A. (1988) 'Wild women: The censure of the suffragette movement', *International Journal of the Sociology of the Law* 16: 179–293.

Young, A. (1991) *Femininity in Dissent*, London: Routledge.

Young, A. (1996) *Imagining Crime*, London: Routledge.

Young, I.M. (1987) 'Impartiality and the civic public: Some implications of feminist critiques of moral and political theory', in S. Benhabib and D. Cornell (eds) *Feminism as Critique*, Minneapolis, MN: University of Minnesota Press, 56–76.

Young, I.M. (1990) *Throwing Like a Girl and Other Essays in Feminist Philosophy and Social Theory*, Bloomington, IN: Indiana University Press.

INDEX

38; rules of inclusion and exclusion 129–31

'femicide' 228, 231

'feminine' values in journalism 22, 31, 35–8, 126

femininity: definitions of 2, 37; idealized 76; and low public status 21–2; topics associated with 14, 41, 45

feminism: and Bakhtin 123–4; and male violence 236–7; on the media agenda 142, 160–73; and objectivity 121–2; and the public sphere 73, 74–8, 80, 105–6; radical 168, 171–2; and reform of news media 161–73; second wave 80–1, 142, 162, 201; specialized groups 166

Feminist Mystique (Friedan) 161, 163–5

feminists: marginalized in child sexual abuse cases 214–15; stereotyping of 162–3

feminization 39, 41–5, 61, 201; and democratization 18–20, 28, 48, 51; of news 32, 93, 95; of newspapers 13–14, 18–23; of panic 176, 178–81; and sexualization 7–8

Ferguson, Sarah, Duchess of York 180

Fiddes, N. 177, 183

film documentary 118–19

film theory 107

Fiske, John 7, 157

'Flapper' 162

Fleming, Dina 245

FMS *see* false memory syndrome

food health scares 142, 174–85

forensic spectacle 82–9

forensics, definition of 82

formats, use of 'soft' and 'hard' 193, 201–2

Fortnight Rule 95–6

Foucault, Michel 110, 150

Fowler, R. 176

Fox, Muriel 164, 165

Fox, Samantha 28, 31

framing, discursive 120, 129–36, 142

Frankfurt School 72

Fraser, Nancy 29, 73, 77

freelance journalists 213–14

Freeman, Jo 166

French Revolution 29

Friedan Betty 160, 166; *The Feminist Mystique* 161, 163–5

Friederichs, Hulda 21

Fuhrman, Mark 85

fun, politics of 29–32

Furness, Betty 164

Gallagher, M. 205–6

Galtung, J. 233

game shows 120

Garrity, Joan, *Total Loving* 23

gatekeepers 147

Geiger, S.N.G. 148

gender: and age 14; and the news agenda 213–15

gender bias, in news reporting 121–2

gender discourse 205, 209–10

gender politics: of journalism 11–137; of news production 186–218; research on media 3–9

gender-neutrality 131

gendered structure 205–11, 216

German female journalists 33

Gingold, Hermione 164

Ginsberg, Allen 47

'Girl Talk' 163–4

girls: news and power 47–70; one of the 33–46

Glazener, Nancy 124

Goff, Trish 55

Goldie, Grace Wyndham 94, 96, 98, 100

Goldwater, Barry 173

Good Sex Guide 25

Gordon, M.T. 254

governability, discourse of 64, 68, 70

Graham, Virginia, 'Girl Talk' 163–4

Gray, John 177

Grierson 98

Grossinger, Tania 164

Guardian 23, 54, 66, 177, 195, 208, 238, 240, 243

Guardian Weekend 28

Gulf War 44

Gunnell, Barbara 69

habeas corpus 74

Habermas Jürgen 83, 106–7; *The Structural Transformation of the Public Sphere* 15, 72, 73, 74–80

Hajdukowski-Ahmed, Maroussia 123

Hall, Stuart 245

Hanisch, Carol 169

Hansen, Miriam 80

'happy talk' 40

'hard' news 4, 7, 13, 22, 132–4, 143;